DATE DUE

THE PROSE OF VACHEL LINDSAY

volume 1

DENNIS CAMP, editor

The Prose of

Vachel Lindsay

complete & with Lindsay's drawings

newly edited by

DENNIS CAMP

volume 1

SPOON RIVER POETRY PRESS
1988

This book is published in part with funds provided by The Illinois Arts Council, a state organization. Our many thanks.

Published by Spoon River Poetry Press; P.O. Box 1443; Peoria, Illinois 61655.

Typesetting by Tom Guttormsson, Minneota (MN) *Mascot.*

Cover design by David R. Pichaske.

ISBN 0-944024-08-4

For Trula . . .

of the Palace of Eve

Introduction

This two-volume edition of Lindsay's published prose is designed to accompany *The Poetry of Vachel Lindsay* (Peoria: Spoon River Poetry Press, 1984-86). With two exceptions, these volumes follow the chronological order of publication. One exception is the closing section of volume two, where the reader will find a selection of Lindsay's prose published in periodicals and newspapers but not collected in his books. These selections follow their own chronological order.

The second exception is the opening work, *A Handy Guide for Beggars*, which was not published in book form until November 1916, although individual stories had appeared in *The Outlook* (1907, 1909, 1911) and in *Twentieth Century Magazine* (1912). Lindsay himself offers the most convincing reason for the break with publication chronology. In his informational brochure, *A Letter about My Four Programmes* (Summer, 1916), he advises would-be readers that the prose in *A Handy Guide* "precedes in point of time the other two prose works [*Adventures While Preaching the Gospel of Beauty* (1914) and *The Art of the Moving Picture* (1915)], and some of the readers chronologically inclined will doubtless read it first" (p. 2). And in Lindsay's self-prepared biography for *Who's Who in America* (all relevant editions), *A Handy Guide* heads the list of the author's books.

I have included full bibliographical information at the beginning of each selection. In the cases of *A Handy Guide for Beggars* and *Adventures While Preaching the Gospel of Beauty,* earlier periodical versions of the stories contain variant readings, many very minor, most generally reflective of an author polishing material. For example, Lindsay changes the name of "Mr. Kind-Heart" in the periodical version of "Death, the Devil, and Human Kindness" to "Mr. Humankindness" in *A Handy Guide.* Lindsay scholars, though, should be aware that some variant readings may be significant, especially when earlier material has been excised. In "A Temple Made with Hands," the opening story of the second part of *A Handy Guide*, the Lindsay narrator announces: "I wanted to preach them a sermon on St. Francis." He demurs, however, with the cryptic explanation: "There was still a quarter in my own pocket" (p. 49). In the version of the story printed in *Twentieth*

Century Magazine, however, Lindsay includes a section appropriately entitled, *"A Speech I Did Not Make"*:

This is what I wanted to say: "Friends across the gulf, throw your money into the street. The hope to do good with it is a fool's hope. Money given away makes paupers, parasites, bootlickers. Throw your money into the bottom of the sea, where men cannot dive for it and the fishes will not tell where it is. Let us enter the great offices and speak so eloquently that men will shut the desk-lids and cut the telephone wires. Let us preach the divine freedom of poverty till the skyscrapers are empty and locked and the keys thrown into the ocean. Let us preach the gospel of going afoot till there shall be neither tramps in box-cars nor aristocrats in Pullman cars. Let us persuade men to turn their backs on the railroad till it becomes a thread of rust. Let us lead forth a great pedestrian immigration, set free, purged of the commerce-made manners and fat prosperity of America, ragged with a beggar's pride, starving, if need be, with a crusader's fervor. Better to die of plague on the highroad, seeing the angels, than to live on iron streets playing checkers with dollars forever and ever.

"But it is absurd,' you say. 'Our business men will not leave business. And the railroads will continue to exist.'

"Well, then, let a few of us go, carrying neither purse nor scrip. Let us get as far from the railroad as possible. Let us be healing the sick imaginations, cleansing the leprous minds, raising the dead aspirations of all our hosts and companions, and casting out the devils of money-lust in those we meet by the way. Let us say to the people that entertain us 'All things worth while have happened while the crops went wrong. The man with house painted and fields in order is in danger of hell fire. It means he has not taken all his time to worship the Christ of Beauty. He has not gathered his children by the fireside to look into some wonderful new doctrine or old tradition, to tell an antique story, or sing a homely song. Be warned, one dollar in your pocket makes you a rich man, and it is God's truth and no mild saying that it is easier for a camel to go through the eye of a needle than for a rich man to enter the kingdom of God.' "

But I did not say any of these things. How could I? There was still a quarter in my own pocket... (June 1912, pp. 47-48)

Finally, inconsistencies in the text, such as "bumble bees" and "bumblebees" or "haymow" and "hay-mow," are typical of Lindsay's writing (and proof-reading), both in his prone and his poetry.

*   *   *

I am grateful to the University of Illinois Rare Book and Manuscript Library for permission to publish "What Grandpa Mouse Said," the frontispiece for volume one, and to Nicholas Cave Lindsay for permission to prepare and publish this edition of his father's prose. Thanks also to the Sangamon State University Library faculty and staff for their continuing support and assistance, especially to Ms. Nancy Stump, who succeeded in acquiring copies of even the most obscure of Lindsay's publications. The esthetic appeal of these volumes is due primarily to publisher David Pichaske, whose skill and taste are self-apparent.

I owe special thanks to Hiram College Library Curator Joanne Sawyer, whose gracious assistance led to the discovery of several early Lindsay publications. And I remain grateful to Catharine Blair and to Catherine Ward, nieces of Vachel Lindsay, for their continuing interest in and support of my work.

As usual, my greatest thanks to Trula: for her encouragement, for her assistance, but especially for her patience.

TABLE OF CONTENTS

A HANDY GUIDE FOR BEGGARS

Especially Those of the Poetic Fraternity

Being sundry explorations, made while afoot and penniless in Florida, Georgia, North Carolina, Tennessee, Kentucky, New Jersey, and Pennsylvania. These adventures convey and illustrate the rules of beggary for poets and some others.

(November 1916)

[Several stories from the first part of the *Handy Guide,* with variant readings, were published in *The Outlook* (New York), including four under the general title "Adventures of a Literary Tramp": "The House of the Loom: A Story of Seven Aristocrats and a Soap-Kettle" (January 2, 1909, pp. 36-39); "The Man with the Apple-Green Eyes" (January 9, 1909, pp. 86-90); "The Gnome" (February 6, 1909, pp. 312-316); and "Man, in the City of Collars" (February 13, 1909, pp. 357-359). *The Outlook* also published "The Man under the Yoke: An Episode in the Life of a Literary Tramp" (June 1, 1907, pp. 243-245) and "Lady Iron-Heels" (October 7, 1911, pp. 335-338). For VL's amplification of the "Dedication and Preface," see "Rules of the Road" in volume two of this edition.

The four long stories in the second part of the *Handy Guide* were published, with variant readings, in *Twentieth Century Magazine* (1912), under the general title "A Religious Mendicant" (June, pp. 45-51; July, pp. 66-72; August, pp. 11-16; September, pp. 31-37).

VL used the *Outlook* and *Twentieth Century* pages to prepare his book, a fact that explains the few variations in spelling ("gray" and "grey") and punctuation in the two parts.

The following poems were used as interludes in the original *Handy Guide* (see "Index of Titles," *The Poetry of Vachel Lindsay*): "Follow the Thistledown," "Columbus," "The Would-Be Merman," "The Tramp's Refusal," "Phidias," "Confucius," "With a Rose, to Brunhilde," "In Lost Jerusalem," "The Town of American Visions," "That Which Men Hail as King," "What the Sexton Said," "Life Transcendent," "In the Immaculate Conception Church," and "That Men Might See Again the Angel-Throng."]

I

VAGRANT ADVENTURES IN THE SOUTH

THE MAN UNDER THE YOKE

It was Sunday morning in the middle of March. I was stranded in Jacksonville, Florida. After breakfast I had five cents left. Joyously I purchased a sack of peanuts, then started northwest on the railway ties straight toward that part of Georgia marked "Swamp" on the map.

Sunset found me in a pine forest. I decided to ask for a meal and lodging at the white house looming half a mile ahead just by the track. I prepared a speech to this effect: —

"I am the peddler of dreams. I am the sole active member of the ancient brotherhood of the troubadours. It is against the rules of our order to receive money. We have the habit of asking a night's lodging in exchange for repeating verses and fairy tales."

As I approached the house I forgot the speech. All the turkeys gobbled at me fiercely. The two dogs almost tore down the fence trying to get a taste of me. I went to the side gate to appeal to the proud old lady crowned with a lace cap and enthroned in the porch rocker. Her son, the proprietor, appeared. He shall ever be named the dog-man. His tone of voice was such, that, to speak in metaphor, he bit me in the throat. He refused me a place in his white kennel. He would not share his dog-biscuit. The being on the porch assured me in a whanging yelp that they did not take "nobody in under no circumstances." Then the dog-man, mollified by my serene grin, pointed with his thumb into the woods, saying: "There is a man in there who will take you in sure." He said it as though it were a reflection on his neighbor's dignity. That I might not seem to be hurrying, I asked if his friend kept watch-dogs. He assured me the neighbor could not afford them.

The night with the man around the corner was like a chapter from that curious document, "The Gospel according to St. John." He "could not afford to turn a man away" because once he slept three nights in the rain when he walked here from west Georgia. No one would give him shelter. After that he decided that when he had a roof he would go shares with whoever asked. Some strangers were good, some bad, but he would risk them all. Imagine this amplified in the drawling wheeze of the cracker sucking his corn-cob pipe for emphasis.

His real name and address are of no consequence. I found later that there were thousands like him. But let us call him "The Man Under the Yoke." He was lean as an old opium-smoker. He was sooty as a pair of tongs. His Egyptian-mummy jaws had a two-weeks' beard. His shirt had not been washed since the flood. His ankles were innocent of socks. His hat had no band. I verily believe his pipe was hereditary, smoked first by a bond-slave in Jamestown, Virginia.

He could not read. I presume his wife could not. They were much embarrassed when I wanted them to show me Lakeland on the map. They had warned me against that village as a place where itinerant strangers were shot full of holes. Well, I found that town pretty soon on the map, and made the brief, snappy memorandum in my notebook: "Avoid Lakeland."

There were three uncertain chairs on the porch, one a broken rocker. Therefore the company sat on the railing, loafing against the pillars. The plump wife was frozen with diffidence. The genial, stubby neighbor, a man from away back in the woods, after telling me how to hop freight-cars, departed through an aperture in the wandering fence.

The two babies on the floor, squealing like shoats, succeeded in being good without being clean. They wrestled with the puppies who emerged from somewhere to the number of four. I wondered if the Man Under the Yoke would turn to a dog-man when the puppies grew up and learned to bark.

Supper was announced with the admonition, "Bring the chairs." The rocking chair would not fit the kitchen table. Therefore the two babies occupied one, and the lord of the house another, and the kitchen chair was allotted to your servant. The mother hastened to explain that she was "not hungry." After snuffing the smoking lamp that had no chimney, she paced at regular intervals between the stove and her lord, piling hot biscuits before him.

I could not offer my chair, and make it plain that some one must stand. I expressed my regrets at her lack of appetite and fell to. Their hospitality did not fade in my eyes when I considered that they ate such provisions every day. There was a dish of salt pork that tasted like a salt mine. We had one deep plate in common containing a soup of luke-warm water, tallow, half-raw fat pork and wilted greens. This dish was innocent of any enhancing condiment. I turned to the biscuit pile.

They were raw in the middle. I kept up courage by watching the children consume the tallow soup with zest. After taking one biscuit for meat, and one for vegetables, I ate a third for good-fellowship. The mother was anxious that her children should be a credit, and shook them too sternly and energetically I thought, when they buried their hands in the main dish.

Meanwhile the Man Under the Yoke told me how his bosses in the lumber-camp kept his wages down to the point where the grocery bill took all his pay; how he was forced to trade at the "company" store, there in the heart of the pine woods. He had cut himself in the saw-pit, had been laid up for a month, and "like a fool" had gone back to the same business. Last year he had saved a little money, expecting to get things "fixed up nice," but the whole family was sick from June till October. He liked his fellow-workmen. They had to stand all he did. They loved the woods, and because of this love would not move to happier fortunes. Few had gone farther than Jacksonville. They did not understand travelling. They did not understand the traveller and were "likely to be mean to him." Then he asked me whether I thought "niggers" had souls. I answered "Yes." He agreed reluctantly. "They have a soul, of course, but it's a mighty small one." We adjourned to the front room, carrying our chairs down a corridor, where the open doorways we passed displayed uncarpeted floors and no furniture. The echo of the slow steps of the Man Under the Yoke reverberated through the wide house like muffled drums at a giant's funeral. Yet the largeness of the empty house was wealth. I have been entertained since in many a poorer castle; for instance, in Tennessee, where a deaf old man, a crone, and her sister, a lame man, a slug of a girl, and a little unexplained boy ate, cooked, and slept by an open fire. They had neither stove, lamp, nor candle. I was made sacredly welcome for the night, though it was a one-room cabin with a low roof and a narrow door.

Thanks to the Giver of every good and perfect gift, pine-knots cost nothing in a pine forest. New York has no such fireplaces as that in the front room of the Man Under the Yoke. I thought of an essay by a New England sage on compensation. There were many old scriptures rising in my heart as I looked into that blaze. The one I remembered most was "I was a stranger, and ye took me in." But though it was Sunday night, I did not quote Scripture to my host.

It was seven o'clock. The wife had put her babies to bed. She sat on the opposite side of the fire from us. Eight o'clock was bedtime, the host had to go to work so early. But our three hearts were bright as the burning pine for an hour.

You have enjoyed the golden embossed brocades of Hokusai. You have felt the charm of Maeterlinck's "The Blind." Think of these, then think of the shoulders of the Man Under the Yoke, embossed by the flame. Think of his voice as an occult instrument, while he burned a bit of crackling brush, and spoke of the love he bore that fireplace, the memory of evenings his neighbors had spent there with him, the stories told, the pipes smoked, the good silent times with wife and children. It was said by hints, and repetitions, and broken syllables, but it was said. We ate and drank in the land of heart's desire. This man and his wife sighed at the fitting times, and smiled, when to smile was to understand, while I recited a few of the rhymes of the dear singers of yesterday and to-day: Yeats and Lanier, Burns and even Milton. This fire was the treasure at the end of the rainbow. I had not been rainbow-chasing in vain.

As my host rose and knocked out his pipe, he told how interesting lumbering with oxen could be made, if a man once understood how they were driven. He assured me that the most striking thing in all these woods was a team of ten oxen. He directed me to a road whereby I would be sure to see half a dozen to-morrow. He said if ever I met a literary man, to have him write them into verses. Therefore the next day I took the route and observed: and be sure, if ever I meet the proper minstrel, I shall exhort him with all my strength to write the poem of the yoke.

As to that night, I slept in that room in the corner away from the fireplace. One comfort was over me, one comfort and pillow between me and the dark floor. The pillow was laundered at the same time as the shirt of my host. There was every reason to infer that the pillow and comfort came from his bed.

They slept far away, in some mysterious part of the empty house. I hoped they were not cold. I looked into the rejoicing fire. I said: "This is what I came out into the wilderness to see. This man had nothing, and gave me half of it, and we both had abundance."

THE MAN WITH THE APPLE-GREEN EYES

Remember, if you go a-wandering, the road will break your heart. It is sometimes like a woman, caressing and stabbing at once. It is a mystery, this quality of the road. I write, not to explain, but to warn, and to give the treatment. Comradeship and hospitality are opiates most often at hand.

I remember when I encountered the outpoured welcome of an Old Testament Patriarch, a praying section boss in a gray log village, one Monday evening in North Florida. He looked at me long. He sensed my depression. He made me his seventh son.

He sent his family about to announce my lecture in the schoolhouse on "The Value of Poetry." Enough apple-cheeked maidens, sad mothers, and wriggling, large-eyed urchins assembled to give an unconscious demonstration of the theme.

The little lamp spluttered. The windows rattled. Two babies cried. Everybody assumed that lectures were delightful, miserable, and important. The woman on the back seat nursed her baby, reducing the noise one third. When I was through shouting, they passed the hat. I felt sure I had carried my point. Poetry was eighty-three cents valuable, a good deal for that place. And the sons of the Patriarch were the main contributors, for before the event he had thunderously exhorted them to be generous. I should not have taken the money? But that was before I had a good grip on my rule.

The Patriarch was kept away by a neighbor who had been seized with fits on Sunday, while fishing. The neighbor though mending physically, was in a state of apprehension. He demanded, with strong crying and tears, that the Patriarch pray with him. Late in the evening, as we were about the hearth, recovering from the lecture, my host returned from the sinner's bed, the pride of priesthood in his step. He had established a contrite heart in his brother, though all the while frank with him about the doubtful efficacy of prayer in healing a body visited with just wrath.

Who would not have loved the six sons, when, at the Patriarch's command, they drew into a circle around the family altar, with their small sister, and the gentle mother with her babe at her breast? It was an achievement to put the look of prayer into such flushed, wilful faces as those boys displayed. They followed their father with the devotion of an Ironside regiment as he lifted up his voice singing "The Son of God goes forth to War." They rolled out other strenuous hymns. I thought they would sing through the book. I looked at the mother. I thanked God for her. She was the only woman in Florida who could cook. And her voice was honey. Her breast was ivory. The child was a pearl. Her whole aspect had the age and the youth of one of De Forest Brush's austere American madonnas. The scripture lesson, selected not by chance, covered the adventures of Jacob at Bethel.

We afterwards knelt on the pine floor, our heads in the seats of the chairs. I peeped and observed the Patriarch with his chair almost in the fireplace. He ignored the heat. He shouted the name of the smallest boy, who answered the roll-call by praying: "Now I lay me down to sleep." The father megaphoned for the next, and the next, with a like response. He called the girl's name, but in a still small voice she lisped the Lord's Prayer. As the older boys were reached, the prayers became individual, but containing fragments of "Now I lay me." The mother petitioned for the soul of the youngest boy, not yet in a state of grace, for a sick cousin, and many a neighborhood cause. The father prayed twenty minutes, while the chair smoked. I forgot the chair at last when he voiced the petition that the stranger in the gates might have visitations on his lonely road, like Jacob at Bethel. Then a great appeal went up the chimney that the whole assembly might bear abundantly the fruits of the spirit. The fire leaped for joy. I knew that when the prayer appeared before the throne, it was still a tongue of flame.

*   *   *

Next morning I spent about seventy cents lecture money on a railway ticket, and tried to sleep past my destination, but the conductor woke me. He put me off in the Okefenokee swamp, just inside the Georgia line. The waters had more brass-bespangled ooze than in mid-Florida; the marsh weeds beneath were lustrous red. I crossed an interminable trestle over the Suwannee River. A fidgety bird was scolding from tie to tie. If the sky had been turned over and the azure boiled to a spoonful, you would have had the intense blue with which he was painted. If the caldron had been filled with sad clouds, and boiled to a black lump, you would have had my heart. Ungrateful, I had forgotten the Patriarch. I was lonely for I knew not what; maybe for my friend Edward Broderick, who had walked with me through central Florida, and had been called to New York by the industrial tyranny which the steel rails represented even here.

We two had taken the path beside the railway in the regions of Sanford and Tampa, walking in loose sand white as salt. An orange grove in twilight had been a sky of little moons. We had eaten not many oranges. They are expensive there. But we had stolen the souls of all we passed, and so had spoiled them for their owners. It had been an exquisite revenge.

We had seen swamps of parched palmettos set afire by wood-burning locomotives whose volcanic smoke-stacks are squat and wide, like those on the engines in grandmother's third reader.

We had met Mr. Terrapin, Mr. Owl, Mrs. Cow, and Master Calf, all of them carved by the train-wheels, Mr. Buzzard sighing beside them. We had met Mr. Pig again at the cracker's table, cooked by last year's forest-fire, run over by last year's train. But what had it mattered? For we together had had ears for the mocking-bird, and eyes for the moss-hung live oaks that mourn above the brown swamp waters.

We had met few men afoot, only two professional tramps, yet the path by the railway was clearly marked. Some Florida poet must celebrate the Roman directness of the railways embanked six feet above the swamp, going everywhere in regions that have no wagon-roads.

But wherever in our land there is a railway, there is a little path clinging to the embankment holding the United States in a network as real as that of the rolled steel, — a path wrought by the foot of the unsubdued. This path wanders back through history till it encounters Tramp Columbus, Tramp Dante, Tramp St. Francis, Tramp Buddha, and the rest of our masters.

All this we talked of nobly, even grandiloquently, but now I walked alone, ignoring the beautiful turpentine forests of Georgia and the sometime accepted merits of a quest for the Grail, the Gleam, or the Dark Tower. Reaching Fargo about one o'clock I attempted to telegraph for money to take me home, beaten. It was not a money-order office, and thirteen cents would not have covered the necessary business details. Forced to make the best of things, I spent all upon ginger-snaps at the combination grocery-store and railway-station. I shared them with a drummer waiting for the freight, who had the figure of Falstaff, and the mustaches of Napoleon third. I did not realize at that time, that by getting myself penniless I was inviting good luck.

After a dreary while, the local freight going to Valdosta came in. Napoleon advanced to capture a ride. A conductor and an inspector were on the platform. He attacked them with cigars. He indulged freely in friendly swearing and slapping on the back. He showed credentials, printed and written. He did not want to wait three hours for the passenger train in that much-to-be-condemned town. His cigars were refused, his papers returned. He took the path to the lumberman's hotel. His defeat appeared to be the inspector's doing.

That obstinate inspector wore a gray stubble beard and a collar chewed by many laundries. He was encompassed in a black garment of state that can be described as a temperance overcoat. He needed only a bulging umbrella and a nose like a pump-spout to resemble the caricatures of the Prohibition Party that appeared in *Puck* when St. John ran for President.

I showed him all my baggage carried in an oil-cloth wrapper in my breast pocket: a blue bandanna, a comb, a little shaving mirror, a tooth-brush, a razor, and a piece of soap. "These," I said, "are my credentials."

Also I showed a little package of tracts in rhyme I was distributing to the best people: *The Wings of the Morning,* or *The Tree of Laughing Bells.* I hinted he might become the possessor of one. I drew his attention to the fact that there was no purse in the exhibit. I divided my last four ginger-snaps with him. I showed him a letter commending me to all pious souls from a leading religious worker in New York, Charles F. Powlison.

Soon we were thundering away to Valdosta! Mr. Temperance climbed to the observation chair in the little box at the top of the caboose, alternately puzzling over my *Wings of the Morning,* and looking out. The caboose bumped like a farm-wagon on a frozen road. The pine-burning stove roared. The negro Adonis on the wood-pile had gold in his teeth. He had eyes like dark jewels set in white marble, and he polished lanterns as black as himself.

"By Jove," I said. "That's the handsomest bit of lacquer this side of the Metropolitan Museum."

"'Sh," said Conductor Roundface, sobering himself. "You will queer yourself with the old man. He wouldn't let that drummer on because *he* swore."

The old man came down. I bridled my profane tongue while he lectured the conductor on the necessity for more interest in the Georgia public schools, and the beauty of total abstinence, and, at last, the Japanese situation. This is a condensed translation of his speech: "I was on the side of the Russians all through the Russo-Japanese war. My friends said, 'Hooray for Japan.' But I say a Japanese is a nigger. I have never seen one, but I have seen their pictures. The Lord intended people to stay where they were put. We ought to have trade, but no immigration. Chinese belong to China. They are adapted to the Chinese climate. Niggers belong to Africa. They are adapted to the African climate. Americans belong to America. They are adapted to the American climate. Why, the mixing that is going on is something scandalous. I had a nigger working for me once that was half-Spaniard and half-Indian. There are just a few white people, and more mulattoes every day. The white people ought to keep their blood pure. Russians are white people. Germans, English, and Americans are white people. French people are niggers. Dagoes are niggers. Jews are niggers. All people are niggers but just these four. There is going to be a big war in two or three years between all the white people and all the niggers. The niggers are going to combine and force a fight, Japan in the lead.''

We reached Valdosta after dark. Conductor and inspector exchanged with me most civil good-bys. Their hospitality had been nepenthe for my poor broken heart. I reconciled myself to sitting in front of the station fireplace all night. I thought my nearest friend was at Macon, one hundred and fifty miles north; a gay cavalier who had read Omar Khayyam with me in college.

Just then an immense, angular, red-haired man sat down in front of the fire. He might have been the prodigal son of some Yankee farmer-statesman. He threw his arms around me, and though I had never seen him before, the Brotherhood of Man was established at once. He cast an empty bottle into the wood-box. He produced another. I would not drink. He poured down one-half of it. It snorted like dish-water going into the sink. He said: ''That's right. Don't drink. This is the first time I ever drank. I have been on a soak two weeks. You see I was in Texas a long time, and went broke. I don't know how I got here.'' ''Well,'' I said, ''we have this fire till they run us out. Enjoy yourself.''

He wept. ''I don't deserve to enjoy anything. Anybody that's made a fool of himself as I have done. I wish I were in Vermont where my wife and babies are buried. Somebody wrote me they were dead and buried just when I went broke.''

Thereafter he was merry. ''There was a man in Vermont I didn't like who kept a fire like this. I went to see him every evening because I liked his fire. He would study and I would smoke.''

He took out two dimes. ''Say, that's my last money. Let's buy two tickets to the next station and get off and shoot up the town.''

A hollow-eyed little man of middle age, grimy like a coal-miner, sat down on the other side of Mr. Vermont. He said he had been flagging trains for so long he could not tell when he began. He said he must wait three hours for a friend. He declined the bottle. He listened to Mr. Vermont's story, told with variations. He put his chin into his hands, his elbows on his knees, and slept. Vermont threw himself on top of the bent back, his face wrapped in his arms, like a

school-boy asleep on his desk-lid. Mr. Flagman slowly awoke, and
cast off his brother, and slept again. Cautiously Vermont waited, to
resume his pillow in a quarter of an hour, and be again cast off.

Mr. Flagman sat up. I asked him if there was a train for Macon
going soon. He said: "The through freight is making up now." He
gave me the conductor's name. I asked if there was any one about
who could write me a pass to Macon. He said, "The pay car has just
come in, and Mr. Grady can give you a pass if he wants to." I went
out to the tracks.

From a little window at the end of the car Mr. Grady was paying the
interminable sons of Ham, who emerged from the African night,
climbed the steps, received their envelopes, and slunk down the steps
into the African night.

At last I showed Mr. Grady my letter from Charles F. Powlison.
Mr. Grady did not appear to be of a religious turn. I asked him
permission to ride to Macon in the caboose of the freight, going out at
one o'clock. I assured him it was beneath my dignity to crawl into the
box-car, or patronize the blind baggage, and I was tired of walking in
swamp. Mr. Grady asked, "Are you an official of the road?"

"No, sir."

"Then what you ask is impossible, sir."

"Oh, my dear Mr. Grady, it is not impossible—"

"I am glad to have met you, sir. Goodnight, sir," and Mr. Grady
had shut the window.

There was the smash, clang, and thud of making up a train. A
negro guided me to the lantern of a freight conductor. The conductor
had the lean frame, the tight jaw, the fox nose, the Chinese skin of a
card-shark. He would have made a name for himself on the Spanish
Main, some centuries since, by the cool way he would have snatched
jewels from ladies' ears and smiled when they bled. He did not smile
now. He gripped his lantern like a cutlass, and the cars groaned.
They were gentlemen in armor compelled to walk the plank by this
pirate with the apple-green eyes. We will call him Mr. Shark.

I put my pious letter into my pocket. "Mr. Shark, I would like to
ride to Macon in the caboose." Mr. Shark thrust his lantern under my
hat-brim. I had no collar, but was not ashamed of that. He said, "I
have met men like you before." He turned down the track shouting
orders. I jumped in front of him. I said, "You are mistaken. You have
not met a man like me before. I am the goods. I am the wise boy from
New York. I have been walking in every swamp in Florida, eating
dead pig for breakfast, water-moccasins for lunch, alligators for
dinner. I would like to tell you my adventures."

"What Grandpa Mouse Said," see p. 204.

Mr. Shark ignored me, and went on persecuting the train.

Valdosta was a depot in the midst of darkness. I hated the darkness. I went into the depot. Vermont was offering Flagman the bottle. He drank.

Flagman asked me: "Can't you make it?"

"No. Grady turned me down. And the conductor turned me down."

Mr. Flagman said, "The sure way to ride in a caboose like a gentleman is to ask the conductor like he is a gentleman, and everybody else is a gentleman, and when he turns you down, ask him again like a gentleman." And much more with that refrain. It was wisdom lightly given, profounder than it seemed. Let us remember the tired flagman, and engrave the substance of his saying on our souls.

I sought the pirate again. I took off my hat. I bowed like Don Caesar De Bazan, but gravely. "I ask you, just as one gentleman to another, to take me to Macon. I have friends in Macon."

Mr. Shark showed a pale streak of smile. "Come around at one o'clock."

My "Thank you" was drowned by a late passenger. It came from Fargo, for Napoleon III dismounted. He said: "Hello. Where are you going, boy?"

"I am just taking the caboose of the through freight for Macon. But I have a few minutes."

"How the devil did you get here, sir?" I told him the story in brief. We were in front of the fire now. "How are you going to make this next train? I would like to go with you."

I could not tell whether he meant it or not. Right beside us Mr. Flagman was asleep for all night, with his elbows on his knees, his chin in his hands. Stretched above Flagman's back was Mr. Vermont, like a school-boy asleep on his desk. I said, "Do you see the gentleman on the bottom of the pile? He is the Grand Lama of Cabooseville. You have to ask him for the password. The man on top is the sublime sub-Lama."

Napoleon looked dubiously at them, and the two bottles in the wood-box. He gave me good words of farewell, finishing with mock-gravity: "Of course I respect you, sir, in not giving the password without orders from your superior, sir."

And now I boarded the caboose, hurrying to surprise the Macon cavalier. He expected me in three weeks, walking. But the caboose did one hundred and fifty miles in thirteen hours, and all the way my heart spun like a glorified musical top. Alas, this is a tale of drink. I filled the coffee-pot and drained it an infinite number of times, all because my poor broken heart was healed. The stove was the only person in the world out of humor. He was mad because his feet were nailed to the floor. He tried to spill the coffee, and screamed, "Now you've done it" every time we rounded a curve. The caboose-door slammed open every seven minutes, Shark and his white man and his negro rushing in from their all-night work for refreshment.

The manner of serving coffee in a caboose is this: there are three tin cups for the white men. The negro can chew sugar-cane, or steal a drink when we do not look. There is a tin box of sugar. If one is serving Mr. Shark, one shakes a great deal of sugar into the cup, and more down one's sleeve, and into one's shoes and about the rocking floor. One becomes sprinkled like a doughnut, newly-fried, and fragrant with splashed coffee. The cinders that come in on the breath of the shrieking night cling to the person. But if you are serving Mr. Shark you do not mind these things. You pour his drink, you eat his bread and cheese, thanking him from the bottom of your stomach, not having eaten anything since the ginger-snaps of long ago. You solemnly touch your cup to his, as you sit with him on the red disembowelled car cushions, with the moss gushing out. You wish him the treasure-heaps of Aladdin or a racing stable in Ireland, whichever he pleases.

Let all the readers of this tale who hope to become Gentlemen of the Road take off collars and cuffs, throw their purses into the ditch, break their china, and drink their coffee from tinware to the health of Mr. Shark, our friend with the apple-green eyes. Yea, my wanderers, the cure for the broken heart is gratitude to the gentleman you would hate, if you had your collar on or your purse in your pocket when you met him. Though there was heavy betting against him, he becomes the Hero in a whirlwind finish. Patriarch and Flagman disputing for second, decision for Flagman.

MACON

The languid town of Macon, Georgia, will ever remain in my mind as my first island of respite after vagrancy. My friend C.D. Russell lent me his clothes, took me to his eating-place, introduced his circle. We settled the destiny of the universe several different ways in peripatetic discourse.

After one has ventured one hundred and fifty miles through everglades and spent twenty-four sleepless hours riding in freight-cabooses the marrow of his bones is marsh, his hair and clothes are moss, cinders and bark, his immortal soul is engine-smoke. Feeling just so, I had entered Russell's law office. He was at court. I sent word by his partner that I had gone to school with him in Ohio, that I had mailed a postal last Sunday from Florida telling him I would arrive afoot in three weeks, — but here I was, already. The word was carried with Southern precision.

"There is a person in the office who went to school with you in Indiana."

"I did not go to school in Indiana."

"He has been walking in Mississippi and Alabama. He wrote you a postal six weeks ago."

"How does he look?"

"Like the devil. He is principally pants and shirt."

The cavalier knew who that was. He found me, took me to his castle, introduced civilization. CIVILIZATION is whiter than the clouds, and full of clear water. One enters it with a plunge. CULTURE is a fuzzy fabric with which one rubs in CIVILIZATION. After I had been intimate with these, I was admitted to SOCIETY: a suit of the cavalier's clothes. I looked like him then, all but head and hands. I regarded myself with awe, as a gorilla would if he found himself fading into a Gibson picture.

A chair is a sturdy creature. I wonder who captured the first one? Who put out its eyes and taught it to stand still? A table-cloth is ritualistic. How nobly the napkin defends the vest, while those glistening birds, the knife, the fork, the spoon, bring one food.

How did these things to eat get here among these hundreds of houses? One would think that if anything to eat were brought among so many men, there would be enough hungry ones to kill each other and spoil it with blood.

Why do people stop eating when they have had just a bit? Why not go on forever?

We were in another room. The cavalier showed on the table what he called his Bible: the letters of Lord Chesterfield. To one who has not slept in all his life, who has lived a thousand years on freight trains, books do not count much. But how ingenious is a white iron bed, how subtle are pillows, how overwhelming is sleep!

THE FALLS OF TALLULAH

(North Georgia)

I

The Call of the Water

The dust of many miles was upon me. I felt uncouth in the presence of the sun-dried stones. Here was a natural bathing-place. Who could resist it?

I climbed further down the cañon, holding to the bushes. The cliff along which the water rushed to the fall's foot was smooth and seemed artificially made, though it had been so hewn by the fury of the cataclysm in ages past.

I took off my clothes and put my shoulders against the granite, being obliged to lean back a little to conform to its angle. I was standing with my left shoulder almost touching the perilous main column of water. A little fall that hurried along by itself a bit nearer the bank flowed over me. It came with headway. Though it looked so innocent, I could scarcely hold up against its power.

But it gave me delight to maintain myself. The touch of the stone was balm to my walk-worn body and dust-fevered feet. Like a sacredotal robe the water flowed over my shoulders and I thought myself priest of the solitude.

I stepped out into the air. With unwonted energy I was able to throw off the coldness of my wet frame. The water there at the fall's foot was like a thousand elves singing. "Joy to all creatures!" cried the birds. "Joy to all creatures! Glory, glory, glory to the wild falls!"

II

The Piping of Pan

I was getting myself sunburned, stretched out on the warm dry rocks. Down over the steep edge, somewhere near the foot of the next descent I heard the pipes of Pan. Why should I dress and go?

I made my shoes and clothes into a bundle, and threw them down the cliff and climbed over, clinging to the steep by mere twigs. I seemed to hear the piping as I approached the terrace at the fall's base. Then the sound of music blended with the stream's strange voice and I turned to merge myself again with its waters.

Against the leaning wall of the cliff I placed my shoulders. The descending current smote me, wrestling with wildwood laughter, threatening to crush me and hurl me to the base of the mountain. But just as before my feet were well set in a notch of the cliff that went across the stream, cut there a million years ago.

It was a curious combination to discover, this stream-wide notch, and above it this wall with the water spread like a crystal robe over it. In the centre of the fall a Cyclops could have stood to bathe, and on the edge was the same provision in miniature for feeble man. And it was the more curious to find this plan repeated in detail by successive cataracts of the cañon, unmistakably wrought by the slow hand of geologic ages. And to see the water of the deep central stream undisturbed in the midst of the fall and still crystalline, and to see it slide down the steep incline and strike each notch at the foot with sudden music and appalling foam, was more wonderful than the simple telling can explain.

Each sheet of crystal that came over my shoulders seemed now to pour into them rather than over them. I lifted my mouth and drank as a desert bird drinks rain. My downstretched arms and extended fingers and the spreading spray seemed one. My heart with its exultant blood seemed but the curve of a cataract over the cliff of my soul.

III

Peril, Vanity, and Adoration

Led by the pipes of Pan, I again descended. Once more that sound, almost overtaken, interwove itself with the water's cry, and I merged body and soul with the stream and the music. The margin of another cataract crashed upon me. In the recklessness of pleasure, one arm swung into the main current. Then the water threatened my life. To save myself, I was kneeling on one knee. I reached out blindly and found a hold at last in a slippery cleft, and later, it seemed an age, with the other hand I was able to reach one leaf. The leaf did not break. At last its bough was in my grasp and I crawled frightened into the sun. I sat long on a warm patch of grass.

But the cliffs and the water were not really my enemies. They sent a wind to give me delight. Never was the taste of the air so sweet as then. The touch of it was on my lips like fruit. There was a flattery in the tree-limbs bending near my shoulders. They said, "There is brotherhood in your footfall on our roots and the touch of your hand on our boughs."

The spray of the splashed foam was wine. I was the unchallenged possessor of all of nature my body and soul could lay hold upon. It was the fair season between spring and summer when no one came to this place. Like Selkirk, I was monarch of all I surveyed. In my folly I seemed to feel strange powers creeping into my veins from the sod. I forgot my near-disaster. I said in my heart, "O Mother Earth majestical, the touch of your creatures has comforted me, and I feel the strength of the soil creeping up into my dust. From this patch of soft grass, power and courage come up into me from your bosom, from the foundation of your continents. I feel within me the soul of iron from your iron mines, and the soul of lava from your deepest fires."

IV

The Blood Unquenchable

The satyrs in the bushes were laughing at me and daring me to try the water again.

I stood on the edge of the rapids where were many stones coming up out of the foam. I threw logs across. The rocks held them in place. I lay down between the logs in the liquid ice. I defied it heartily. And my brother the river had mercy upon me, and slew me not.

Amid the shout of the stream the birds were singing: "Joy, joy, joy to all creatures, and happiness to the whole earth. Glory, glory, glory to the wild falls."

I struggled out from between the logs and threw my bundle over the cliff, and again descended, for I heard the pipes of Pan, just below me there, too plainly for delay. They seemed to say "Look! Here is a more exquisite place."

The sun beat down upon me. I felt myself twin brother to the sun. My body was lit with an all-conquering fever. I had walked through tropical wildernesses for many a mile, gathering sunshine. And now in an afternoon I was gambling my golden heat against the icy silver of the river and winning my wager, while all the leaves were laughing on all the trees.

And again I stood in a Heaven-prepared place, and the water poured in glory upon my shoulders.

* * *

Why was it so dark? Was a storm coming? I was dazed as a child in the theatre beholding the crowd go out after the sudden end of a solemn play. My clothes, it appeared, were half on. I was kneeling, looking up. I counted the falls to the top of the cañon. It was night, and I had wrestled with them all. My spirit was beyond all reason happy. This was a day for which I had not planned. I felt like one crowned. My blood was glowing like the blood of the crocus, the blood of the tiger-lily. And so I meditated, and then at last the chill of weariness began to touch me and in my heart I said, "Oh Mother Earth, for all my vanity, I know I am but a perishable flower in a cleft of the rock. I give thanks to you who have fed me the wild milk of this river, who have upheld me like a child of the gods throughout this day."

Around a curve in the cañon, down stream, growing each moment sweeter, I heard the pipes of Pan.

V

The Gift of Tallulah

Go, you my brothers, whose hearts are in sore need of delight, and bathe in the falls of Tallulah. That experience will be for the foot-sore a balm, for the languid a lash, for the dry-throated pedant the very cup of nature. To those crushed by the inventions of cities, wounded by evil men, it will be a washing away of tears and of blood. Yea, it will be to them all, what it was to my heart that day, the sweet, sweet blowing of the reckless pipes of Pan.

THE GNOME

Let us now recall a certain adventure among the moonshiners.

When I walked north from Atlanta Easter morning, on Peachtree road, orchards were flowering everywhere. Resurrection songs flew across the road from humble blunt steeples.

Stony Mountain, miles to the east, Kenesaw on the western edge of things, and all the rest of the rolling land made the beginning of a gradual ascent by which I was to climb the Blue Ridge. The road mounted the watershed between the Atlantic and the gulf.

An old man took me into his wagon for a mile. I asked what sort of people I would meet on the Blue Ridge. He answered, "They make blockade whisky up there. But if you don't go around hunting stills by the creeks, or in the woods away from the road, they'll be awful glad to see you. They are all moonshiners, but if they likes a man they loves him, and they're as likely to get to lovin' you as not."

When I was truly in the mountains, six days north of Atlanta, a day's journey from the last struggling railway, the road wound into a certain high, uninhabited valley. Two days back, at a village I entered just after I had enjoyed the falls of Tallulah, I had found a letter from my new friend John Collier whom I had met in Macon and Atlanta. It contained a little money, which he insisted I should take, to make easier my way. I was inconsistent enough to spend some of it, instead of returning it or giving it "to the poor."

I invested seventy-five cents in brogans made of the thickest leather. I had thought they were conquered the first day. But now one of them bit a piece out of my heel. John Collier has done noble things since. On my behalf, for instance, he climbed Mount Mitchell with me, and showed me half the glory of the South. Then and after, he has helped my soul with counsel and teaching. But he should not have corrupted a near-Franciscan with money for hoodoo brogans. Though it was fairly warm weather, if ever I rested five minutes, the heavy things stiffened like cooling metal.

The little streams I crossed scarcely afforded me a drink. Their dried borders had the footprints of swine on them.

Lameness affects one's vision. The thick woods were the dregs of the landscape, fit haunt for the acorn-grubbing sow. The road following the ridges was a monster's spine.

Those wicked brogans led me where they should not. Or maybe it was just my destiny to find what I found.

About four o'clock in the afternoon, after exploring many roads that led to futile nothing, I was on what seemed the main highway, and dragged myself into the sight of the first mortal since daybreak. He seemed like a gnome as he watched me across the furrows. And so he was, despite his red-ripe cheeks. The virginal mountain apple-tree, blossoming overhead, half covering the toad-like cabin, was out of place. It should have been some fabulous, man-devouring devil-bush from the tropics, some monstrous work of the enemies of God.

The child, just in her teens, helping the Gnome to plant sweet potatoes, had in her life planted many, and eaten few. Or so it appeared. She was a crouching lump of earth. Her father dug the furrow. She did the planting, shovelling the dirt with her hands. Her face was sodden as any in the slums of Chicago. She ran to the house a ragged girl, and came back a homespun girl, a quick change. It must not be counted against her that she did not wash her face.

The Gnome talked to me meanwhile. He had made up his mind about me. "I guess you want to stay all night?"

"Yes."

"The next house is fifteen miles away. You are welcome if what we have is good enough for you. My wife is sick, but she will not let you be any bother."

I wanted to be noble and walk on. But I persuaded myself my feet were as sick as the woman. I accepted the Gnome's invitation.

Let the readers with a detective instinct note that his hoe-handle was two feet short, and had been whittled a little around the top to make it usable. It was at best an awkward instrument. (The mystery will soon be solved.)

We were met at the door by one my host called Brother Joseph—a towering shape with an upper lip like a walrus, for it was armed with tusk-like mustaches. He was silent as King Log.

But the Gnome said, "I have saved up a month of talk since the last stranger came through." With ease, with simplicity of word, with I know not how much of guile, he gave fragments of his life: how he had lived in this log house always, how his first wife died, how her children were raised by this second wife and married off, how they now enjoyed this second family.

He showed me the other fragment of the hoe-handle. "I broke that over a horse's head the last time I was drunk. I always get crazy. When I come to, I do not remember anything about it. The last time I fought with my cousin. When I knocked down his horse he drew his knife. I drew *this* knife. My wife said I fought like a wild hog. I sliced my cousin pretty bad. He skipped the country, for he cut out one of my lungs and two of my ribs. I lost two buckets of blood. It took the doctor a long time to put my insides back."

From this hour forward he struggled between the luxury of being even more confidential, and the luxury of being cautious like a lynx. I squirmed. Despite his abandon, he was watching me.

I put one hand in my pocket. I found a diversion, a pair of eyeglasses. I had chanced on them in the bushes at Tallulah. The droop of his eyelids as he put them on was exquisite. He paced the floor. I had a review of his appearance. He was like a thin twist of tobacco. He had been burned out by too-sharp whisky. The babies clapped their hands as he strutted. He was like a third-rate Sunday-school teacher in a frock coat in the presence of the infant class. He was glad to keep the glasses, yet asked questions with a double meaning, implying I had stolen them in Atlanta, and fled these one hundred miles. We were gay rogues, and we knew it.

"Get up! Make some coffee and supper!" he shouted to the figure on the bed in the black corner of the cabin. He kept his jaw tight on his pipe, speaking to her in the gnome language. She replied in kind, snorting and muffling her words, without moving lips or tongue, and keeping her teeth on her snuff-stick. She stumbled up, groaning, with both hands on her head. She had once been a woman. She had lived with this thing too long. All the trappings that make for home had grown stale and weird about her. The scraps of rag-carpet on the floor were rat eaten. The red calico window curtains were vilely dirty from the years of dust and the leak of many rains. The benches were battered, unsteady. The door-latch was gone. The door was held in place by a stone. She stood before me, her hair hanging straight across her face or down her collar, or flying about or tied behind in a dreadful knot. She stood before me, but as long as I was in that house she did not look at me, she did not speak to me.

There was no stove. The Gnome said: "Wife don't like a stove. She had rather cook the way she learned." We rolled in the back-log for her and coaxed up the embers. We sat at one side of the hearth. We exchanged boastful adventures. She crawled into the fireplace to nurse the corn-bread and coffee and pork to perfection and place the Dutch oven right.

Have you heard your grandmother speak of the Dutch oven? It is a squat kettle which is set in the embers. When it is hot, the biscuit dough is put in and the lid replaced. Slowly the biscuits become ambrosia. Slowly the watching cook is baked.

The Devil was in my host. By his coaxing hospitality he made it seem natural that a woman deadly sick should serve us. The rest of the family could wait. It did not matter if the tiny one cried and pulled the mother's skirt. She smote it into silence and fear, then carried it to the black corner where the potato planter herded the rest of the babies, helped by King Log, the walrus-headed.

The Gnome said, "I quit drinking ever since I had that fight I told you about. I don't dare drink. So I take coffee."

You should have seen him flooding himself with black coffee, drinking from a yellow bowl. I said to myself: "He will surely turn to the consolation of liquor anon. He will beat his wife again. He will drive his children into the woods. This woman must fight the battle for her offspring till her black-snake hair is white. Or maybe that insane knife will go suddenly into her throat. She may die soon with her hair black,—and red."

We ate with manly leisure. We were sated. The mother prepared the second meal, and called the group from the black corner. She made ready her own supper. I see her by the fire, the heavy arm shielding her face, the hunched figure a knot of roots, — a palpable mystery about her, making her worthy of a portrait by some new Rembrandt. It is the tragic mystery born of the isolation of the Blue Ridge and the juice of the Indian corn. Let us not forget the weapon with which she fights the flame, the quaint long shovel.

Let us watch her at the table, breaking her corn-bread alone, her puffy eyelids closed, her cheek-bones seeming to cut through the skin. There is something of the eagle in her aspect because of her Roman nose, and her hands moving like talons. It is not corn-bread that she tears and devours. She is consuming her enemies, which are Weariness, Squalor, Flat and Unprofitable Memory, Spiritual Death. She is seeking to forget that the light of the hearthstone that falls on her dirty but beautiful babies is kindled in hell.

The Gnome spoke of his hogs. A Middle West farmer can talk hogs, and the world will admire him the more. But a mediaeval swine-herd dare not. It is self-betrayal.

My host grew affectionate, grandfatherly. He told of a solid acre of mica on top of a mountain. He speculated that it was a mile deep. He put a chunk into my pocket for me to carry to Asheville to interest great capitalists. He offered me fifty per cent on the profits. I took out a copy of the *Tree of Laughing Bells* from my pocket. I reviewed the tale contained in the book, in words I thought the Gnome would understand. Then he read it for himself with the "specs." He was proud of having learned to read out of the Bible, with no schooling.

He seemed particularly impressed with the length of the journey of the hero of the poem, who flew "to the farthest star of all." He looked at me with conceited shrewdness. "I played hookey myself, when I was a kid. I rode and walked forty-five miles that day. I was mighty glad to get back to my mammy the day after. I never wanted to run away again." He shook his pipe at me. "You are just a run-away boy, that's what you are."

He said something favorable about me to his wife, in the gnome language. She stood up. She shrilled back a caution. She showed her dirty teeth at him. But there was something he was bursting to tell me. He was essentially too reckless to conceal a scret long, even a life-and-death secret. He began: "I still raise a little corn."

The Walrus gave a sort of watch-dog bark. The Gnome reluctantly accepted the caution. He pointed sharply to the bed farthest from the black corner of the room.

"That's for you."

"Isn't there a shed or a corn-crib where I can sleep?"

"No, you don't get out of this house to-night. There aren't any sheds or cribs."

I looked helplessly around that single-roomed cabin. Not fear, but modesty, overcame me. I was expected to retire first. But King Log, the Walrus, perceiving my diffidence, set me an example. He rapidly hauled a couch off the porch and tumbled into it, first undressing as far as his underwear. With a quilt almost to his chin, and covering his pretty pink feet, he was a decent spectacle.

Happily I also wore underwear, and was soon under my quilt. I stole a look at the potato planter. I realized that she was the maiden present. Be pleased, O brothers, to observe that she has been aware of her age and state. She has huddled up to the fire, with her back to us; she has hidden her face on her knees. At last she piles ashes on the embers and finds a place in the black corner in the cot full of children. Her father and mother take the cot between.

Next morning was Sunday, a week since Easter. Only when a man has sadly mangled feet, and blood heated by many weeks of adventure, can he find luxury such as I found in the icy stream next morning. The divine rivulet on the far side of the field had been misnamed "Mud Creek." It was clear as a diamond.

Always carrying a piece of soap in my hip pocket, I was able to take a complete scour. Not content with this (pardon me), I did scrub shirt, socks, underwear, and bandanna. I hung them on the bushes, thanking God for the wind. Taking my before-mentioned credentials from my pocket, I made myself into a gentleman. When I dressed at last, my clothes were a little damp, but I knew that an hour's walking would put all to rights. As I held the bushes aside I saw a crib-like structure that made me shake more than the damp clothes. Was it a still, or was it not a still?

In my innocence I could not tell. But I remembered the warning, "Don't go pokin' round huntin' stills by the creeks."

As I hurried to the house my host carelessly appeared from the region of my bathing-place. He was whittling with his historic knife. I suppose he had noted my actions enough to restore his confidence. Anyway, the shame of being unwashed was his only visible emotion. He said, "I always bathe in hot water."

"So do I, when I am not on the road."

Still he was abashed. He took an enormous chew of tobacco to vindicate himself.

After breakfast the wife helped the Walrus to drag the cot out of doors. When she was alone on the porch I told her how sorry I was she had been obliged to cook for me. I thanked her for her toil. But she hurried away, without a pause or a glance. She kissed one of those miry faced babies. She walked into the house, leaving me smirking at the hills. She growled something at the host. He came forth. He pointed out the road, over the mountains and far away. He broke off a blossoming apple-sprig and whittled it.

"So you've been to Atlanta?" he asked.

"Yes."

"I was there once. What hotel did you use?"

"The Salvation Army."

"I was in the United States Hotel."

Still I was stupid. He continued:

"I was there two years."

He put on his glasses. He threw down the apple-sprig, and, looking over the glasses, he made unhappy each blossom in his own peculiar way. He continued: "I was in the United States Hotel, for making blockade whisky. I don't make it any more." He spat again. "I don't even go fishin' on Sunday unless—"

He had made up his mind that I was a customer, not a detective.

"Unless what?"

"Unless a visitor wants a mess of fish."

But I did not want a mess of fish. Repeatedly I offered money for my night's lodging. This he declined with real pride. *He maintained his one virtue intact.* And so I thought of him, just as I left, as a man who kept his code.

The John Collier brogans were easier that morning, partly because I had something new on my mind, no doubt.

I thought of the Gnome a long time. I thought of the wife, and wondered at her as a unique illustration of the tragic mysteries of the human race. If she screams when seven devils enter into the Gnome, no one outside the house will hear but the apple-tree. If she weeps, only the wind in the chimney will understand. If she seeks justice and the law, King Log, the Walrus, is her uncertain refuge. If she desires mercy, the emperor of that valley, the king above King Log, is a venomous serpent, even the Worm of the Still.

But now the road unwound in glory. I walked away from those serpent-bitten dominions for that time. I was one with the air of the sweet heavens, the light of the ever-enduring sun, the abounding stillness of the forest, and the inscrutable Majesty, brooding on the mountains, the Majesty whom ignorantly we worship.

THE HOUSE OF THE LOOM

A Story of Seven Aristocrats and a Soap-Kettle.

With no sorrow in my heart, with no money in my pocket, with no baggage but a lunch, the most dazzling feature of which was a piece of gingerbread, I walked away from a windswept North Carolina village, one afternoon, over the mountain ridges toward Lake Toxaway. I turned to the right once too often, and climbed Mount Whiteside. There was a drop of millions of miles, and a Lilliputian valley below like a landscape by Charlotte B. Coman. I heard some days later that once a man tied a dog to an umbrella and threw him over. Dog landed safely, barking still. Dog was able to eat, walk, and wag as before. But the fate of the master was horrible. Dog never spoke to him again.

Having no umbrella, I retraced my way. I stepped into the highway that circumscribes the tremendous amphitheatre of Cashier's Valley. I met not a soul till eight o'clock that night. The mountain laurel, the sardis bloom, the violet, and the apple blossom made glad the margins of the splendidly built road; and, as long as the gingerbread lasted, I looked upon these things in a sort of sophisticated wonder.

This was because the gingerbread was given me by a civilized man, to whom John Collier had written for me a letter of introduction: Mr. Thomas G. Harbison, Botanical Collector; American tree seeds a specialty.

Back there by the village he was improving the breed of mountain apples by running a nursery. He was improving the children with a school he taught without salary, and was using the most modern pedagogy. Something in his manner made me say, "You are like a doctor out of one of Ibsen's plays, only you are optimistic." Then we talked of Ibsen. He debated art versus science, he being a science-fanatic, I an art-fanatic. He concluded the argument with these words: "You are bound to be wrong. I am bound to be wrong. What is the use of either of us judging the other?" That is not the mountain way of ending a discussion.

For the purposes of the tale, as well as for his own merits, we must praise this civilized man who entertained me a day and a half so well. His mountain cottage was a permanent civilized camp. Without intruding on his privacy, we can show what that means. Cross a few states to the west with me.

Have you watched the camps of the up-to-date visitors, in the oldest parts of Colorado? They begin with tent, axe, blanket, bacon, and frying-pan, as miners do. In ten summers, though they climb as much as the miners, wear uglier boots, and rougher clothes, their tents are highly organized. They are convenient and free from clutter as the best New York flat. The axe has multiplied rustic benches, bridges, shelters. It has made a refrigerator in the stream. The frying-pan has changed into a camp-stove and a box of white granite dishes. The blanket flowers and Mariposa lilies that made the aspen groves celestial have been gathered in jardinières.

Meanwhile, in the big houses of the veteran miners of the villages are the axe, the blanket, and the frying-pan, though their lords have been through half a dozen fortunes since pioneer days. Those houses have the single great advantage of a rich tradition. They seem to grow up out of the ground.

Musing these matters, I munched my gingerbread, walking past sweet waterfalls, groves of enormous cedars, many springs, and one deserted cabin. I was homesick for that great civilized camp, New York, and the sober-minded pursuit of knowledge there.

But civilization lost her battle at twilight, when I swallowed my last gingerbread crumb. Immediately I was in the land beyond the nowhere place, willing to sleep twelve hours by a waterfall, or let the fairies wake me before day. The road went deeper into savagery. I blundered on, rejoicing in the fever of weariness. In the piercing light of the young stars, the house that came at last before me seemed even more deeply rooted in the ground than the oaks around it. What new revelation lies here? Knock, knock, knock, O my soul, and may Heaven open a mystery that will give the traveller a contrite heart.

Let us tell a secret, even before we enter. If, with the proper magic in our minds, we were guests here, a year or a day, we might write the world's one unwritten epic. All day, in one of these tiny rooms, amid appointments that fill the spirit with the elation of simple things, we would write. At evening we would dream the next event by the fire. The epic would begin with the opening of the door.

There appeared a military figure, with a face like Henry Irving's in contour, like Whistler's in sharpness, fantasy, and pride.

"May I have a night's lodging? I have no money."

"Come in. . . . We never turn a man away."

We were inside. He asked: "What might be your name?" I gave it. He gave his. The circle by the fire did not turn their heads, but presumably I was introduced. One child ran into the kitchen. My host gave me her chair. All looked silently into the great soap-kettle in the midst of the snapping logs.

I have a high opinion of the fine people of the South, and gratefully remember the scattering of gentlefolk so good as to entertain me in their mansions. But in this cottage, with one glance at those fixed, flushed faces, I said: "This is the best blood I have met in this United States." The five children were night-blooming flowers. There were hints of Doré in the shadow of the father, cast against the log walls of the cabin. He sat on the little stairway. He was a better Don Quixote than Doré ever drew.

I said, "Every middle-aged man I have met in Florida, Georgia, and North Carolina has been a soldier, and I suppose you were."

He looked at me long, as though the obligation of hospitality did not involve conversation. He spoke at last: "I fought, but I could not help it. It was for home, or against home. I fought for this cabin."

"It is a beautiful cabin."

He relented a bit. "We have kept it just so, ever since my great-grandfather came here with his pack-mule and made his own trail. I— — hated the war. We did not care anything about the cotton and niggers of the fire-eaters. The niggers never climbed this high."

I changed the subject. "This is the largest fireplace I have seen in the South. A man could stand up in it."

He stiffened again. *This is not the South. This is the Blue Ridge.*

An inner door opened. It was plain the woman who stood there was his wife. She had the austere mouth a wife's passion gives. She had the sweet white throat of her youth, that made even the candle-flame rejoice. She looked straight at me, with ink-black eyes. She was dumb, like some one struggling to awake.

"Everything is ready," she said at length to her husband.

He turned to me: "Your supper is now in the kitchen, 'if what we have is good enough.'" It was the usual formula for hospitality.

I turned to the wife. "My dear woman, I did not know that this was going on. It is not right for you to set a new supper at this hour. I had enough on the road."

"But you have walked a long way." Then she uttered the ancient proverb of the Blue Ridge. "'A stranger needs takin' care of.'"

In the kitchen there was a cook-stove. Otherwise there was nothing to remind one of the world this side of Beowulf. I felt myself in a stronghold of barbarian royalty.

"Do you do your own spinning and weaving?"

She lifted the candle, lighting a corner. "Here are the cards and the wools." She held it higher. "There is the spinning wheel."

"Where is the loom?"

"Up stairs, just by where you will sleep."

I knew that if there was a loom, it was a magic one, for she was a witch of the better sort, a fine, serious witch, and a princess withal.

Her ancestors wore their black hair that simple way when their lords won them by fighting dragons. She was prouder than the pyramids. If the epic is ever written, let it tell how the spinner of the wizard wools did stand to serve the stranger, that being the custom of her house. This was a primitive camp indeed. There was no gingerbread. There was not one thing to remind me of the last table at which I had eaten. But every gesture said, "Good prince, you are far from your court. Therefore, this, our royal trencher, is yours. May you find your way to your own kingdom in peace." But for a long time her lips were still. She had the spareness of a fertile, toiling mother. And, ah, the motherhood in her voice when she said at last, "My son, you are tired."

Let the epic tell that, when the stranger returned to the fireplace, a restless, expectant silence settled down upon the circle. There was portent in the hiss of the flames. When I spoke to the children they only stared at me as at a curious shadow. Their lips moved not. The eldest, about seventeen, had inherited, no doubt, his love of strange brewing. He looked sideways into the soap-kettle. I said to myself, "He sees more hippogriffs than steam-engines." He eyed every move of the circle with restless approval or disapproval. Every chip his little brother threw on the fire seemed to be a symbol of some precious thing sacrificed, every curl of steam seemed to have something to do with the destiny of the house.

He took out of his pocket a monthly magazine. It was the sort that costs ten cents a year. No doubt, had he gone to school to the admirable man who gave me gingerbread, he would have learned to read scientific and technical monthlies. But a magazine of any sort is a terribly intrusive thing at this juncture. The boy, and a sister just a little younger, read in a loud whisper to one another an advertisement they did not want me to hear. At their stage of culture it was impossible to read silently. The advertisement, if I remember, went about this way: —

"Free, free, free! A sewing machine! Send us a two-cent stamp, your name and address, mentioning the name of this magazine. We will tell you how to get an up-to-date sewing machine absolutely free. This offer is good for thirty days."

They wrote a most unscholarly letter, spelling it aloud. It required their total and united culture to produce it. When the girl returned to the fire, she was provoked by her pride into an astonishing flush. How it set off her temples, with their pattern of azure veins! With her lotus-leaf hands, the hands of Hathor, goddess of love, she cooled her cheeks again and again. There is something of breeding in the very color of blood. Come, brothers of the road, all who travel with me in fancy, will you not join the knighthood of the soap-kettle? Come, ladies in mansions, will you not be one with us? None of you could have gainsaid the maiden-in-chief of the assembly. She wore her homespun as Zenobia, princess of Palmyra, wore her splendors. With her arms around her two gypsy younger sisters she smiled at last into the soap-kettle. When the epic is written, let it use words of marvelling, speaking of her hair, so pale, so electrical, set in a thick, ingenious coronal.

All the little children stood up. "Uncle," they shouted. Hoofs sounded by the door. A man entered without knocking. When he saw me he became ceremonious as a Mandarin.

"This is a traveller," said my host.

The messenger indulged in inquiries about my welfare, journey, and destination. My host interrupted.

"How's mother? We have watched late to know."

"She is much worse." And the messenger went on to say that she might not live two days, and the doctor was a careless, indifferent dog, treating her as though she were an ordinary old woman.

"Does he still give her strychnine?"

"He won't deny it." The messenger explained that the doctor thought strychnine in small doses was good for old people. The scientist who gave me gingerbread should have been there to champion the doctor. In the eyes of his judges that night he was suspected of poisoning or treating with criminal folly, royalty itself.

The younger doctor was miles away, and might refuse to make the trip. The two loyal sons seemed paralyzed because the time for decision and the time for mourning came together. There were long silences, interrupted by my host repeating in a sort of primitive song, *"I can't think of anything except my dying mother. I can't think of anything except mother is going to die."*

At last, with his brother's consent, the messenger galloped and galloped away, to find his only hope, the younger physician. As the wife gave me the candle, sending me up stairs, I looked back at the family circle.

Helpless grief made every face rigid. I looked again at the eldest daughter. The moving shadows embroidered on her breast intricate symbols of the fair years, passing by in the ghost of tapestry, things that happened in the beginning of the world. Let the epic tell that when the stranger slept there was a magic loom by his bed that wove that history again in valiant colors, showing battles without number, and sieges, and interminable sunny love-tales, and lotus-handed ladies whispering over manuscript things too fine to be told, and ruddy warriors sitting at watch-fires on battlements eternal; and let the epic tell how, in the early dawn, the stranger half awoke, yet saw this tapestry hung round the walls. If one could remember every story for which the pictures stood, he might indeed write the world's unwritten epic. The last tapestry to be hung changed from gold to black warp and woof upon which was written that because of a treacherous prime minister who served a poisoned wine, the Empress of the White Witches was perishing before her time, and the young wizard, with the counter-spell, was riding night and day, but all the palace knew he would arrive too late.

At breakfast the faces were stolid and white as frost. The father answered me only when I said good-by.

He said he hardly knew whether I had had anything to eat, or whether any one had been good to me. "You just had to take care of yourself." The son, feeling the demand of hospitality in his father's voice, walked to the road with me. He asked if I was walking to Asheville.

"Yes, by way of Mount Toxaway and Brevard."

He told me it was good walking all the way, and added, in a difficult burst of confidence, "I am going to Asheville."

"Why not come along with me?" I asked. I meant it heartily.

He said he had to take horseback, and then the railway. He had to be there to-morrow.

"What's the hurry?"

"I have to witness in a whisky case, an internal revenue case."

He said it like a Spanish Protestant called before the inquisition.

I said to my soul: "These were the revelations of a night and a morning. What deeper troubles were in the House of the Loom that you did not know?"

All through the country there had been that night what is called a black frost. By the roadside it was deep and white as the wool on a sheep. But it left things blighted and black, and destroyed the chances of the fruit-bearing trees. All the way to Mount Toxaway I met scattered mourners of the ill-timed visitation.

But the simple folly of spring was in me, and the strange elation of gratitude. My soul said within itself: "A money-claim has definite limits, but when will you ever discharge your obligation to the proud and the fine in the House of the Loom? You intruded on their grief. Yet they held their guest sacred as their grief."

MAN, IN THE CITY OF COLLARS

A Not Very Tragic Relapse into the Toils of the World, and of Finance.

Having been properly treated as a bunco man by systematic piety in a certain city further south, I had double-barrelled special recommendations sent to a lofty benevolence in Asheville, from a religious leader of New York, the before-mentioned Charles F. Powlison.

It was with confidence that I bade good-by to the chicken-merchant who drove me into the city. I entered the office of the black-coated, semi-clerical gentleman who had received the Powlison indorsements. My stick pounded his floor. The heels of my brogans made the place resound. But he gave all official privileges. He received me with the fine manly handclasp, the glitter of teeth, the pat on the back. He insisted I use the shower bath, writing room, reading table. Then I suggested a conference among a dozen of his devouter workers on the relation of the sense of Beauty to their present notion of Christianity or, if he preferred, a talk on some aspect of art to a larger group.

He took me into his office. He shut the door. He was haughty. He made me haughty. I give the conversation as it struck me. He probably said some smart things I do not recall. But I remember all the smart things I said.

He denounced labor agitators in plain words. I agreed. I belonged to the brotherhood of those who loaf and invite their souls.

He spoke of anarchy. I maintained that I loved the law.

He very clearly, and at length, assaulted Single Tax. I knew nothing then of Single Tax, and thanked him for light. He denounced Socialism. Knowing little about Socialism at that time, I denounced it also, having just been converted to individualism by a man in Highlands.

The religious leader spoke of his long experience with bunco men. I insisted I wanted not a cent from him, I was there to do him good. I had letters of introduction to two men in the city; one of them, an active worker in the organization, had already been in to identify me. A third man was coming to climb Mount Mitchell with me.

He doubted that I was a bona fide worker in his organization. Then came my only long speech. We will omit the speech. But he began to see light. He took a fresh grip on his argument. He said: "There is a man here in Asheville I see snooping around with a tin box and a butterfly net. They call him the state something-ologist. He goes around and—and—*hunts bugs*. But do you want to know what I think of a crank like that?" I wanted to know. He told me.

"But," I objected, "I am not a scientist. I am an art student."

He expressed an interest in art. He gave a pious and proper view of the nude in art. It took some time. It was the sort of chilly, cautious talk that could not possibly bring a blush to the cheek of ignorance. I assured him his decorous concessions were unnecessary. I was not expounding the nude.

There was an artist here, and Asheville needed no further instruction of the kind, he maintained. The gentleman had won some blue ribbons in Europe. He painted a big picture (dimensions were given) and sold it for thousands (price was given).

"He is holding the next one, two feet longer each way, for double the money."

I told him if he felt there was enough art in Asheville, we might do something to popularize the poets.

In reply he talked about literary cranks. He spoke of how Thoreau, with his long hair and ugly looks, frightened strangers who suddenly met him in the woods. I thanked him for light on Thoreau. . . . But he had to admit that my hair was short.

He suspected I was neither artist nor literary man. I assured him my friends were often of the same opinion.

"But," he said bitterly, "do you know sir, by the tone of letters I received from Mr. Powlison I expected to assemble the wealth and fashion of Asheville to hear you. I expected to see you first in your private car, wearing a dress-suit."

I answered sternly, "Art, my friend, does not travel in a Pullman."

He threw off all restraint. "Old shoes," he said, "old shoes." He pointed at them.

"I have walked two hundred miles among the moonshiners. They wear brogans like these." But his manner plainly said that his organization did not need cranks climbing over the mountains to tell them things.

"Your New York letter did not say you were walking. It said you 'would arrive.'"

He began to point again. "Frayed trousers! And the lining of your coat in rags!"

"I took the lining of the coat for necessary patches."

"A blue bandanna round your neck!"

"To protect me from sunburn."

He rose and hit the table. "And no collar!"

"Oh yes, I have a collar." I drew it from my hip pocket. It had had a two hundred mile ride, and needed a bath.

"I should like to have it laundered, but I haven't the money."

"*Get* the money."

"No," I said, "but I will get a collar."

I entered a furnishing and tailor shop around the corner. I asked for the proprietor. He showed me collars.

"Two for a quarter?"

"Yes."

"Now I have here a little brochure I sell for twenty-five cents. In fact it is a poem, well worth the money. I will let you have it for half price, that is, one collar."

"We are selling collars."

"I am selling the poem."

I turned my Ancient Mariner eye on him. I recited the most mesmeric rhymes.

He repeated, "We are selling collars."

Evidently the eye was out of order. I tried argument.

"Don't you think I need a collar?"

"Yes."

"Don't you think this one would fit this shirt?"

"Yes."

"I renew my offer."

He sternly put the box away.

So I said, "If I must face my friends in Asheville without this necessary ornament, you shall blush. I have done my duty, and refuse to blush."

I looked up a scholar from Yale, Yutaka Minakuchi, friend of old friends, student of philosophy, in which he instructed me much, first lending me a collar. He became my host in Asheville. It needs no words of mine to enhance the fame of Japanese hospitality. . . .

And I had a friend in a distant place, whom, for fancy's sake, we will call the Caliph Harounal-Raschid. Let him remain a mystery. We will reveal this much. Had he known the truth, he would have sent Greek slaves riding on elephants, laden with changes of raiment. He discerned, at least, that I was in a barbarous land, for at length a long package containing a sword arrived from the court of the Caliph (to speak in parables). I exchanged the weapon at a pawnshop for *money,* all in one bill—*money*—against which I had so many times sworn eternal warfare, which had been my hoodoo in the past, and was destined to be again. But this time, such are the whims of fate, the little while it was with me it brought me only good.

I entered the furnishing store. The proprietor was terribly busy, but my glittering eye was in condition. I persuaded him, by dint of repetition, to show me his collars. I treated him as though we had not met.

"Fifteen cents apiece?"

"Yes."

"I will take *one*." I gave the bill. He had to send a boy out for the change. I put the silver in my pocket, and rattled it. He wrapped up the collar, while I studied his cheeks. He blushed like a maid, bless his tender heart, and in his sweet confusion he knew that I knew it.

The streets of Asheville kept shouting to me: "Let us praise Man, when he builds cities, and grows respectable, and cringes to money, and becomes a tailor, and loves collars with all his heart."

THE OLD LADY AT THE TOP OF THE HILL

It was a bland afternoon. I had been crossing a green valley in North Carolina. Every man I passed had that languid leanness slanderously attributed to the hookworm by folk who have no temperament. Yet some bee of industry must have stung these fellows into intermittent effort this morning, yesterday, last week or last year.

Here were reasonably good barns. Here were fences, and good fences at that. Here were mysterious crops, neither cotton nor corn. One man was not ploughing with a mule. No, sir. He was ploughing with a sort of horse. . . .

At last I mounted the northern rim of the circle of steep hills that kept the place as separate from the rest of the world as a Chinese wall. I met her on the crest. She advanced slowly, looking on the ground, leaning at the hips as do the very aged, but not grotesquely. Her primly made dress and sunbonnet were dull dark blue. With her walking-stick she meditatively knocked the little stones from her path. The staff had a T-shaped head. It was the cane Old Mother Hubbard carries in the toy book.

And now she looked up and said with a pleasant start, "Why, good evening, young stranger."

"Good evening, kind lady."

"Where have you been, my son?"

"Why, I am following my nose to the end of the world. I have just walked through this enterprising valley."

She looked into the dust and meditated awhile. Then she said: "It's getting late. No one has let you in?"

"No one."

"How about that house by the bridge?" She pointed with her cane.

"The lady said she had a sick child."

"Nonsense, nonsense. Do you see that little Ardella by that corner of the ploughed field near the house? She don't run like a sick child. . . . Did you ask at the next place, the one that has a green porch?" She pointed again with her cane.

"The woman said she had no spare bed."

"But she has. I slept in it last week. . . . And that last house before you start up this hill?"

"The woman said she had to take care of saw-mill hands."

"Did she tell you *that?*"

"Yes, ma'am."

The old lady ruminated again, leaning on her stick. At length she said: "Sit down. I want to tell you something." There we were, Grandmother and newly adopted grandson, on a big sunlit rock.

I give only the spirit of her words. She discounted in that precious mountain dialect, so mediaeval, so Shakespearean with its surprising phrases that seem at first the slang of a literary clan, till one learns they are the common property of folk that cannot read. It is a manner of speech all too elusive. Would that I had kept a note-book upon it! But somewhat to this intent she spoke, and in a tone gentler than her words: —

"They thought I would never find out about this, or they would not have treated you so. That woman in the last house is my daughter-in-law. She has only two saw-mill hands, and they're no trouble. That's my house anyway. It was my mother's before me. No one dares turn strangers away when I am there. There's an empty bed up stairs, and another in the hall."

She turned about and pointed in the direction in which I had been walking. "Just ahead of you, around that clump of trees, is a hospitable family. If they will not take care of you, it is because they have a good excuse. If they cannot take you in, ask no further. Come back to my place, and" (she spoke with a Colonial Dame air) "*I will make you welcome.*"

"What sort of mountaineer is this?" I asked myself. "The hospitality is the usual thing, but the grandeur is exotic."

We chatted awhile of the sunset. Then I accompanied her to the edge of the hill.

Under her sacred hair her face retained girl-contours. The wrinkles were not too deep. She seemed not to have changed as mothers often do, when, under decades of inevitable sorrow, the features are recarved into the special mask of middle age, and finally into the very different mask of senility. She had yet the authority of Beauty. She wore her white hair with a Quakerish-feminine skill most admirably adapted to that ancient forehead. I divined she had learned that at sixteen. What a long time to be remembering.

We were spirits that at once met and understood. She said: "My son, I have walked all my life across this valley, or up this hill, or toward that green mountain where you are going. I never walked as far as I wanted to. But walking even so short a path makes for consolation."

Now she laid aside antique grandeur and took on plain vanity.

"Do you know how old I am?"

"About eighty-five."

"I'm ninety-two years old, young man, and I'm going to live ten years more."

It was getting late. I said, "I am glad indeed to have met you."

She answered, "I am sorry my valley has not been kind."

I ventured to ask, "So it's *your* valley?"

I had touched a raw nerve. I was completely shaken by the suddenness of her answer.

"Mine! Mine! Mine!" she shrieked. Kneeling, she beat up the dust of the road with her cane. And then "Mine! Mine! Mine!" shaking her outstretched arms over that amphitheatre, as though she would drag it all to her breast.

She was out of breath and trembling. At length she smiled, and added so quietly it seemed another person. "And they shall not take it away from me."

I helped her to her feet. She was once more the Martha Washington sort. . . . I remember her last sentence. In a royal tone, that was three times an accolade, in a motherly tone that was caressing and slow she half-sung the pretty words: —

"Good evening, young man. I wish you well."

The man at the next house took me in. In the course of the evening he assured me that the old lady did own the valley, and that she ruled it with a rod of iron. The family graveyard was full of heirs who had grown to old age and died of old age hoping in vain to outlive, and to inherit her authority.

LADY IRON-HEELS

I

The Seven Suspicions

One Saturday in May I was hurrying from mountainous North Carolina into mountainous Tennessee. Because of my speed and air of alarm, I was followed by the Seven Suspicions. I was either a revenue detective in pursuit of moonshiners, or a moonshiner pursued by revenue detectives, or a thief hurrying out of hot territory, or a deputy sheriff pursuing a thief, or a pretended non-combatant hurrying toward a Tennessee feud, actually an armed recruit, or I had just killed my family's hereditary enemy and was eluding his avengers, or I had bought some moonshine whisky and was trying to get out of a bad region before nightfall. These suspicions implied that the inhabitants admired me. Yet I hurried.

I came upon one article of my creed, the very next day, Sunday. But Saturday was a season of panic, preparation, and trial.

The article of my creed that I won as my reward might be stated in this fashion: *"Peace is to be found, even in a red and bleeding rose."*

I was accustomed to the feudist and the assassin. Such people had been good to me, and I had walked calmly through their haunts. But now the smothering landscape seemed to double every natural fear. The hills were so steep and so close together that only the indomitable corn and rye climbed to the top to see the sun. The road was in the bed of a scolding rivulet. People in general travelled horseback. Cross-logs for those afoot bridged high above the streams every half mile. There was a primeval something about the heavy chains of the cross-logs, binding them to the trees, that suggested the forgotten beginning of an iron people, some harsh iron-willed Sparta. This impression was strengthened by the unpainted dwellings, hunched close to the path, with thick walls to resist siege.

In the prose sketches in this book I have allowed myself a story-teller's license only a little. Sometimes a considerable happening is introduced that came the day before, or two days after. In some cases the events of a week are told in reverse order.

Lady Iron-Heels is obviously a story, but embodies my exact impression of that region in a more compressed form than a note-book record could have done.

The other travel-narratives are ninety-nine per cent literal fact and one per cent abbreviation.

What first fixed these outlaws here, as in a nest, with a ring of houseless open country round them? A traveller was more shut from the horizon than in the slums of Chicago. The road climbed no summits. It writhed like a snake. And there were snakes sunning themselves on every other cross-log. *And there was never a flower to be seen.*

An old woman, kindly enough, gave this beggar a noon-meal for the asking, but the landscape had struck into me so I almost feared to eat the bread. For this fear I sternly blamed my perverse imagination. Refreshed in body only, I crept like a fascinated fly, dragged by occult force toward a spider's den. I felt as though I had reached the very heart of the trap when I stepped into the streets of the profane village of Flagpond, Tennessee.

It was early in the afternoon. The feudal warriors had come to the place on horseback, dressed in poverty-stricken Saturday finery: clothes tight and ill-dyed, with black felt hats that should have slouched, but did not. The immaculate rims stood out in queer precision. The wearers sat in front of the three main stores, looking across the street at one another. Since there was no woman in sight, every one knew that the shooting might begin at any time. The silence was deadly as the silence of a plague. I checked my pace. I ambled in a leisurely way from store to store, inquiring the road to Cumberland Gap, the distance to Greenville, and the like. I was on the other side of the circle of dwellings pretty soon, followed by the Seven Suspicions, shot from about seventy-five lean countenances, which makes about five hundred and twenty-five suspicions.

One of the most indescribable and haunting things of that region was that all the women and children were dressed in a certain dead-bone gray.

About four o'clock I had made good my escape. I had begun to mount rolling, uninhabited hills. At twilight I entered a plain, and felt a new kind of civilization round me. It would have been shabby in Indiana. Here it was glorious. They had whitewashed fences, and white-painted cottages, glimmering kindly through the dusk. Some farm machinery was rusting in the open. I climbed a last year's straw-stack, and slept, with acres of stars pouring down peace.

II

The Tailor and the Florist

Now the story begins all over again with the episode of the

well-known tailor and the unknown florist. Just off the main street of Greenville, Tennessee, there is a log cabin with the century old inscription, ANDREW JOHNSON, TAILOR. That sign is the fittest monument to the indomitable but dubious man who could not cut the mantle of the railsplitter to fit him. I was told by the citizens of Greenville that there was a monument to their hero on the hill. So I climbed up. It was indeed wonderful—a weird straddling archway, supporting an obelisk. The archway also upheld two flaming funeral urns with buzzard contours, and a stone eagle preparing to screech. There was a dog-eared scroll inscribed, "His faith in the people never wavered." Around all was, most appropriately, a spiked fence.

But I was glad I came, because near the Tailor's resting-place was a Florist's grave, on which depends the rest of this adventure, and which reaches back to the beginning of it. It had a wooden headstone, marked "John Kenton of Flagpond, Florist. 1870-1900." And in testimony to his occupation, a great rosebush almost hid the inscription. Any man who could undertake to sell flowers in Flagpond might have it said of him also, "His faith in the people never wavered."

And now in my tramping the spirit of John Kenton, or some other Florist, seemed to lead me. My season of panic, preparation, and trial was over. It was indeed Sunday on this planet for awhile. I passed bush after bush of the same sort as that marking Kenton's place of sleep. The sight of them was all that I had to give me strength till noon. I had had neither breakfast nor supper. People would have fed this poor tramp, but I love sometimes the ecstasy that comes with healthy fasting. And now that I reflect upon it, it was indeed appropriate that the Religion of the Rose should begin with abstinence.

I have burdened you further back with an elaborate description of the landscape of Flagpond. Now that landscape was repeated with the addition of roses. And what a difference they made! They quenched the Seven Suspicions. They made gray dresses seem rather tolerable. On either side loomed the steepest cornfields yet, but they did not make me tremble now.

At noon I turned aside where a log cabin on stilts, leaning against its own chimney, stood astride a little gully. It was about as big as a dove-cote. Straggling rose-hedges led to the green-banked spring at the foot of a ladder that took the place of steps. The old lady that came to the door was a dove in one respect only; she was dressed in gray.

She was drawn to the pattern of the tub-like peasants of the German funny paper *Simplicissimus*. I told her my name was

Nicholas. She took it for granted that I wanted my dinner, and asked me up the ladder without ado. She did an unusual thing. She began to talk family affairs. "You must be kin to Lawyer Nicholas of Flagpond. . . . He defended my son ten years ago . . . in a trial for murder."

I said: "I am no kin to Lawyer Nicholas, but I hope he won his case."

"No. My son is in the state's prison for life. . . . He surely killed Florist Kenton."

But she added, as if it nullified all guilt, "they were both drunk."

She was busy cooking at the open fireplace. She turned to the boy, about ten years old. "Call your Ma and your Aunt to dinner." He climbed the steep and shouted. Presently two figures came over the ridge. The larger woman took the boy's hand.

"That's my daughter-in-law, the boy's mother," said Mrs. Simplicissimus.

I judged the second figure to be a woman of about twenty-eight. She carried a fence-rail on her shoulder. She was straight as an Indian. The old woman said: *"That's my daughter. She was going to marry John Kenton."* The only influences that could have induced a mountain-woman to unburden so much, were the roses, just outside the door, leaping in the wind.

The procession soon reached us The wood-carrier threw the log into the yard. "There's firewood," she sang. She vaulted over the fence, displaying iron-heeled brogans, thick red stockings, and a red-lined skirt. There was a smear of earth on cheek and chin. Her face was sunburned, dust-mired roseleaf. She swept off her hat. She bowed ironically. She said: "Howdy. What might be your name?"

I did not tell my name.

She fell on her knees. She drank from her hands at the spring. I could feel the cold water warring with the sunshine in her sinews. She would never have done with splashing eyelids and ears, and cheeks and red arms and throat. The rosebushes behind her leaped in the wind. The boy and his mother and the grandmother knelt at that same place and splashed after that same manner. Then the grandmother nudged me.

"Wash," she said.

I washed.

We climbed into that dove-cote block-house on stilts. We ate like four plough-horses and a colt. We consumed corn-bread and fat pork, then corn-bread and beans, then corn-bread and butter. I ate supper, breakfast, and dinner in three quarters of an hour.

III

A Brief Siesta

Working a farm of fields that stand on edge, without men to help, and without much machinery, makes women into warriors or kills them. The grandmother and mother were no longer women. Even when they caressed the boy their faces were furrowed with invincible will-power. But Lady Iron-Heels still a woman, was confused in the alternative of manhood or death. She was indeed a flower not yet torn to pieces by the wind, greatly shaken, and therefore blooming the faster.

There was a red ribbon streaming over the gray rag-carpet. Lady Iron-Heels stooped, gave the ribbon a jerk, and a banjo came snarling from under the bed.

She sat on the warring colors of the crazy-quilt, and played a dance-tune, storming the floor with one heel. She grew pensive. She sang: —

"We shall rest in the fair and happy land
Just across on the ever-green shore,
Sing the song of Moses and the Lamb (by and by)
And dwell with Jesus evermore."

Her neck had a yellow handkerchief round it. A brown lock swept across her leaping throat. Her cheeks and chin were bold as her iron heels. Underneath the precious silken sunburn, the blood was beating, beating, and trying to thicken into manhood to fight off death.

After the music the ladies dipped snuff in the circle around the dim fire.

IV

"That's All the Church I Get"

I made a great palaver to Iron-Heels about giving me the banjo ribbon. She consented easily. Coquetry was not her specialty.

"What might be your name?" she asked.

There was no dodging now. The old woman spoke up as though to save me pain: "His name is Nicholas. But he is no kin to Lawyer Nicholas of Flagpond."

After a long silence the girl said: "We came from Flagpond, once upon a time."

She had been looking out the door at the clear bowl of the spring, and the reflection of the tall bushes, leaping in the wind.

I thought to myself: "She herself was John Kenton's chief rose." I thought: "He had her in mind when he set these ameliorating bushes through the wild." Possibly the girl could not read or write. Yet she was royal.

Democracy has the ways of a jackdaw. Democracy hides jewels in the ash-heap. Democracy is infinitely whimsical. Every once in a while a changeling appears, not like any of the people around, a changeling whose real ancestors are aristocratic souls forgotten for centuries. As the girl's eyes narrowed, she became Queen Thi, the masterful and beautiful potentate of immemorial Egypt whose face I have seen in a museum, carved on a Canopic jar. She was Queen Thi only an instant, then she became a Tennessee girl again, with the eyes of a weary doe.

She said: "Them roses give me comfort. That's all the church I get."

I asked: "Why are there so many roses between here and Greenville and none near Flagpond?"

It was her turn not to speak. The old woman as though to save her pain, answered: "The flowers of these parts were all brought in by John Kenton. He lived in Flagpond, but could not sell them there."

And the mother of the little boy, the man-woman, whose husband had killed Kenton, broke her long silence: "The only flowers we have to-day are these he brought. I think we would die without them. . . . How do we get through the winter?"

Lady Iron-Heels and her sister-in-law took a swig of whisky from the jug under the table, and lifted up their hoes from the floor. The boy whimpered for a drink. They said: "Wait till you are a man." All three climbed the hill.

Lady Iron-Heels was the last to go over the ridge. She saw me gather buds from both those bushes by the spring. She made a gesture of salute with her hoe.

I never travelled that way again. I passed by quickly; therefore I had a glimpse of what she was intended to be. "He that loseth his life shall find it." I see her many a time when I am looking on scattered rose-leaves. She was a woman, God's chief rose for man. She was scorned and downtrodden, but radiant still. I am only saying that she wore the face of Beauty when Beauty rises above circumstance.

The buds that I had gathered did not fall to pieces till I had passed by Daniel Boone's old trail on through Cumberland Gap, on over big hill Kentucky into the Blue Grass. On the way I wrote this, their poor memorial, the Canticle of the Rose: —

It is an article of my creed that the petals of this flower of which we speak are a medicine, that they can almost heal a mortal wound.

The rose is so young of face and line, she appears so casually and humbly, we forget she is an ancient physician.

Yet so much tradition is wrapped around her stalk, it is strange she is not a mummy. Her ashes can be found in the tombs of the Pharoahs, in everlasting companionship with the ashes of the lotus and the papyrus plant. Her dust travels on every desert wind.

No love-song can do without her.

No soldier and no priest can scorn her. There were the Wars of the Roses. And there was a Rose in Sharon. Our wandering brother Dante found a great rose in Paradise.

There are white roses, sweet ghosts under the pine. There are yellow roses, little suns in the shadow. But the normal bloom is red, flushed with foolish ardors, laughing, shaking off the gossamer years. She remembers Love, but not too well, if love is pain. There is no yesterday that can daunt her and keep her dear heart-laughter down. In springtime her magic petals bring God to the weary and give Heaven's strength to the wavering of heart.

She can turn the slave to a woman, the woman to something a little more than mortal. Oh, how bravely, with the same life-giving red, with the last of her virgin strength, she blooms and blooms on almost every highway. We find her on the road to Benares, on the road to Mecca, on the road to Rome, and on the road to Nowhere, in Tennessee.

Her red petals can almost heal a mortal wound.

II

A MENDICANT PILGRIMAGE IN THE EAST

A TEMPLE MADE WITH HANDS

I

The Dwelling-place of Faith, Hope, and Charity

I had walked twelve miles before noon. Then I had eaten four slices of bread and butter on merciful doorsteps. At four-thirty, having completed twenty-one miles, I entered the richest village in the United States, a village that is located in New Jersey. I was so weary I was ready to sleep in the gutter, and did not care if the wagons ran over me. I should have walked through to the green fields before I looked for hospitality. I knew that the well meant deeds of the city cannot equal the kindness of the most commonplace farm-hand. Yet I lingered.

I purchased a feast of beefsteak and onions at an obscure Jewish restaurant and felt myself once more a man. But it was now too late to leave town. The rule of the country is—one must ask for his night's lodging before five o'clock. After that, things are growing dark, and people may be afraid of you.

After paying for beefsteak and onions, I had twenty-five cents. This twenty-five cents was all that remained after a winter's lecturing on art and poetry in Manhattan. I am satisfied that the extra money, over and above all paid debts, brought me some of the ill-luck of the night. As I have before observed, money is a hoodoo on the road. Until a man is penniless he is not stripped for action.

A sign at the lunch-counter advertised: "Furnished rooms, fifty cents."

I asked the proprietor to cut the price. He dodged the issue. "Say, why don't you go up there to the mission? They will sell you a good bed cheap."

"For a quarter?"

"Something like that."

"Show me the place."

As of old the Jew pointed out the way of salvation. The Gentile followed it and reached the dwelling-place of Faith, Hope, and Charity.

"What do you want?" The questioner, evidently in charge of the place, was accoutred in stage laboring-man style. Maybe his paraphernalia was intended to put him on a level with wayfarers. He wore a slouch hat, a soft shirt, and no necktie. His clothes had the store freshness still. They looked rather presumptuous in that neat, well-stocked reading room.

"I want a cheap bed."

"We do not sell beds."

"I was told you did."

"We give them away."

"All right."

"But you have to work."

"Very well."

"Do you want to leave early in the morning?" (The place was evidently a half-way house for tramps.)

"Yes. I want to leave early in the morning."

"Then you will have to split kindling two hours to-night."

"Show me the kindling."

II

Splitting Kindling

In the basement I throned myself on one block while I chopped kindling on another. Before me, piled to the first story, was a cellarful of wood, the record of my predecessors in toil. I gathered that the corporal's guard of the unemployed who stayed at the mission that night, and had been there two or three days, had finished their day's assignment of splitting. They completely surrounded me, questioned me with the greatest curiosity, and put me down as a terrific liar, for I answered every question with simple truth.

As soon as the melodramatic workingman-boss went up stairs, one of them said, "Don't work so fast. It's only a matter of form this late at night. They want to see if you are willing, that's all."

I chopped a little faster for this advice. Not that I was out of humor with the advisers, — though I should have been, for they were box-car tramps.

One of them, having an evil and a witty eye, said, "If I was goin' west like you, I'd start about ten o'clock to-night and be near Buffalo before morning."

Another, a mild nobody, professed himself a miller. He told what a wonderful trick it was to say, "Leddy, I'm too tired to work till I eat," and after eating, to walk away.

The next, a carriage painter of battered gentility, told endless stories of the sprees that had destroyed him. Another, a white frog with a bald head and gray mustache, quite won my heart. He said, "Wait till you get a nice warm bath after service. Then you'll sleep good."

To my weary and addled brain the mission was like one of those beautiful resting-places in Pilgrim's Progress. It became my religion, just to split kindling. I failed to apprehend what infinitesimal nobodies these fellows around me were. I should have disliked them more.

The modern tramp is not a tramp, he is a speed-maniac. Being unable to afford luxuries, he must still be near something mechanical and hasty, so he uses a dirty box-car to whirl from one railroad-yard to another. He has no destination but the cinder-pile by the water-tank. The landscape hurrying by in one indistinguishable mass and the roaring of the car-wheels in his ears are the ends of life to him. He is no back-to-nature crank. He is a most highly specialized modern man. All to keep going, he risks disease from these religious missions, from foul box-cars, and foul comrades. He risks accident every hour. He is always liable to the cruelty of conductor or brakeman and to murder by companions.

He runs fewer risks in the country, yet his aversion to the country is profound. He knows all that I know about country hospitality, that it can be purchased by the merest grain of courtesy. Yet most of the farm-people that entertained me had not seen a tramp for months.

To account for some of the happenings of this tale I will only add that a speed-maniac at either end of the social scale is not necessarily a hustler, personally. But in one way or another he is sure to be shallow and artificial, the grotesque, nervous victim of machinery. And a "Mission," an institution built by speed-maniacs who use automobiles for speed-maniacs who use box-cars, is bound to be absurd beyond words to tell it.

III

The Sermon on the Mount

I loved all men that night, even the fellow in melodramatic laboring-man costume, who appeared after two hours to drive us animals up stairs into one corner of the chapel, where a dozen of our kind had already assembled from somewhere.

On the far side of that chapel sat the money-fed. The aisle was a great gulf between them and us. I smiled across the gulf indulgently, imagining by what exhortations to "Come and help us in our problem" those uncomfortable persons had been assembled. An unmitigated clergyman rose to read a text.

I presume this clergyman imagined Christ wore a white tie and was on a salary promptly paid by some of our oldest families. But I share with the followers of St. Francis the vision of Christ as a man of the open road, improvident as the sparrow. I share with the followers of Tolstoi the opinion that when Christ proclaimed those uncomfortable social doctrines, he meant what he said.

The clergyman read: "Blessed are the poor in spirit, for theirs is the kingdom of heaven."

"Blessed are they that mourn, for they shall be comforted."

"Blessed are the meek, for they shall inherit the earth."

He read much more than I will quote. Here is the final passage: —

"Ye have heard how it hath been said: 'An eye for an eye and a tooth for a tooth.' But I say unto you that you resist not evil. But whosoever shall smite thee on thy right cheek, turn to him the other also. And if any man will sue thee at the law, and take away thy coat, let him have thy cloak also. And whosoever shall compel thee to go a mile, go with him twain. Give to him that asketh thee, and to him that would borrow of thee, turn not thou away."

This Pharisee smugly assumed that he was authorized by the Deity to explain away this scripture. And he did it, as the reader has heard it done many a time.

The Pharisee was followed by a fat Scribe who tried to smile away what the other fellow had tried to argue away. The fat one then called on the assembly to bow, and exhorted the repentant to hold up their hands to be prayed for.

I held up my hand. Was I not eating the bread of the mission? And then I felt like a sinner anyway.

"Thank God," said the fat one.

After a hymn, testimonies were called for. I felt the spirit move me, but some one had the floor. Across the gulf she stood, an exceedingly well-dressed and blindly devout sister. She glanced with a terrified shrinking at the animals she hoped to benefit. She said:—

"There has been one great difficulty in my Christian life. It came with seeking for the Spirit. Sometimes we think it has come with power, when we are simply stirred by our own selfish desires. Our works will show whether we are moved by the Spirit."

I wanted to preach them a sermon on St. Francis. But how could I? There was still a quarter in my own pocket. Meanwhile there rose a saint with a pompadour and blocky jaws. He was distinctly inferior in social position to a great part of the saints. It was probable he had given that testimony many times. But he did not want the meeting to drag. He spake in a loud voice: "I was saved from a drunkard's life, in this mission, eighteen years ago, and ever since, not by my own power, but by the grace of God, I have been leading a God-fearing and money-making life in this town." That was his exact phrase, "a money-making life." His intention was good, but he should have been more tactful. The Pharisee looked annoyed.

IV

A Screaming Farce

I advise all self-respecting citizens to skip this section. It is nothing but over-strained, shabby farce.

The throng melted. Scribe and Pharisee, Dives, Mrs. Dives, and their satellites went home to their comfortable beds. Many of the roughs on our side of the house found somewhere else to stay. The fellow dressed like a workingman in a melodrama sought the consolations of his own home. Had the last authority departed? Were we to have anarchy? The Frog, in his gentlest manner, sidled up to make friends again.

"Now you can have your nice warm bath, you two." I looked around. There were two of us then. Beside me, fresh from a box-car was a battered scalawag. The Frog must have let him in at the last moment.

We three climbed to the bath-room.

"Wait a minute," said the Amphibian. He disappeared. I opened my eyes, for this creature spake with a voice of authority. The box-car scalawag grinned sheepishly.

There was a scuffling overhead, a scratch and a rumble. We two looked up just in time to dodge the astonishing vision of a clothes-horse descending through a trap-door by a rope. At the upper end of the rope was the absurd bald head of our newly achieved superintendent.

"Hello, Santy Claus," said the box-car tramp. "Whose Christmas present is this?"

The Frog shouted: "Put your shoes and hats in the corner. If you have any tobacco, put it in your shoes. Hang everything else on the clothes-horse."

I obeyed, except that I had no tobacco. The rascal by my side had a plenty, and sawdusted the bath-room floor with some of it, and the remainder went into his foot-gear. Then we two, companions in nakedness, watched the Frog haul up our clothes out of sight. He closed the trap-door with many grunts.

Then this Amphibian, this boss, descended and entered the bath-room. He was a dry-land Amphibian. He had never taken a bath himself, but was there to superintend. He seemed to feel himself the accredited representative of all the good people behind the mission, and no doubt he was.

"Can it be possible," I asked myself, "that they have chosen this creature to apply their Christianity?"

The Frog said to my companion: "Git in the tub."

Then he turned on the water, regulated the temperature, and watched as though he expected one of us to steal the faucets from the wash-bowl. He threw a gruesome rag at the tramp, and allowed him to scrub himself. The creature bathing seemed well-disposed toward the idea, and had put soap on about one-third of his person when the Frog shouted: "I've got to get up at four-thirty."

The scalawag took the hint and rose like Venus from the foam. He splashed off part of it, and rubbed off the rest with a towel that was a fallen sister of the wash-rag.

The Frog was evidently trying to enforce, in a literal way, regulations he did not understand. He wiped out the bath-tub most carefully with the unclean wash-rag. Then he provided the scalawag with a shirt for night-wear. The creature put it on and said: —

"Ain't I a peach?"

He was.

The nightie was an old, heavily-starched dress-shirt, once white. Maybe it had once been worn by the Scribe or the Pharisee. But it had not been washed since. The rascal cut quite a figure as he took long steps down the corridor to bed, piloted by the hurrying Amphibian. He was a long-legged rascal, and the slivered remainders of that ancient shirt flapped about him gloriously.

I was hustled into the tub after the rascal. I was supervised after the same manner. "Now wash," boomed the Amphibian. He threw at me the sloppy rag of my predecessor.

I threw it promptly on the floor.

"I don't use a wash-rag," I said.

"Hurry," croaked the Frog. *And he let the water out of the tub.* He handed me the towel the scalawag had used. I had not, as a matter of fact, had a bath, and I was quite footsore.

"I do not want that towel," I said.

"You're awful fancy, aren't you?" sneered the Frog.

Wherever I was damp, I rubbed myself dry with my bare hands, being skilled in the matter, meanwhile reflecting that there is nothing worse than a Pharisee except a creature like this. I wondered if it was too late to rouse a mob among the better element of the town, neither saints nor sinners, but just plain malefactors of great wealth, and have this person lynched. There were probably multi-millionnaires in this town giving ten-dollar bills to this mission, who were imagining they were giving a free bath to somebody.

I wanted to appeal to some man with manicured hands who had grown decently rich robbing the widow and the orphan and who now had the leisure to surround himself with the appurtenances of civility and the manners of a Chesterfield.

"I am through with the poor but honest submerged tenth. Rich worldlings for mine," I muttered.

"Put these on," squeaked the Frog. His manner said, "See how good we are to you." He held out the treasure of the establishment, a night-garment retained for fastidious new-arrivals, newly-bathed. Of course, no one else was supposed to bathe.

Was the garment he held out a slivered shirt? Nay, nay. It was a sort of pajama combination. Hundreds of men had found shelter, taken a luxurious bath, and put them on. They were companions in crime of the towel and the wash-rag. Let us suppose that three hundred and sixty-five men wore them a year. In ten years there would have been about three thousand six hundred and fifty bathed men in them. That did not account for their appearance.

"What makes them so dirty?" I asked.

No answer.

"Can't I wear my underclothes to bed instead of these?"

"No."

"Why?"

"Sulphur."

"What do you mean by sulphur?"

"Your clothes are up stairs being fumigated."

"Can't I get my socks to-night I always wash them before I go to bed."

"No. It's against the law of the state. And you would dirty up these bowls. I have just scrubbed them out."

"I will wash them out afterward."

"I haven't time to wait. I must get up at four-thirty."

"But why fumigate my clean underwear, and give me dirty pajamas?"

The Frog was getting flabbergasted. "I tell you it's the law of New Jersey. You are getting awful fancy. If I had had my way, you would never have been let in here."

"Blessed are the meek, for they shall inherit the earth," I said to myself, and put on the pajamas.

This insanitary director showed me my bed. It was in a long low room with all the windows closed, where half a score were asleep. The sheets had never, never, never been washed. Why was it that in a mission so shiny in its reading room, and so devout in its chapel, so melodramatic with its clean workman-boss, in the daytime, these things were so?

The lights went out. I kicked off the pajamas and slept. I awoke at midnight and reflected on all these matters. I quoted another scripture to myself: "I was naked, and ye clothed me."

V

The Highway of Our God

At six o'clock I was called for breakfast. My sulphur-smelling clothes were on my bed. I put them on with a light heart, for after all I had slept well, and my feet were not stiff. The quarter was still in my trousers' pocket. I presume that hoodoo quarter had something to do with the bad breakfast.

The Amphibian was now cook. He gave each man a soup-plate heaped with oat-meal. If it had been oats, it would have been food for so many horses. Had the Frog been up since four-thirty preparing this?

The price of part of that horse-feed might have gone into something to eat. There was a salty blue sauce on it that was called milk. And there was dry bread to be had, without butter, and as much bad coffee as a man could drink.

A person called the bookkeeper arrived with the janitor. I made my formal farewells to those representatives of the law, before whom the Amphibian melted with humility. The scalawag who had bathed with me tipped me a wink, and tried to escape in my company. But I bade him good-by so firmly that the authorities noticed, and the brash creature remained glued to his chair. He probably had to do his full share of kindling before he escaped.

I went forth from that place into the highway of our God, who dwelleth not in temples made with hands, neither is worshipped with men's hands, as though He needed anything, seeing He giveth to all men life and breath and all things.

I said in my heart: "I shall walk on and on and find a better, a far holier shrine than this at the ends of the infinite earth."

ON BEING ENTERTAINED ONE EVENING BY COLLEGE BOYS

I walked across the bridge from New Jersey into Easton, Pennsylvania, one afternoon. I discovered there was a college atop of the hill. In exchange for a lecture on twenty-six great men based on a poem on the same theme, that I carried with me, the boys entertained me that night. They did not pay much attention to the lecture. Immediately before and after was a yell carnival. There was to be a game next day. They were cheering the team and the coach with elaborate reiteration. All was astir.

But for all this the boys spoke to me gently, gave me the privileges of the table, the bathroom, the dormitory. The president of the Y.M.C.A. lent me a clean suit of pajamas. He and two other young fellows delighted my vain soul, by keeping me up late reciting all the poems I knew.

I record these things for the sake of recording one thing more, the extraordinary impression of buoyancy that came from that school. It was inspiring to a degree, a draught of the gods. Coming into that place not far from the centre of hard-faced Easton-town I realized for the first time what sheltered, nurtured boy-America was like, and what wonders may lie beneath the roofs of our cities.

NEAR SHICKSHINNY

I

Leaving New Jersey I kept from all contact with money, and was consequently turning over in memory many delicious adventures among the Pennsylvania-German farmers. After crossing that lovely, lonely plateau called Pocono Mountain, I descended abruptly to Wilkesbarre by a length of steep automobile road called Giant Despair.

It was a Sunday noon in May. Wilkesbarre was a mixture of Sabbath calm and the smoke of torment that ascendeth forever. One passed pious faces too clean, sooty faces too restless. I hurried through, hoping for more German farmers beyond. But King Coal had conspired against the traveller, and would not let him go. The further west I walked, the thicker the squalor and slag heaps, and the presence of St. Francis seemed withdrawn from me, though I had been faithful in my fashion.

King Coal is a boaster. He says he furnishes food for all the engines of the earth. He says he is the maker of steam. He says steam is the twentieth century. He holds that an infinite number of black holes in the ground is a blessing.

He may say what he likes, but he has not excused himself to me. He blasts the landscape. Never do human beings drink so hard to forget their sorrow as in the courtyards of this monarch. To dig in a mine makes men reckless, to own one makes them tormentors.

I had a double reason for hurrying on. My rules as a mendicant afoot were against cities and railroads. I flattered myself I was called and sent to the agricultural laborer.

When the land grew less black and less inhabited, I mistakenly rejoiced, assuming I should soon strike the valleys where grain is sown and garnered. Yet the King was following me still, like a great mole underground. There was no coal on the surface. The land was rusty-red and ashen-gray, — as though blasted by the torch of a Cyclops and only yesterday cooled by the rain. The best grain that could have been scattered among such rocks with the hope of a crop was a seed of dragon's teeth.

How long the desolation continued! Toward the end of the day in the midst of the nothingness, I came upon a saloon full of human creatures roaring drunk. Otherwise there was not so much as a shed in sight.

Four vilely dirty little girls came down the steps carrying beer. One of them, too intoxicated for her errand, entrusted her can to her companions. They preceded me toward the smoke-veiled sun by a highway growing black again with the foot-prints of the King.

Now there was a deafening explosion. I sat down on a rock examining myself to see if I was still alive. The children pattered on. My start seemed to amuse them immensely. I followed toward the new civil war, or whatever it was.

Just over the crest and around the corner I encountered the King's never-varying insignia, the double-row of "company houses."

Every dwelling was as eternally and uniformly damned as its neighbor, making the eyes ache, standing foursquare in the presence of the insulted daylight. Every porch and railing was jig-sawed in the same ruthless way. Every front yard was grassless. Everything was made of wood, yet seemed made of iron, so black it was, so long had it stood in the wasting weather, so steadily had it resisted the dynamite now shaking the earth.

There they stood, thirty houses to the left, thirty to the right, with what you might call a street between, whose ruts were seemingly cut by the treasure-chariots of the brimstone princes of the nether world.

Two-thirds of the way through, several young miners were exploding giant powder. As I approached I saw another was loading his pistol with ball-cartridges and shooting over the hills at the sun. He did not put it out.

The group of children with the beer served these knights of dynamite, holding up the cans for them to drink. The little cup-bearers were then given pennies. They scurried home.

By their eyes and queer speech I guessed that these children were Poles, or of some other race from Eastern Europe. I guessed the same about the men celebrating. Every porch on both sides of that street held some heavy headed creatures from presumably the same foreign parts. They were, no doubt, good citizens after their peculiar fashion, but with countenances that I could not read. Though the next explosion seemed to jolt the earth out of its orbit, they merely blinked.

I said to myself, "This is not the fourth of July. Therefore it must be the anniversary of the day when 'Freedom shrieked' and 'Kosciuszko fell.'"

I reached the end of the street; nothing beyond but a hollow of hills and a dubious river, enclosing a new Tophet, that I learned afterwards was Shickshinny. It was late. I wanted to get beyond to the green fields.

I zigzagged across that end of the street to folk on the front porches that I thought were Americans. Each time I vainly attempted conversation with some dumb John Sobieski in Sunday clothes. I wondered what were the Polish words for bread, shelter, and dead broke.

II

The Son of King Coal

Some spick and span people came out on the porch of the last house. Possibly they could understand English. I went closer. They were out and out Americans.

So I looked them in the eye and said: "I would like to have you entertain me to-night. I am a sort of begging preacher. I do not take money, only food and lodging."

"A beggin' preacher?"

"My sermon is in poetry. I can read it to you after supper, if that will suit."

"What sort of poetry?" asked the man.

"I can only say it is my own."

"Why I just LOVE poetry," said the woman. "Come in."

"Come up," said the man, and hustled out a chair.

"I'll go right in and get supper," said the wife. She was a breezy creature with a loud musical voice. She doubtless developed it by trying to talk against giant powder.

I told the man my story, in brief.

After quite a smoke, he said, "So you've walked from Wilkesbarre this afternoon. Why, man, that's seventeen miles."

I do not believe it was over fourteen.

He continued, "I'm awful glad to see a white man. This place is full of Bohunks, and Slavs, and Rooshians, and Poles and Lickerishes (Lithuanians?). They're not bad to have around, but they ain't Cawcasians. They all talk Eyetalian."

The fellow's manner breathed not only race-fraternity, but industrial fraternity. It had no suggestion of sheltered agricultural caution. It was sophisticated and anti-capitalistic. It said, "You and I are against the system. That's enough for brotherhood."

Now that he stood and refilled his pipe from a tobacco box nailed just inside the door, I saw him as in a picture-frame. He had powerful but slanting shoulders. He was so tall he must needs stoop to avoid the lintel. With his bent neck, he looked as though he could hold up a mine caving in. His general outlines seemed to be hewn from fence-rails, then hung with grotesque muscles of loose leather. His eyebrows were grown together. From looking down long passage-ways his eyes were marvelously owl-like. He was cadaverous. He had a beak nose. He had a retreating chin but, breaking the rules of phrenology, he managed to convey the impression of a driving personality. He looked like an enormous pickaxe,

He calmly commented: "Them Polacks waste powder awful. Not only on Sunday, for fun, but down in the mine they use twice too much. And they can't blast the hardest coal, either. . . . And they're always gettin' careless and blowin' themselves to hell and everybody else. It's awful, it's awful," he said, but in a most philosophic tone.

He lowered his voice and pointed with his pipe stem: "Them people that live in the next house are supposed to be Cawcasians, but they haven't a marriage license. They let their little girl go for beer this afternoon, for them fellows explodin' powder over there. 'Taint no way to raise a child. That child's mother was a well-behaved Methodist till she married a Polack, and had four children, and he died, and they died, and some say she poisoned them all. Now she's got this child by this no-account white man. They live without a license, like birds. Yet they eat off weddin's."

"Eat off weddings?"

"Yes," he said. "These Bohunks and Lickerishes all have one kind of a wedding. It lasts three days and everybody comes. The best man is king He bosses the plates."

"Bosses the plates?"

"Yes. They buy a lot of cheap plates. Every man that comes must break a plate with a dollar. The plate is put in the middle of the floor. He stands over it and bangs the dollar down. If he breaks the plate he gets to kiss and hug the bride. If he doesn't break it, the young couple get that dollar. He must keep on givin' them dollars in this way till he breaks the plate. Eats and plates and beer cost about fifty dollars. The young folks clear about two hundred dollars to start life on."

"And," he continued, "the folks next door make a practice of eatin' round at weddin's without puttin' down their dollars."

I began to feel guilty.

"It's a good deal like my begging supper and breakfast of you." He hadn't meant it that way. "No," he said, "you're takin' the only way to see the country. Why, man, I used to travel like you, before I was married, except I didn't take no book nor poetry no nothin', and wasn't afeered of box-cars the way you are. . . . I been in every state in the Union but Maine. I don't know how I kept out of there. . . . I've been nine years in this house. I don't know but what I see as much as when I was on the go. . . .

"That fellow Gallic over there that was shootin' that pistol at the sky killed a man named Bothweinis last year and got off free. It was Gallic's wedding and Bothweinis brought fifty dollars and said he was goin' to break all the plates in the house. He used up twelve dollars. He broke seven plates and kissed the bride seven times. Then the bride got drunk. She was only fifteen years old. She hunted up Bothweinis and kissed him and cried, and Gallic chased him down towards Shickshinny and tripped him up, and shot him in the mouth and in the eye. . . . The bride didn't know no better. . . . He was an awful sight when they brought him in. The bride was only a kid. These Bohunk women never learn no sense anyway. They're not smart like Cawcasian women, and they fade in the face quick."

He reflected: "My wife's a wonderful woman. I have been with her nine years, and she learns me something every day, and she still looks good in her Sunday clothes."

He became lighter in tone again. "What these Bohunks need is a priest and a church to make them behave. They mind a priest some, if he is a good priest. They're all Catholics, or no church. . . ."

"Seems though sometimes a man's GOT to shoot. Some of them devils over there used to throw rocks at my door, but one Sunday I filled 'em full of buckshot and they quit. The justice upheld me. I didn't have to pay no fine. They've been pretty good neighbors since, pretty good neighbors."

There was a sound as though the flagstones of eternity had been ripped up. He saw I didn't like it and said consolingly, "They'll stop and go to supper pretty soon. They eat too much to do anything but set, afterwards. They don't have nothin' to eat in the old country but raw turnips. Here they stuff themselves like toads. I don't see how they save money the way they do. The mine owners squeeze the very life out of 'em and they wallow in beer. I've always made big money, but somehow never kept it. Me and my wife are spenders. But I ain't afraid, for I am the only man on the street that can dig the hardest coal. I could dig my way out of hell with my pick, and by G— once I did it, too."

The wife came to the door newly decked in an elaborate lace waist, torn, alas, at the shoulder. Husband was right. She looked good. She announced radiantly: "Come to supper."

Then she rushed down between the houses and shouted: "Jimmy and Frank, come here! What you doin'? Get down off that roof. What you doin', associatin' with them Polack children? What you doin' with them switches?" Then she swore heartily, as unto the Lord, and continued, "They're helpin' them Polack kids switch that poor little drunk American child. Come down off that coal shed!"

They slunk into sight. She snatched their switches from them.

"Who started it?"

Jimmy admitted he started it. He looked capable of starting most anything, good or bad. He had eyes like black diamonds, a stocky frame, and the tiny beginnings of his mother's voice.

"I don't know whether to lick you or not," she said judicially. Finally: "Go up to bed without supper."

Jimmy went.

She addressed us in perfect good humor, as a musical volcano might: "Come and eat."

III

The Daughter of the King

Never did I see beefsteak so thick. There was a garnish of fried onions. There was a separate sea of gravy. There was a hill of butter, a hill of thickly sliced bread. There was a delectable mountain of potatoes. That was all. These people were living the simple life, living it in chunks.

At table, as everywhere, the husband solemnly deferred to the wife. She was to him a druid priestess. And so she was radiant, as woman enthroned is apt to be. Of course, no young lady from finishing school would have liked the way we tunnelled and blasted our way through the provender. We were gloriously hungry and our manners were a hearty confession of the fact.

My passion for the joys of the table partially sated, I began to realize the room. There were hardly any of the comforts of home. There was a big onyx time-piece, chipped, and not running. Beside it was a dollar alarm-clock in good trim.

There were in the next room, among other things, two frail gilt parlor chairs, almost black. The curtains were streaked with soot and poorly ironed. She said she had washed them yesterday. But, she continued, "I just keep cheerful, I don't keep house. Doesn't seem like I can, this street is so awful dirty and noisy and foreign."

"Yet you like it," said the husband.

"Yes," she said, "that's because I'm half Irish. The Irish were born for excitement."

"What's *your* ancestry?" I asked the husband.

"My father was a mountain white. Moved here from North Carolina, and dug coal and married a Pennsylvania Dutch lady."

"It's your turn," she said to me. "You are a preacher?"

"That's a kind of an excuse I make."

"You can't be any worse than the preacher we had here," continued the wife. "He lived down toward Shickshinny. He preached in an old chapel. He wouldn't start a Sunday school. We needed one bad enough. He just married folks. He hardly ever buried them. They say he was afraid. And," she continued, with a growing tone of condemnation, "it's a preacher's BUSINESS to face death.

"Just about the time two of our children died of diphtheria, was when he came to these parts. He was a Presbyterian, and I was raised a Presbyterian, and he wouldn't preach the funeral of my two babies. He promised to come, and we waited two hours. So I just read the Bible at the grave."

This she recounted with a bitter sense of insult.

"And the same day he locked up his mother, too."

"Locked up his mother?"

"Yes. Some said he wanted to visit a woman he didn't want her to know about. They said he was afraid she would follow him and spy. He locked up the old lady, and she about yelled the roof off, and the neighbors let her out.

"And then," continued my hostess, "when he was dying, he sent for a Wilkesbarre priest."

"Sent for a priest?" I exclaimed, completely mystified.

"Yes," she whispered. "He must have been a Catholic all the time. And the priest wouldn't come either. *That's what that old preacher got for being so mean.*"

She continued: "That preacher wasn't much meaner than the man is in the company store."

She was bristling again.

"He won't deliver goods up here unless you run a big bill. If I want anything much while big Frank here is at work, I have to take Jimmy's little play express-wagon and haul it up."

And now she was telling me of her terrible fright three days ago, down at the company store, when there was a rumor of an accident in one of the far tunnels of the mine.

"All the foreign women came running down the hill, half-crazy. I am used to false alarms, but I could hardly get up to this house with my goods. I was expecting to see big Frank brought in, just like he was before little Frank was born, eight years ago."

Little Frank lifted his face from its business of eating to listen.

"The first thing that boy ever saw was his father on the floor there, covered with blood."

"You don't remember it, Frank?" asked his father, grinning.

"Nope."

The wife continued: "There was only one doctor came. We had a time between us. The other doctor was tendin' the men husband had dug out. The coal fell on them and mashed them flat. It couldn't quite mash husband. He's too tough," she said, lovingly. "He grabbed his pick and he tunnelled his way through, with the blood squirting out of him."

Husband grinned like a petted child. He said: "It wasn't quite as bad as that, but I was bloody, all right."

She continued with a gesture of impatience: "This IS cheerful Sunday night talk. Let's try something else. What kind of a poem are you goin' to read?"

"It tells boys how to be great men, but it's for fellows of from fifteen to twenty. You'll have to save it for your sons till they grow a bit."

She was at the foot of the stairway like a flash.

"Son, dress and come down to supper."

Son was down almost as soon as she was in her chair, pulling on a stocking as he came. And he was hungry. He ate while we talked on and on.

IV

The Grandsons of the King

After the supper the dishes waited. The wife said: "Now we will have the poetry." I said in my heart, "Maybe this is the one house in a hundred where the seed of these verses will be sown upon good ground."

We went into the parlor, distinguished as such by the battered organ. The mother had Frank and Jimmy sit in semicircle with her and big Frank, while I plunged into my rhymed appeal. After the dynamite of the day I did not hesitate to let loose the thunders. I did not hesitate to pause and expound: — the poem being, as I have before described, many stanzas on heroes of history, with the refrain, ever and anon: *God help us to be brave*. No, kind and flattering reader, it was NOT above their heads. Earnestness is earnestness everywhere. The whole circle grasped that I really expected something unusual of those boys with the black-diamond eyes, no matter what kind of perversity was in them at present.

I said, in so many words, as a beginning, that nitro-glycerine was not the only force in the world, that there is also that dynamite called the power of the soul, and that detonation called fame.

But I did not dwell long upon my special saints, Francis of Assisi and Buddha, nor those other favorites who some folk think contradict them: Phidias and Michael Angelo. I dwelt on the strong: Alexander, Caesar, Mohammed, Cromwell, Napoleon, and especially upon the lawgivers, Confucius, Moses, Justinian; and dreamed that this ungoverned strength before me, that had sprung from the loins of King Coal, might some day climb high, that these little wriggling, dirty-fisted grandsons of that monarch might yet make the world some princely reparation for his crimes.

After the reading the mother and father said solemnly, "it is a good book."

Then the wife showed the other two pieces of printed matter in the household, a volume of sermons, and a copy of *The House of a Thousand Candles.* You have read that work about the candles. The sermons were by the Reverend Wood M. Smithers. You do not know the Reverend Mister Smithers? He has collected in one fair volume all the sermons that ever put you to sleep, an anthology of all those discourses that are just alike.

She said she had read them over and over again to the family. I believed it. There was butter on the page. I said in my heart: "She is not to be baffled by any phraseology. If she can get a kernel out of Wood M. Smithers, she will also derive strength from my rhyme."

She promised she would have each of the boys pick out one of the twenty-six great men for a model, as soon as they were schooled enough to choose. She put the poem in the kitchen table drawer, where she kept some photographs of close relatives, and I had the final evidence that I had become an integral part of the family tradition.

V

On to Shickshinny

They sent me up to bed. I put out the lamp at once, lest I should see too much. I went to sleep quickly. I was as quickly awakened. Being a man of strategies and divertisements, I reached through the blackness to the lamp that was covered with leaked oil. I rubbed this on my hands, and thence, thinly over my whole body. Coal oil too thick makes blisters; thin enough, brings peace.

I remember breakfast as a thing apart. Although the table held only what we had for supper, warmed over, although the morning light was grey, and the room the worse for the grey light, the thing I cannot help remembering was the stillness and tenderness of that time. Father and mother spoke in subdued human voices. They had not yet had occasion to shout against the alarums and excursions of the day. And the sensitive faces of the boys, and the half-demon, half-angel light of their eyes stirred me with marvelling and reverence for the curious, protean ways of God.

And now I was walking down the steeps of Avernus into Shickshinny, toward the smoke of torment that ascends forever. Underfoot was spread the same dark leprosy that yesterday had stunted flower and fruit and grass-blade.

I hated King Coal still, but not so much as of yore.

DEATH, THE DEVIL, AND HUMAN KINDNESS
The Shred of an Allegory

I

The Undertaker

Curious are the agencies that throw the true believer into the occult state. Convalescence may do it. Acts of piety may do it. Self-mortification may do it.

After reading my evening sermon in rhyme in the house of the stranger, I had slept on the lounge in the parlor. The lounge had lost some of its excelsior, and the springs wound their way upwards like steel serpents. So strenuous had been the day I could have slumbered peacefully on a Hindu bed of spikes.

I awoke refreshed, despite several honorable scars. What is more important I left that house with faculties of discernment.

I did not realize at first that I was particularly spiritualized. I was merely walking west, hoping to take in Oil City on my route. Yet I saw straight through the bark of a big maple, and beheld the loveliest. . . but I have not time to tell.

Then I heard a fluttering in a patch of tall weeds and discovered what the people in fairyland call . . . but no matter. We must hurry on.

At noon your servant was on the front step of a store near a cross-roads called Cranberry, Pennsylvania. The store was on the south side of the way by which I had come. I sat looking along wagon tracks leading north, little suspecting I should take that route soon.

On one side overhead was the sign: "Fred James, Undertaker." On the other: "Fred James, Grocer."

"And so," I thought, *"I am going to meet, face to face, one of the eternal powers.* He may call himself Fred James all he pleases. His real name is Death."

I met the lady Life, once upon a time, long ago. She had innocent blue eyes. Alone in the field I felt free to kiss the palm of her little hand, under the shadow of the corn.

It has nothing to do with the tale, but let us here reflect how the corn-stalk is a proud thing, how it flourishes its dangerous blades, guarding the young ear. It will cut you on the forehead if the wind is high. Above the blades is the sacred tassel like a flame.

Once, under that tassel, under those dangerous blades, I met Life, and for good reason, bade her good-by. After her solemn words of parting, she called me back, and mischievously fed me, from the pocket of her gingham apron, crab apples and cranberries. Ever since that time those fruits have been bitter delights to my superstitious fancy.

And here I was at CRANBERRY cross-roads, with a funeral director's sign over my head. A long five minutes I meditated on the mystery of Life and Death and cranberries. A fat chicken, apparently meditating on the same mystery, kept walking up and down, catching gnats.

At length it was revealed to me that when things have their proper rhythm Life and Death are interwoven, like willows plaited for a basket. Somewhat later in the afternoon I speculated that when times are out of joint, it is because Death reigns without Life for a partner, with the assistance of the Devil rather. But do not remember this. It anticipates the plot.

One does not hasten into the presence of the undertaker. One rather waits. HE was coming. I did not look round. Even at noon he cast a considerable shadow.

The shadow dwindled as he sat on the same step and asked: "What road have you come?" His non-partisan drawl was the result, we will suppose, of not knowing which side of the store the new customer approached.

"I came from over there. I have been walking since sunrise."

He had some account of my adventures, and my point of view as a religious mendicant. I knew I would have to ask the further road of him, but disliked the necessity. He waited patiently while I watched my friend, the fat chicken, explore an empty, dirty, bottomless basket for flies.

"I want to go west by way of Oil City," I finally said.

He answered: "Oil City is reached by the north road, straight in front of you as you sit. It is about an hour's walk to the edge of it. It is a sort of trap in the mountains. When you get in sight of it, *keep on going down.*" This he said very solemnly.

He put his hand on my shoulder: "Come in and rest and eat first. It won't cost you a cent."

I was hungry enough to eat a coffin handle, and so I looked at him and extended my hand. He was a handsome chap, with a grey mustache. His black coat was buttoned high. He was extra neat for a country merchant, and chewed his tobacco surreptitiously. His face was not so bony and stern as you might think.

I gave him an odd copy of the *Tree of Laughing Bells,* still remaining by me. He looked at the outside long, doing the cover more than justice. Then he opened it, with a certain air of delicate appreciation. I urged him to postpone reading the thing till I was gone.

His store was high and long and narrow and cool. There was a counter to the west, a counter to the east. Behind the western one were tall coffin cupboards. As he proudly opened and shut them, one could not but notice the length of his fingers and their dexterity. He showed plain coffins and splendid coffins. He unscrewed the lid of one, that I might see the silky cushions within. They looked easier than last night's lounge.

As he stepped across what might be called the international date line of the store, and entered the hemisphere of groceries, he began to look as though he would indulge in a merry quip. A faint flush came to his white countenance, that shone among the multi-colored packages.

Before us were the supplies of a rural general store, from the kitchen mop to the blue parlor vase. Hanging from the ceiling was an array of the flamboyant varnished posters of the seedsmen, with pictures of cut watermelons, blood-red, and portraits of beets, cabbages, pumpkins.

I read his home-made sign aloud: "I guarantee every seed in the store. Pansy seeds a specialty."

"Not that they all grow," he explained. "But the guarantee keeps up the confidence of the customers. I have made more off of vegetable and flower seeds this year than caskets.''

He pulled out a chip plate and fed me with dried beef, sliced thin. He smiled broadly, and set down a jar. The merry quip had arrived. ''Why,'' he asked, ''is a stick of candy like a race-horse?'' I remained silent, but looked anxious to know. Delighted with himself, he gave the ancient answer, and with it several sticks of candy. Kind reader, if you do not know the answer to the riddle, ask your neighbor.

There was no end of sweets. He skilfully sliced fresh bread, and spread it with butter and thick honey-comb. With much self-approval he insisted on crowding my pockets with supper.

''Nobody knows how they will treat you around Oil City. *I go often, but never for pleasure. Only on funeral business.*''

He gave me pocketfuls of the little animal crackers, so daintily cut out, that used to delight all of us as children. Since he insisted I take something more, I took figs and dates.

He held up an animal cracker, shaped like a cow, and asked: ''When was beefsteak the highest?'' I ventured to give the answer.

Death is not a bad fellow. Let no man cross his grey front stoop with misgiving. The honey he serves is made by noble bees. Yet do not go seeking him out. No doubt his acquaintance is most worth while when it is casual, unexpected, one of the natural accidents. And he does not always ask such simple riddles.

II

The Trap without the Bait

It was about two o'clock when the north road left the cornfields and reached the hill crests above the city. How the highway descended over cliffs and retraced itself on ridges and wound into hollows to get to the streets! At the foot of the first incline I met a lame cat creeping, panic-stricken, out of town.

Oil City is an ugly, confused kind of place. There are thousands like it in the United States.

I reached the post-office at last. *There was no letter for me at the general delivery. I was expecting a missive.* And now my blistered heels, and my breaking the rule to avoid the towns, and my detour of half a day were all in vain.

Oil City, in her better suburbs, as a collection of worthy families in comfortable homes, may have much to say for herself. But as a corporate soul she has no excuse. The dominant, shoddy architecture is as eloquent as the red nose of a drunkard. I do not need to take pains to work her into my allegory. The name she has chosen makes her a symbol. No doubt others reach the very heart of her only to find it empty as the post-office was to me. Baffling as this may be, there is another risk. Escape is not easy.

Almost out of town at last, I sat down by the fence, determined not to stir till morning. I said, "I can sleep with my back against this post."

I had just overtaken the lame cat, and she now moved past me over the ridge to the cornfields. She seemed most unhappy. I looked back to that oil metropolis. *I wondered how many had lived and died there when they would have preferred some other place.*

III

A Mysterious Driver

A fat Italian came by in a heavily-tired wagon. The wagon was loaded with green bananas. The fruit-vendor stopped and looked me over. He most demonstratively offered me a seat beside him. He had a Benvenuto Cellini leer. He wore one gold earring. He looked like the social secretary of the Black Hand.

He was apparently driving on into the country. Therefore I suffered myself to be pulled up on to the seat. Around the corner we came to green fields and bushes, and I thanked the good St. Francis and all his holy company.

I said to my charioteer: "As soon as you get a mile out, let me down. I do not want to get near any more towns for awhile."

"Allaright," he said. On his wrist was tattooed a blue dagger. The first thing he did was unmerciful. He went a yard out of his way to drive over the lame cat which had stopped in despair, just ahead of us. Pussy died without a shriek. Then the cruel one, gathering by my manner that I was not pleased with this incident, created a diversion. He reproved his horse for not hurrying. It was not so much a curse as an Italian oration. The poor animal tried to respond, but hobbled so, his master surprised me by checking the gait to a walk. Then he cooed to the horse like a two hundred pound turtledove.

In a previous incarnation this driver must have been one of the lower animals, he had so many dealings with such. Some rocks half the size of base-balls were piled at his feet. A ferocious dog shot out from a cottage doorway. With lightning action he hurled the ammunition at the offender. The beast retreated weeping aloud from pain. And Mr. Cellini showed his teeth with delight.

And now, after passing several pleasant farm-houses, where I ran a chance for a free lodging for the asking, I was vexed to be suddenly driven into a town. We hobbled, rattled on, into a wilderness thicker every minute with fire-spouting smoke-stacks.

"This ees Franklin," said my charioteer. "Nice-a-town. MY town," he added earnestly. "I getta reech (rich) to-morrow."

He began to cross-examine the writer of this tale. I counselled myself not to give my name and address, lest I be held for ransom.

After many harmless inquiries, he asked in a would-be ingratiating manner, "Poppa reech?"

"No. Poor."

"Poppa verra reech?"

"No. Awfully poor. But happy and contented."

"Where your Poppa leeve?"

"My father is the Man in the Moon."

That answer changed him completely. I seemed to have given the password. I had joined whatever it was he belonged to. He gave me three oranges as a sign.

I had hoped we would drive past the smoke and fire. But he turned at right angles, into the midst of it, and drove into a big black barn. He waved me good-by in the courtliest manner, as though he were somebody important, and I were somebody important.

Pretty soon I asked a passer-by the nearest way to the suburbs. I had to walk on the edges of my feet they were so tired. The street he pointed out to me was nothing but a continuation of tar-black, coughing, out-of-door ovens, side by side, shoulder to shoulder, on to the crack of doom. I presume, in the language of this vain world, they were coke ovens.

I opened my eyes as little as possible and breathed hardly at all. Then, by way of diversion, I nibbled animal crackers, first a dog, then a giraffe, then a hippopotamus, then an elephant.

Those ovens looked queerer as the street led on. There were subtle essences abroad when the smoke cleared away, and when the great roar ceased there were vague sounds that struck awe into the heart. I may be mistaken, but I think I know the odor of a burning ghost on the late afternoon wind, and the puffing noise he makes.

As the cinders crunched, crunched, underfoot, the conviction deepened: "These ovens are not mere works of man. Dying sinners snared and corrupted by Oil City are carried here when the city has done its work—carried in the wagon of Apollyon, under bunches of green bananas. Body and soul they are disintegrated by the venomous oil; they crumble away in the town of oil, and here in the town of ovens, the fragments are burned with unquenchable fire.''

Now it was seven o'clock. The street led south past the aristocratic suburbs of Franklin, and on to the fields and dandelion-starred roadside.

IV

The Allegory Breaks Down.
My Friend Humankindness with the Green Galluses

I hoped for a farm-hand's house. Only in that sort will they give free lodging so near town. And, friends, I found it, there on the edge of the second cornfield. The welcome was unhesitating.

I looked at my host aghast. To satisfy my sense of the formal, he should have had the dignity to make him Father Adam, and lord of Paradise. How could one round out a day that began loftily with Death, and continued gloriously with some one mighty like the Devil, with this inglorious type now before me? He wrecked my allegory. There is no climax in Stupidity.

Just as the colorless, one-room house had stove, chimney, cupboard, adequate roof, floor, and walls, so the owner had the simplified, anatomical, and phrenological make-up of a man. He had a luke-warm hand-clasp. He smoked a Pittsburg stogy. He had thick vague features and a shock of drab hair. The nearest to a symbol about him was his new green galluses. I suppose they indicated I was out in the fields again.

If his name was not Stupidity, it was Awkwardness. He kept a sick geranium in an old tomato can in the window. He had not cut off the bent-back cover of the can. Just after he gave me a seat he scratched his hand, as he was watering the flower, and swore softly.

Yet one must not abuse his host. I hasten to acknowledge his generous hospitality. If it be not indelicate to mention it, he boiled much water, and properly diluted it with cold, that the traveller might bathe. The bath was accomplished out of doors beneath the shades of evening.

Later he was making preparations for supper, with dull eyes that looked nowhere. He made sure I fitted my chair. He put an old comfort over it. It was well. The chair was not naturally comfortable; it was partly a box.

After much fumbling about, he brought some baked potatoes from the oven. The plate was so hot he dropped it, but so thick it would not break.

He picked up the potatoes, as good as ever, and broke some open for me, spreading them with tolerable butter, and handing them across the table. Then I started to eat.

"Wait a minute," he said. He bowed his head, closed his dull eyes, and uttered these words: "The Lord make us truly thankful for what we are about to receive. Amen."

I have been reproved by some of the judicious for putting so much food in these narratives. Nevertheless the first warm potato tasted like peacocks' tongues, the next like venison, and the next like ambrosia, and the next like a good warm potato with butter on it. One might as well leave Juliet out of Verona as food like this out of a road-story. As we ate we hinted to each other of our many ups and downs. He mumbled along, telling his tale. He did not care whether he heard mine or not.

He had been born near by. In early manhood he had been taken with the oil fever. It happened in this wise:—He had cut his foot splitting kindling. Meditating ambition as he slowly recovered, he resolved to go to town. He sold his small farm and wasted his substance in speculation. At the same time his young wife and only child died of typhoid fever. He was a laborer awhile in the two cities to the northeast. Then he came back here to plough corn.

He had been saving for two years, had made money enough to go back "pretty soon" and enter what he considered a sure-thing scheme, that I gathered had a close relation to the oil business. He said that he had learned from experience to sift the good from the bad in that realm of commerce.

He put brakes on the slow freight train of his narrative. "I was about to explain, when you ast to come in, that I don't afford dessert to my meals often."

"If you will excuse me," I said, emptying my pockets, "these figs, these dates, these oranges, these animal crackers were given me by Death, and the Devil. Eat hearty."

"Death and the Devil. What kind are they?"

"They're not a bad sort. Death gave me honey for dinner, and the Devil did no worse than drive me a little out of my way."

He smiled vaguely. He thought it was a joke, and was too interested in the food itself to ask any more questions.

The balmy smokeless wind from the south was whistling, whistling past the window, and through the field. How much one can understand by mere whispers! The wind cried, "Life, life, life!" Some of the young corn was brushing the walls of the cottage, and armies on armies of young corn were bivouacing further down the road, lifting their sacred tassels toward the stars.

There was no change in the expression of the countenance of my host, eating, talking, or sitting still in the presence of the night. I may have had too poor an estimate of his powers, but I preached no sermon that evening.

But, like many a primitive man I have met, he preached me a sermon. He had no bed. He gave the traveller a place to sleep in one corner and himself slept in the opposite corner. The floor was smooth and clean and white, and the many scraps of rag carpet and the clean comfort over me were a part of the sermon. Another part was in his question before he slept: "Does the air from that open window bother you?"

I assured him I wanted all there was, though from the edge of the world.

He had awkwardly folded his new overcoat, and put it under my head. . . . And so I was beginning to change his name from Stupidity and Awkwardness to Humankindness.

Though in five minutes he was snoring like Sousa's band, I could not but sleep. When I awoke the sun was in my eyes. It shone through the open door. Mr. Humankindness was up. The smell of baked potatoes was in the air. Outside, rustled the corn. The wind cried, "Life, life, life."

THE OLD GENTLEMAN WITH THE LANTERN
(AND THE PEOPLE OF HIS HOUSEHOLD)

I

The Savage Necklace

The reader need not expect this book to contain any nicely adjusted plot with a villain, hero, lawyer, papers, surprise, and happy ending. The highway is irrelevant. The highway is slipshod. The highway is as the necklace of a gipsy or an Indian, a savage string of pebbles and precious stones, no two alike, with an occasional trumpery suspender button or peach seed. Every diamond is in the rough.

I was walking between rugged farms on the edge of the oil country in western Pennsylvania.

The road, almost dry after several days of rain, was gay with butterfly-haunted puddles. The grotesque swain who gave me a lift in his automobile for a mile is worth a page, but we will only say that his photograph would have contributed to the gaiety of nations — that he was the carved peach-stone on the necklace of the day.

There was a complacent cat in a doorway, that should have been named "scrambled eggs and milk," so mongrel was his overcoat. There was a philosophic grasshopper reading inscriptions in a lonely cemetery, with whom I had a long and silent interchange of spirit. Even the graveyard was full of sun.

On and on led the merry morning. At length came noon, and a meal given with heartiness, as easily plucked as a red apple. For half an hour after dinner in that big farm-house we sat and talked religion.

O pagan in the cities, the brand of one's belief is still important in the hayfield. I was delighted to discover this household held by conviction to the brotherhood of which I was still a nominal member. Their lingo was a taste of home. "Our People," "Our Plea," "The pious unimmersed." Thus did they lead themselves into paths of solemnity.

Then, in the last five minutes of my stay, I gave them my poem-sermon. The pamphlet made them stare, if it did not make them think.

Splendor after splendor rolled in upon the highway from the four corners of heaven. Why then should I complain, if about four o'clock the prosy old world emerged again?

The wagon-track now followed a section of the Pennsylvania railroad, and railroads are anathema in my eyes when I am afoot. There appeared no promising way of escape. And now the steel rails led into a region where there had been rain, even this morning. More than once I had to take to the ties to go on. When the mud was at all passable I walked in it by preference, fortifying myself with these philosophizings: —

"Cinders are sterile. They blast man and nature, but the black earth renews all. Mud upon the shoes is not a contamination but a sign of progress, eloquent as sweat upon the brow. Who knows but the feet are the roots of a man? Who knows but rain on the road may help him to grow? Maybe the stature and breadth of farmers is due to their walking behind the plough in the damp soil. Only an aviator or a bird has a right to spurn the ground. All the rest of us must furrow our way. Thus will our cores be enriched, thus will we give fruit after our kind."

Whistling pretty hard, I made my way. And now I had to choose between my rule to flee from the railroad, and my rule to ask for hospitality before dark.

At length I said to myself: "I want to get into a big unsophisticated house, the kind that is removed from this railroad. I want to find an unprejudiced host who will listen with an open mind, and let me talk him to death."

To keep this resolve I had to hang on till near eight o'clock. The cloudy night made the way dim. At length I came to a road that had been so often graded and dragged it shed water like a turtle's shell. It crossed the railway at right angles and ploughed north. I followed it a mile, shaking the heaviest mud from my shoes. Led by the light of a lantern, I approached a dim grey farm-house and what would have been in the daytime a red barn.

II

By the Light of the Lantern

The lantern was carried, as I finally discovered, by an old man getting a basket of chips near the barn gate. He had his eye on me as I leaned over the fence. He swung the lantern closer.

"My name is Nicholas," I said. "I am a professional tramp."

"W-e-l-l," he said slowly, in question, and then in exclamation.

He flashed the lantern in my face. "Come in," he said. "Sit down."

We were together on the chip-pile. He did not ask me to split kindling, or saw wood. Few people ever do.

In appearance he was the old John G. Whittier type of educated laboring man, only more eagle-like. He spoke to me in a kingly prophetic manner, developed, I have no doubt, by a lifetime of unquestioned predominance at prayer-meeting and at the communion table. It was the sonorous agricultural holy tone that is the particular aversion of a certain pagan type of city radical who does not understand that the meeting-house is the very rock of the agricultural social system. As far as I am concerned, if this manner be worn by a kindly old man, it inspires me with respect and delight. In a slow and gracious way he separated his syllables.

"Young man, you are per-fect-ly wel-come to shel-ter if we are on-ly sure you will not do us an in-ju-ry. My age and ex-per-ience ought to count for a lit-tle, and I assure you that most free travel-ers abuse hos-pi-tal-ity. But wait till my daugh-ter-in-law comes."

I was shivering with weariness, and my wet feet wanted to get to a stove at once. I did not feel so much like talking some one to death as I had a while back.

By way of passing the time, the Patriarch showed me his cane. "Pre-sen-ted at the last old set-tel-ers' picnic because I have been the pres-i-dent of the old-settlers' association for ten years. Young man, why don't you carry a cane?"

"Why should I?"

"Won't it help you to keep off dogs?"

I replied, "A housekeeper, if she is in a nervous condition, is apt to be afraid of a walking-stick. It looks like a club. To carry something to keep off dogs is like carrying a lightning-rod to keep off lightning. I encounter a lot of barking and thunder, but have never been bitten or blasted."

And while I was thus laboring for the respect of the Patriarch, the daughter-in-law stepped into the golden circle of the lantern light. She had just come from the milking. I shall never forget those bashful gleaming eyes, peering out from the sunbonnet. Her sleeves were rolled to the shoulder. Startling indeed were those arms, as white as the foaming milk.

She set down the bucket with a big sigh of relaxation. She pushed back the sunbonnet to get a better look. The old man addressed her in an authoritative and confident way, as though she were a mere adjunct, a part of his hospitality.

"Daugh-ter, here is a good young man—he LOOKS like a good young man, I think a stew-dent. You see he has books in his pock-et. He wants a night's lodging. Now, if he *is* a good young man, I think we can give him the bed in the spare room, and if he is a bad young man, I think there is enough rope in the barn to hang him before day-light."

"Yes, you can stay," she said brightly. "Have you had supper?"

It is one of the obligations of the road to tell the whole truth. But in this case I lied. The woman was working too late.

"Oh yes, I've had supper," I said.

And she carried the milk into the darkness.

In the city, among people having the status indicated by the big red barn and the enormous wind-mill and a most substantial fence, this gleaming woman would have languished in shelter. She would have played at many philanthropies, or gone to many study clubs or have had many lovers. She would have been variously adventurous according to her corner of the town. Here her paramour was WORK. He still caressed her, but would some day break her on the wheel.

The old man sent me toward the front porch alone. There was a rolling back of the low gray clouds just then, and the coming of the moon. The moon's moods are so many. To-night she took the forlornness out of the restless sky. She looked domestic as the lantern.

III

You Ought to be Ashamed of Yourself

I was on the porch, scraping an acquaintance with the grandmother. She held a baby in her lap. They sat in the crossing of the moonlight and the lamplight.

There was no one to explain me. I explained myself. She eyed me angrily. She did not want me to shake hands with the baby. She asked concerning her daughter-in-law.

"And did she say you could stay?"

"She did."

The grandmother brought a hard fist down on the arm of the chair: "I'd like to break her neck. She's no more backbone than a rabbit."

I do not distinctly remember any bitter old man I have met in my travels. She was the third bitter old woman. Probably with the same general experiences as her husband, she had digested them differently. She was on the shelf, but made for efficiency and she was not run down.

In her youth her hair was probably red. Though she was plainly an old woman, it was the brown of middle age with only a few streaks of gray. Under her roughness there were touches of a truly cultured accent and manner. I would have said that in youth she had had what they call opportunities.

I asked: "Isn't the moon fine to-night?"

She replied: "Why don't you go to work?"

I answered: "I asked for work in the big city till I was worn to a thread. And you are the first person who has urged it on me since I took to tramping. I wonder why no one ever thought of it before."

She smiled grudgingly.

"What kind of work did you try to do in the city?"

"I wanted to paint rainbows and gild sidewalks and blow bubbles for a living. But no one wanted me to. It is about all I am fit for."

"Don't talk nonsense to me, young man!"

"Pardon me, leddy—I am a writer of rhymes."

"The nation's going to the dogs," she said. I suppose I was the principal symptom of national decay.

Just then a happy voice called through the house, "Come to supper."

"That's for you," said the grandmother. "You ought to be ashamed of yourself."

IV

Gretchen-Cecilia, Waitress

I went in the direction of the voice, delighted, not ashamed. There, in that most cleanly kitchen, stood the white-armed milkmaid, with cheeks of geranium red. She had spread a table before me in the presence of mine enemy. I said: "I did not ask for supper. I told you I had eaten."

"Oh, I knew you were hungry. Wait on him, Gretchen-Cecilia."

My hostess scurried into the other room. She was in a glorious mood over something with which I had nothing to do.

Gretchen-Cecilia came out of the pantry and poured me a glass of warm milk. I looked at her, and my destiny was sealed forevermore—at least for an hour or so. The sight of her brought the tears to my eyes.

I know you are saying: "Beware of the man with tears in his eyes." Yes, I too have seen weeping exhibitions. I remember a certain pious exhorter. The collection followed soon. And I used to hear an actor brag about the way he wept when he looked upon a certain ladylike actress whom we all adore. He vividly pictured himself with a handkerchief to his devoted cheeks, waiting in the wings for his cue. He had belladonna eyes. At the risk of being classed with such folk, I reaffirm that I was a little weepy. I insist it was not gratitude for a sudden square meal—if truth be told, I have had many such—it was the novel Gretchen-Cecilia.

It took a little conversation to show that Gretchen-Cecilia was a privileged character. She had little of the touch of the farm upon her. She was the spoiled pet of the house, and the index of their prosperity—what novelists call the third generation. She had a way of lifting her chin and shoving her fists deep into her apron pockets.

I said: "I have a fairy-tale to read to you after supper."

And she said: "I like fairy-tales." And then, redundantly: "I like stories about fairies. Fairy stories are nice."

It was no little pleasure to eat after nine hours doing without, and to dwell on beauty such as this after so many days of absence from the museums of art and the curio shops. Every time she brought me warm biscuits or refilled my tumbler, she brought me pretty thoughts as well.

She was nine years old, she told me. Her eyes were sometimes brown, sometimes violet. Her mouth was half a cherry, and her chin the quintessence of elegance. Her braids were long and rich, her ribbons wide and crisp.

Maidenhood has distinct stages. The sixteenth year, when unusually ripe, is a tender prophecy. Thirteen is often the climax of astringent childhood, with its especial defiance or charm. But nine years old is my favorite season. It is spring in winter. It is sweet sixteen through walls of impregnable glass. This ripeness dates from prehistoric days, when people lived in the tops of the trees, and almost flew to and from the nests they built there, and mated much earlier than now.

As I finished eating, the mother brought the little brother into the room saying, "Gretchen-Cecilia, watch the baby." Then she smiled on me and said: "When she washes the dishes, you can hold him."

She had on a fresh gingham apron, blue, with white trimmings. I judged by the squeak, she had changed her shoes.

"Who's coming?" I asked, when the mother had left.

"Papa. He goes around the state and digs oil wells, and is back at the end of the week."

I was washing the dishes when Grandma came in. She frowned me away from the dishpan. She said, "Gretchen-Cecilia, wipe the dishes."

The baby howled on the floor. I was not to touch him. Gretchen-Cecilia tried to comfort him by saying, "Baby, dear dear baby; baby, dear dear baby."

"Do you realize, young man," asked Grandma, "that I, an old woman, am washing your dishes for you?"

I was busy. I was putting my wet stockinged feet on a kindling-board in the oven, and my shoes were curling up on the back of the stove.

"Young man—"

"Yessum—"

"*Where's your wife?*"

I replied, "I have no wife, and never did have." Then I ventured to ask, "May I have the hand of Gretchen? I want some one who can wipe dishes while I wash them."

"But I'm not grown up," piped the maiden. It seemed her only objection.

I said: "I will wait and wait till you are seventeen."

The old lady had no soul for trifles. She intoned, like conscience that will not be slain: *"Where's your wife?"*

But I said in my heart: "Madam, you are only a suspender-button upon the necklace of the evening."

V

"Papa Has Come!"

There was a scurry and a flutter. Gretchen threw down her dish-rag, leaving Grandma a plate to wipe.

I heard the grandfather say, "Wel-come, son, wel-come indeed!" The young wife gave a smothered shriek, and then in a minute I heard her exclaim, "John, you're a scamp!"

I put on my hot shoes and went in to see what this looked like. Gretchen-Cecilia was somewhere between them, and then on her father's shoulder, mussing his hair. And the mother took Gretchen down, as John said in reply to a question: —

"Business is good. Whether there's oil or not, I dig the hole and get paid."

This man was now standing his full height for his family to admire. He was one I too could not help admiring. He had an open sunburned face, and I thought that behind it there was a non-scheming mind, that had attained good fortune beyond the lot of most of the simple. He was worth the dressing up the family had done for him, and almost worthy of Gretchen's extra crisp hair ribbons.

His wife put her arms around his neck and whispered something, evidently about me. He watched me over his shoulder as much as to say: —

"And so it's a stray dog wants shelter? No objections."

He unwrapped his package. It was an extraordinary doll, with truly truly hair, and Gretchen-Cecilia had to give him seven kisses and almost cry before he surrendered it.

He pulled off his boots and threw them in the corner, then paddled up stairs and came down in his shoes. For no reason at all Gretchen-Cecilia and her mother chased him around the kitchen table with a broom and a feather duster, and then out on to the back porch.

VI

Conferences

The grandfather called me into the front room and handed me a book.

"Yer a schol-ar. What do you think of that?"

It was a history of the county. The frontispiece was a portrait of Judge Somebody. But the book naturally opened at about the tenth page, on an atrocious engraving of this goodly old man and his not ill-looking wife. He breathed easier when I found it. It was plainly a basis of family pride. I read the inscription.

"So you two are the oldest inhabitants?" I asked.

"The oldest per-pet-ual in-habitants. I was born in this coun-ty and have nev-er left it. My wife is some young-er, but she has nev-er left it, since she married me."

Even the old lady grew civil. She tapped a brooch near her neck. "They gave me this breast-pin at the last old settlers' picnic."

The old man continued: "All the old farm is still here in our hands, but mostly rented. It brings something, something. Our big income is from my son's well-digging. He never speculates and he makes money."

It seemed a part of the old man's pride to have even the passing stranger realize they were well-fixed. In a furtive attempt to do justice to their station in life they had a tall clock in the corner, quite new and beautiful. And, as I discovered later, there was upstairs a handsome bath-room. The rest of that new house was clean and white, but helplessly Spartan.

The old folk were called to the back porch. At the same time I heard the mother say, "Show the man your doll."

And in came the little daughter like thistle-down.

We were in that white room at opposite ends of the long table, and nothing but the immaculate cloth stretching between us. She sat with the doll clutched to her breast, looking straight into my eyes, the doll staring at me also. The girl was such a piece of bewitchment that the poem I brought to her about the magical *Tree of Laughing Bells* seemed tame to me, and everyday. That foolish rhyme was soon read and put into her hands. It seemed to give her an infinite respect for me. And any human creature loves to be respected.

On the back porch the talking grew louder.

"Papa is telling them he wants to rent the rest of the farm and move us all to town," explained Gretchen.

It was the soft voice of the young wife we heard: "Of course it will be nice to be nearer my church."

And then the young father's voice: "And I don't want Gretchen to grow up on the farm."

And the old man's voice, still nobly intoned: "And as I say, I don't want to be stub-born, but I don't want to cross the coun-ty line."

Gretchen banged the door on them and we crossed the county line indeed. We told each other fairy-tales while the unheeded murmur of debate went on.

When it came Gretchen's turn, she alternated Grimm, and Hans Andersen and the legends of the Roman Church. I had left the railroad resolved to talk some one to death, and now with all my heart I was listening. She knew the tales I had considered my special discoveries in youth: "The Amber Witch," "The Enchanted Horse," "The Two Brothers." She also knew that most pious narrative, *Elsie Dinsmore.* She approved when I told her I had found it not only sad but helpful in my spiritual life. She had found it just so in hers.

VII

The Spare Room

With her eyes still flashing from argument, the grandmother took me up stairs. She gave me a big bath-towel, and showed me the bath-room, and also my sleeping place. I asked her about the holy pictures hanging near my bed. She explained in a voice that endeavored not to censure: "My daughter-in-law is of German-Cath-olic descent, and she is *still* Catholic."

"What is *your* denomination?" I asked.

"My husband and son and I are Congregationalists."

She did not ask it of me, but I said: "I am what is sometimes disrespectfully called a 'Campbellite.'"

But the old lady was gone.

After a boiling bath I lay musing under those holy pictures. My brother of the road, when they put you in the best room, as they sometimes do, and you look at the white counterpane and the white sheets and the cosey appointments, do you take these brutally, or do you think long upon the intrinsic generosity of God and man?

I have laid hold of hospitality coldly and greedily in my time, but this night at least, I was thankful. And as I turned my head in a new direction I was thankful most of all for the unexpected presence of the Mother of God. There was her silvery statue near the foot of my bed, the moonlight pouring straight in upon it through the wide window. It spoke to me of peace and virginity.

And I thought how many times in Babylon I had gone into the one ever open church to look on the crowned image of the Star of the Sea. Though I am no servitor of Rome I have only adoration for virginity, be it carved in motionless stone, or in marble that breathes and sings.

A long long time I lay awake while the image glimmered and glowed. The clock downstairs would strike its shrill bell, and in my heart a censer swung.

VIII

Morning

There was a pounding on the door and a shout. It was the young husband's voice. "It's time to feed your face."

They were at the breakfast-table when I came down. My cherished memory of the group is the picture of them with bowed heads, the grandfather, with hand upraised, saying grace. It was ornate, and by no means brief. It was rich with authority. I wanted to call in all the mocking pagans of the nation, to be subdued before that devotion. I wanted to say: "Behold, little people, some great hearts still pray."

I stood in the door and made shift to bow my head. Yet my head was not so much bowed but I could see Gretchen-Cecilia and her mother timidly cross themselves. In my heart I said "Amen" to the old man's prayer. But I love every kind of devotion, so I crossed myself in the Virgin's name.

The tale had as well end here as anywhere. On the road there are endless beginnings and few conclusions. For instance I gathered from the conversation at the breakfast-table they were not sure whether they would move to the city or not. They were for the most part silent and serene.

There were pleasant farewells a little later. Gretchen-Cecilia, when the others were not looking, gave me, at my earnest solicitation, a tiny curl from the head of her doll that had truly truly hair.

I walked on and on, toward the ends of the infinite earth, though I had found this noble temple, this shrine not altogether made with hands. I again consecrated my soul to the august and Protean Creator, maker of all religions, dweller in all clean temples, master of the perpetual road.

THE WAR BULLETINS

(July-August 1909)

[The *War Bulletins* were reprinted in the *Village Magazine,* 3rd and 4th editions (1925), with an introductory essay, a VL letter to Joel Elias Spingarn, and Spingarn's reply. I have reprinted the essay and the two letters under *"The Village Magazine,* 3rd edition" (q.v.). *War Bulletin Four* was the booklet of poems entitled *The Tramp's Excuse and Other Poems:* see *The Poetry of Vachel Lindsay,* pp. 1-68. *The Sangamon County Peace Advocate* (*Poetry,* pp. 69-76) officially ended VL's "war." VL's essay "The Golden-Faced People" was first printed, with variant readings, in *The Crisis* (November 1914), pp. 36-42. The following is reproduced with VL's spelling, punctuation, and capitalization.]

WAR BULLETIN NUMBER ONE

Springfield, Ill., July 19, 1909

Why a War Bulletin?

I have spent a great part of my few years fighting a soul battle for absolute liberty, for freedom from obligation, ease of conscience; independence from commercialism. I think I am farther from slavery than most men. But I have not complete freedom of speech. In my daily round of work I find myself taking counsel to please the stupid, the bigoted, the conservative, the impatient, the cheap. A good part of the time I can please these people, having a great deal in common with all of them. — but —

The things that go into the War Bulletin please me only. To the Devil with you, average reader. To Gehenna with your stupidity, your bigotry, your conservatism, your cheapness and your impatience!

In each new Bulletin the war shall go faster and further. War! War! War!

The Golden-Faced People

A Story of the Chinese Conquest of America

And yet it is not a Story. It is an Essay. All purely literary critics pray consider yourselves defied. When you have read the piece twice you may write to me and say what you think the moral is.

He was a Laundryman who ironed shirts superbly, yet as though it were a mere incident. His picked English showed him to be no ordinary Coolie. I thought we had been friends for some months. But now old Yellow-Arms clutched my week's washing because I had lost my half of his red ticket. I showed him for the tenth time the name on the linen. I was in a hurry to dress for the banquet. Pushing the money toward him, I jumped for the exit with my goods. He turned out the gas. I heard him scramble over the counter. He was between me and the door. He hit me with the handle of his broom. I thought then that I made for the alley through the side entrance.

I found myself in a long iron-floored passage, thick with yellow fog. Just as suddenly I was in a packed assembly room where the walls blazed with dragon embroidered lanterns. I turned around. The door of iron behind me was closed. My pursuer was not in sight.

The place looked like a sort of Heathen Temple, But no—the next thing that caught my eye was the Phrase *"In the year of Christ."* It appeared that this fantastic gathering was about to dedicate with speeches and ceremonies, a tablet inscribed, "In the year of Christ two thousand eight hundred and nine Lin Kon was born. This memorial is set up on the one hundreth anniversary of his birth, in honor of his meritorious and superior career. He was the emancipator of the white man."

The shirt washer had hit me pretty hard. He had knocked me through that iron door into the next Millennium. A person quite like him sat in the pew at one side of the platform. Despite the crowd, the rest of his bench was empty. He blinked there, in surprising majesty.

I was being escorted toward the tablet. I was being introduced to half a score of speakers of the evening, there grouped. Then I was proclaimed to the audience as one who had studied the Chinese conquest with zeal. I laid down my laundry bundle. I was in a whirlwind of astonishing impressions. And it was no longer a bundle, but had shrunk into a manuscript in my own handwriting. I opened it. I read to the crowd something after this fashion:

"When our fathers taught the Golden People mechanics, in the sordid ages of the world, the White Man was the leader of Civilization." There was a mighty cheer. The audience rose, a kaleidscope of whirling colors. Gongs were beaten. Fans were thumped against the seats till they were splinters. I continued: "Our fathers were not scared, when the Golden Men instituted their thorough-going compulsory education, nor when they put up their immortal Universities from Canton to Lhassa. But that was the crucial hour, the pivot of history. Then in the Chinese Psychology, the religion of Science took the place of the religion of learning, which had been with them from the days of Shen and Yao. In their laboratories were hatched the medical lodges and inventors' secret societies, infamous and sublime. They sent forth whirlwinds of tracts with sociological, hygienic, biological remedies for China. These became well nigh inspired in the eyes of sects and sub-sects who prayed over their crucibles in their little back rooms, with the frenzy of Mohammedans entering battle.

"Private lists were compiled of high families prone to opium, or vice, or bad citizenship, and all others prone to crime or stupidity. When the storm broke, these were sure to fall, whatever the apparent quarrel. Two provinces below the normal were almost wiped out. Over every temple door and city gate appeared the quotation from the scientific Conspirator Dah Win, "Science and Heaven are one." Revolutionary banners proclaimed his more terrible saying, "None but superior men are fit to live." Every Revolution means the annihilation of some class. Here all perished but the subtle, the wise and the strong.

"In the Counter Revolution science apparently returned to her kitchen and work bench. The simple worship of Heaven was restored with high Christian elements. The scholar sipped his tea, quoted the Sermon on the Mount, quoted the Apostle Paul, quoted Mencius again; and practically every Chinaman was a scholar. The Golden Man retained, indeed, the most scientific family relations. But he had learned to justify them by the five Classics. His Revolution had not been in vain. When he nodded, Asia had to kneel. He dominated, not by conquest, but apparently by his sedate carriage, his level glance, his deliberate fan.

"Their novelists showed to the judicious that the Golden people were still human and their deep burrowing sociologists made their sins seem black, but how could we realize it, who only met them in public matters? How could we resist the well disposed iron-boned gentlemen? To be sure we had made great steps since the sordid ages, but beside them, we seemed to have been retrograding. To be sure, we had sculpture and architecture greater than theirs, but they had taught us to apologize for them, by showing at the right moment dazzling textiles, ceramics and bronzes. We had a power in music they could not master, but they hinted it was a mark of national effeminacy. They spoke of their jades and mosaics, their new schools of pantomine and drama. We had a Poetry of our own, but they made the poems collected by Confucius more loved by the world.

"Indeed, said one of their scholars to his prince, 'In the presence of the well rounded daily life of China, how brash seem the unclothed inventions of this whey-faced democracy where the weakling or diseased are tolerated for their votes and praised for their perverseness, where forever and forever the fairest things are tarnished with stupidity.'

"Yet the Golden faced men came to our land with that apparent humility that hides, one knows not what. They were hired servants of our public: scientific road builders, park architects, expert accountants, linguists, lecturers. Later they came as establishers of immemorial ceremonies in the Courts of our Governors, who found the ways of the Golden People indispensable for the glory of their administrations. They became valuable political advisers. Ceremony blended into intrigue. Politeness became the poisoned sword of politics and left the puzzled voters out of the Government.

"Many Europeans, not in the pay of the Chinese, have maintained that our first fifty years as a Chinese Province were the greatest in our history. When the Pagodas began to rise, when the so-called Orange-toned school of City-building, first carried by the Japanese into China, was brought here with distinctly Chinese changes, all our best spirits felt the fertilizing effect. Our young scholars, returning from Peking with the highest degrees, had the faculty of finding every man of talent and firing his zeal for creative work till he was like an amber flame. Our common people did not fare so well, but knew it not. In the words of one of our historians, 'They moved about anemic and restless like the petted white monkeys that eat sweetmeats in the palaces of India.'

"Gradually the strength of the Golden-faced became an ingenious tyranny. They protested they meant us well, and individually many of them did; but, collectively, we were the weaker, because our social system was more impure, and so we had to go down through caste and serfdom to slavery. Only when it was too late did we know of the system of engines in the Chinese laboratories especially constructed to insure our obedience.

"In our endless nightmare we scarcely noted the young sage who was traveling around the world with his group of students, like Confucius, seeking that magistrate who would allow him to set up his ideal government. Indeed, in his majestic and superior doctrines the great Lin Kon was nearer to Confucius than to any other teacher."

A spiritual wind swept through the audience. Again they burst through the shame of showing emotion. They rocked in their seats and wept and shouted. They thanked heaven and thanked God for Lin Kon.

Indeed, it was a curious audience, not only in the luxuriant color of the gowns of the women and children, embroidered with large turkey-cocks, eagles, and roses, in the stately blue and gray robes of the men, and the mesmeric glitter of the young girls' heavy jewelry; but the Eurasian aspect of these things stimulated the wildest speculations within me as I read.

The Eurasian face is unmistakeable. I looked down at my own hands. Had they not grown yellower since I passed through the iron doors? I wore a robe like some of the rest, with a picture of a palanquin embroidered large upon my breast.

There were few truly white people in the audience. I found myself shrinking from them. There seemed a sort of nakedness about their celery-color. The heads of the men became more nobly formed in proportion as their eyebrows straightened, and their hair grew Chinese black. The proudest of the women were plainly those with facial contours sleek as carved jade, and complexions neither gold nor silver, yet both.

The audience seemed to be in sympathy with me whatever I said. The name of Lin Kon set burning every drop of white blood still there. The proudest with the humblest stamped and shouted. But the cheering increased when I counselled patience with present vexations.

"It was in these provinces," I continued, "that Lin Kon saw men and women chained to what was actually a state auction block, though defended under a technical name. He saw our fathers sold into hard labor, our mothers into destruction. He had been born on the hardy plains of Central China where people had a rough sort of equality. Kneeling before the sacred Image of Equality in this very town, he swore by the justice of heaven he would sometime hit the curse of slavery and hit it hard.

"And the story will be told tonight how, because of the martyred, canonized, immortal Lin Kon, we have an equal place before the law. I must be brief. I have been asked to say a few words on the issues of the hour. At the mass meeting of the Orientals of the whole city, to celebrate Lin Kon this afternoon, great pains were taken to keep white men off the platform or the Committees, though it was a public not a social occasion. We have been indignant. We have declared it was like playing Hamlet without the melancholy Dane. We have maintained that our voices should not necessarily have defiled their ears neither should our rejoicings have made them sad. But we can celebrate here. We have one great privilege sufficient for rejoicing. Equality before the Law. Putting aside daily vexations the next step is to attain commercial equality. We do not want social equality, neither do we want the color line rubbed out. Our highest dream is that by patience and dignity, by more care for ethics and ceremony, by a sweeter Christianity, to attain a sort of spiritual rank with the conservative, everlasting race that still dominates.''

I was sitting by the Chinaman now. By an impreceptible gesture he had drawn me to his side as I folded the manuscript. I knew that he shrank from me as from a leper, yet his grin was an accolade. He whispered, ''Servant, can you come with me?'' I answered, ''Honorable Sir, I am with you''. We threaded the packed aisles. Through sheer vanity, my heart pumped like a fire-engine. My cheeks seemed scalded with the blood in them. I knew every speaker left behind envied me, would rather have my place than have made the oration of the year. How soft and cool was the night air!

Under the dingy street lamps of the White Man's quarters, there was a sad radiant dignity about my companion, that put an aching in my cheeks and a choking in my throat I had not known since childhood. I said in my heart, as his measured words flashed upon me, ''I would be willing to be skinned alive to be like him. He justifies the ages.'' Yet he was simple enough in conversation.

With slow dignity we entered the brilliant celestial streets. I had no eye for the pageantry, for he was saying, ''Servant, I was anxious to hear the rest of your speakers, but am due at the other banquet. I am going to proclaim tonight, as the watchword of re-construction the saying of the great Lin Kon, ''The superior man shows malice toward none and Charity for all.'' In addition I shall read them, if you are willing, the section of your manuscript in which you counsel ''sweet Christianity.'' It is good for both races to know that such a word has been given tonight.

I answered, ''I will feel a terrible shame Master, if you become absurd for my sake.'' He made a gesture as though my words were tossed aside. His face glowed with a determination to be just. Aspirations lofty and immemorial had formed his forehead and purged his eyes of cunning and scorn. But I went on, ''You cannot make me a hero in your assembly. Whatever you and I may say in public, we know a white criminal is made more famous in a day, by the golden newspapers than a white sage can become by endless talk of sweet Christianity. Whatever linen he wears he is hated still.''

Before the statue of Equality at the edge of the park we paused. She was a vast Sphynx-like creature. The animals beneath her claws were like those that guard the Ming Tombs. Her half shut eyelids held unfathomable thought. Many men who passed by saluted her gravely, so I presumed it was a custom. I did it with silent bitterness, my friend with words of hope.

We were at the door of the banquet hall—Indeed, I loved the man—I handed him my manuscript. It crackled strangely. He disappeared into the lobby, but not too soon for me to see that it was no longer my manuscript but once more my bundle of laundry, now burst open. He moved abstractedly—A handkerchief fell on the floor then some socks—The string trailed behind him. "Come back", I called in a panic "Master! Master!". I shook my fan at him. It changed to the missing half of the laundry ticket. "Stop him!" I demanded of the lackey at the door, a white man of course. "Give him this little red ticket and get the bundle. The young bucks will accuse him of opium. He will lose face.

I tried to push the lackey in. . . It was like pushing against a pillar . . . He said, "The Honorable Sir is in the hands of his friends. He would not take my ticket. It was a fan again. Somehow I concluded the lackey was to blame for all this. . . I said, "Here you stand dressed up to lick boots, and you get in your tricks on the sly. The old man is your friend and mine. Why should you make him absurd? The devil take all jugglers. Why don't you go into a white man's business?"

"Carrying palanquins?" he asked, indicating the grinning group of servants at the foot of the steps. . . Each of these white men had a picture of a palanquin embroidered on his breast even as I. . . That then was my calling. . . "Proud puppy! Proud puppy!" they shouted at me. . .

I sought the more deserted streets, where under the new moon I dully wondered over mechanical ingenuities overlaid with oriental grace. Everything was antique. Bronze was tarnished. . . Stone balustrades were mossy, oaken doorways had faced the rain for centuries. . .

"What does this mean, servant?" What does this mean, chalk nose?" A Chinese boy, indeed a handsome youth, with a gilded cap, thrust a newspaper under my eyes. The headlines declared, "Makes A Speech On Absolute Social Equality. Later tries to break into the Celestial banquet to Lin Kon."

"Masters, it's a lie! a lie!" I called to the crowd. It was useless. The whole Yellow Race seemed to pursue, led by the Alcibiades in the gilded cap. I do not know how I reached our assembly hall. A half score pushed into the room after me. They seemed unable to tell which one I was. They shouldered up the aisle laying right and left with their swords, while a venerable white man was in the midst of this sentence: "The great Lin Kon has often been compared to Confucius." But already the youth in the gilded cap had struck him on the mouth, then beheaded him. Would our people never resist?

what unspeakable fear paralyzed them? Was it the blue phosphorescent crystals on the sword hilts?

I was broken hearted like a child who finds his father suddenly cruel. The Alcibiades appeared to grow before my eyes, to become impossibly emaciated and tall, yet with broad square shoulders. His sword stretched out cutting down my wailing people like weeds.

I turned. I wrenched desperately at the rings on the iron doors. Now I was in the yellow fog once more, crawling on the iron floored passageway. I felt if I could get to the other end I could awake. My feet and hands were like magnets clinging to the floor.

> *   *   *   *   *

"Well! Well! You brought him to, doctor. I thought that broom had finished him".

I was back in the twentieth century, in the laundry shop. I was on the counter by the window. Friends in festive attire were flocking around me, good fellows all, the blooded youth of the town.

Three or four policemen held the door. Outside a mob howled and peered. Across the street dangled three men, hanged by the neck till they were dead. An officer pointed to the nearest.

"That's your Chinaman", he said "The report was out that he killed you."

"Who hung him?"

"The mob."

"Who are the other two?"

"One is a Greek."

"What did he do?"

The Irishman laughed. "I dunno", he said. "These foreigners have to keep out of the way, I suppose." Then, by way of information, "The Greeks are an awful ignorant people."

"Who is the third man?"

"Oh, that's just a nigger."

"Why did they hang him?"

"I dunno. I guess he was too free with his lip. Damn a nigger anyway. They are all alike. There was a negro in Indiana the other day—", and he told the usual story.

"You treat your coons differently up here," said a southerner. "We don't lynch 'em in our country unless we know they're guilty". And squinting up his eyes at the mob: "We don't leave the dirty work to the poor white trash."

I found myself able to stand and receive the congratulations of the company. "Now wash the blood off your head, old man", continued the Southerner, "and we will go home with you and get you ready for the banquet yet."

Sure enough there was my laundry bundle on the counter. I opened it. The shirt was not soiled where it would show. We managed to dodge the crowd by using the side door. In my room I made a quick change. We were only fifty minutes late. Fortunately we had white waiters. And the southerner saved the day by his opening speech on Lincoln as an example of the survival of the fittest, accompanied by a eulogy of Darwin. The other speakers were able to follow the pace especially since a good part of the audience were fired with champagne. I managed to spill wine all over my shirt bosom. The Southerner said it served me right. He is one of these Local Option orators.

War Bulletin number two will contain an attack on Conventional Christianity as it is practiced in the remote and nefarious village of Morristown New Jersey, the wealthiest little burg in the United States. The paper will contain many a lesson for those who make sudden and ill-considered attempts to be good.

WAR BULLETIN NUMBER TWO

Springfield, Ill., Aug. 4, 1909

PRICE-Henceforth the Bulletins are as free as
bread and butter in a hospitable house. He
who helps to pass the fire of the Bulletins from
mind to mind, has done the greatest Favor
possible to do for the publisher hereof.
Writers and speakers, please steal my ideas.

Why I Fight?

All at once there rose a thought in me, and I asked myself "What
art thou afraid of? Wherefore like a coward dost thou forever pip and
whimper, and go cowering and trembling? Despicable biped! what is
the sum total of the worst that lies before thee? Well, death, and say
the pangs of Tophet too, and all that the Devil and man may will or
can do against thee! Hast thou not a heart; canst thou not suffer what
so it be, and as a child of Freedom, though outcast, trample Tophet
itself under thy feet, while it consumes thee? Let it come then; I will
meet it and defy it." And as I thought there rushed like a stream of
fire over my whole soul; and I shook base fear away from me forever.
I was strong; of unknown strength a spirit; almost a God. *Ever from
that time the temper of my misery was changed: not fear or whining
sorrow was it, but indignation, and grim fire-eyed defiance.*

So writes Thomas Carlyle in Sartor Resartus in the chapter called
"The Everlasting No."

One hour after reading this passage I wrote the Introduction to War
Bulletin Number One.

Now follows a personal adventure in a Presbyterian Mission in
Morristown, New Jersey.

An Adventurer Gets Religion

The Gentleman Adventurer had walked twelve miles before noon. Then he had eaten four slices of bread and butter on merciful doorsteps. At 4:30 he was ravenous, having completed twenty-one miles. Reaching a wealthy village he purchased a feast of beefsteak and onions at an obscure Jewish restaurant. After paying for it he had twenty-five cents. There was a sign at the cash desk; *"Furnished Rooms for Fifty cents."* He asked the proprietor to cut the price. The Hebrew dodged the issue.

"Say, why don't you go up here to the mission? They will sell you a good bed cheap."

"For a quarter?"

"Something like that."

"Show me the place."

As of old the Jew pointed out the way of Salvation. The Gentile followed it, and reached the dwelling place of Faith, Hope and Charity.

"What do you want?"

The questioner looked like a Boss Carpenter. Maybe his paraphernalia was to put him on a level with wayfarers. He wore a slouch hat, a soft shirt and no necktie. They looked rather incongruous in that neat, well stocked reading room.

"I want a cheap bed."

"We don't sell beds."

"I was told you did."

"We give them away."

"All right."

"But you have to work."

"Very well."

"Do you want to leave early in the morning?"

"Yes."

"Then you will have to split kindling two hours tonight."

"Show me the kindling."

Because he had been walking a world highway all day the Adventurer, though deadly tired, was not afraid of work. Down in the basement he sat on one block while he chopped kindling on another. Before him, piled to the first story was a cellar full, split by his predecessors in toil. He gathered that the men out of work, who stayed at the mission had just finished their days assignment of that toil. As soon as the Carpenter went up-stairs, one of them said:

"Don't split so fast, its only a matter of form this late at night. They want to see if you are willing to work, that's all."

The Adventurer split a little faster for this advice. But he rather liked the advisers. They were box car tramps, the kind who look for work when it is not there, the kind who never tramp at all. They thought the Gentleman Adventurer an idiot when he confessed that he had walked all day. But they were friendly. The younger, having an evil and witty eye said. "If I was goin' west like you I'd start about ten o'clock tonight and I'd be near Buffalo before morning."

Another, a mild nobody, professed himself a miller. He told what a wonderful trick it was to say, "Leddy, I'm too tired to work till I eat," and after eating, to walk quickly away.

The next, a carriage painter of battered gentility, told endless stories of the sprees that had destroyed him.

The last, a white frog with a bald head and grey mustache, won the Gentleman's heart.

"Wait till you get a nice warm bath after service. Then you'll sleep good."

The Adventurer forgave these fellows for being nobodies. It was grand, just to be with them, with a roof overhead. He was intoxicated with weariness. The place was like the Interpreter's House in Pilgrim's Progress. It became his religion just to split kindling.

He loved all men, even the Boss Carpenter, who appeared after two hours to drive the animals up-stairs into one corner of the chapel where a dozen of their kind had already assembled from somewhere.

In the center of that chapel sat the respectables. The aisle was a great gulf between them. The Adventurer smiled across the gulf indulgently, imagining by what exhortations to "Come and help us in our problem," they had been brought.

An Unmitigated Clergyman rose to read a text he did not understand.

But because he had been walking a world highway all day the Adventurer understood.

Blessed are the poor in spirit for theirs is the Kingdom of Heaven.
Blessed are they that mourn, for they shall be comforted.
And the Adventurer found peace.
Blessed are the meek for they shall inherit the earth.
For that brief hour, all the world belonged to the Adventurer.

The Unmitigated Clergyman read the latter end of that greatest sermon this side of the stars:

Ye have heard how it hath been said "an eye for an eye and a tooth for a tooth." But I say unto you that ye resist not evil. But whosoever shall smite thee on thy right cheek turn to him the other also. And if any man will sue thee at the law and take away thy coat let him have thy cloak also. And whosoever shall compel thee to go a mile, go with him twain. Give to him that asketh thee, and to him that would borrow of thee, turn thou not away.

And the text went home. The Adventurer experienced the terrible beneficence, the soul consuming paradox and the mystery of the Sermon on the Mount. He placed himself at the command of the world, and called not one rag upon his back his own, not one muscle of his sunburned body, not one fibre of his soul. He was lost in wonder and scarcely noted the reader's comments with their colossal blasphemies. He scarcely noted the clergyman's smug assumption that he was deep in the confidence of the Deity, authorized to explain away and make of none effect the literalness of this scripture. The Adventurer lost his power of criticism and hate, or he would have noted the text reader was the sort that can never forgive a person with dusty trousers and soiled finger nails for being in the world at all.

The authorities behind the mission must have realized the gulf between such a preacher and such outcasts. He was followed by a fat Pharisee whose genial ways were to be the remedy.

We bring railing accusation against these ministers only because it is a necessity of the tale. They had placed themselves in an artificial social situation, that must perforce make temporary hypocrites of almost any of us who are not saints of the highest sort.

The hardy Pharisee, — let us forgive him remembering we also are dust, — smiled unctuously upon the fallen. He took one special beatitude for his portion: *Blessed are the meek, for they shall inherit the earth.*

He explained it away in fifteen minutes, then called on the assembly to bow, and exhorted the repentant to hold up their hands to be prayed for. The Adventurer humbled himself and held up his hand. "Thank God," said the Pharisee.

After a hymn testimonies were called for.

The Adventurer started to rise, but a sister across the gulf had the floor. She glanced with a terrified shrinking at the animals she hoped to benefit. She said:

"There has been one great difficulty in my Christian life, it came with seeking for the Spirit. Sometimes we think it has come with power, when we are simply stirred by our own selfish desires. Our works will show whether we are truly moved by the spirit."

The Adventurer sincerely approved of her saying and was summoning courage to continue in the same vein when a saint across the gulf with blocky jaws and pompadour hair anticipated him. It was probable he had given the testimony many times. He did not want the meeting to drag, that was all. So he spoke in a loud voice: —

"I was saved from a drunkard's life in this mission, eighteen years ago, and ever since, not by my own power, but by the grace of God, I have been leading a God fearing and money making life in this town."

The meeting was now ended with a hymn and benediction.

The Adventurer for sundry reasons considered a money making life the height of abominations. So that was the kind of Christians they were trying to make here! Immediately there fell from his eyes as it had been scales. Grimly he watched the Scribe and Pharisee shaking hands with each sinner. So those were the ministers of the grace he had received!

The Scribe spoke with dry curiosity to the Adventurer: Where did you come from?

The Adventurer quoted scripture:

"From going to and fro in the earth and walking up and down in it."

The throng melted. Scribe and Pharisee went home to their comfortable beds. The Boss Carpenter sought the consolation of his own home. These three do not appear again in this history.

The Gentleman Adventurer did not at this moment understand that the building was left completely at the mercy of the lost, that it was mob rule for the rest of the night. As in all anarchies, a dictator with a show of legitimacy was speedily to appear. He rejoiced when the Frog, in the gentlest manner, sidled up to make friends again.

"Now you two can have your nice warm bath."

The Adventurer looked around. There were two of them then! Beside him fresh from a box car stood a battered scalawag. The Frog must have let him in at the last moment.

The three climbed to the bathroom.

"Wait a minute," said the Frog. The Frog disappeared. The Adventurer opened his eyes, for the Frog spoke with a voice of authority. The Scalawag grinned at the Adventurer sheepishly.

There was scuffling overhead, a scratch and a rumble. The two looked up just in time to dodge the astonishing vision of a clothes horse descending through a trap door by a rope. At the upper end of the rope was the absurd bald head of the Frog.

"Hello Santa Claus," said the Adventurer. "Whose Christmas present is this?"

The Frog shouted "Put your shoes and hats in the corner. If you have any tobacco put it in your shoes. Hang everything else on the clothes horse."

The astonished Adventurer obeyed the Frog, except that he had no tobacco. The Rascal had a plenty, and sawdusted the bath-room floor with some of it, and the remainder went into his footgear. These companions in nakedness watched the frog haul up their clothes out of sight, and close the trap door with many grunts.

The Frog re-entered the bath room. He was a dry land frog. He had never taken a bath himself, but he was there to superintend. He seemed to feel himself the accredited representative of the Boss Carpenter, the Scribe and the Pharisee, "Could it be possible," asked the Adventurer of himself, "that they have chosen this creature to apply their Christianity?"

The Frog said to the box-car scalawag, "Git in the tub."

Then the Frog turned on the water, regulated its temperature and watched as though he expected the scalawag to steal the faucets. He threw a grewsome rag at him and allowed him to scrub himself. The Scalawag seemed disposed to wash and had scrubbed about a third of his person when the Frog shouted, "I've got to get up at four thirty."

The Scalawag took the hint, and toweled himself with a towel that was a fallen sister of the wash rag.

The Frog evidently was trying to enforce regulations he did not understand, for he wiped out the bath tub most carefully, with the uncleaned wash rag. Then he provided the Scalawag a shirt for night wear. The creature put it on and said:

"Ain't I a peach?"

He was.

The nightie was an old heavily starched dress-shirt, once white. Maybe it had once been worn by the Boss Carpenter, the Scribe or the Pharisee. But it had not been washed since. The Rascal cut quite a figure as he took long steps down the corridor to bed, piloted by the hurrying Frog. He was a longlegged Rascal, and the slivered remainders of that ancient shirt flapped about him gloriously.

The Gentleman Adventurer was hustled into the tub after the Rascal. He was supervised after the same manner. "Now wash," boomed the Frog. He threw at him the sloppy rag of his predecessor.

The Adventurer threw it on the floor.

"I don't use a wash rag," he said.

"Hurry," croaked the frog. And he let the water out of the tub. He handed him the towel the Scalawag had used.

I don't want that towel," said the Gentleman Adventurer.

"You're awful fancy, aren't you?" sneered the frog.

The Adventurer rubbed himself dry with his bare hands, being skilled in the matter, meanwhile reflecting that there is nothing worse than a saint, except a sinner. He wondered if it was too late to rouse a mob among the better element of the town, neither saints nor sinners, but just plain malefactors of great wealth, and have this person lynched. He knew it was the wealthiest village in New Jersey. He desired to appeal to some man with manicured hands who had grown decently rich robbing the widow and orphan, and now had leisure to surround himself with the appurtenances of civility and the manners of a Chesterfield. "Rich worldlings for mine," muttered the Adventurer.

"Put these on," squeaked the Frog. His manner said, "See how good we are to you." He held out a treasure of the establishment, a night garment retained for fastidious new arrivals. Was it a slivered shirt? nay, nay. It was a sort of pajama combination. Hundreds of men had found shelter, taken a luxurious bath and put them on. They were companions in crime of the towel and wash rag. Let us suppose that three hundred and sixty five men wore them a year. In ten years there would have been about 3650 bathed men in them. That did not account for them.

"What makes them so dirty," asked the Adventurer.

No answer.

"Can't I wear my under clothes to bed instead of these?"

"No."

"Why?"

"Sulphur."

"What do you mean by sulphur?"

"Your clothes are up stairs being fumigated."

"Can't I get my socks tonight?" I always wash them before I go to bed."

"No. Its against the law of the state. And you would dirty up these bowls, I have just scrubbed them out."

"I will wash them out afterward."

"I havn't time to wait, I must get up at 4:30."

"But why fumigate my clean underwear and give me dirty pajamas?"

The frog was getting flabbergasted. "I tell you it's the law of New Jersey. You are getting awful fancy. If I had had my way you would never have been let in here."

"*Blessed are the meek,*" said the Gentleman Adventurer, and put on the pajamas.

The Unsanitary Director showed him his bed. It was a long low room with all the windows closed, where half a score were asleep. The sheets had never, never, never been washed. Why was that mission so shiny in its reading room and chapel, these other things being so?

The lights went out. The Adventurer kicked off the Pajamas and slept. He awoke at midnight, and reflected on all these matters. And he whispered a curious thing to the darkness: "I was naked and ye clothed me."

At six o'clock he was called for breakfast. His sulphur smelling clothes were on his bed. The Frog was now cook. He gave each man a soup plate heaping with oatmeal. If it had been oats it would have been food for so many horses. Had the frog been up since 4:30 preparing this?

The price of part of that horse feed might have gone into something to eat. There was a salty blue sauce on it, that was called milk. And there was dry bread to be had, without butter, and as much bad coffee as a man could drink.

After waiting an hour for the front door to be unlocked by the arriving janitor it dawned on the Adventurer that for all night there had been no one in the mission that the authorities could trust with keys.

A person called the bookkeeper arrived with the janitor. The Adventurer made his formal farewells to those representatives of law, before whom the Frog melted with humility. The Scalawag who had bathed with the Adventurer tipped him a wink and tried to escape in his company. But the Gentleman bade him good-by so firmly that the authorities noticed, and the brash creature remained glued to his chair. He probably had to do his full share of kindling before he escaped.

And the Adventurer went forth from that place into the highway of our God, who dwelleth not in temples made with hands, neither is worshipped with men's hands, as though He needed any thing.

If you have any friends in Morristown please forward them this Bulletin.

War Bulletin number three will contain an essay entitled, The Creed of a Beggar.

War Bulletin number four will be the last for some time. It will be in the form of a seventy page book of my verses entitled "The Tramps Excuse," which I will give with both hands to anyone who will confess that he reads poetry, who will try to read it through twice, who will write me a brief letter when he is done.

WAR BULLETIN NUMBER THREE

Springfield, Ill., Aug. 30, 1909

The Creed of a Beggar

I believe in God, the creeping fire, the august and whimsical Creator, maker of all religions, dweller in all clean shrines.

I am convinced that the great religions: Christianity, Judaism, Mohammedism, Confucianism, Buddhism, are absolutely different from one another in core and essence, though God made them all. I choose Christianity.

I believe in Christ the Socialist, the Beautiful, the personal savior from sin, the Singing Immanuel.

I believe in that perilous maddening flower, the Holy Ghost.

I believe in the Sermon on the Mount as the one test of society, though I scarcely expect to live up to it one hour in my life.

I believe in all institutions that are the result of reading the words of Christ and meditating upon him.

I believe the hope for the union of Christians is my special inheritance, since all my people were pupils of Alexander Campbell.

I believe in the Far-Flung Battle line of Christian Missions, and pray for its advance.

I believe in the Unitarians. I believe in all the Evangelical Protestants, especially the Disciples of Christ. I believe in the Mass, the Eucharist, the Virgin Mary.

I take for my brother the Lord Buddha remembering with happy tears the hours when he was my master. I take for my friend the founder of Christian Science. I can not accept her teachings, but I can rejoice in the peculiar presence I have found in her churches.

In a special sense I take St. Francis for my master, and pray that I may attain to his divine immolation.

I believe that Beggary is the noblest occupation of man.

I believe in the hospitality of my fellow human, for it has never failed me.

It May Be, Brother

I have never seen a miracle. I have never seen anyone raised from the dead. I do not want to be raised from the dead. Heaven is no goal for me. The kingdom of God on earth is vastly more significant. Let me do a little for the success of the race, a great deal for myself, and then sleep forever.

I have never seen Heaven or Hell except in visions. Visions are not infallible. *They are parables of the day, consolations of the hour.* I think man should use Faith only when he must. Vision is better than Faith, but Experience is better than Vision. I do not believe in the infallibility of any Book, Teacher or Church. Thereby hangs a story. In the first Khandaka of the Mahavagga is found this passage concerning Buddha: "And the Blessed One having remained at Uruvela as long as he thought fit, went forth to Benares. Now Upaka, the naked ascetic saw the Blessed One travelling on the road between Gaya and the Bodhi tree; and when he saw him he said to the Blessed One, 'Your countenance, my friend, is serene; your complexion is pure and bright. In whose name, friend, have you retired from the world? Who is your teacher? Whose doctrine do you profess?'

When Upaka the naked ascetic has spoken thus the Blessed One addressed him in the following stanzas: "I have overcome all foes. I am all wise. I am free from stains in every way. I have left everything and have attained emancipation by the destruction of desire. Having myself gained knowledge, whom should I call my master? I have no teacher. No one is equal to me. In the world of men and of Gods, no being is like me. I am the Holy one in this world. I am the highest teacher. I alone am the absolute Sambuddha. I have gained coolness by the extinction of all passion and have obtained Nirvana. To found the kingdom of Truth I go to the city of Benares. I will beat the drum of the immortal in the darkness of this world."

"You profess then, friend, to be the holy and absolute VICTORIOUS ONE"?

Buddha said: "Like me are all the victorious who have reached the extinction of sensuality, individuality, delusion and ignorance. I have overcome all states of sinfulness, therefore Upaka, am I the VICTORIOUS ONE."

When he had spoken thus, Upaka the naked ascetic replied: "It may be so friend," shook his head, took another road and went away.

I am as Upaka, the naked ascetic. I do not believe in infallibility. It may be so, friend, but I shake my head, and take another road.

I believe in God, the Creeping Fire. I have met him. He has scorched the walls of my arteries. I believe in the terrible flower of the Holy Ghost. I have eaten of it. I believe in Christ the Socialist, for I have seen the Sermon on the Mount many times illustrated by my hosts on the road.

Orthodox Theologian! I hear you say to me, "Why this is a rag of a creed." Yes sir. The creed of a beggar. Will you give me the Whole Garment of Truth? I am searching for it with tears: men always give me bread, never the truth. Like that disreputable Ulrich Brendle, I am setting out for the Great Nothing, yet tap you on the shoulder and say, "can you let me have a loan? Can you spare an ideal or two?"

Scientific Socialist! I hear you say "Why this is a more than ample creed. Omit your traditions. The Sermon on the Mount is enough. It is the perfect garment." I answer, "Yes indeed, but I am a beggar. I would not look well in that glistening white samite. A careless effort to live up to it would make me into a damned complacent hypocrite, intoxicated with my good intentions. So I walk in the rags of my superstition and leave the Sermon at Home. But on the road I meet it again. My hosts live up to its doctrines till they make me forget what I really am: Upaka, the naked ascetic, Brendle the Disreputable."

A Confession

Let me declare that I love money. At work in the city I have the usual human feeling that I am not getting all the cash my work deserves. I am just as deferential as you, good reader, to people of wealth especially if they have used their leisure to acquire culture, or sweet religious merit. I have the usual shrinking from the man whose father did not obtain for him early in life an environment of porcelain bath tub and full dinner pail. I realize that this bulletin is a hothouse production, the conservatory was built with other men's dollars. In my usual speeches as a Y.M.C.A. man, an Anti-Saloon man and a Disciple of Christ I am apt to say the things that don't disturb business. I am sorry this is so. But on the road I eat of the Perilous Flower and preach the sermon for strangers.

Sermon for Strangers

Strangers in the city, throw your money into the street. The hope to ''do good with it'' is a fool's hope. Money given away makes paupers, parasites, bootlickers. It gives scientific cold philanthropy a chance to lift its hydra head. Throw your money into the street and let it draw the flies if it will.

Let us enter the great offices and shut the desk lids and cut the telephone wires. Let us see that the skyscrapers are empty and locked, and the keys thrown into the river. Let us break up the cities. Let us send men on a great migration: set free, purged of the commerce-made manners and fat prosperity of America; ragged with the beggar's pride, starving with the crusador's fervor. Better to die of plague on the highroad, seeing the angels, than live on iron streets playing checkers with dollars forever and ever.

''But it is absurd,'' you say. ''They will not leave business. There will be no plague.''

Well then, let a few of us go, carrying neither purse nor scrip. Let us be healing the sick imaginations, cleansing the leprous minds, raising dead aspirations, casting out the devils of money-lust, in those we meet by the way. Let us meditate upon the abstinences of those monks of the Highway: Buddha, Christ and St. Francis. Hospitality is the most sacred thing in the world. Box car tramps that came before us have hardened men's hearts with their deceits. They had no right to the road. They had no message. This is our message *Oh Strangers in the Country*.

Waste not your precious youth in industry. America is too rich already. She lacks most those things that come to idle men. Satan finds work for busy hands to do. You hate the kings in oil and grain and cattle and the like. Behind clean bodies, quick and nerved with wire, their souls squat like giant spiders ready to spring; Sons of the Giant Spider Mammon. And you sirs, are tiny spiders of the same breed. All you who raise grain are petty imitation wheat kings. Your little souls are full of the venom of covetousness. You are subscribers to the business axioms that make this a Land of Death. If any man has a dollar in his pocket let him throw it away, lest it transform him into spiritual garbage.

All great things have happened while the crops went wrong. Abraham Lincoln went into the white house carrying the debts of his youth. Scotland knows how wretched a farmer was Robert Burns, the poet of the plough for all time.

Oh farmers, so jealous for your grain, give all your time to fields of cloud and air. There the harvests truly are plenteous and the laborers few. The man with a house painted and fields in order is in danger of hell fire. It means he has not taken all his time to worship the Christ of Beauty and His free grace, he has not gathered his children by the fireside to carve something lovely that has not the damning touch of machinery upon it, to look into some wonderful new doctrine or old tradition, to tell an antique story or sing a homely song. Be warned, one dollar in your pocket makes you a rich man, and it is God's truth, and no mild saying, that *it is easier for a camel to go through the eye of a needle than for a rich man to enter the kingdom of God.*

The Flower of the Amaranth

For good or ill I have eaten of the flower of the Holy Spirit, the most dangerous bloom in the Universe. There are days when visions come in cataracts. With these pictures burning heart and conscience away, I would compass Heaven and Earth to make one proselyte. I would go through smoke and flame to prove that these my visitations came to me. The martyr's crown would be sweeter than honey.

I have beside me a letter from a man in New York on whose opinion I set great store. After some strong reproof, good for my soul, he tells me some people think me "clairvoyant." It makes me drunk to call me clairvoyant. There used to be an art student who called me "great magician." He divined the shortest road to my vanity.

If I had been born among an unscientific people, say the Mohammedans, I would have attempted a Koran. I would have tried to draw the world-conquering sword. One more fanatic would have died the death upon the burning sands. Or should I have been so fortunate as to stir those Arabians who had in them the making of great statesmen, in a whirlwind half a generation long we might have established a new Islam. Fortunately I have a rag of conscience left. Fortunately I have no powers of leadership. Fortunately, this is a scientific age. Fortunately I have studied art and know that all good picture-makers see the wonders in the air before they make them.

Let me give thanks to God for my artist friends, those who have given their hearts to the Christ of Beauty, though they may not call on His name. They serve Him by their work. To them every day is a revelation to be written or painted. To them the faces of man and nature are an ever-changing vision in the rainbow-light of the eternal sun.

They too see genii in the night, taller than any that encountered the Arabian. But they are not troubled by the Scripture Writing fever, the desire to be infallible, that eats into me. They do not want to go to the city of Benares to beat the drum of the immortal in the darkness of this world. They do not want to put on the whole armour of God.

All these I should have attempted had I not mingled with artists so intimately and now that I am banished from them it is by co-operating with the useful zealots, socialists, Local Optionists, Single Taxers, Y.M.C.A., men, that I am able to find a safe vent for my fancies, to refrain from shouting new pictures of Heaven and the Deep from the housetops. People call me a radical, but for similar reasons, I am even more of a conservative, a worshipper of tradition, especially the story of religion as it is revealed in architecture and ritual from the Sphinx to the little Catholic churches of Springfield. My eyes are trained by long study to read justly the religious emotions and the precise tremble of the nerves when the Hiroglyphic was cut, the altar rail gilded. These designs live side by side in the streets of my mind, as in the streets of History.

I open my heart and quench the mad new fire, that comes of too much eating of the Amaranth. I receive the storm of old wine pouring down from the boats of the grey prophets who ride in a fleet in the ancient skies. In the spray of that fairy cataract, I see the virgin Mary and accept her as a vision that grew in the bosom of all my fathers back from the day when Isis, the first Madonna, nourished the sun god, Horus.

How one can brood over the strange statue-groups in the museums! There is Athena, the wisest of virgins, the spiritual mother of Athens. But the Virgin was born in her sharpest potency in Nazareth, glorified in the Medieval Catholic ages and finally crowned by the shrewd priests of Rome, who but followed the aspirations of the ages and builded better than they knew.

I cannot resist her. Many times a week I enter the church of the Immaculate Conception or of St. Agnes here and offer her my heart. He who is afraid to kneel when the desire comes, will not get the joy out of the shrines of the earth. There is a certain portion of every clean shrine that is not made with hands.

The church of Rome belongs to me, to do with as I will. I do not belong to her. I do not go in by Peter's Gate. I am the thief that climbs over the wall. I am as the outlaw David, who ate the temple bread that it was not lawful for him to lay hand upon.

Newman is my heart's delight. I honor any man who takes a step from one religion to another. He who is a Methodist because his father was, is worse than an infidel. He who is the son of an infidel, and receives the gift of the Holy Ghost at a camp meeting mourners' bench, is a dear child of the Lord. But more of Newman. Reading his Apologia I began clearly to understand that there was such a thing as systematic Dogma in the world, row upon row of immemorial bricks, regularly laid with a mortar of logic between, and the bottom row resting on nothing, mud, or infinity, as you please. I realized that this bottom row was arbitrarily chosen, and I examined myself, I looked over my religion and decided that I had arbitrarily chosen the doctrine of Tran-substantiation, and the doctrine of the Union of Christians. The first binds me in a deep sympathy with the Mass. The second holds me in my hereditary brotherhood, with which I have a deeper sympathy—the Disciples of Christ; and as long as there are two dogmas in me, I have no right to censure the man with a hundred.

The Union of Christians—a tremendous doctrine. How are we going to have it in that future day when all Asia does lip service either to Peter or Paul? There will be a Christ with an elephant's head carved in India that the West will abhor, which true disciples should not shrink from. There will be a Christ guarded by gilded dragons in China that the West will revile, but the true disciple should not scorn. In Japan there will be a Christ meditating upon a terrace in Heaven, done in bronze and set on a high mountain, and thinking thoughts that seem foolishness to Glasgow or Rome or Chicago. But they will not seem foolishness to the true Disciple. Oh far flung battle line of Christian missions, you fight better than you understand, you build better than you know! The missionaries dying on the field are like angels crucified in the stars that the whole sky may be redeemed. But the new earth they are bringing will hold much they have not planned.

For God is an august and whimsical Creator, maker of all religions, dweller in all clean shrines.

An Exhortation

Having had an invisible world made visible to me, I cannot but counsel others to seek for the like. Some such experience awaits you, reader, as is related in the story of "The Boats and the Prophets." The meaning, the actors, the scenery will differ, will contradict mine, but the splendor awaits. Brother, for your own soul's sake, open your eyes and rebuild for yourself a kingdom of God on earth, a house not made with hands. *Do not consider the raw pictures fresh from the sky infallible guides for yourself or others.* Do not get drunk upon them, the consolations of an hour, parables of a day, but rigidly test them by experience, by the traditions of the church Universal and the dreams of all the reformers who are bringing down the angels to men.

The Boats of the Prophets.

This is the night my ship comes in,
Tho wine is pouring down!
Glory and pain! The Angels' blood
Anoints the teeming town
And the mighty flagship sways and dips.
I thank my God with fevered lips
My prophet brings a thousand ships
And the dream of a burning crown.

A proud hungry composer with the roll of a rejected oratorio under his arm—"Queen Esther" walked back and forth on the outer edge of Brooklyn bridge usually used by wagons only. He wanted to get close to the water. He was bent on suicide. With conscious dramatic egotism, he chanted these lines of the Queen in the oratorio:

"And so will I go in unto the king, which is not according to the law: and if I perish, I perish."

He looked at the green-black water then to the roofs of the East side with their brown glowing shadows, then to the real New York beyond with the cold white lights cutting their way through the blackness. The only people on the footbridge were two policemen far away. They could not hear the song. They could not see him. He could scarcely hear himself. There were roaring street cars in the passageways allotted to them.

He shouted his song in defiance at the steel cables rising in network to the dizzy bridge-towers. The towers, winged with cable-nets were arrogantly hovering above the cities. They were eagles above anthills. They were not unlike two cyclop ships of war lashed end to end. But before an hour had gone he had seen ships of the air so vast and real that Brooklyn Bridge and Williamsburg Bridge were as broken fishnets cast overboard from them.

It was at the stroke of twelve that he grew silent. He covered his face with his hands. Then he looked into the water. Then he looked up, and what he saw destroyed the thought of suicide. The Milky Way came floating down, every grey glimmer a thread of stars, a heavenly necklace. The jewels became tiny boats, then titan ships, each necklace a fleet, falling with speed and glory toward the bridge and the cities, spreading sails that were as wings. When the pageant well-nigh reached the bridge-towers, each boat took a place as though anchored invisibly, and was a thing of conscious life, and trembled, a carrier dove of God, held in leash, eager to be gone. They were arrayed in ranks, mast above mast, fleet behind fleet into the sky and the ships farthest away were greatest of all. The masts were purple, the ragged sails were pale lavender, the hulls were built of bars of crystal light more real than the bridge cables. The musician's opened eyes could penetrate the hulls of those farthest away. He saw that only a few near him had inhabitants or cargo. These had their sides splashed with red-purple. They bore cargoes of wine in open jars. These wine-ships carried each a solitary sailor, asleep beside his mast.

The heart of the musician was like a tongue of flame within him. The tears of mortal fear were upon his face. He saw in the countenances of the captains trouble and loneliness beyond his own, and written beneath the lines of care, the lines of courage to endure. His fear slowly left him. There was established a brotherhood between his soul and the souls of the ancient sleepers.

The old men awoke, tottering among the wine-jars, toiling with them to the edge of the ships. There were many pauses. There was much kneeling and muttering prayer. They were tall as the tallest of mortals, but beside their stupendous masts they were little men. Their black rough robes and white beards were stained from their work. Some had Chinese faces. Some had Hebrew faces. Some had Hindu faces. Some had Greek faces. Many had faces of those he knew were born in giant planets of distant suns they were so strangely and strongly made.

All began pouring down the wine from the ships. It's fragrance filled the air. It rolled up from the streets of New York and Brooklyn in a purple mist that in a moment hid those cities. The fleet rose upon the rising cloud-sea that swept above him.

He breathed the mists. The fury and glory of ancient Prophecy entered into him. The perfume was the Word of God in his breast. He felt like Elisha of old when the mantle fell on his shoulders from the ascending chariot. He felt as Isaiah did when one of the Seraphim laid upon his lips the live coal from the altar. The musician said, without knowing why, "here am I, Lord, send me."

As his eyes grew accustomed to it he saw through the mist, how the old men fainted now, or slept with faces like ashes, amid their overturned jars. There was no one to lay hand to rope or wheel. But the faithful boats, slaves of an unknown law, rose to the ranks of the empty fleets above. Slowly the whole pageant stole away, winding in long lines higher and faster into the sky, hiding at last behind the stars.

When he looked on the cities, the mist had settled. Towers appeared above it. It ran in the streets a network of swirling rivers. He felt himself led down into these currents, bearing within him a contrite heart. He went down into that great baptism, and it carried him for twelve hours where it would.

Forty others, who would not bow down the knee to Baal, who had stood in the solitary places, were able to see the ships and the wine. There was a struggling sculptor who had been looking to the stars through his open skylight. There was a struggling dramatist, who had been half asleep upon the roof of a tenement when the vision came. There was a priest of the Paulist Fathers who was praying for the city. There was a Rabbi in the Ghetto who was reading the Psalms of Imprecation, and pondering over the afflictions of Israel. There was an upright Chinese trader transcribing in exquisite archaic characters his essay on the decay of Truth in a room above his brother's gambling den. There was a proud little actress, not eighteen years old, of divine promise, who had refused to make her way wrongfully, who slept unmolested on a perilous stairway and woke in time to see the crystal boats. Forty people in all, of whom the world was not worthy had had their spiritual eyes opened to this wonder and had said in their hearts, "Here am I, Lord, send me," and had gone down into the great baptism. Each thought himself the only one who saw it. They did not meet each other, except for one whom the musician encountered at the west end of the bridge, his father in music, living in the same garret near by at the foot of the bridge.

This father in music was a cadaverous, grey German. He had been world-renowned once. He had eaten opium and gone to the gutter. He had been saved by a wild Bowery Evangelist and a relative, a faithful physician.

The two composers walked together with lofty silence and noble laughter, following the purple currents. In the mist, brick and iron became fragile dreams, thin husks of gleaming fruit. How could they help being happy, when every building had a soul which stood naked for them to read and the face of every passer-by likewise showed his innermost greatness? As the day came the crowds poured to the business heart of the city, every passing face transfigured, three times as divine as men appear by common day.

And the two said subtle things, kind things, witty things, holy things to one another about all they saw.

At noon they were again on Brooklyn Bridge. The mist was fading fast. Again the bridge piers were materialism omnipotent, taloned and cruel eagles, with steel beaks and granite bones. Only a few threads of purple cloud blew about them.

The young man asked the old, "What is the mist?"

The other said, "It is the Blood of the Archangels, who have gone into all the universe to preach the gospel to every star. At this moment they hang upon crosses in the uttermost planets of the uttermost suns for the sins of the Universe. They are forsaken of God as was Christ their elder brother. By the winds of mystery, by trans-substantiation their blood enters the wine jars of the Prophets, who are their proclaimers. We who see the mist should understand that by this redeeming blood shall come the New Earth, The New Heaven and the New Universe."

And the old man told him one hundred other things that these imply till the young composer tightened the roll of the manuscript of Queen Esther and threw it into the river. He took hold of his master's arm and said with a smile: "Now we are going to my honorable garret, and eat of my honorable dry crust. Then you may do as you please, but I am going to sleep on my honorable bare floor for eleven hours. When I arise I will sketch my first oratorio, my first real music. I shall call it "The Prophets.""

The Boats of the Prophets is first of all a story. I hope the foregoing sermons have not interfered with its art value.

If the reader of this Bulletin is earnestly desirous to relate my creed to a series of autobiographical poems, my foolish map of the Universe and my foolish Cosmic System, it can be done in a certain fashion by reading the last section of The Tramp's Excuse. (War Bulletin Number Four) a book of about eighty pages which I will give with both hands to anyone who will write to me and confess that he reads poetry, who will try to read it through twice, who will send me a brief letter when he is done. *I am indeed anxious for serious response to this offer, and exhort my friends to stir up the godly, or on their own account send me names, addresses and credentials. I want to plant the Tramp's Excuse where it will take root and grow.*

Bulletin Number Five, not to be issued for some time, will be a defense of the Young Men's Christian Association.

WAR BULLETIN NUMBER FIVE

Springfield, Ill., Thanksgiving Season, 1909

A Defense of the Y.M.C.A.

This War Bulletin contains a little story to show what markedly inefficient service is done by the Beer Barrel on Thanksgiving Day to make plain to the Italian citizen the meaning of the President's Proclamation. I need not say that hymns are seldom heard in the saloons on Sunday. I need not add that on Thanksgiving Day no one is set apart to read a Psalm. Yet the Bartenders have the nerve to serve Turkey and Cranberries.

The Brand of Commercial Infamy is set upon every retail liquor dealer. Only the wholesale dealers attempt to buy respectability. The most hardened Americans know it and let the retail business alone. The Brewers employ the unassimilated foreigner who can speak English, yet is not yet sensitive to American Ideals because he does not belong to the American Reading Public. His child is learning to read something besides the liquor papers and often, as a consequence learning to abhor his business. (In the story below they are still an ingenuous, happy family, with no Puritanism to disturb them.)

The leader of the colony becomes not only the saloonkeeper, but at the same time becomes to his whole flock the interpreter of the Pilgrim Fathers, George Washington, Abraham Lincoln, the Democratic and Republican Machines, and the President's Thanksgiving Proclamation. American History is read through the bottom of the Beer Mug. The unfortunate Italian, Slav, Pole, Lithuanian imagines he is in the land of the Free, when he is merely in the hands of that International Person, sometimes called Beelzebub.

This purports to be a defense of the Y.M.C.A. I might state it more concretely: Seldom is anyone shot or stabbed in the Y.M.C.A. One can find there many well-thumbed American Periodicals and books, and discover what a Thanksgiving Proclamation means. There that dirty animal called man can take a bath, and make himself a bit more like an angel. When Turkey and Cranberries are served, a little prayer is said. The law does not prohibit the selling of Y.M.C.A. privileges to minors. Really now, this means something. I will defer further defense of the Y.M.C.A. to War Bulletin Number Six.

Give a Reception to Reps!

[*Clipping from State Register*]

St. Louis, Mo., Nov. 5 — Paul Reps, immigrant Russian laborer, was the hero and guest of honor this afternoon in an unique celebration. His hostesses were among the wealthiest social leaders of St. Louis. A fortnight ago Reps wrote Mrs. W.K. Kavanaugh, wife of the president of the Lake-to-the-Gulf Deep Waterways Association, that he would become a citizen to-day, asking whether she could arrange a celebration in his honor that day — the greatest of his life. Reps has spent $12 in court fees and was willing to expend $15 if Mrs. Kavanaugh and friends would come and sing patriotic songs. Reps' letter said it was a disgrace as mostly immigrants in such an event, induced by politicians to take naturalization, drink much beer and fight.

The use of a hall and pipe organ were donated to Mrs. Kavanaugh. Besides Reps, wife and three children, those at the celebration included Mrs. Kavanaugh, Mrs. Kreismann, wife of the mayor; Mrs. Edward L. Pertorious, wife of the newspaper publisher and Mrs. Wallace C. Captain. The hostesses sang "America" and other patriotic and war songs.

Upon inquiry the Editor of the Bulletin finds that citizen Reps is thoroughly deserving of his honors. I take this chance to bid him Godspeed in his citizenship. I congratulate the hostesses as well.

Now there is a touch of humor in it, as in all healthful events, but isn't it a good idea — giving a Reception to Reps? Hearken, all you society ladies in our small towns! St. Louis has set the fashion — carry it further. In the railroad cutting down near the bridge the Italians are blasting the rock. Some day you will use the railroad. Maybe the Garibaldi of America is there. Exercise your ingenuity. Find some way to meet him on a patriotic basis. As the phrase goes: give a Reception to Reps.

The Lithuanians are digging in the mine just two miles away. They are blowing themselves to pieces all that you may have coal in the cellar and a warm Reception Room. So put some roses in the vase on the piano, get some kind of an introduction to the colony, and give a Reception to Reps.

When the brilliant Jew from the Bleeding Ghettos of Russia comes here with his violin, his Psalms and his Talmud, remember the God of Abraham, and David and St. Paul, and give a reception to Reps. This would be especially fitting at Thanksgiving time, when we so much need a substitute for the devouring saloon, where the Jew will scarcely go and the others go only for their hurt. In the name of Martha Washington, the Lady of the White House, and Nancy Hanks, the lady of the Log Cabin, let us devise a new Custom and do something in a Social and Patriotic way for these obscure but patient Pilgrim Fathers. At the Thanksgiving season, if no other time, give a reception to Reps!

How the Ice Man Danced

"What sought they thus afar,
Bright jewels of the mine,
The wealth of seas, the spoils of war?
They sought a faith's pure shrine."

Just two years ago tomorrow, in New York City, nineteen hundred and seven, upon Thanksgiving evening a band of exiles moored their bark in a wild Italian bar room. We were five young artists, an Australian, a "Pennsylvania Dutchman," two New Englanders and your servant, who tells the tale—exiles from the peculiar beauties of life that money can buy. We had wandered about Union Square, Washington Square and the streets between. The bar room was the first place stomach and soul could be fed, under the circumstances.

We had been well-nigh mobbed by self-conscious street urchins dressed as jesters, as dukes, as soldiers. We had been screamed at by little girls constumed as queens or gypsies, or wearing their brother's trousers. Some of the children enjoyed themselves with reasonable human vanity, dusty little butterflies, bedraggled little peacocks. But the gang leaders were filled with money lust to the point of hysteria. As is the custom in almost all New York holidays, they held out their hands crying "Gimme five cents." "Just a penny." "Aw, gimme some money." "You're rich. Gimme ten cents." One boy dressed as an Indian kept on our trail across Washington Square. "Just one penny, Aw just one cent for Thanksgiving!" He was hoping to rasp us into liberality. But one of the New Englanders destroyed the creature's assurance by saying—"Sonny, we can't help it if we're broke.'' ''And you mustn't whine if you want me to shell out.''

The infant had the face of a bitter old man. He could never enjoy a lesson in manners. He ran away, shouting for all the world to hear—''Short sports,'' ''Short sports.''

We reached the saloon. We took a table near the bar. Between us and the crowd of Italians eating near the kitchen was a stretch of sawdust floor, the stove, and the billard table. Italy and America were literally and spiritually far apart that Thanksgiving night.

A company of six scuffled in, demanding drink. A half blind man would have supposed them three scrub women hobnobbing with delicate boys of seventeen. They fancied they looked so. But they were men dressed as women, women as men. Never believe in Rosalind again. It is no disguise to mass the hair under the cap in slatternly tightness. That will not conceal its sex nor keep the insulted locks from straying. No matter how full the trousers, they cannot conceal the taper from the hip to the foot. They cannot mend the simpering step. The Dutchman said: ''We might concede that was a real maid of all work, that big blonde in the spotted skirt.'' Just then the creature turned his blue chin our way. It made his golden wig outrageous. ''I'll take it back,'' said the Dutchman.

We turned to our affairs. One New Englander a Mystic, cut up his spaghetti. The rest of us were eclectic in method. We all agreed with the other New Englander Cotton Mather that ''spaghetti was not invented by a gentleman,'' and enjoyed it anyway. Four of us could afford the usual Italian Restaurant claret. That means that I, the fifth am a fool-tetotaler. I hate the alcoholic beverages, and all their works. Three of us could afford Turkey. The evening was by agreement a ''Dutch treat.'' We ate our pockets empty while the Australian told us stories, about the ''bush'' and the ''stations,'' which are the same as ranches and how the cattlemen drive with twenty foot whips, instead of in the fashion of our classic cowboys; and about the art of rabbit poisoning; and how Australia is only a few square miles smaller than the United States. We likewise spake with our best wit, and fancied the tavern light gave the flash of which Omar speaks, the flash exceeding the darkness of certain temples.

The waitress tried to get us to take chances on an ancient gold stop watch, belonging to a family friend in distress. The raffle was to occur in one week, with elaborate precautions against fraud, one hundred chances at ten cents apiece. She told the sad story of her friend's life. We were not interested. The Dutchman changed the subject.

Pointing to the bar, he said, ''Those people are having a happy Thanksgiving. It is plain they have a good deal to be thankful for.''

"Yes" she answered. "To-day is the holiday. Gurruls is always glad
for a holiday,'—smiling and pointing to the crowd, "They are gurrul
friends of ours." The waitress was the daughter of the proprietor.
The whole event had the atmosphere of a family lark. The waitress
turned away. One of the girls laughed at us, like MacMonnie's
Bacchante. Cotton Mather assured us that there was the sacred blood
of Tuscany in her Aurora face. The other New Englander said
"probably she is a Sicilian. Most of these Dagoes are." And three of
us agreed. The front door opened slowly.

From the kitchen came a yell;—*"Look out, you're pinched!"*
Though it was a bit of pleasantry, the six ran out professing to be
terrified by the couple just whirling in from the sidewalk—a woman in
brown trousers and coat and a mesenger-boy's hat; and a man in a
big blue dress and a scarf. The newcomer in skirts grasped at the
hand of the "Tuscan" girl, she gave him a terrific slap and joined her
friends in the street—many others were leaving at the sight of the
newcomers, yet many remained. Meanwhile the messenger-boy
frowned, hastening to hide most of her person behind a table beside a
grey old man. We had not noticed that old man before. The
Dutchman appeared to know him. The Dutchman and the Mystic
were the frequenters of the place. One of them quoted:

"There were men with hoary hair
Amid that pilgrim band:
Why had they come to wither there
Away from their childhood's land?

You must answer in rhyme." "Cheap labor's in demand,"
answered the Australian. "To establish the black hand," said your
servant. "That grey man is the proprietor," said the Mystic, not
falling into the game. "He is the father or father-in-law, or something
of most of these people here."

The man in the blue skirt was dancing in the long floor-space by the
bar, between us and the Italian tables. The only aristocratic thing
about him was his mustache. The Earl of Pawtucket might wear such
a one. For the rest, his towering shoulders, his long arms, red neck,
chapped hands, tremendous feet and half-hewn face betokened a
good man to cut up ice, lift it out of the wagon, and if necessary carry
it up six flights of stairs. The four of us agreed to call him *the ice man.*

The ice man lifted his skirts. He kicked the sawdust all over the cat.
He danced and drank at once. He jumped into the air. He sprawled.
He saved his face by "doing the split," placing one leg flat on the
floor in front, one straight behind him. Italy and America cheered.
Applause was sweet. He slid to his feet stiff-legged, going down the

same way. He did it half a dozen times. "He must have been a circus actor before he fell into the ice business," said the Australian.

A toad of a man, a Blear Derelict came in and drank. The ice man kicked over his head. He kicked off his hat. He shook hands to show it was kindly meant. He stepped back onto the small dog who thereupon yelped. A mastiff big as a bear, and solemn as Henry the Eighth came rolling down the little black stair. We whispered to each other, "He is a detective in disguise." Without a sound he licked the small dogs nose and ears. The small dog ceased whining. The comforter rolled up-stairs again, well-nigh overturning our table on the way.

The ice man took another drink. He rolled on the floor, rending his garments in ecstacy. He shook out that part of the padding of his chest which stood for matronly charm. It was two aprons rolled up. One of the daughters of the household restored them to his bosom. This suggested an interchange of sugary compliment, pointed and liberal. At length the lady retreated with her hands over her ears.

The woman in the messenger-boy hat rose and danced with him. The Pennsylvania Dutchman observed, "Do you notice that perfectly delicious droop of her eyes?"

They came nearer. His voice changed. "Why he is at least eight years younger than she is. She is forty, if a day. She is his wife, more than likely. She put on those togs to keep him out of mischief."

He was red, that ice man, as though he had been boiled. He perspired like a hand in the field. Yet she let him kiss her. Then she broke away, found his scarf, and tied the funny thing over his head, hiding his mustache, and making him look more like a woman. It was plain by her gesture she was pleading with him to go home. The room reeked with garlic, cold turkey, beer, and primitive man. The stove was a blast furnace. We paid the reckoning. We had figured closely. It cleaned up all but two of us. We rose to go, just as a hurdy-gurdy hand organ began to play outside. The ice man hearkened dramatically, threw off his scarf, and opened both doors. All the children of the neighborhood had begun to dance in front of the place. There are squares in Europe where the doves gather whenever the crumbs are scattered. The babies gather in New York whenever the hurdy-gurdy plays.

The sharp air was a delight. We moved our chairs against the wall, and sat down again. This drama evidently had a second act. We looked out. Our hearts leaped to see the children swaying, swaying, and to hear the rhythm of their sliding feet upon the stones.

"This is the sort of thing Henri likes," I said. I was once a Henri student.

The ice man scattered the infants like sparrows. He hitched himself to the hurdy-gurdy. He dragged it into the barroom beside our table, almost against the wall.

The doors were shut on the children. The hurdy-gurdy man still turned the crank, utterly insensible to all things around. His wife still shook her tamborine. She was a heavy, marefaced creature, in an interesting condition.

The ice man loved the music. He danced a sort of can-can, exposing socks and man's garters, then a man's union suit, half hidden by borrowed lingerie. He felt especially wicked. He did it again, while Italy to the south of him, and the United States to the north of him, laughed at the simplicity of his naughtiness.

The Blear Derelict had been blocked in the corner by the hurdy-gurdy. He was standing with his untasted beer at his chin. He was bobbing philosophically, saying something no one could hear. The music stopped. We heard him murmur to the dancer, "You're a damned fake. You're a— —"

The music as suddenly resumed, for the hurdy-gurdy man had had a drink. No one cared for the philosopher. He was an outsider, too drunk to feel snubbed.

The woman did not desire to give up her tamborine, but the ice man wanted it, and was of course, able to take it away. This made her angry. She fought all her battles that evening without the help of her mate. He looked straight at the wall, straight through the wall, whatever happened, and ground and ground and ground the hand organ.

The ice man hit everyone on the head with the tamborine. He threw it up and caught it. He stepped on it. He skipped daintily around it. He passed it around for dimes. Only two of us could contribute. The Italians were liberal. He shook the dimes into the sawdust, and we helped to pick them up. The music stopped a moment as he gave them to the hand organist.

The philosopher in the corner shouted "You're a damned fake." The music started again.

The ice man danced with another daughter of the proprietor. She looked to be a wholesome and healthy spirit. Her face was merriment itself. The Dutchman said to us: "You would not suppose that lady could emit as choice a lot of hair-curling swearwords as any gentleman present, but she can." The ice man thought her charming. He hugged her outrageously. She struggled away. He sent a kick after her retreating figure, which missed its errand only a little. She did not swear. She laughed at him from behind a table. Apparently but only apparently, his social prestige was not disturbed. He passed the tamborine again. The two wealthy artists gave the rest of their fortune. The others put in pieces of bread. The ice man threw out the bread with frowns. He gave the money to the man. He would not give up the tamborine. The woman wrestled for it, showing dog-teeth as she snarled. Her husband ground and ground the machine and was always looking at the wall.

The woman apparently gave up, biding her time. It was only nine o'clock. But the Australian said "We must go pretty soon." The Dutchman said "It is a highly decorative evening, but enough is enough." The ice man sang in Italian about Christopher Columbus. Everybody smiled, but no one laughed. His wife caught him off guard. She helped the hurdy-gurdy woman snatch the tamborine. She begged him to go home. She was muffling the funny scarf over his head. She was close to us. There were tears on her quivering face. We exchanged gay waves of the hand with the company as we went into the street. Passing out, we saw the ice man turning hot water into the tamborine from the coffee boiler on the stove. We approached Washington Square. The Australian said "by all the rules, there will be a fight back there, in a few minutes, and a scalded ice man."

South of Washington Square the steeple of the Judson Memorial church rises into the sky, bearing an electric cross, which is half the glory of that region at night. Cotton Mather looked up at it and said, "By Jove this is Thanksgiving day. I knew it, but I didn't realize it enough to wake up in time for services this morning. And I swore last Thanksgiving day I would go to church this time. It is a good old custom That cross—"

An Indian burst upon our trail. He began to pursue us. "Aw gimme a nickel for Thanksgiving." Then he recognized us and snarled, "Huh. Short sports. Five sports, and not a cent." But he ceased to follow. He had learned our ways.

The last of August I announced that War Bulletin Number four—the Book of Poems entitled the Tramp's Excuse, would be given to whoever asked. I received many applications from strangers both in the city and out and supplied all comers and still had enough left to crowd a copy or so onto my friends. Now the edition of three hundred is exhausted and the offer is withdrawn.

Every man in the United States ought to publish a War Bulletin and a Personal Creed. There are no two of us alike in the important parts of our souls, so every Bulletin and Creed should be different.

We would think less of each other no doubt, but be on an honest and solid basis for progress.

In the name of Ultimate Humanity then, Oh Friends, mine Enemies—print out your naked souls! Let us have several million War Bulletins!

From THE VILLAGE MAGAZINE

First Edition

(Summer, 1910)

[The following essays are reprinted in the 2nd, 3rd, and 4th eds. unless otherwise noted. With a few exceptions, all are published in handwritten capital letters. In the 2nd, 3rd, and 4th eds., "An Editorial on the Taj Mahal, for the Local Building Contractor" is set in conventional type (with minor variant readings). In the 4th ed., two essays are reset (with minor variants) in conventional type: "An Editorial for the Wise Man in the Metropolis Concerning the Humble Agricultural Village in Central Illinois" and "An Editorial for the Art Student Who Has Returned to the Village." The text of the 4th ed. is used here unless otherwise noted. The essays are reproduced with VL's spelling, punctuation, and capitalization.]

ON CONVERSION

In protracted meeting the burden of a certain kind of sin rolls off the shoulders as it did in PILGRIM'S PROGRESS, when Christian knelt at the cross. Priceless ecstasy often comes down from the clouds. I have gone through this convulsion, as have many of my friends, and it counts as a milestone on the journey. But there are other conversions, and other kinds of sin to be rid of. The pilgrimage to complete civilization is a long one. In America the repentance the Christian most needs is least mentioned in his hour of prayer. If he would truly be reconciled to God he must be rid of his sins against loveliness.

Villages as a whole are thus converted, when they go dry. Church bells are rung, the children march, the women pray. The boozers are black with wrath. But the place is inevitably converted from the stupidity and ugliness of the saloon. The citizens would stare if you told them they had been converted to the God of Beauty, yet they have taken the first great step in his praise.

The parsonages are repainted, more children's shoes are sold by the store around the corner, the Fourth of July procession is nearer to a pageant. There is increasing of laughter in the fields, less heartbreak in the dark. The village belles become sacred vestals. More good hats and dresses are seen, more flower gardens are planted. No man has read Shelley's ["]Hymn to Intellectual Beauty,["] no man has purchased a history of painting, a history of architecture, a textbook on landscape gardening or village improvement. Yet instinctively they build their altars to the unknown God, the radiant One, He whom ignorantly they worship should be declared unto them in his fullness.

[Punctuation in brackets added by editor; VL's spelling "ecstacy" corrected by editor.]

AN EDITORIAL ON THE HOLINESS OF BEAUTY
FOR THE VILLAGE PASTOR

Where there is loveliness . . . there is God

Some men think when they have said "consider the lilies" they have used the only proof-text that will establish the rights of the aesthetic in theology. That text they take in a weak way. The reason can be found by studying their parlors, where the idea of that which is fine has never stepped beyond some sugary Easter-card. They are ignorant of the rainbow color, the dignity, the sculptural line, of *The Book*. The gospels begin with the heavenly hosts singing of glory, with the Magnificat of Mary, with the gold frankincense and myrrh of the wise, and end with a blaze of Resurrection light. There is hardly a parable but is passionate with that adoration of nature which is the beginning of art. "Behold a sower went forth to sow." "I am the vine and ye are the branches." Such phrases build cathedrals.

Why should not the Bible make your village of heavenly aspect, as it has many an old-world town? Remember the Romanesque and Gothic architects, and repent.

Take up the worn book for this evening considering only those things which make for the peculiar fullness of life which is the goal of art. See how dry or puzzling texts take on power. Consider Adam, the park architect. Consider the tenderness, innocence and wildness of Eden in its first estate, which all Christian sweethearts dream they can restore. Consider man, made in the image of God, in the beginning a creator of star-worlds of his own, and the fall of man but a turning of the back upon loveliness, and a choosing to disobey the spirit that yet walks in quiet gardens in the cool of the day. Consider Moses, the Angelo of statesmanship, the inspired sculptor of the laws. Consider that the Decalogue gives the gentle buds of human nature a chance to bloom, sheltered from lust and covetousness and death. It is the intent of the Ten Commandments that all lovable things shall be nurtured to delight our eyes, with the *Presence* among them of which no image dare be made, on which no limitation can be set. The Sabbath is not a period of deadly inertia, but of artistic incubation, the time when Deity and man ponder some new world-dream. Consider Leviticus and Numbers champion a ministry, a peculiar priesthood, in which public health, national ritual and cleanliness are all bound together, to secure for the nation both holiness and splendor.

What is the Song of Songs but the cry of the lover of God-consecrated beauty? The book of Ecclesiastes is by an Omar Khayyam as stately as the Persian, in the end more devout, giving the final philosophy of the rose and the vine, an exhortation to consecrate the dear glory of youth in its beginning "Remember now thy Creator in the days of thy youth."

Consider David [,] harper, shepherd, ruddy and of a fair countenance. He was indeed from the village of Bethlehem, yet there he began the writing of Psalms more gorgeous than the church-pictures of Venice, and expressing in another medium, the same purpose: to worship the Lord with glorious works of art. Lest I should be suspected of writing a commentary, I go no further. Theology is not my specialty. And I hope I have not interfered with the theology of any parsonage. I hope each pastor will search this matter to the end in his own way, till, in the end he has a St. John's vision of the splendors of the new earth. Meanwhile, since your village is lovely, make it transcendently so, for the glory of the Lord.

[Punctuation in brackets added by editor. "INDEX" note in 2nd ed. (included in the "Table of Contents and General Elucidation" section of the 3rd and 4th eds.): "My good friend Harriet Monroe has done me the honor to frame this editorial and hang it in her office."]

AN EDITORIAL FOR THE WISE MAN IN THE METROPOLIS
CONCERNING THE HUMBLE AGRICULTURAL VILLAGE
IN CENTRAL ILLINOIS.

"Scene I A desert place enter three witches." Thus many people
would begin if they expressed their feelings about the village to which
they have not returned for fifteen years. And so certain smoke
smothered suburbs of the metropolis could be described but if any
have the notion that the Illinois agricultural town is today a
tobacco-soaked railway station, surrounded by "general" stores,
they are to be immediately surprised the blasted heath is no
more.   We will look out of the window in some region where corn,
wheat and sunshine are rampant. The sky-line of the shops a few rods
away, is jagged as of old but if we get off the train and go close, we
note that they no longer have rickety porches with loose boards and
nails. They have cement steps and platforms. The window displays
are pretty good. Within we find all neatly kept, with the same sort of
goods as the same sized trading places on one of the arteries of
Chicago. The old "general" emporiums. The James Whitcomb Riley
and A.B. Frost type linger along the street, but are going soon. Most
places have expanded into shining little department stores, or have
separated into the harness shop, the dry goods house, the
confectionery, and the like. Chewing tobacco is still for sale, but rural
free delivery has disbanded the Central Cuspidor Club that used to
tarnish yesterday's postoffice. Gossip itself is on a larger basis,
because of the country telephone, a peculiar device, differing from
the town telephone in that all the neighbors can talk to each other at
once. In the evening everyone takes down the receiver. The
conversation goes round the circle, as it used to do at the
post-office-store, but the group is larger, and the ladies join in. The
loafing is done at home.   The most fastidious customers use their
automobiles for quick shopping, and can get to the big town almost as
readily as to the village. The local merchant spruces up to keep their
trade, and welcomes the travelling salesmen of the best houses, who
haunt the erstwhile sleepy hotel. In the drug store window is just the
same high pile of the latest Collier's, McClure's, The American,
Everybody's, Success, Life, The Outlook and the rest that you find
around the corner in Los Angeles or San Francisco, Tampa or New
York.   We cannot walk down this row of buildings without passing
a newspaper office. When the rural editor asserts himself, as in the
Illinois Free Press, published at Litchfield, or the Fulton County

Democrat, published at Lewistown, he is indeed a joy. If we beg an armload of country exchanges, take them to the hotel and clip them for unique passages, we will be exhilarated and instructed. A great part of the local news is church news. There is too much of this to clip any of it. But if we seek out interesting bits of gossip, philosophy, and indications of civic patriotism, we will have some such a collection as follows. Some of the clippings will throw difficulties in the way of theories which I shall air afterward, but as Newman has said "Ten thousand difficulties do not make one doubt." The collection was made mainly last April with a few later additions. There could be found few better introductions to the outer court of the village, than the village paper.

[The following are newspaper clippings.]

THE BAYLIS GUIDE.

Philander Chaney, of New Salem, made his second delivery of Stark fruit trees at Baylis Friday and Saturday. The customers seemed well pleased and there were several extra trees with each order, even small orders. The Stark Nursery, of which he is agent, has some very choice varieties—not common—such as, of apples, Delicious, King David, Stayman, Wine Sap; of plums, the Gold and Shiro; they have also a fine variety of pears, peaches, cherries, etc.; of small fruits, Cumberland raspberry and other varieties, gooseberry, currents, grapes, ornamental hedge, etc.

Fulton County Democrat

The Oquawka Journal says the Jake Bricker farm near Rozetta has 15 Genitian apple trees that are so heavily loaded that if nothing happens to them between now and fall they will yield at least 150 bushels. That is something unusual in Illinois this fall.

Sheriff Basel with his wamus on, in his bare feet and with a yawn consented that out-door Sunday evening union meetings could be held in front of the court house during the heated term.

A traveling man whose route takes him to many cities in several states said to this editor the other day: "You have not the most prosperous town I know, but you do have more real pretty and well-behaved young girls than I ever saw in a city of near Lewistown's population. There must be something peculiar in the climate here, or in some other important feature of your city's environments." The editor could only reply: "It's been so for 60 years."

West Point Journal

Geo. W. Bailey holds the palm for potatoes. On Monday of this week, while plowing in his garden he plowed up a peck of Early Ohio potatoes that were planted last spring. They were not over six inches from the surface and are large and firm and as fine as any potato that ever went on the table. —Carthage Republican.

Gee. That's nothing, we stuck a fork into a hill of potatoes yesterday, which had been in the ground all winter, and eleven bushels ran out before we could stop up the hole. —Carthage Democrat.

Charles Rice of Durham came after a load of lumber Wednesday and used a six horse team. That is the most horses we have seen hitched in one regular team in a long time. It reminds one of the teams the freighters use in the west. If his wagon tongue held out he got home all right as he had six cracker jacks of horses.

Carthage Republican

Donald Stewart showed us an old lion cage on his farm. It is used as an oat bin at present. "Van Amberg's Circus and Menagerie", can be plainly read on it yet. Mr. Clark, who owned the farm before the Stewart's, bought the cage from the old circus, forty or fifty years ago some say. Geo. Garrett says the show had a riot with the sawmill men at Montrose and got all "whipped to pieces" and had to pull out for Carthage in the night, at which latter place Mr. Clark bought the cage. How about it Mr. Editor and when was it. We will venture that there is not another rat bin like it in Hancock county and probably not in the state.

Meredosia Budget

The thrill of spring now runs along the backbone of the calf. He'll buck and dance upon the mead and hoist his hinder calf. He'll dream of blooming clover fields and waving curly dock, gambol with his rigid tail stuck up at 6 o'clock. The blithesome meadow lark will sing the glories of the dawn and the robins will turn somersets upon the greening lawn. The spring intoxicated colt will do-si-do about, the festive frog will wake up to help the Weather Bureau out, the poor consumer will rejoice and hope for better luck, and the trusts will sit around and damn the coming garden truck. —Sounds like Bliss.

Fulton County Democrat

A business man tells us that during the rush trade of a Saturday one lady kept a clerk two hours trying to fit her with a pair of shoes while several customers could not be waited upon. On the following Monday this lady brought back the shoes she had worn all day, because they pinched her feet, and changed them for a new pair. The scuffed shoes are still on hands. This dealer belongs to Bro. Cleaver's church and can't properly express his views of that customer.

Illinois Free Press

On The Fence.

I want to charm the mayor,
  And the corporation, too;
I want to please the whiskey men,
  Yet keep the church in view.
It's business sense to suit the dry,
  And not offend the wet;
So I'm going to trim between the two,
  And suit em both, you bet.
O, it's the fence for mine
  To save my precious skin;
I'll not come out, on either side,
  Till I see which one will win.
Two years ago, I tried this plan,
  But it did'nt seem to work;
The whiskey men looked doubtful,
  And the drys called me a shirk;
But I'm satisfied the scheme is right,
  It's got to work, by Jing!
So it's "whoop-hurray" for both of them
  I'll make the echoes ring,
For it's the fence for mine,
  I'll save my precious skin:
And not declare for either side
  Till I see which one will win.

Fulton County Democrat

Mt. Pleasant, the ancient Indian battle ground of Fulton county, forever until the crack of doom, no doubt, will keep up its traditions, by spells, as the storm center of human cussedness in Fulton county. No better people live than the farmers about that commanding bluff of the Illinois river. But the youngsters just so often have to "blow off steam," or have it blow off their heads. That explains why some of the grandest soldiers of the civil war came from that section, with brave old Corporal Lem Potts, to carry the flag into Dixie. Mt. Pleasant had not been in eruption for a long time until on a recent Sunday evening when the Epworth League was in session with 10 or 15 older people present. We are told that some ungodly imp invaded the scene to settle, then and there, between the earnest prayers and sweet old songs, the dire problem as to some neighborhood tittle-tattle. There were, we are told, harsh and awful words and threats, for the house of God. And some fierce sinner pealed off his coat and offered to "lick the feller (or felleress) who had said so and so." But no blood was shed. The old editor has been in two or three Mt. Pleasant shindies. We know it is very improper to confess the fact—that the preachers will condemn this attitude—but from ancient inherited cussedness he always feels aggrieved and lonesome when he misses Mt. Pleasant in eruption.

The Barry Record
   An attention has been called by different ones to the littered and untidy condition of our alleys, and a hope expressed that the Record would impress upon the people the need of each property owner and tenant looking after their premises and making them as presentable as possible. All should have civic pride enough to do this, as it not only means health and cleanliness for our citizens, but makes a good impression on all strangers who visit our city.

The Rushville Times
   —Rushville people who have visited the city cemetery this spring have noted and commented upon the fine work done there by Ross McKee, the sexton, and since the new addition has been put under fence it adds greatly to the attractiveness of the whole cemetery. Mr. McKee has just completed the job of building 130 rods of wire fence, and he has seeded the two plowed ridges on the south to oats and clover to keep down the weeds.

Carthage Democrat
   —One of the cannons recently received by the G.A.R. of this city has been mounted and was this afternoon placed in a commanding position in the public square at the northeast corner of the court house.

Clayton Enterprise

So far as dirt roads are concerned, the modest simple inexpensive split log drag is the main solution. But it must be worked by a man with some brains. The time to do the business is in the spring and early summer. A days work now is worth six days' next fall.

Hull Enterprise

Some Cleaner Anyhow.

———————

The clean-up day got many an old can, bottle, broken dish, etc., off the streets and alleys. There were some who took the notice lightly and did not prepare the junk for hauling, but most residents appreciate the effort of the town board and gathered up the rubbish in convenient places.

West Point Journal

West Point is a modern town, the size being considered, as can be found in this section of the state. We boast of having better side walks and more concrete ones than any town of this size in Hancock or the surrounding counties. When a stranger comes to town we take him around to see ''our'' electric light plant and boast on what good service they are giving us.

A few days ago a gentleman went to a residence in this town and seeing an electric light switch beside the door, took it to be a door bell attachment. No amount of turning would get any response, so he finally knocked on the door.

Dallas City Review

J.E. Williams county superintendent of schools, was a visitor to our city Thursday and made us a pleasant call. Mr. Williams is a candidate for renomination as will be seen by an announcement in another column. During his administration of that office he has builded up the schools of the county in a most favorable manner. He has also started in to learn the rising generation how to raise corn; and if through his efforts the yield of corn in Hancock county could be raised ten bushels per acre his name would be handed down to future generations.

Fulton County Democrat

The streets are a whole lot handsomer and more comfortable, thanks to Street Superintendent Braden.

Every evening the court house square is pretty well crowded with men, women and children with no other attraction than to meet a sober, orderly, well dressed and handsome company. The hotter the evenings, the bigger the crowd, because it is pleasanter in the breezy square than even in pleasant homes.

Particularly jolly are the many happy babies in their go-carts that enliven the scene. And of such is the kingdom of heaven!

The old editor once in a while has a sudden desire to be rich—very rich. It's when a sweet country or town girl passing him on the street with a rare smile drawls out her delicious' salutation: "Howdy d-i-e-w!" we then wish to be rich so that one by one we could give each of these dear girls a shining silver dollar.

Hull Enterprise

Tony, The Convict.

———————————

Tony, The Convict, was put on at the city hall by a home talent company of New Canton Tuesday night and was quite a pleasing event. A number of short readings between acts by one of the young ladies, was the main feature of the evenings entertainment.

———————————

The County Scribe

We people of Birmingham feel that we are fortunate again. Through the efforts of our school an evening's entertainment of the *strictest* order has been billed for this town, on Saturday evening, April 16th. The trio, who will give the program, are known as the State Normal Entertainers.

The Mendon Dispatch

—The play, "Arthur Eustes, or a Mother's Love," given by the Mendon Dramatic Club Saturday evening at the opera house drew a good audience. Those taking part did well, having their parts well committed. Emmett Ebrgott, as the Dutchman, kept the audience in a roar of laughter. If some of the players would talk louder it would be much better.

Griggsville Press

The city council at its meeting Monday night, decided to permit the children to skate on the sidewalks with their roller skates within a block of the business section. This is the right thing to do, as it is healthfᵤl exercise for the youngsters but they should not take advantage of the privilege by monopolizing the walks. The council also voted to contract for the purchase of cement for the construction of walks this spring, and also to make a new contract with the electric company for lighting the streets of the city.

Last Friday was Winn apple day in the city schools, when C.G. Winn presented the pupils with two barrels of lucious apples. The quantity was sufficient for each child to have several of them and all enjoyed the treat immensely. Mr. Winn also made an interesting and instructive talk before the pupils of the north building, concerning his late trip through the west. — Griggsville Press.

Calhoun County Republican
Won't Mix.

With all the splendid advice which has been written about the "uplift of the farmer" there has not been much of an uncomplimentary character; and yet the following probably represents the views of many a far-seeing farmer.

"If city people think things are so all-fired fine on the farms," writes Mr. Benning, a South Dakota Farmer, "why don't they pack up and try it? Attractions of farm life are dreams, and nobody has them except city folks, Life on the farm is hard work year in and year out, and nobody but a millionaire could get anything else out of it. If I had money enough I could enjoy life, in the meanwhile the farm would go to pot. But I want to tell you that if I had money enough to enjoy life on a farm I would go to the city to do it. And I reckon that if all the farmers in this country came into possession of such an amount of money at the same time there would'nt be population enough left in three weeks to bring the cows home.

And about this transfer of labor from the factories to the farms; it will never take place. I hired a young man who was a clerk in a wholesale drug establishment. His job wasn't agreeing with his health and he decided to become a farmer. Now, the country is no place for broken down humanity unless they have money enough to pay their board, and even then salt meat in hot water is likely to disturb their digestive organs. This young man I hired had to work for his living. He had the grit, too, and stuck to his task in the field until he fell of exhaustion, and we never knew there was anything the matter with him.

I got the doctor, and he sent the clerk back to the city. He told him the only work he was fit for was store work. And not only that, but the young man pined for excitement all the time he was at my place, and I could see with half an eye that he would'nt keep at farming.

It's fine talk the people are making who want to uplift the farm, but they have got in the wrong stall. The only way country life could be improved would be to do away with about half the work. I don't think that is possible. Farm work is different from other work. It takes more time. Machinery has made a great change, but I don't believe there can be many more inventions that will reduce the amount of work. Cows must be milked and pigs must be fed. There will always be the haying in haying time and harvesting in harvesting time — too much work in the summer and plenty in the winter.

My wife says she's used to work and that's why she can stay on the farm. She says she doesn't want to attend any art classes or play bridge. She says if she did want to play bridge and such things, she would go to the city to do it.

It seems to me that it isn't possible to improve country life by injecting city life into it. The two won't mix.

Meredosia Budget

Not so many years ago "farmer" was about as scornful a slang term as could be applied to anybody who blundered, stumbled, or "got in bad." But what would the average man in the streets say to-day if somebody shouted to him "You farmer?" Wouldn't he throw his chest out and spring a smile as braod as if he owned a gold mine? He certainly would. The farmer doesn't wear his hayseed in his hair any longer. He sells it and buys an automobile. And when doctor, lawyer, merchant, chief, point their finger at him and say, "You're it," he merely throws in the speed clutch and smiles back along the wind.

The LaHarper
Helpful Citizens.
The most humble citizen can be most helpful in building up the town and its business enterprises if he will. When we see the goods piled up on our station platform from the mail order houses of the larger cities for our farmer friends, we wonder that it is so. Surely no man owning a farm within the trading circle of LaHarpe, but what knows the value of that farm is largely in being in close proximity to a good town. The better the town the greater value is the land about it. We heard of a humble citizen, a laborer, whose income is not large, as he depends wholly upon his skill and labor to carry on his contract work, yet this man turned in over $5,000 last year to our merchants. He got every dollar of his supplies from home dealers. He could have gone to other towns or to the city for his supplies, but he was and is patriotic enough to give support to home dealers and build up the town and thereby enhance his own property values. This is no idle assertion but facts. The same patriotic concern from all the farmers and others, would make our town almost self-supporting and bring prosperity and profit to all. The few dollars saved, if there is any saving, in buying from home, is lost in the conditions which follow the trading from home habit. We know our merchants can meet all competition if given the opportunity.

Fulton County Democrat
The Cuba baseball "Cubs" have won everyone of the nine games played this season with teams from larger cities. Cuba is very proud of its triumphant athletes. Yet there would be a nice taste in the mouths of many excellent Cuba men and women if the boys would cut out the Sunday games. Pastor Zeller makes this confession and very considerate appeal to members of his church:
"It has been reported (by people who should not attend Sunday base ball themselves) that some of the members of the Christian church are found at the game Sunday afternoons. There is no command in the New Testament which reads Keep holy the Sunday. However, we know that God has always required one-seventh of our time for spiritual development, and there is certainly not much of that at a Sunday baseball game. Sunday games are for people who make no profession of Christianity, and they bring no shame to the church by attending Sunday baseball. But my brother or sister in the church, what influence can you hope to exercise for Christ with your neighbor when he knows you are out rooting for the ball team on Sunday? Think it over."

[VL's essay resumes here.]

These are brave words for a pastor to his recreant church members.

No other organization in rural life can compare with the church. In the city a woman can belong to endless secular sisterhoods. Even a man can be member of a political gang, a socialist local, a labor union, a dancing set, a literary society, a board of directors, an athletic club. But on the prairie the church has no rivals. She is in a sense, every one of these, in herself.   It is after the traveller has walked *three blocks from the railroad and the business section* that he encounters the public square, verdant as paradise, planted thick with maples, enshrining a sturdy band-stand, with tolerably clean youngsters playing all about. Across the streets, towering over fairy cottages, are the Methodist, Baptist, Presbyterian and Disciple meeting-houses. These are the sentinels of the scene, *and the arbiters of the community's destiny.*   Why is everything so lovely? There are no stores. The yards are deep, with no fences. Roses, poppies and hollyhocks come in season. Cement sidewalks, of which every village statesman boasts at this hour, add a touch of unifying gray, and provide against the rainy day with a sense of anticipated coziness. They lead out to the nearest farm houses, that are always white, with barns always red, fences always in order, with immense, well mowed yards, having little pretense of flower beds, but stately and rich with evergreens. And there may be near by a really big park, that is a camping ground in summer, where the very lords of chautauqua appear. As we look further down the road, then out over the vast fields, flat as the ocean at dead calm, we acknowledge that Illinois can still be called a prairie state, but as we return to the square, top heavy with trees, passing the side streets with reverend avenues planted by the first settlers, we realize that the word no longer means desolation.   Simplicity and space, and shade and soft grass, and cozy houses and clean walks and serene steeples may make no lasting impression if we visit only one square. But after invading several score, they form a sort of landscape gardening system in the memory, a panorama of civilized democracy from villages near Danville across the state to villages near Quincy only in coal mining townlets is the charm broken. There is an unconscious birth of beauty in the agricultural hamlet that gives one who has searched long for the key to democracy's beauty-sense, and watched patiently for her art development, a hope and an inspiration, and on some bright spring Sunday noon, if we return to the square, and all those churches, like great cornucopias, pour forth processions of cupid-like babes, virgins in floating white and heroically built men—to · the man with faith in his land, hope has become prophecy.   But let us take off our wings, and in an every-day way study the church ascendency. These four denominations represent old feuds. Curious indeed are the theological discussions we could unearth if we chose. Yet the paramount fact is the unity and not the separateness of the church, in the social system. When traditional quarrels persist, the preachers often conspire to have their way, unobserved. Thus church entertainments, protracted meetings, lectures and socials are apt to be arranged so as not to conflict. The town, en masse is the guest of each group in turn, and no matter what side a man takes in theology, he is somewhere enmeshed in the omnipresent social net. Not only, at a crisis, does united Christendom vote the town dry, and finance a law and order crusade, but every hour the pastors are leaving their marks for culture and cleanness upon some raw rebellious element of the place. They are the embodiment of the public opinion which wins year in and year out. Religious revival, which in its rhythm of reappearance makes the main drama of village existence, completely floods out and drowns any last remnant of opposition.   The pastor's library is mostly those new world-books, paper-covered, but systematic, scholarly and electrical, representing the evangelization of all nations in this generation, the new sort of Bible-study classes, Sunday School methods, the sociological crisis in the cities in its relation to the church, the year-book of the militant Anti-Saloon league; and the rest is commentaries. Fed from this library, he thunders at the community, of a Sunday, in the voice of the wide religious world. In short, he is the same pastor we meet in the city, but has the advantage of no competition from other orators. Even when he seeks to be in abeyance for awhile, the church as an institution looms up, still testifying to the importance of things spiritual.   Few people stop to think what an all around human appeal is furnished by the meeting house machinery. There is the graded Sunday School where one can join a class of one's own years and kind, be they chirping children, or moralizing middle aged mothers. In the dry towns the Young Men's Bible Classes are full, and almost every small town in Illinois is dry. But the Bible Class for older men is the institution we would emphasize. There gather the very fathers of the township, patriarchs of weight, and prosperity, to read of Paul before Agrippa, or Christ feeding the multitude. The discussion begins timidly and stupidly. But often in the end these great human engines are at work on these matters with full power, revealing the seasoned philosophy and high mysticism of their nobly disciplined lives.   The Sunday School is only one device. There is the Pastor's Aid Society, the

Missionary Society, the W.C.T.U., the Endeavor Society, The Men's Brotherhood, the Church Social.   Let us look closer at the Church Social. Here is entertainment for all but the too-proud or the too-bookish. The spirit of the occasion is that of rejoicing before the Lord. Everyone is well dressed, no one too well. The small boys play tag, and get in everyone's way. They jostle against the prim little girls, that stand in conversational half-circles, spreading their fluffy skirts. Pretty soon the able-bodied persons from seven till seventy form a big circle and play Jacob and Ruth, which game can become a wild scramble or a graceful pantomine, according to the moods of the ever-changing couples in the center. It is a kind of natural dancing, *not* so called. This game dissolves into spin the plate, or drop the handkerchief. Meanwhile people having enough exercise drift into the chairs at the side. The committee takes the hint, and a little girl recites for the flushed company; maybe the Sunday School Superintendent exhibits himself as an impromptu story-teller. Subsequently ice cream and cake are passed around by a committee, mainly the young converts, aware that this is a sort of happy initiation. Meanwhile the old folks gossip about the grand-children, and the grand-children about their dolls, while the mists of romance swim before the eyes of the sets of boys and girls of match-making age. The more conventional news of the day is roared from mouth to mouth till the hall is like a cave of the sea, while all the passions in Shakespere lie underneath the so called gossip that flies on stealthy wings.   Now a long table is made from the short tables and two companies are formed and a great game of Jenkins is started. When the crowd is in fine nervous fettle on each side, the art of finding the quarter becomes the trick of captains with second sight, which the captains actually develop, to their own astonishment.   While this evening was young there waited outside on the steps the boys not yet converted. Maybe they threw in a bit of gravel or a potato for the humor of the thing, but more likely they peeped in with high-beating hearts and lumps in their throats. In the city, in such a situation, some one could say, "Come on fellows, let's go to the Devil," or words of that kind, and the inevitable bar room with its leering cordiality would claim them for the night. But here, in the saloonless village, they still haunt the social. No other lights are as bright as these. Sooner or later the ring-leader sneaks in and joins the Jacob and Ruth circle or the Jenkins game. All his Godly kin are lying in wait. An angel-hearted girl, maybe, is watching without seeming to watch. The pastor does not allow the incident to escape him. And the fellow, erstwhile intractable as a Mexican broncho is converted before the next protracted meeting is over. His gang have nothing to do but meekly follow suit. To continue to be Devil's advocate argues an individuality worthy of a bronze medal.   The church has a code of daily conduct that is passionately espoused by the young convert. He never turns entirely away from it, though it seems to fade in off seasons. It is actually the trellis upon which his soul grows, however, he may weave in and out. It is a system of being bad and good. The sinners have their points of conduct as well as the saints.   The children are in two sets from infancy, the one composed of those who run the streets after dark, wild little satyrs, and the other group the more sober stay-at-homes, who take to the code from the cradle. Both go regularly to Bible School. That Sunday truce is part of the game. Saint and sinner are apt to be intimate friends. They cannot be gradually separated as in the city, with the saloon dominating one group and the church the other. Conversion comes to all alike, from fifteen to eighteen, as naturally as marriage a little later. Almost all settle down to sober maturity.   It is the proper thing for half grown male sinners to be quite shabbily or quite loudly dressed, get drink by express, play cards interminably. They organize dances when it is possible, but they cannot get the people they like best to come. They indulge in semi-clandestine amours with the more reckless girls. They conform to the full pattern of iniquity by going to the city and bringing back sodden tales of adventure. Yet they would never think of shooting up a store as in the west, or fighting knife-duels, as in the mountains of the south.   The respectable young lady, not yet converted, and technically a sinner, will not dance, and indicates her technical sinfulness by saying she wishes her folks would let her. She has no testimony to offer at Epworth League or Christian Endeavor. She indulges in reckless speech against the saints, and allows the wild young men, who make bold to get drunk, to think they are heroes. She is willing to be seen with them more than a new convert could possibly approve. Repentance is bound to smite her in time. She is constantly exposed to the lightning of the Lord.   While the saints must abstain from the city theatre and vaudeville, while they are supposed to avoid as a pestilence, the dance, Sunday baseball and playing cards, they are accorded all the privileges of the town. Their joys are many. They attend the band concerts, lectures, kinetescope shows, recitals; take part in amateur theatricals, Christmas and Easter entertainments, fish frys, log rollings, and taffy pullings. They are permitted by the holy inquisition, known otherwise as the Sewing Society, to go to ice cream soda fountains, week-day baseball, kissing parties, buggy rides, hay rides, skating rinks. They may read anything they please, gossip, and if boys, they can swear mildly and chew tobacco unobtrusively.   Oh, big city wise man, while you are permitted to smile, you must not sit in the seat of the scorner. Judge the game as a whole. Every constitution and by-laws is arbitrary, with queer details it is as dangerous to try surgery upon as the birthmark in Hawthorne's tale. The rules of baseball, of the Chinese court, of West Point, of the Talmud, must be respected in their place. The true soul asks, "Is the game played with spirit?" "Does it make them happy?" "Is the seasoned player a credit to human nature?"

Once conversion, maturity and marriage are reached, there are a multitude of enterprises the village code does not hinder. In fact, it represents the tastes and limitations of the average married folks; it is an instinctive device to get the passionate aspiring and rebellious young safely to the threshold of the householder period. After that comes farm making, family building, road dragging, street making, politics and the like, all mellowed and sanctified by the church, without any specific provisions.   The principal world-criticism of the cross-roads-meeting-house ideal round which this system is built, is that it has produced only *one* type of man. I meet an example of him in most any small place. The other males are only variations. The father of his people, often the grand-father, towering and sunburned, he has gradually developed from the man who farms with his feet to the man who farms with his brain. Maybe he has reached the class of "retired farmers." There is a powerful kind of city potentate whose education is complete when he leaves college, who at forty appears to have thrown to Moloch most of the fair fancies he should have cherished. He exhausts most of his idealism in being legal in business. If we are to judge by the kind of metropolis he makes, there is little fine flavor or rich depth in the meditations of his age. But this other leader of men, this teacher of the Farmers' Bible Class and chairman of the prayer meeting committee and the board of trustees of the village church, has found a means of development in his mere citizenship in state and church. In his soul is the decalogue, the Declaration of Independence and the Constitution of the United States. If you want to arouse him, appeal to these, and not to any new doctrine. He knows why thunder came from Horeb, and why the Civil War was fought. If you want his political allegiance, argue the present crisis from something Andrew Jackson said. His position as a stubborn and perpetual dry voter is an integral part of his adamant Americanism. He is nearer to the ancient Roman type of farmer-patriot that the fathers of the republic had in mind, than any other breathing man. Rugged though he is, the choirs of village belles in their white dresses, the endless rows of sweet-faced grand-children in the infant class, singing the praises of God in little voices are the most cherished of the white harvests of his life. Because he is in line with our simple democratic traditions, and gets his education from the four seasons and the Book of God and the open sky, and has been doing so for a century, he is in line for his final development. There are endless subtle touches of maturity. All signs show, that in this generation or the next, the century plant will bloom. He and his fathers have constructed the vistas of neat homes, that make every street. He and his kin have planted these brooding trees, have laid out the square, now so smoothly rolled. He has financed the new school building, the electric light plant, the chautauqua grounds, the new town hall. Out of his secret soul comes the sense of space, cleanliness, and permanency that pervades the square. He was on the committee that laid the cement walks binding the whole village together with one grey ribbon. His taste has raised in strong and severe style these sentinel church buildings. Because of these, his accumulated labors, done in one spirit through many years, the air is saturated with tantalizing spiritual suggestion. All signs cry, "Tomorrow, Tomorrow!" These villages are the fortunate islands in the wild sea of commerce. In one or two rare moments they have brought to me the elusive charm of dead and immortal Hellas with such a different root and stalk the perfume was the same once or twice as I have spoken, as is my custom, in their pulpits, looking down into the Sabbath-stilled faces of the young, the whole place was turned to a nowhere of ivory and gold; that bright army of perfectly carved countenances became Greek before my eyes, though mine was a mighty Puritan cause. The church became a wonderland pervaded by the trance of classic, not Hebraic immortality. While quoting with all my heart the invectives of the prophets, there ran through my fancy Swinburne's mesmeric lines:

"The bountiful infinite west, the happy memorial places
Full of the stately repose and the Lordly delight of the dead,
Where the fortunate islands are lit with the light of ineffable faces
And the sound of a sea without wind is about them, and sunset is
    red."

You say "overdone;" you object; you insist the church is an everyday place. Yes, but there is something in her everydayness that makes higher vision possible.   There was, no doubt, in new England such an atmosphere as this just before she ripened. I anticipated that many things will soon happen in the villages that will grieve and puzzle the Sewing Society. There is a chance that not only simple loveliness, but a supreme unique culture will ripen under these trees. It is my hope that it will be a culture even more of the eye than of the mind.   Some one of these villages, apparently no more sensitive than the rest, is going to be gradually aware of herself, is going to take special pains with her talented children. Teaching them, no matter how far they explore the world for special training, to concentrate the finest product of their matured life to their birthplace. Some village pastor is going to have a vision of his responsibility as the custodian of a ripening civilization, and the developer of the special personality of a town, as well as the watchdog of its morals. He will search for the divine fires of artistic impulse as well as the tears of social repentance in the eyes of the wilder children of the place.   Not always will the talented prodigal remain in the big city in the forlorn hope to conquer it with sculpture and song. Amid the clangors of babel, amid the husks of commerce, he will be perishing with beauty-hunger, and return at length to his own people. He and his comrades will bring with them crafts, song, landscape gardening, painting, drama, architecture. The town certainly will tolerate these and adopt them in time, and consecrate each as a means of grace as she has the electric light and the cement sidewalk.   Oh, wise man of the noise-world, you know industrial civilization has bitter war immediately ahead, but do you know that in the village is being conserved already that loveliness which may heal the wounded and bind up the broken-hearted?

["INDEX" note in 2nd ed. (included in the "Table of Contents and General Elucidation" section of the 3rd and 4th eds.): "The above is the principal editorial of the first imprint of The Village Magazine 1910. It is perhaps interesting, because it quotes from many newspapers of the Spoon River Region, four years before the Anthology appeared. They help to indicate what I have always maintained, that Edgar Lee Masters and myself see Central Illinois with much the same eyes. The editorial for the Wise Man in the metropolis does not express my present view of American civilization. I was much nearer to Masters in 1914 when Spoon River appeared, than in 1910 when this editorial was written."

The 2nd, 3rd, and 4th eds. include in the margins eleven plates from VL's *The Spring Harbinger* (see *Poetry,* pp. 77-82).]

TAJ MAHAL
AGRA INDIA.
M.V.LINDSAY.
1906.

AN EDITORIAL ON THE TAJ MAHAL,
FOR THE LOCAL BUILDING
CONTRACTOR

I copied this, the Taj Mahal, from a photograph, adding the border that some of the page might be my own. I have never visited the place except in spirit, yet I almost see that famous dome when I turn my eyes toward Dawn, toward the eternal, richly varied East, where faith is weird and tremendous, where Islam waits her judgment day, where man is ever old.

Friend, let us toil that this our raw and rasping western nation may be redeemed, and wear such white robes of marvel, such minarets of quiet snow. Through our great missionaries we send the East the gospel of brotherhood. Let us not be too full of spiritual self-sufficiency. Let us receive in return from them the silent gospel of beauty. It is not that we are to imitate these special forms, or carry on the Arabesque tradition. We are rather to interpret our own land in that rare hour when it is serene. Let it remain the free young West, yet become a land where sacred rivers have place.

Build for that day the cross-roads church, the lone farm house, the wooden bridge. Seemingly perishable materials, if wrought with rejoicing and love, can make indeed a deathless land. The place whose tiny town hall is a gem, will be prepared against making its first skyscraper a Tower of Babel and a blasphemy.

AN EDITORIAL FOR THE LOCAL STATESMAN,
WHEN THE CROSS-ROADS BECOMES A BIG CITY.

Some day the place outgrows itself. Some day they cease fighting about the mayor's hens, that scratched the Baptist minister's flower bed, and legislating about the hitchrails around the public square. The mayor buys his chicken. The hitchrails are gone forever[.] The town also outlives a part of that spontaneous bloom which this book seeks to cherish; and the honorable deliberation which might have been made the basis of a true philosophy, the leisure which might have given birth to classic design, are seemingly destroyed by the stridencies of trade and graft. The churches now have competition in temples frankly dedicated to Moloch and insanity; Mammon, Astarte and all their abominations.

Though the place seems a small Chicago trimmed in brass, it is not completely destroyed. I have often been thrilled and comforted by hearing natives describe our Springfield, for instance, as "a little, overgrown country town." As long as such is the case, she is still at the parting of the ways, and can turn from the broad road that leadeth to Chicago, and take the narrow one that leadeth to green fields and mystery, and eternal life.

Yet wait. It seems to me I have heard even Chicago described as "a little overgrown country town." As long as such is her case, in any phase of her life, we can hope on. Let her controlling citizens visit the villages whence they came, and surprise themselves with the growing spiritual treasuries there[.] Then let them consider how such grace can abound in Chicago.

[Punctuation in brackets added by editor. This essay is not included in 2nd, 3rd, and 4th eds.]

AN EDITORIAL FOR THE ART STUDENT WHO HAS
RETURNED TO THE VILLAGE.

No matter what your study, if you pursued it to the bitter end, you found yourself lured from Chicago to New York. Thence you were led to London, Paris, Berlin or Munich. The only thing that could hold you back was lack of funds. Assuming you went this path, as so many of my acquaintances have done you finally found yourself in culture, a citizen of Europe.   The first two sentences of the Gettysburg address are graven on every native soul. So you have come back all the way to the old home. Many good patriots, not knowing the treasures accumulating at the cross-roads since they left, have compromised on New York or Chicago. They are an example to you in your hours of defeat, for they are happy in the cities. Many sensitive fellows keep laughing, though they use all their strength to produce delicate, highly wrought work. To be true to democracy is also their task, as they know. They fail, but smile.   It is *indeed difficult to discover the taste of the man in the street. He seems, from the standpoint of culture, to be a mechanical toy, amused by clockwork.* He is clipped to a terrible uniformity by the sharp edges of life. He knows who won the last baseball game and who may be the next president. He knows the names of the grand opera singers he has heard on the phonograph. He turns over luxuriously in his subconscious soul the tunes he has heard on the self-playing piano in front of the vaudeville theatre. He will read a poem if it is telegraphed across the country, with a good newspaper story to start it. All of his thinking is done by telegraph and fancies that are too delicate to be expressed by the comic supplement seldom reach him. Dominated by a switch-board civilization, he moves in grooves from one clock-work splendor to another. He reads the same set of magazines from New York to San Francisco. The magazines are great, yet they make for uniformity.   What a task then has the conscientious art-democrat, to find the individual, delicate, immortal soul of this creature, dressed in a Hart, Schaffner and Marx suit and trying to look like a Hart, Schaffner and Marx advertisement! *For the most part, the really trained man can find little common ground.* When Poe's poems went the rounds of the newspapers, when the World's Fair stirred the land for a season, when the servant in the house had his triumph, when Markham for a moment was heard, democracy and art seemed to meet. But think of the thousands of enterprises just as fine, but lacking advertising value, or mere size, that have been scornfully ignored by Mister Hart, Schaffner-Marx! *They were poured forth with joy; by the European standard they would have been immortal. By our relentless standard, which we can never escape, they are valueless as the dollar bills of the Southern Confederacy.*   The city craftsmen who have really embraced the problem of the mob, determined to be masters whether they are Orthodox or not, are to be commended. They are on the whole as well placed as the village designer, but no more so. It is a noble thing to build a successful skyscraper, but there will be the same art laughter in your heart if you give some grace to the wheat elevator at the way-station. Once in a while an O. Henry becomes a story writer, still remaining a journalist, exquisitely combining the two. But it is just as exquisite and meritorious a thing to edit the Fulton County Democrat at Lewistown.   Our most conspicuous advertising and magazine artists, men of immense ingenuity turn out a sort of cover design that could be stepped on by a fire-engine horse, shot through by currents from an electric chair, run through a rolling mill, pushed off a tower or baked in a pie and come out still singing, like the four and twenty blackbirds. And in all seriousness this work has chances to survive the centuries, along with the pyramids because it expresses precisely the mood of high-class-ready-made-clothing-democracy. It is just like Chicago, where Adams meets Randolph Street. It is as near to history as anything written by Ida Tarbell.   We who want to be democrats, yet avoid these phases, have an opportunity in the cross-roads that gave us birth. There we can be true to grand-father's log cabin and at the same time remember the Erectheum and the Temple of Nikko. There we meet the real citizen, three generations before he is ironed out into a mechanical toy. *His crudity is plain, but his delicacy is apparent also. His sound culture-tendencies and false tendencies can be sorted out.* At home we encounter institutions just beginning to bloom, absolutely democratic, yet silken and rich; no two villages quite alike, all with chances of developing intense uniqueness, *while all the rest of America speaks one iron speech.*   Of course staying at home has its drawbacks. Your work goes down, technically, through lack of the skilled criticism you once knew. You lose some chances of recognition from the growing art circles of the metropolis. *But your life is now thoroughly dedicated to the proposition that all men are created equal in taste. You are engaged in a joyous Civil War testing whether your work, or any work so conceived and so dedicated can long endure. Just as much real civilization hangs upon your success as hung upon the fighting of the private soldier at Gettysburg.*   Oh, all you students that I have loved, whose work I have enviously admired, who are now back home grubbing at portraits, though they are not your specialty; or designing billboards, though they are not your divine call; or acting on the committee to paper the church and buying bad paper to please them; or back on the home newspaper that will not often print your short novels; or singing in the old choir for no salary at all; or composing advertisements in the real estate office and neglecting your lyrics; or taking charge of the Sunday School orchestra and curing them of the Moody-Sankey habit—greeting, and God-speed to you! If you have any cherished beauty-enterprise, undertake it where you are. *You will find no better place in all America.*   It is easier for me to preach than to cut the grass in my own front yard. It is easier to hand out art advice than to make a first rate irrelevant section. Maybe the interest of this work depends upon the irrelevant departments, yet there as elsewhere my lettering is rude, my drawing thin, my verse uneven. However casual the magazine, I hope you like it. Oh game and joyous craftsman, it is likely that I will enjoy whatever *you* attempt that comes under *my* eye. Whether you are making a picture or a book, a newspaper, a tombstone or a statue, a park, a skating rink or a world's fair, I will grant you your thesis, accept your intention, laugh at your joke, frown at your sermon, find light where your ecstacy is recorded, from where the love of form is shown, line where line begins to display its power, and color where the edge of the rainbow begins to gleam.

["INDEX" note in 2nd ed. (included in the "Table of Contents and General Elucidation" section of the 3rd and 4th eds.): "Edward J. Wheeler filled me with pride and vanity by quoting this editorial in Current Literature." Wheeler's essay, "Illinois Art Revivalist," was published in *Current Literature* (March 1911), pp. 320-323.

The 2nd, 3rd, and 4th eds. include in the margins four plates from VL's *The Spring Harbinger* (see *Poetry,* pp. 77-82).]

A CALL FOR LETTERS.

The less you agree with the underlined parts of the address to the art-student, the more the perpetrator will be pleased. Do him the service to analyze your objections, and write them out. Be explicit: firstly, secondly, thirdly and tenthly. He will welcome essays ten pages long. The editor wants your notion of a visible civilization. He hopes to expand those propositions in the art student editorial to a treatise of much greater length, reconstructed, to meet good critics half way. The editor will take the same pains and pleasure, in classifying and studying the letters, that he has in producing the present magazine. As a matter of fact, he suspects that an ample reply from his readers is the main sober justification for thus much printer's ink. This is, of course, the first and last number of The Village Magazine. The editor hopes to make his next essay not only a reply to your every letter, but a treatise ripe enough to win publication in the conventional ways.

Bad habits are stubborn, but The Village Magazine is possibly the editor[']s last gratuitous tract, his farewell appearance as an Ishmaelite.

[Punctuation in brackets added by editor. This essay is not included in 2nd, 3rd, and 4th eds.]

ADVENTURES WHILE PREACHING THE GOSPEL OF BEAUTY

(Fall, 1914)

DEDICATED to Miss Sara Teasdale

[*Adventures* was published in the fall, 1914, by Mitchell Kennerley, the six chapters having been serialized in Kennerley's magazine *The Forum* (September 1913-February 1914). The five "Proclamations" were first published in *Farm and Fireside*, Vol. 36 (1913), as follows: January 18, p. 25; February 1, p. 28; February 15, p. 33; March 1, p. 35; and August 16, p. 15. A sixth Proclamation from *Farm and Fireside* (March 29, 1913, p. 17) is included in volume two of this edition.

The following poems were used as interludes in the original *Adventures* (see "Index of Titles," *The Poetry of Vachel Lindsay*): "Upon Returning to the Country Road," "Heart of God," "The Kallyope Yell," "On the Road to Nowhere," "Kansas," "Here's to the Spirit of Fire," "What Grandpa Mouse Said," "The Flute of the Lonely," "The Shield of Faith," "The Rose of Midnight," "The Path in the Sky," "Epilogue to the Adventures While Preaching the Gospel of Beauty."]

I

I Start on My Walk

As some of the readers of this account are aware, I took a walk last summer from my home town, Springfield, Illinois, across Illinois, Missouri, and Kansas, up and down Colorado and into New Mexico. One of the most vivid little episodes of the trip, that came after two months of walking, I would like to tell at this point. It was in southern Colorado. It was early morning. Around the cliff, with a boom, a rattle and a bang, appeared a gypsy wagon. On the front seat was a Romany, himself dressed inconspicuously, but with his woman more bedecked than Carmen. She wore the bangles and spangles of her Hindu progenitors. The woman began to shout at me, I could not distinguish just what. The two seemed to think this was the gayest morning the sun ever shone upon. They came faster and faster, then, suddenly, at the woman's suggestion, pulled up short. And she asked me with a fraternal, confidential air, "What you sellin', what you sellin', boy?"

If we had met on the first of June, when I had just started, she would have pretended to know all about me, she would have asked to tell my fortune. On the first of June I wore about the same costume I wear on the streets of Springfield. I was white as paper from two years of writing poetry indoors. Now, on the first of August I was sunburned a quarter of an inch deep. My costume, once so respectable, I had gradually transformed till it looked like that of a showman. I wore very yellow corduroys, a fancy sombrero and an oriflamme tie. So Mrs. Gypsy hailed me as a brother. She eyed my little worn-out oil-cloth pack. It was a delightful professional mystery to her.

I handed up a sample of what it contained—my *Gospel of Beauty* (a little one-page formula for making America lovelier), and my little booklet, *Rhymes to Be Traded for Bread.*

The impatient horses went charging on. In an instant came more noises. Four more happy gypsy wagons passed. Each time the interview was repeated in identical language, and with the same stage business. The men were so silent and masterful-looking, the girls such brilliant, inquisitive cats! I never before saw anything so like high-class comic opera off the stage, and in fancy I still see it all:—those brown, braceleted arms still waving, and those provocative siren cries:—"What you sellin', boy? What you sellin'?"

I hope my Gospel did them good. Its essential principle is that one should not be a gypsy forever. He should return home. Having returned, he should plant the seeds of Art and of Beauty. He should tend them till they grow. There is something essentially humorous about a man walking rapidly away from his home town to tell all men they should go back to their birthplaces. It is still more humorous that, when I finally did return home, it was sooner than I intended, all through a temporary loss of nerve. But once home I have taken my own advice to heart. I have addressed four mothers' clubs, one literary club, two missionary societies and one High School Debating Society upon the Gospel of Beauty. And the end is not yet. No, not by any means. As John Paul Jones once said, "I have not yet begun to fight."

I had set certain rules of travel, evolved and proved practicable in previous expeditions in the East and South. These rules had been published in various periodicals before my start. The home town newspapers, my puzzled but faithful friends in good times and in bad, went the magazines one better and added a rule or so. To promote the gala character of the occasion, a certain paper announced that I was to walk in a Roman toga with bare feet encased in sandals. Another added that I had travelled through most of the countries of Europe in this manner. It made delightful reading. Scores of mere acquaintances crossed the street to shake hands with me on the strength of it.

The actual rules were to have nothing to do with cities, railroads, money, baggage or fellow tramps. I was to begin to ask for dinner about a quarter of eleven and for supper, lodging and breakfast about a quarter of five. I was to be neat, truthful, civil and on the square. I was to preach the Gospel of Beauty. How did these rules work out?

The cities were easy to let alone. I passed quickly through Hannibal and Jefferson City. Then, straight West, it was nothing but villages and farms till the three main cities of Colorado. Then nothing but desert to central New Mexico. I did not take the train till I reached central New Mexico, nor did I write to Springfield for money till I quit the whole game at that point.

Such wages as I made I sent home, starting out broke again, first spending just enough for one day's recuperation out of each pile, and, in the first case, rehabilitating my costume considerably. I always walked penniless. My baggage was practically nil. It was mainly printed matter, renewed by mail. Sometimes I carried reproductions of drawings of mine, *The Village Improvement Parade,* a series of picture-cartoons with many morals.

I pinned this on the farmers' walls, explaining the mottoes on the banners, and exhorting them to study it at their leisure. My little pack had a supply of the aforesaid *Rhymes to Be Traded for Bread.* And it contained the following Gospel of Beauty:

The Gospel of Beauty

Being the new "creed of a beggar" by that vain and foolish mendicant Nicholas Vachel Lindsay, printed for his personal friends in his home village—Springfield, Illinois. It is his intention to carry this gospel across the country beginning June, 1912, returning in due time.

I

I come to you penniless and afoot, to bring a message. I am starting a new religious idea. The idea does not say "no" to any creed that you have heard. . . . After this, let the denomination to which you now belong be called in your heart "the church of beauty" or "the church of the open sky." . . . The church of beauty has two sides: the love of beauty and the love of God.

II

The New Localism

The things most worth while are one's own hearth and neighborhood. We should make our own home and neighborhood the most democratic, the most beautiful and the holiest in the world. The children now growing up should become devout gardeners or architects or park architects or teachers of dancing in the Greek spirit or musicians or novelists or poets or story-writers or craftsmen or wood-carvers or dramatists or actors or singers. They should find their talent and nurse it industriously. They should believe in every possible application to art-theory of the thoughts of the Declaration of Independence and Lincoln's Gettysburg Address. They should, if led by the spirit, wander over the whole nation in search of the secret of democratic beauty with their hearts at the same time filled to overflowing with the righteousness of God. Then they should come back to their own hearth and neighborhood and gather a little circle of their own sort of workers about them and strive to make the neighborhood and home more beautiful and democratic and holy with their special art. . . . They should labor in their little circle expecting neither reward nor honors. . . . In their darkest hours they should be made strong by the vision of a completely beautiful neighborhood and the passion for a completely democratic art. Their reason for living should be that joy in beauty which no wounds can take away, and that joy in the love of God which no crucifixion can end.

The kindly reader at this point clutches his brow and asks, "But why carry this paper around? Why, in Heaven's name, do it as a beggar? Why do it at all?"

Let me make haste to say that there has been as yet no accredited, accepted way for establishing Beauty in the heart of the average American. *Until such a way has been determined upon by a competent committee,* I must be pardoned for taking my own course and trying any experiment I please.

But I hope to justify the space occupied by this narrative, not by the essential seriousness of my intentions, nor the essential solemnity of my motley cloak, nor by the final failure or success of the trip, but by the things I unexpectedly ran into, as curious to me as to the gentle and sheltered reader. Of all that I saw the State of Kansas impressed me most, and the letters home I have chosen cover, for the most part, adventures there.

Kansas, the Ideal American Community! Kansas, nearer than any other to the kind of a land our fathers took for granted! Kansas, practically free from cities and industrialism, the real last refuge of the constitution, since it maintains the type of agricultural civilization the constitution had in mind! Kansas, State of tremendous crops and hardy, devout, natural men! Kansas of the historic Santa Fé Trail and the classic village of Emporia and the immortal editor of Emporia! Kansas, laid out in roads a mile apart, criss-crossing to make a great checker-board, roads that go on and on past endless rich farms and big farm-houses, though there is not a village or railroad for miles! Kansas, the land of the real country gentlemen, Americans who work the soil and own the soil they work; State where the shabby tenant-dwelling scarce appears as yet! Kansas of the Chautauqua and the college student and the devout school-teacher! The dry State, the automobile State, the insurgent State! Kansas, that is ruled by the cross-roads church, and the church type of civilization! The Newest New England! State of more promise of permanent spiritual glory than Massachusetts in her brilliant youth!

Travellers who go through in cars with roofs know little of this State. Kansas is not Kansas till we march day after day, away from the sunrise, under the blistering noon sky, on, on over a straight west-going road toward the sunset. Then we begin to have our spirits stirred by the sight of the tremendous clouds looming over the most interminable plain that ever expanded and made glorious the heart of Man.

I have walked in eastern Kansas where the hedged fields and the orchards and gardens reminded one of the picturesque sections of Indiana, of antique and settled Ohio. Later I have mounted a little hill on what was otherwise a level and seemingly uninhabited universe, and traced, away to the left, the creeping Arkansas, its course marked by the cottonwoods, that became like tufts of grass on its far borders. All the rest of the world was treeless and riverless, yet green from the rain of yesterday, and patterned like a carpet with the shadows of the clouds. I have walked on and on across this unbroken prairie-sod where half-wild cattle grazed. Later I have marched between alfalfa fields where hovered the lavender haze of the fragrant blossom, and have heard the busy music of the forging bumble bees. Later I have marched for days and days with wheat waving round me, yellow as the sun. Many's the night I have slept in the barn-lofts of Kansas with the wide loft-door rolled open and the inconsequential golden moon for my friend.

These selections from letters home tell how I came into Kansas and how I adventured there. The letters were written avowedly as a sort of diary of the trip, but their contents turned out to be something less than that, something more than that, and something rather different.

Thursday, May 30, 1912. In the blue grass by the side of the road. Somewhere west of Jacksonville, Illinois. Hot sun. Cool wind. Rabbits in the distance. Bumblebees near.

At five last evening I sighted my lodging for the night. It was the other side of a high worm fence. It was down in the hollow of a grove.

It was the box of an old box-car, brought there somehow, without its wheels. It was far from a railroad. I said in my heart "Here is the appointed shelter." I was not mistaken.

As was subsequently revealed, it belonged to the old gentleman I spied through the window stemming gooseberries and singing: "John Brown's body." He puts the car top on wagon wheels and hauls it from grove to grove between Jacksonville and the east bank of the Mississippi. He carries a saw mill equipment along. He is clearing this wood for the owner, of all but its walnut trees. He lives in the box with his son and two assistants. He is cook, washerwoman and saw-mill boss. His wife died many years ago.

The old gentleman let me in with alacrity. He allowed me to stem gooseberries while he made a great supper for the boys. They soon came in. I was meanwhile assured that my name was going into the pot. My host looked like his old general, McClellan. He was eloquent on the sins of preachers, dry voters and pension reformers. He was full of reminiscences of the string band at Sherman's headquarters, in which he learned to perfect himself on his wonderful fiddle. He said, "I can't play slow music. I've got to play dance tunes or die." He did not die. His son took a banjo from an old trunk and the two of them gave us every worth while tune on earth: *Money Musk, Hell's Broke Loose in Georgia, The Year of Jubilee, Sailor's Hornpipe, Baby on the Block, Lady on the Lake,* and *The Irish Washerwoman,* while I stemmed gooseberries, which they protested I did not need to do. Then I read my own unworthy verses to the romantic and violin-stirred company. And there was room for all of us to sleep in that one repentant and converted box-car.

Friday, May 31, 1912. Half an hour after a dinner of crackers, cheese and raisins, provided at my solicitation by the grocer in the general store and post-office, Valley City, Illinois.

I have thought of a new way of stating my economic position. I belong to one of the leisure classes, that of the rhymers. In order to belong to any leisure class, one must be a thief or a beggar. On the whole I prefer to be a beggar, and, before each meal, receive from toiling man new permission to extend my holiday. The great business of that world that looms above the workshop and the furrow is to take things from people by some sort of taxation or tariff or special privilege. But I want to exercise my covetousness only in a retail way, open and above board, and when I take bread from a man's table I want to ask him for that particular piece of bread, as politely as I can.

But this does not absolutely fit my life. For yesterday I ate several things without permission, for instance, in mid-morning I devoured all the cherries a man can hold. They were hanging from heavy, breaking branches that came way over the stone wall into the road.

Another adventure. Early in the afternoon I found a brick farmhouse. It had a noble porch. There were marks of old-fashioned distinction in the trimmed hedges and flower-beds, and in the summer-houses. The side-yard and barn-lot were the cluckingest, buzzingest kind of places. There was not a human being in sight. I knocked and knocked on the doors. I wandered through all the sheds. I could look in through the unlocked screens and see every sign of present occupation. If I had chosen to enter I could have stolen the wash bowl or the baby-buggy or the baby's doll. The creamery was more tempting, with milk and butter and eggs, and freshly pulled taffy cut in squares. I took a little taffy. That is all I took, though the chickens were very social and I could have eloped with several of them. The roses and peonies and geraniums were entrancing, and there was not a watch dog anywhere. Everything seemed to say *Enter in and possess!''*

I saw inside the last door where I knocked a crisp, sweet, simple dress on a chair. Ah, a sleeping beauty somewhere about!

I went away from that place.

Sunday, June 1, 1912. By the side of the road, somewhere in Illinois.

Last night I was dead tired. I hailed a man by the shed of a stationary engine. I asked him if I could sleep in the engine-shed all night, beginning right now. He said "Yes." But from five to six, he put me out of doors, on a pile of gunny sacks on the grass. There I slept while the ducks quacked in my ears, and the autos whizzed over the bridge three feet away. My host was a one-legged man. In about an hour he came poking me with that crutch and that peg of his. He said "Come, and let me tell your fortune! I have been studying your physiognifry while you were alseep!" So we sat on a log by the edge of the pond. He said: "I am the Seventh Son of a Seventh Son. They call me the duck-pond diviner. I forecast the weather for these parts. Every Sunday I have my corner for the week's weather in the paper here." Then he indulged in a good deal of the kind of talk one finds in the front of the almanac.

He was a little round man with a pair of round, dull eyes, and a dull, round face, with a two weeks' beard upon it. He squinted up his eyes now. He was deliberate. Switch engines were going by. He paused to hail the engineers. Here is a part of what he finally said: "You are a Child of Destiny." He hesitated, for he wanted to be sure of the next point. "You were born in the month of S-e-p-t-e-m-b-e-r. Your preference is for a business like clerking in a store. You are of a slow, *pigmatic* temperament, but I can see you are fastidious about your eating. You do not use tobacco. You are fond of sweets. You have been married twice. Your first wife died, and your second was divorced. You look like you would make a good spiritualist medium. If you don't let any black cats cross your track you will have good luck for the next three years."

He hit it right twice. I *am* a Child of Destiny and I *am* fond of sweets. When a prophet hits it right on essentials like that, who would be critical?

An old woman with a pipe in her mouth came down the railroad embankment looking for greens. He bawled at her "Git out of that." But on she came. When she was closer he said: "Them weeds is full of poison oak." She grunted, and kept working her way toward us, and with a belligerent swagger marched past us on into the engine-room, carrying a great mess of greens in her muddy hands.

There was scarcely space in that little shed for the engine, and it was sticking out in several places. Yet it dawned on me that this was the wife of my host, that they kept house with that engine for the principal article of furniture. Without a word of introduction or explanation she stood behind me and mumbled, "You need your supper, son. Come in."

There was actually a side-room in that little box, a side-room with a cot and a cupboard as well. On the floor was what was once a rug. But it had had a long kitchen history. She dipped a little unwashed bowl into a larger unwashed bowl, with an unwashed thumb doing its whole duty. She handed me a fuzzy, unwashed spoon and said with a note of real kindness, "Eat your supper, young man." She patted me on the shoulder with a sticky hand. Then she stood, looking at me fixedly. The woman had only half her wits.

I suppose they kept that stew till it was used up, and then made another. I was a Child of Destiny, all right, and Destiny decreed I should eat. I sat there trying to think of things to say to make agreeable conversation, and postpone the inevitable. Finally I told her I wanted to be a little boy once more, and take my bowl and eat on the log by the pond in the presence of Nature.

She maintained that genial silence which indicates a motherly sympathy. I left her smoking and smiling there. And like a little child that knows not the folly of waste, I slyly fed my supper to the ducks.

At bedtime the old gentleman slept in his clothes on the cot in the kitchenette. He had the dog for a foot-warmer. There was a jar of yeast under the table. Every so often the old gentleman would call for the old lady to come and drive the ducks out, or they would get the board off the jar. Ever and anon the ducks had a taste before the avenger arrived.

On one side of the engine the old lady had piled gunny-sacks for my bed. That softened the cement-floor foundation. Then she insisted on adding that elegant rug from the kitchen, to protect me from the fuzz on the sacks. She herself slept on a pile of excelsior with a bit of canvas atop. She kept a cat just by her cheek to keep her warm, and I have no doubt the pretty brute whispered things in her ear. Tabby was the one aristocratic, magical touch: — one of these golden coon-cats.

The old lady's bed was on the floor, just around the corner from me, on the other side of the engine. That engine stretched its vast bulk between us. It was as the sword between the duke and the queen in the fairy story. But every so often, in response to the old gentleman's alarm, the queen would come climbing over my feet in order to get to the kitchen and drive out the ducks. From where I lay I could see through two doors to the night outside. I could watch the stealthy approach of the white and waddling marauders. Do not tell me a duck has no sense of humor. It was a great game of tag to them. It occurred as regularly as the half hours were reached. I could time the whole process by the ticking in my soul, while presumably asleep. And while wating for them to come up I could see the pond and a star reflected in the pond, the star of my Destiny, no doubt. At last it began to rain. Despite considerations of fresh air, the door was shut, and soon everybody was asleep.

The bed was not verminiferous. I dislike all jokes on such a theme, but in this case the issue must be met. It is the one thing the tramp wants to know about his bunk. That peril avoided, there is nothing to quarrel about. Despite all the grotesquerie of that night, I am grateful for a roof, and two gentle friends.

Poor things! Just like all the citizens of the twentieth century, petting and grooming machinery three times as smart as they are themselves. Such people should have engines to take care of them, instead of taking care of engines. There stood the sleek brute in its stall, absorbing all, giving nothing, pumping supplies only for its own caste; — water to be fed to other engines.

But seldom are keepers of engine-stables as unfortunate as these. The best they can get from the world is cruel laughter. Yet this woman, crippled in brain, her soul only half alive, this dull man, crippled in body, had God's gift of the liberal heart. If they are supremely absurd, so are all of us. We must include ourselves in the farce. These two, tottering through the dimness and vexation of our queer world, were willing the stranger should lean upon them. I say they had the good gift of the liberal heart. One thing was theirs to divide. That was a roof. They gave me my third and they helped me to hide from the rain. In the name of St. Francis I laid me down. May that saint of all saints be with them, and with all the gentle and innocent and weary and broken!

II

Walking Through Missouri

Tuesday Morning, June 4, 1912. In a hotel bedroom in Laddonia, Missouri. I occupy this room without charge.

Through the mercy of the gateman I crossed the Hannibal toll-bridge without paying fare, and the more enjoyed the pearly Mississippi in the evening twilight. Walking south of Hannibal next morning, Sunday, I was irresistibly reminded of Kentucky. It was the first real "pike" of my journey, — solid gravel, and everyone was exercising his racing pony in his racing cart, and giving me a ride down lovely avenues of trees. Here, as in dozens of other interesting "lifts" in Illinois, I had the driver's complete attention, recited *The Gospel of Beauty* through a series of my more didactic rhymes till I was tired, and presented the *Village Improvement Parade* and the *Rhymes to Be Traded for Bread* and exhorted the comradely driver to forget me never. One colored horseman hitched forward on the plank of his breaking-cart and gave me his seat. Then came quite a ride into New London. He asked, "So you goin' to walk west to the mountains and all around?" "Yes, if this colt don't break my neck, or I don't lose my nerve or get bitten by a dog or anything." "Will you walk back?" "Maybe so, maybe not." He pondered a while, then said, with the Bert Williams manner, *"You'll ride back. Mark my words, you'll ride back!"*

He asked a little later, "Goin' to harves' in Kansas?" I assured him I was not going to harvest in Kansas. He rolled his big white eyes at me: "What in the name of Uncle Hillbilly *air* you up to then?"

In this case I could not present my tracts, for I was holding on to him for dear life. Just then he turned off my road. Getting out of the cart I nearly hung myself; and the colt was away again before I could say "Thank you."

Yesterday I passed through what was mostly a flat prairie country, abounding in the Missouri mule. I met one man on horseback driving before him an enormous specimen tied head to head with a draught-horse. The mule was continually dragging his good-natured comrade into the ditch and being jerked out again. The mule is a perpetual inquisitor and experimenter. He followed me along the fence with the alertest curiosity, when he was inside the field, yet meeting me in the road, he often showed deadly terror. If he was a mule colt, following his mare mamma along the pike, I had to stand in the side lane or hide behind a tree till he went by, or else he would turn and run as if the very devil were after him. Then the farmer on the mare would have to pursue him a considerable distance, and drive him back with cuss words. 'Tis sweet to stir up so much emotion, even in the breast of an animal.

What do you suppose happened in New London? I approached what I thought a tiny Baptist chapel of whitewashed stone. Noting it was about sermon-time, and feeling like repenting, I walked in. Behold, the most harmoniously-colored Catholic shrine in the world! The sermon was being preached by the most gorgeously robed priest one could well conceive. The father went on to show how a vision of the Christ-child had appeared on the altar of a lax congregation in Spain. From that time those people, stricken with reverence and godly fear, put that church into repair, and the community became a true servant of the Lord. Infidels were converted, heretics were confounded.

After the sermon came the climax of the mass, and from the choir loft above my head came the most passionate religious singing I ever heard in my life. The excellence of the whole worship, even to the preaching of visions, was a beautiful surprise.

People do not open their eyes enough, neither their spiritual nor their physical eyes. They are not sensitive enough to loveliness either visible or by the pathway of visions. I wish every church in the world could see the Christ-child on the altar, every Methodist and Baptist as well as every Catholic congregation.

With these thoughts I sat and listened while that woman soloist sang not only through the Mass, but the Benediction of the Blessed Sacrament as well. The whole surprise stands out like a blazing star in my memory.

I say we do not see enough visions. I wish that, going out of the church door at noon, every worshipper in America could spiritually discern the Good St. Francis come down to our earth and singing of the Sun. I wish that saint would return. I wish he would preach voluntary poverty to all the middle-class and wealthy folk of this land, with the power that once shook Europe.

Friday, June 7, 1912. In the mid-afternoon in the woods, many miles west of Jefferson City. I am sitting by a wild rose bush. I am looking down a long sunlit vista of trees.

Wednesday evening, three miles from Fulton, Missouri, I encountered a terrific storm. I tried one farm-house just before the rain came down, but they would not let me in, not even into the barn. They said it was "not convenient." They said there was another place a little piece ahead, anyway. Pretty soon I was considerably rained upon. But the "other place" did not appear. Later the thunder and lightning were frightful. It seemed to me everything was being struck all around me: because of the sheer downpour it became pitch dark. It seemed as though the very weight of the rain would beat me into the ground. Yet I felt that I needed the washing. The night before I enjoyed the kind of hospitality that makes one yearn for a bath.

At last I saw a light ahead. I walked through more cataracts and reached it. Then I knocked at the door. I entered what revealed itself to be a negro cabin. Mine host was Uncle Remus himself, only a person of more delicacy and dignity. He appeared to be well preserved, though he was eighteen years old when the war broke out. He owns forty acres and more than one mule. His house was sweet and clean, all metal surfaces polished, all wood-work scrubbed white, all linen fresh laundered. He urged me to dry at his oven. It was a long process, taking much fuel. He allowed me to eat supper and breakfast with him and his family, which honor I scarcely deserved. The old man said grace standing up. Then we sat down and he said another. The first was just family prayers. The second was thanksgiving for the meal. The table was so richly and delicately provided that within my heart I paraphrased the twenty-third Psalm, though I did not quote it out aloud: "Thou preparest a table before me in the presence of mine enemies" — (namely, the thunder and lightning, and the inhospitable white man!).

I hope to be rained on again if it brings me communion bread like that I ate with my black host. The conversation was about many things, but began religiously; how *"Ol' Master in the sky gave us everything here to take keer of, and said we mussent waste any of it."*

The wife was a mixture of charming diffidence and eagerness in offering her opinion on these points of political economy and theology.

After supper the old gentleman told me a sweet-singing field-bird I described was called the "Rachel-Jane." He had five children grown and away from home and one sleek first voter still under his roof. The old gentleman asked the inevitable question: "Goin' west harvestin'?"

I said "No" again. Then I spread out and explained *The Village Improvement Parade*. This did not interest the family much, but they would never have done with asking me questions about Lincoln. And the fact that I came from Lincoln's home town was plainly my chief distinction in their eyes. The best bed was provided for me, and warm water in which to bathe, and I slept the sleep of the clean and regenerated in snowy linen. Next morning the sun shone, and I walked the muddy roads as cheerfully as though they were the paths of Heaven.

Sunday Morning, June 9, 1912. I am writing in the railroad station at Tipton, Missouri.

A little while back a few people began to ask me to work for my meals. I believe this is because the "genteel" appearance with which I started has become something else. My derby hat has been used for so many things, — to keep off a Noah's flood of rain, to catch cherries in, to fight bumblebees, to cover my face while asleep, and keep away the vague terrors of the night, — that it is still a hat, but not quite in the mode. My face is baked by the sun and my hands are fried and stewed. My trousers are creased not in one place, but all over. These things made me look more like a person who, in the words of the conventional world, *"ought to work."*

Having been requested to work once or twice, I immediately made it my custom to offer labor-power as a preliminary to the meal. I generally ask about five people before I find the one who happens to be in a meal-giving mood. This kindly person, about two-thirds of the time, refuses to let me work. I insist and insist, but he says, "Aw, come in and eat anyway." The man who accepts my offer of work may let me cut weeds, or hoe corn or potatoes, but he generally shows me the woodpile and the axe. Even then every thud of that inevitably dull instrument seems to go through him. After five minutes he thinks I have worked an hour, and he comes to the porch and shouts: "Come in and get your dinner."

Assuming a meal is worth thirty-five cents, I have never yet worked out the worth of one, at day-laborer's wages. Very often I am called into the house three times before I come. Whether I work or not, the meals are big and good. Perhaps there is a little closer attention to *The Gospel of Beauty,* after three unheeded calls to dinner.

After the kindling is split and the meal eaten and they lean back in their chairs, a-weary of their mirth, by one means or another I show them how I am knocking at the door of the world with a dream in my hand.

Because of the multitudes of tramps pouring west on the freight trains, — tramps I never see because I let freight cars alone, — night accommodations are not so easy to get as they were in my other walks in Pennsylvania and Georgia. I have not yet been forced to sleep under the stars, but each evening has been a scramble. There must be some better solution to this problem of a sleeping-place.

The country hotel, if there is one around, is sometimes willing to take in the man who flatly says he is broke. For instance, the inn-keeper's wife at Clarksburg was tenderly pitiful, yea, she was kind to me after the fashion of the holiest of the angels. There was a protracted meeting going on in the town. That was, perhaps, the reason for her exalted heart. But, whatever the reason, in this one case I was welcomed with such kindness and awe that I dared not lift up my haughty head or distribute my poems, or give tongue to my views, or let her suspect for a moment I was a special IDEA on legs. It was much lovelier to have her think I was utterly forlorn.

This morning when I said good-bye I fumbled my hat, mumbled my words and shuffled my feet, and may the Good St. Francis reward her.

When I asked the way to Tipton the farmer wanted me to walk the railroad. People cannot see "why the Sam Hill" anyone wants to walk the highway when the rails make a bee-line for the destination. This fellow was so anxious for the preservation of my feet he insisted it looked like rain. I finally agreed that, for the sake of avoiding a wetting, I had best hurry to Tipton by the ties. The six miles of railroad between Clarksburg and Tipton should be visited by every botanist in the United States. Skip the rest of this letter unless you are interested in a catalogue of flowers.

First comes the reed with the deep blue blossoms at the top that has bloomed by my path all the way from Springfield, Illinois. Then come enormous wild roses, showing every hue that friend of man ever displayed. Behold an army of white poppies join our march, then healthy legions of waving mustard. Our next recruits are tiny golden-hearted ragged kinsmen of the sunflower. No comrades depart from this triumphal march to Tipton. Once having joined us, they continue in our company. The mass of color grows deeper and more subtle each moment. Behold, regiments of pale lavender larkspur. 'Tis an excellent garden, the finer that it needs no tending. Though the rain has failed to come, I begin to be glad I am hobbling along over the vexatious ties. I forget my resolve to run for President.

Once I determined to be a candidate. I knew I would get the tramp-vote and the actor-vote. My platform was to be that railroad ties should be just close enough for men to walk on them in natural steps, neither mincing the stride nor widely stretching the legs.

Not yet have we reached Tipton. Behold a white flower, worthy of a better name, that the farmers call "sheep's tea." Behold purple larkspur joining the lavender larkspur. Behold that disreputable camp-follower the button-weed, wearing its shabby finery. Now a red delicate grass joins in, and a big purple and pink sort of an aster. Behold a pink and white sheep's tea. And look, there is a dwarf morning glory, the sweetest in the world. Here is a group of black-eyed Susans, marching like suffragettes to get the vote at Tipton. Here is a war-dance of Indian Paint. And here are bluebells.

"Goin' west harvestin'?"

"I have harvested already, ten thousand flowers an hour."

JUNE 10, 1912. 3 p.m. Three miles west of Sedalia, Missouri. In the woods. Near the automobile road to Kansas City.

Now that I have passed Sedalia I am pretty well on toward the Kansas line. Only three more days' journey, and then I shall be in Kansas, State of Romance, State of Expectation. Goodness knows Missouri has plenty of incident, plenty of merit. But it is a cross between Illinois and northern Kentucky, and to beg here is like begging in my own back-yard.

But the heart of Kansas is the heart of the West. . . . Inclosed find a feather from the wing of a young chicken-hawk. He happened across the road day before yesterday. The farmer stopped the team and killed him with his pitchfork. That farmer seemed to think he had done the Lord a service in ridding the world of a parasite. Yet I had a certain fellow-feeling for the hawk, as I have for anybody who likes chicken.

This walk is full of suggestions for poems. Sometimes, in a confidential moment, I tell my hosts I am going to write a chronicle of the whole trip in verse. But I cannot write it now. The traveller at my stage is in a kind of farm-hand condition of mind and blood. He feels himself so much a part of the soil and the sun and the ploughed acres, he eats so hard and sleeps so hard, he has little more patience in trying to write than the husbandman himself.

If that poem is ever written I shall say, — to my fellow-citizens of Springfield, for instance: — "I have gone as your delegate to greet the fileds, to claim them for you against a better day. I lay hold on these furrows on behalf of all those cooped up in cities."

I feel that in a certain mystical sense I have made myself part of the hundreds and hundreds of farms that lie between me and machine-made America. I have scarcely seen anything but crops since I left home. The whole human race is grubbing in the soil, and the soil is responding with tremendous vigor. By walking I get as tired as any and imagine I work too. Sometimes the glory goes. Then I feel my own idleness above all other facts on earth. I want to get to work immediately. But I suppose I am a minstrel or nothing. (There goes a squirrel through the treetops.)

Every time I say "No" to the question "Goin' west harvestin'?" I am a little less brisk about reciting that triad of poems that I find is the best brief exposition of my gospel: (1) *The Proud Farmer,* (2) *The Illinois Village* and (3) *The Building of Springfield.*

If I do harvest it is likely to be just as it was at the Springfield water-works a year ago, when I broke my back in a week trying to wheel bricks.

JUNE 12, 1912. On the banks of a stream west of the town of Warrensburg, Missouri.

Perhaps the problem of a night's lodging has been solved. I seem to have found a substitute for the spare bedrooms and white sheets of Georgia and Pennsylvania. It appears that no livery stable will refuse a man a place to sleep. What happened at Otterville and Warrensburg I can make happen from here on, or so I am assured by a farmhand. He told me that every tiniest village from here to western Kansas has at least two livery-stables and there a man may sleep for the asking. He should try to get permission to mount to the hay-mow, for, unless the cot in the office is a mere stretch of canvas, it is likely to be (excuse me) verminiferous. The stable man asks if the mendicant has matches or tobacco. If he has he must give them up. Also he is told not to poke his head far out of the loft window, for, if the insurance man caught him, it would be all up with the insurance. These preliminaries quickly settled, the transient requests a buggy-robe to sleep in, lest he be overwhelmed with the loan of a horse-blanket. The objection to a horse-blanket is that it is a horse-blanket.

And so, if I am to believe my friend with the red neck, my good times at Warrensburg and Otterville are likely to continue.

Strange as it may seem, sleeping in a hayloft is Romance itself. The alfalfa is soft and fragrant and clean, the wind blows through the big loft door, the stars shine through the cottonwoods. If I wake in the night I hear the stable-boys bringing in the teams of men who have driven a long way and back again to get something; — to get drunk, or steal the kisses of somebody's wife or put over a political deal or get a chance to preach a sermon; — and I get scraps of detail from the stable-boys after the main actors of the drama have gone. It sounds as though all the remarks were being made in the loft instead of on the ground floor. The horses stamp and stamp and the grinding sound of their teeth is so close to me I cannot believe at first that the mangers and feed-boxes are way down below.

It is morning before I know it and the gorged birds are singing "shivaree, shivaree, Rachel Jane, Rachel Jane" in the mulberry trees, just outside the loft window. After a short walk I negotiate for breakfast, then walk on through Paradise and at the proper time negotiate for dinner, walk on through Paradise again and at six negotiate for the paradisical haymow, without looking for supper, and again more sleepy than hungry. The difference between this system and the old one is that about half past four I used to begin to worry about supper and night accommodations, and generally worried till seven. Now life is one long sweet stroll, and I watch the sunset from my bed in the alfalfa with the delights of the whole day renewed in my heart.

Passing through the village of Sedalia I inquired the way out of town to the main road west. My informant was a man named McSweeny, drunk enough to be awfully friendly. He asked all sorts of questions. He induced me to step two blocks out of my main course down a side-street to his "Restaurant." He said he was not going to let me leave town without a square meal. It was a strange eating-place, full of ditch-diggers, teamsters, red-necked politicians and slender intellectual politicians. In the background was a scattering of the furtive daughters of pleasure, some white, some black. The whole institution was but an annex to the bar room in front. Mr. McSweeny looked over my book while I ate. After the meal he gathered a group of the politicians and commanded me to recite. I gave them my rhyme in memory of Altgeld and my rhyme in denunciation of Lorimer, and my rhyme denouncing all who cooperated in the white slave trade, including sellers of drink. Mr. McSweeny said I was the goods, and offered to pass the hat, but I would not permit. A handsome black jezebel sat as near us as she dared and listened quite seriously. I am sure she would have put something in that hat if it had gone round.

"I suppose," said Mr. McSweeny, as he stood at his door to bow adieu, "you will harvest when you get a little further west?"

That afternoon I walked miles and miles through rough country, and put up with a friendly farmer named John Humphrey. He had children like little golden doves, and a most hard-working wife. The man had harvested and travelled eight years in the west before he had settled down. He told me all about it. Until late that night he told me endless fascinating stories upon the theme of that free man's land ahead of me. If he had not had those rosy babies to anchor him, he would have picked up and gone along, and argued down my rule to travel alone.

Because he had been a man of the road there was a peculiar feeling of understanding in the air. They were people of much natural refinement. I was the more grateful for their bread when I considered that when I came upon them at sunset they were working together in the field. There was not a hand to help. How could they be so happy and seem so blest? Their day was nearer sixteen than eight hours long. I felt deathly ashamed to eat their bread. I told them so, with emphasis. But the mother said, "We always takes in them that asks, and nobody never done us no harm yet."

That night was a turning point for me. In reply to a certain question I said: *"Yes. I am going west harvesting."*

I asked the veteran traveller to tell me the best place to harvest. He was sitting on the floor pulling the children's toes, and having a grand time. He drew himself up into a sort of oracular knot, with his chin on his knees, and gesticulated with his pipe.

"Go straight west," he said, "to Great Bend, Barton County, Kansas, the banner wheat county of the United States. Arrive about July fifth. Walk to the public square. Walk two miles north. Look around. You will see nothing but wheat fields, and farmers standing on the edge of the road crying into big red handkerchiefs. Ask the first man for work. He will stop crying and give it to you. Wages will be two dollars and a half a day, and keep. You will have all you want to eat and a clean blanket in the hay."

I have resolved to harvest at Great Bend.

III

Walking into Kansas

It has been raining quite a little. The roads are so muddy I have to walk the ties. Keeping company with the railroad is almost a habit. While this shower passes I write in the station at Stillwell, Kansas.

JUNE 14, 1912. I have crossed the mystic border. I have left Earth. I have entered Wonderland. Though I am still east of the geographical centre of the United States, in every spiritual sense I am in the West. This morning I passed the stone mile-post that marks the beginning of Kansas.

I went over the border and encountered—what do you think? Wild strawberries! Lo, where the farmer had cut the weeds between the road and the fence, the gentle fruits revealed themselves, growing in the shadow down between the still-standing weeds. They shine out in a red line that stretches on and on, and a man has to resolve to stop eating several times. Just as he thinks he has conquered desire the line gets dazzlingly red again.

The berries grow at the end of a slender stalk, clustered six in a bunch. One gathers them by the stems, in bouquets, as it were, and eats off the fruit like taffy off a stick.

I was gathering buckets of cherries for a farmer's wife yesterday. This morning after the strawberries had mitigated I encountered a bush of raspberries, and then hedges on hedges of mulberries both white and red. The white mulberries are the sweetest. If this is the wild West, give me more. There are many varieties of trees, and they are thick as in the East. The people seem to grow more cordial. I was eating mulberries outside the yard of a villager. He asked me in where the eating was better. And then he told me the town scandal, while I had my dessert.

A day or so ago I hoed corn all morning for my dinner. This I did cheerfully, considering I had been given a good breakfast at that farm for nothing. I feel that two good meals are worth about a morning's work anyway. And then I had company. The elderly owner of the place hoed along with me. He saved the country, by preaching to me the old fashioned high tariff gospel, and I saved it by preaching to him the new fashioned Gospel of Beauty. Meanwhile the corn was hoed. Then we went in and ate the grandest of dinners. That house was notable for having on its walls really artistic pictures, not merely respectable pictures, nor yet seed-catalogue advertisements.

That night, in passing through a village, I glimpsed a man washing his dishes in the rear of a blacksmith shop. I said to myself: "Ah ha! Somebody keeping bach."

I knew I was welcome. There is no fear of the stranger in such a place, for there are no ladies to reassure or propitiate. Permission to sleep on the floor was granted as soon as asked. I spread out *The Kansas City Star,* which is a clean sheet, put my verses under my head for a pillow and was content. Next morning the sun was in my eyes. There was the odor of good fried bacon in the air.

"Git up and eat a snack, pardner," said my friend the blacksmith. And while I ate he told me the story of his life.

I had an amusing experience at the town of Belton. I had given an entertainment at the hotel on the promise of a night's lodging. I slept late. Over my transom came the breakfast-table talk. "That was a hot entertainment that young bum gave us last night," said one man. "He ought to get to work, the dirty lazy loafer," said another.

The schoolmaster spoke up in an effort not to condescend to his audience: "He is evidently a fraud. I talked to him a long time after the entertainment. The pieces he recited were certainly not his own. I have read some of them somewhere. It is too easy a way to get along, especially when the man is as able to work as this one. Of course in the old days literary men used to be obliged to do such things. But it isn't at all necessary in the Twentieth Century. Real poets are highly paid." Another spoke up: "I don't mind a fake, but he is a rotten reciter, anyhow. If he had said one more I would have just walked right out. You noticed ol' Mis' Smith went home after that piece about the worms." Then came the landlord's voice: "After the show was over I came pretty near not letting him have his room. All I've got to say is he don't get any breakfast."

I dressed, opened the doorway serenely, and strolled past the table, smiling with all the ease of a minister at his own church-social. In my most ornate manner I thanked the landlord and landlady for their extreme kindness. I assumed that not one of the gentle-folk had intended to have me hear their analysis. 'Twas a grand exit. Yet, in plain language, these people "got my goat." I have struggled with myself all morning, almost on the point of ordering a marked copy of a magazine sent to that smart schoolmaster. *"Evidently a fraud!"* Indeed!

"Goin' wes' harvesin'?"

"Yes, yes. I think I will harvest when I get to Great Bend."

JUNE 18, 1912. Approaching Emporia. I am sitting in the hot sun by the Santa Fé tracks, after two days of walking those tracks in the rain. I am near a queer little Mexican house built of old railroad ties.

I had had two sticks of candy begged from a grocer for breakfast. I was keeping warm by walking fast. Because of the muddy roads and the sheets of rain coming down it was impossible to leave the tracks. It was almost impossible to make speed since the ballast underfoot was almost all of it big rattling broken stone. I had walked that Santa Fé railroad a day and a half in the drizzle and downpour. It was a little past noon, and my scanty inner fuel was almost used up. I dared not stop a minute now, lest I catch cold. There was no station in sight ahead. When the mists lifted I saw that the tracks went on and on, straight west to the crack of doom, not even a water-tank in sight. The mists came down, then lifted once more, and, as though I were Childe Roland, I suddenly saw a shack to the right, in dimensions about seven feet each way. It was mostly stove-pipe, and that pipe was pouring out enough smoke to make three of Aladdin's Jinns. I presume some one heard me whistling. The little door opened. Two heads popped out, "Come in, you slab-sided hobo," they yelled affectionately. "Come in and get dry." And so my heart was made suddenly light after a day and a half of hard whistling.

At the inside end of that busy smoke-stack was a roaring redhot stove about as big as a hat. It had just room enough on top for three steaming coffee cans at a time. There were four white men with their chins on their knees completely occupying the floor of one side of the mansion, and four Mexicans filled the other. Every man was hunched up to take as little room as possible. It appeared that my only chance was to move the tins and sit on the stove. But one Mexican sort of sat on another Mexican and the new white man was accommodated. These fellows were a double-section gang, for the track is double all along here.

I dried out pretty quick. The men began to pass up the coffee off the stove. It strangled and blistered me, it was so hot. The men were almost to the bottom of the food sections of their buckets and were beginning to throw perfectly good sandwiches and extra pieces of pie through the door. I said that if any man had anything to throw away would he just wait till I stepped outside so I could catch it. They handed me all I could ever imagine a man eating. It rained and rained and rained, and I ate till I could eat no more. One man gave me for dessert the last half of his cup of stewed raisins along with his own spoon. Good raisins they were, too. A Mexican urged upon me some brown paper and cigarette tobacco. I was sorry I did not smoke. The men passed up more and more hot coffee.

That coffee made me into a sort of thermos bottle. On the strength of it I walked all afternoon through sheets and cataracts. When dark came I slept in wet clothes in a damp blanket in the hay of a windy livery-stable without catching cold.

Now it is morning. The sky is reasonably clear, the weather is reasonably warm, but I am no longer a thermos bottle, no, no. I am sitting on the hottest rock I can find, letting the sun go through my bones. The coffee in me has turned at last to ice and snow. Emporia, the Athens of America, is just ahead. Oh, for a hot bath and a clean shirt!

A mad dog tried to bite me yesterday morning, when I made a feeble attempt to leave the track. When I was back on the ties, he seemed afraid and would not come closer. His bark was the ghastliest thing I ever heard. As for his bite, he did not get quite through my shoe-heel.

EMPORIA, KANSAS, JUNE 19, 1912. On inquiring at the Emporia General Delivery for mail, I found your letter telling me to call upon your friend Professor Kerr. He took my sudden appearance most kindly, and pardoned my battered attire and the mud to the knees. After a day in his house I am ready to go on, dry and feasted and warm and clean. The professor's help seemed to come in just in time. I was a most weary creature.

Thinking it over this morning, the bathtub appears to be the first outstanding advantage the cultured man has over the half-civilized. Quite often the folk with swept houses and decent cooking who have given my poems discriminating attention, who have given me good things to eat, forget, even when they entertain him overnight, that the stranger would like to soak himself thoroughly. Many of the working people seem to keep fairly clean with the washpan as their principal ally. But the tub is indispensable to the mendicant in the end, unless he is walking through a land of crystal waterfalls, like North Georgia.

I am an artificial creature at last, dependent, after all, upon modern plumbing. 'Tis, perhaps, not a dignified theme, but I retired to the professor's bathroom and washed off the entire State of Missouri and the eastern counties of Kansas, and did a deal of laundry work on the sly. This last was not openly confessed to the professor, but he might have guessed, I was so cold on the front porch that night.

I shall not soon lose the memory of this the first day of emergence from the strait paths of St. Francis, this first meeting, since I left

Springfield, with a person on whom I had a conventional social claim. I had forgotten what the delicacy of a cultured welcome would be like. The professor's table was a marvel to me. I was astonished to discover there were such fine distinctions in food and linen. And for all my troubadour profession, I had almost forgotten there were such distinctions in books. I have hardly seen one magazine since I left you. The world where I have been moving reads nothing but newspapers. It is confusing to bob from one world to the other, to zig-zag across the social dead-line. I sat in the professor's library a very mixed-up person, feeling I could hardly stay a minute, yet too heavy-footed to stir an inch, and immensely grateful and relaxed.

Sooner or later I am going to step up into the rarefied civilized air once too often and stay there in spite of myself. I shall get a little too fond of the china and old silver, and forget the fields. Books and teacups and high-brow conversations are awfully insinuating things, if you give them time to be. One gets along somehow, and pleasure alternates with pain, and the sum is the joy of life, while one is below. But to quit is like coming up to earth after deep-sea diving in a heavy suit. One scarcely realizes he has been under heavier-than-air pressure, and has been fighting off great forces, till he has taken off his diving helmet, as it were. And yet there is a baffling sense of futility in the restful upper air. I remember it once, long ago, in emerging in Warren, Ohio, and once in emerging in Macon, Georgia: — the feeling that the upper world is all tissue paper, that the only choice a real man can make is to stay below with the great forces of life forever, even though he be a tramp — the feeling that, to be a little civilized, we sacrifice enormous powers and joys. For all I was so tired and so very grateful to the professor, I felt like a bull in a china shop. I should have been out in the fields, eating grass.

SUNDAY MORNING, JUNE 23, 1912. I am writing on the top of a pile of creosote-soaked ties between the Santa Fé tracks and the trail that runs parallel to the tracks. Florence, Kansas, is somewhere ahead.

In the East the railroads and machinery choke the land to death and it was there I made my rule against them. But the farther West I go the more the very life of the country seems to depend upon them. I suppose, though, that some day, even out West here, the rule against the railroad will be a good rule.

Meanwhile let me say that my Ruskinian prejudices are temporarily overcome by the picturesqueness and efficiency of the

Santa Fé. It is double-tracked, and every four miles is kept in order by a hand-car crew that is spinning back and forth all the time. The air seems to be full of hand-cars.

Walking in a hurry to make a certain place by nightfall I have become acquainted with these section hands, and, most delightful to relate, have ridden in their iron conveyances, putting my own back into the work. Half or three-fourths of the employees are Mexicans who are as ornamental in the actual landscape as they are in a Remington drawing. These Mexicans are tractable serfs of the Santa Fé. If there were enough miles of railroad in Mexico to keep all the inhabitants busy on section, perhaps the internal difficulties could be ended. These peons live peacefully next to the tracks in houses built by the company from old ties. The ties are placed on end, side by side, with plaster in the cracks, on a tiny oblong two-room plan. There is a little roofed court between the rooms. A farmer told me that the company tried Greek serfs for a while, but they made trouble for outsiders and murdered each other.

The road is busy as busy can be. Almost any time one can see enormous freight-trains rolling by or mile-a-minute passenger trains. Gates are provided for each farmer's right of way. I was told by an exceptional Mexican with powers of speech that the efficient dragging of the wagon-roads, especially the "New Santa Fé Trail" that follows the railroad, is owing to the missionary work of King, the split-log drag man, who was employed to go up and down this land agitating his hobby.

When the weather is good, touring automobiles whiz past. They have pennants showing they are from Kansas City, Emporia, New York or Chicago. They have camping canvas and bedding on the back seats of the car, or strapped in the rear. They are on camping tours to Colorado Springs and the like pleasure places. Some few avow they are going to the coast. About five o'clock in the evening some man making a local trip is apt to come along alone. He it is that wants the other side of the machine weighed down. He it is that will offer me a ride and spin me along from five to twenty-five miles before supper. This delightful use that may be made of an automobile in rounding out a day's walk has had something to do with mending my prejudice against it, despite the grand airs of the tourists that whirl by at midday. I still maintain that the auto is a carnal institution, to be shunned by the truly spiritual, but there are times when I, for one, get tired of being spiritual.

Much of the country east of Emporia is hilly and well-wooded and hedged like Missouri. But now I am getting into the range region.

Yesterday, after several miles of treeless land that had never known the plough, I said to myself: "Now I am really West." And my impression was reinforced when I reached a grand baronial establishment called "Clover Hill Ranch." It was flanked by the houses of the retainers. In the foreground and a little to the side was the great stone barn for the mules and horses. Back on the little hill, properly introduced by ceremonious trees, was the ranch house itself. And before it was my lord on his ranching charger. The aforesaid lord created quite an atmosphere of lordliness as he refused work in the alfalfa harvest to a battered stranger who bowed too low and begged too hard, perhaps. On the porch was my lady, feeding bread and honey to the beautiful young prince of the place.

I have not yet reached the wheat belt. Since the alfalfa harvest is on here, I shall try for that a bit.

SUNDAY AFTERNOON, JUNE 30, 1912. In the spare room of a Mennonite farmer, who lives just inside the wheat belt.

This is going to be a long Sunday afternoon; so make up your minds for a long letter. I did not get work in the alfalfa. Yet there is news. I have been staying a week with this Mennonite family shocking wheat for them, though I am not anywhere near Great Bend.

Before I tell you of the harvest, I must tell you of these Mennonites. They are a dear people. I have heard from their reverent lips the name of their founder, Menno Simonis, who was born about the time of Columbus and Luther and other such worthies. They are as opposed to carnal literature as I am to tailor-made clothes, and I hold they are perfectly correct in allowing no fashion magazines in the house. Such modern books as they read deal with practical local philanthropies and great international mission movements, and their interdenominational feelings for all Christendom are strong. Yet they hold to their ancient verities, and antiquity broods over their meditations.

For instance I found in their bookcase an endless dialogue epic called *The Wandering Soul,* in which this soul, seeking mainly for information, engages in stilted conversation with Adam, Noah, and Simon Cleophas. Thereby the Wandering Soul is informed as to the orthodox history and chronology of the world from the Creation to the destruction of Jerusalem. The wood-cuts are devotional. They are worth walking to Kansas to see. The book had its third translation into Pennsylvania English in 1840, but several American editions had existed in German before that, and several German editions in Germany. It was originally written in the Dutch language and was popular among the Mennonites there. But it looks as if it was printed by Adam to last forever and scare bad boys.

Let us go to meeting. All the women are on their own side of the aisle. All of them have a fairly uniform Quakerish sort of dress of no prescribed color. In front are the most pious, who wear a black scoop-bonnet. Some have taken this off, and show the inevitable "prayer-covering" underneath. It is the plainest kind of a lace-cap, awfully coquettish on a pretty head. It is intended to mortify the flesh, and I suppose it *is* unbecoming to *some* women.

All the scoop-bonnets are not black. Toward the middle of the church, behold a cream-satin, a soft gray, a dull moon-gold. One young woman, moved, I fear, by the devil, turns and looks across the aisle at us. An exceedingly demure bow is tied all too sweetly under the chin, in a decorous butterfly style. Fie! fie! Is this mortifying the flesh? And I note with pain that the black bonnets grow fewer and fewer toward the rear of the meeting house.

Here come the children, with bobbing headgear of every color of the rainbow, yet the same scoop-pattern still. They have been taking little walks and runs between Sunday-school and church, and are all flushed and panting. But I would no more criticise the color of their headgear than the color in their faces. Some of them squeeze in among the black rows in front and make piety reasonable. But we noted by the door as they entered something that both the church and the world must abhor. Seated as near to the men's side as they can get, with a mixture of shame and defiance in their faces, are certain daughters of the Mennonites who insist on dressing after the fashions that come from Paris and Kansas City and Emporia. By the time the rumors of what is proper in millinery have reached this place they are a disconcerting mixture of cherries, feathers and ferns. And somehow there are too many mussy ribbons on the dresses.

We can only guess how these rebels must suffer under the concentrated silent prayers of the godly. Poor honest souls! they take to this world's vain baggage and overdo it. Why do they not make up their minds to serve the devil sideways, like that sly puss with the butterfly bow?

On the men's side of the house the division on dress is more acute. The Holiness movement, the doctrine of the Second Blessing that has stirred many rural Methodist groups, has attacked the Mennonites also. Those who dispute for this new ism of sanctification leave off their neckties as a sign. Those that retain their neckties, satisfied with what Menno Simonis taught, have a hard time remaining in a state of complete calm. The temptation to argue the matter is almost more than flesh can bear.

But, so far as I could discover, there was no silent prayer over the worst lapse of these people. What remains of my Franciscan soul was hurt to discover that the buggy-shed of the meeting-house was full of automobiles. And to meet a Mennonite on the road without a necktie, his wife in the blackest of bonnets, honking along in one of those glittering brazen machines, almost shakes my confidence in the Old Jerusalem Gospel.

Yet let me not indulge in disrespect. Every spiritual warfare must abound in its little ironies. They are keeping their rule against finery as well as I am keeping mine against the railroad. And they have their own way of not being corrupted by money. Their ministry is unsalaried. Their preachers are sometimes helpers on the farms, sometimes taken care of outright, the same as I am.

As will later appear, despite some inconsistencies, the Mennonites have a piety as literal as any to be found on the earth. Since they are German there is no lack of thought in their system. I attended one of their quarterly conferences and I have never heard better discourses on the distinctions between the four gospels. The men who spoke were scholars.

The Mennonites make it a principle to ignore politics, and are non-resistants in war. I have read in the life of one of their heroes what a terrible time his people had in the Shenandoah valley in the days of Sheridan. . . . Three solemn tracts are here on my dresser. The first is against church organs, embodying a plea for simplicity and the spending of such money on local benevolences and world-wide missions. The tract aptly compares the church-organ to the Thibetan prayer-wheel, and later to praying by phonograph. A song is a prayer to them, and they sing hymns and nothing but hymns all week long.

The next tract is on non-conformity to this world, and insists our appearance should indicate our profession, and that fashions drive the poor away from the church. It condemns jewels and plaiting of the hair, etc., and says that such things stir up a wicked and worldly lust in the eyes of youth. This tract goes so far as to put worldly pictures under the ban. Then comes another, headed Bible Teaching on Dress. It goes on to show that every true Christian, especially that vain bird, the female, should wear something like the Mennonite uniform to indicate the line of separation from "the World." I have a good deal of sympathy for all this, for indeed is it not briefly comprehended in my own rule: "Carry no baggage"?

These people celebrate communion every half year, and at the same time they practise the ritual of washing the feet. Since Isadora

Duncan has rediscovered the human foot aesthetically, who dares object to it in ritual? It is all a question of what we are trained to expect. Certainly these people are respecters of the human foot and not ashamed to show it. Next to the way their women have of making a dash to find their gauzy prayer-covering, which they put on for grace at table and Bible-lesson before breakfast, their most striking habit is the way both men and women go about in very clean bare feet after supper. Next to this let me note their resolve to have no profane hour whatsoever. When not actually at work they sit and sing hymns, each Christian on his own hook as he has leisure.

My first evening among these dear strangers I was sitting alone by the front door, looking out on the wheat. I was thrilled to see the fairest member of the household enter, not without grace and dignity. Her prayer covering was on her head, her white feet were shining like those of Nicolette and her white hymn-book was in her hand. She ignored me entirely. She was rapt in trance. She sat by the window and sang through the book, looking straight at a rose in the wall-paper.

I lingered there, reading *The Wandering Soul* just as oblivious of her presence as she was of mine. Oh, no; there was no art in the selection of her songs! I remember one which was to this effect:

> ''Don't let it be said:
> 'Too late, too late
> To enter that Golden Gate.'
> Be ready, for soon
> The time will come
> To enter that Golden Gate.''

On the whole she had as much right to plunk down and sing hymns out of season as I have to burst in and quote poetry to peaceful and unprotected households.

I would like to insert a discourse here on the pleasure and the naturalness and the humanness of testifying to one's gospel whatever that gospel may be, barefooted or golden-slippered or iron-shod. The best we may win in return may be but a kindly smile. We may never make one convert. Still the duty of testifying remains, and is enjoined by the invisible powers and makes for the health of the soul. This Mennonite was a priestess of her view of the truth and comes of endless generations of such snow-footed apostles. I presume the sect ceased to enlarge when the Quakers ceased to thrive, but I make my guess that it does not crumble as fast as the Quakers, having more German stolidity.

Let me again go forward, testifying to my particular lonely gospel in the face of such pleasant smiles and incredulous questions as may come. I wish I could start a sturdy sect like old Menno Simonis did. They should dress as these have done, and be as stubborn and rigid in their discipline. They should farm as these have done, but on reaching the point where the Mennonite buys the automobile, that money and energy should go into the making of cross-roads palaces for the people, golden as the harvest field, and disciplined well-parked villages, good as a psalm, and cities fair as a Mennonite lady in her prayer-covering, delicate and noble as Athens the unforgotten, the divine.

The Mennonite doctrine of non-participation in war or politics leads them to confine their periodic literature to religious journals exclusively, plus *The Drover's Journal* to keep them up to date on the prices of farm-products. There is only one Mennonite political event, the coming of Christ to judge the earth. Of that no man knoweth the day or the hour. We had best be prepared and not play politics or baseball or anything. Just keep unspotted and harvest the wheat.

''Goin' wes' harvesin'?''

I have harvested, thank you. Four days and a half I have shocked wheat in these prayer-consecrated fields that I see even now from my window. And I have good hard dollars in my pocket, which same dollars are against my rules.

I will tell you of the harvest in the next letter.

IV

In Kansas: The First Harvest

MONDAY AFTERNOON, JULY 1, 1912. A little west of Newton, Kansas. In the public library of a village whose name I forget.

Here is the story of how I came to harvest. I was by chance taking a short respite from the sunshine, last Monday noon, on the porch of the Mennonite farmer. I had had dinner further back. But the good folk asked me to come in and have dessert anyway. It transpired that one of the two harvest hands was taking his farewell meal. He was obliged to fill a contract to work further West, a contract made last year. I timidly suggested I might take his place. To my astonishment I was engaged at once. This fellow was working for two dollars a day, but I agreed to $1.75, seeing my predecessor was a skilled man and twice as big as I was. My wages, as I discovered, included three rich meals, and a pretty spare room to sleep in, and a good big bucket to bathe in nightly.

I anticipate history at this point by telling how at the end of the week my wages looked as strange to me as a bunch of unexpected ducklets to a hen. They were as curious to contemplate as a group of mischievous nieces who have come to spend the day with their embarrassed, fluttering maiden aunt.

I took my wages to Newton, and spent all on the vanities of this life. First the grandest kind of a sombrero, so I shall not be sun-struck in the next harvest-field, which I narrowly escaped in this. Next, the most indestructible of corduroys. Then I had my shoes re-soled and bought a necktie that was like the oriflamme of Navarre, and attended to several other points of vanity. I started out again, dead broke and happy. If I work hereafter I can send most all my wages home, for I am now in real travelling costume.

But why linger over the question of wages till I show I earned those wages?

Let me tell you of a typical wheat-harvesting day. The field is two miles from the house. We make preparations for a twelve-hour siege. Halters and a barrel of water and a heap of alfalfa for the mules, binder-twine and oil for the reaper and water-jugs for us are loaded into the spring wagon. Two mules are hitched in front, two are led behind. The new reaper was left in the field yesterday. We make haste. We must be at work by the time the dew dries. The four mules are soon hitched to the reaper and proudly driven into the wheat by the son of the old Mennonite. This young fellow carries himself with proper dignity as heir of the farm. He is a credit to the father. He will not curse the mules, though those animals forget their religion sometimes, and act after the manner of their kind. The worst he will do will be to call one of them an old cow. I suppose when he is vexed with a cow he calls it an old mule. My other companion is a boy of nineteen from a Mennonite community in Pennsylvania. He sets me a pace. Together we build the sheaves into shocks, of eight or ten sheaves each, put so they will not be shaken by an ordinary Kansas wind. The wind has been blowing nearly all the time at a rate which in Illinois would mean a thunderstorm in five minutes, and sometimes the clouds loom in the thunderstorm way, yet there is not a drop of rain, and the clouds are soon gone.

In the course of the week the boy and I have wrestled with heavy ripe sheaves, heavier green sheaves, sheaves full of Russian thistles and sheaves with the string off. The boy, as he sings *The day-star hath risen,* twists a curious rope of straw and reties the loose bundles with one turn of the hand. I try, but cannot make the knot. Once all sheaves were so bound.

Much of the wheat must be cut heavy and green because there is a liability to sudden storms or hail that will bury it in mud, or soften the ground and make it impossible to drag the reaper, or hot winds that suddenly ripen the loose grain and shake it into the earth. So it is an important matter to get the wheat out when it is anywhere near ready. I found that two of the girls were expecting to take the place of the departing hand, if I had not arrived.

The Mennonite boy picked up two sheaves to my one at the beginning of the week. To-day I learn to handle two at a time and he immediately handles three at a time. He builds the heart of the sheaf. Then we add the outside together. He is always marching ahead and causing me to feel ashamed.

The Kansas grasshopper makes himself friendly. He bites pieces out of the back of my shirt the shape and size of the ace of spades. Then he walks into the door he has made and loses himself. Then he has to be helped out, in one way or another.

The old farmer, too stiff for work, comes out on his dancing pony and rides behind the new reaper. This reaper was bought only two days ago and he beams with pride upon it. It seems that he and his son almost swore, trying to tinker the old one. The farmer looks with even more pride upon the field, still a little green, but mostly golden. He dismounts and tests the grain, threshing it out in his hand, figuring the average amount in several typical heads. He stands off, and is guilty of an aesthetic thrill. He says of the sea of gold: "I wish I could have a photograph of that." (O eloquent word, for a Mennonite!) Then he plays at building half a dozen shocks, then goes home till late in the afternoon. We three are again masters of the field.

We are in a level part of Kansas, not a rolling range as I found it further east. The field is a floor. Hedges gradually faded from the landscape in counties several days' journey back, leaving nothing but unbroken billows to the horizon. But the hedges have been resumed in this region. Each time round the enormous field we stop at a break in the line of those untrimmed old thorn-trees. Here we rest a moment and drink from the water-jug. To keep from getting sunstruck I profanely waste the water, pouring it on my head, and down my neck to my feet. I came to this farm wearing a derby, and have had to borrow a slouch with a not-much-wider rim from the farmer. It was all the extra headgear available in this thrifty region. Because of that not-much-wider rim my face is sunburned all over every day. I have not yet received my wages to purchase my sombrero.

As we go round the field, the Mennonite boy talks religion, or is silent. I have caught the spirit of the farm, and sing all the hymn-tunes I can remember. Sometimes the wind turns hot. Perspiration cannot keep up with evaporation. Our skins are dry as the dryest stubble. Then we stand and wait for a little streak of cool wind. It is pretty sure to come in a minute. "That's a nice air," says the boy, and gets to work. Once it was so hot all three of us stopped five minutes by the hedge. Then it was I told them the story of the hens I met just west of Emporia.

I had met ten hens walking single-file into the town of Emporia. I was astonished to meet educated hens. Each one was swearing. I would not venture, I added, to repeat what they said.

Not a word from the Mennonites.

I continued in my artless way, showing how I stopped the next to the last hen, though she was impatient to go on. I inquired "Where are you all travelling?" She said "To Emporia." And so I asked, "Why are you swearing so?" She answered, "Don't you know about the Sunday-school picnic?" I paused in my story.

No word from the Mennonites. One of them rose rather impatiently.

I poured some water on my head and continued: "I stopped the last hen. I asked: "Why are you swearing, sister? And what about the picnic?" She replied: "These Emporia people are going to give a Sunday-school picnic day after to-morrow. Meantime all us hens have to lay devilled eggs."

"We do not laugh at jokes about swearing," said the Mennonite driver, and climbed back on to his reaper. My partner strode solemnly out into the sun and began to pile sheaves.

Each round we study our shadows on the stubble more closely, thrilled with the feeling that noon creeps on. And now, up the road we see a bit of dust and a rig. No, it is not the woman we are looking for, but a woman with supplies for other harvesters. We work on and on, while four disappointing rigs go by. At last appears a sunbonnet we know. Our especial Mennonite maid is sitting quite straight on the edge of the seat and holding the lines almost on a level with her chin. She drives through the field toward us. We motion her to the gap in the hedge.

We unhitch, and lead the mules to the gap, where she joins us. With much high-minded expostulation the men try to show the mules they should eat alfalfa and not hedge-thorns. The mules are at last tied out in the sun to a wheel of the wagon, away from temptation, with nothing but alfalfa near them.

The meal is spread with delicacy, yet there is a heap of it. With a prayer of thanksgiving, sometimes said by Tilly, sometimes by one of the men, we begin to eat. To a man in a harvest-field a square meal is more thrilling than a finely-acted play.

The thrill goes not only to the toes and the finger-tips, but to the utmost ramifications of the spirit. Men indoors in offices, whose bodies actually require little, cannot think of eating enormously without thinking of sodden overeating, with condiments to rouse, and heavy meats and sweets to lull the flabby body till the last faint remnants of appetite have departed and the man is a monument of sleepy gluttony.

Eating in a harvest field is never so. Every nerve in the famished body calls frantically for reinforcements. And the nerves and soul of a man are strangely alert together. All we ate for breakfast turned to hot ashes in our hearts at eleven o'clock. I sing of the body and of the eternal soul, revived again! To feel life actually throbbing back into one's veins, life immense in passion, pulse and power, is not over-eating.

Tilly has brought us knives, and no forks. It would have been more appropriate if we had eaten from the ends of swords. We are finally recuperated from the fevers of the morning and almost strong enough for the long, long afternoon fight with the sun. Fresh water is poured from a big glittering can into the jugs we have sucked dry. Tilly reloads the buggy and is gone. After another sizzling douse of water without and within, our long afternoon pull commences.

The sun has become like a roaring lion, and we wrestle with the sheaves as though we had him by the beard. The only thing that keeps up my nerve in the dizziness is the remembrance of the old Mennonite's proverb at breakfast that as long as a man can eat and sweat he is safe. My hands inside my prickling gloves seem burning off. The wheat beards there are like red-hot needles. But I am still sweating a little in the chest, and the Mennonite boy is cheerfully singing:

> "When I behold the wondrous cross
> On which the Prince of Glory died,
> My richest gain I count but loss
> And pour contempt on all my pride."

Two-thirds round the field, methinks the jig is up. Then the sun is hidden by a friend of ours in the sky, just the tiniest sort of a cloud and we march on down the rows. The merciful little whiff of dream follows the sun for half an hour.

The most terrible heat is at half-past two. Somehow we pull through till four o'clock. Then we say to ourselves: "We can stand this four-o'clock heat, because we have stood it hotter."

'Tis a grim matter of comparison. We speed up a little and trot a little as the sun reaches the top of the western hedge. A bit later the religious hired man walks home to do the chores. I sing down the rows by myself. It is glorious to work now. The endless reiterations of the day have developed a certain dancing rhythm in one's nerves, one is intoxicated with his own weariness and the conceit that comes with seizing the sun by the mane, like Sampson.

It is now that the sun gracefully acknowledges his defeat. He shows through the hedge as a great blur, that is all. Then he becomes a mist-wrapped golden mountain that some fairy traveller might climb in enchanted shoes. This sun of ours is no longer an enemy, but a fantasy, a vision and a dream.

Now the elderly proprietor is back on his dancing pony. He is following the hurrying reaper in a sort of ceremonial fashion, delighted to see the wheat go down so fast. At last this particular field is done. We finish with a comic-tragedy. Some little rabbits scoot, panic-stricken, from the last few yards of still-standing grain. The old gentleman on horseback and his son afoot soon out-manoeuvre the lively creatures. We have rabbit for supper at the sacrifice of considerable Mennonite calm.

It was with open rejoicing on the part of all that we finished the field nearest the house, the last one, by Saturday noon. The boy and I had our own special thrill in catching up with the reaper, which had passed by us so often in our rounds. As the square in mid-field grows smaller the reaper has to turn oftener, and turning uses up much more time than at first appears.

The places where the armies of wheat-sheaves are marshalled are magic places, despite their sweat and dust. There is nothing small in the panorama. All the lines of the scene are epic. The binder-twine is invisible, and has not altered the eternal classic form of the sheaf. There is a noble dignity and ease in the motion of a new reaper on a level field. A sturdy Mennonite devotee marching with a great bundle of wheat under each arm and reaching for a third makes a picture indeed, an essay on sunshine beyond the brush of any impressionist. Each returning day while riding to the field, when one has a bit of time to dream, one feels these things. One feels also the essentially patriarchal character of the harvest. One thinks of the Book of Ruth, and the Jewish feasts of ingathering. All the New Testament parables ring in one's ears, parables of sowing and reaping, of tares and good grain, of Bread and of Leaven and the story of the Disciples plucking corn. As one looks on the half-gathered treasure he thinks on the solemn words: ''For the Bread of God is that which cometh down out of Heaven and giveth life unto the World,'' and the rest of that sermon on the Bread of Life, which has so many meanings.

This Sunday before breakfast, I could fully enter into the daily prayers, that at times had appeared merely quaint to me, and in my heart I said ''Amen'' to the special thanksgiving the patriarch lifted up for the gift of the fruit of the land. I was happy indeed that I had had the strength to bear my little part in the harvest of a noble and devout household, as well as a hand in the feeding of the wide world.

What I, a stranger, have done in this place, thirty thousand strangers are doing just a little to the west. We poor tramps are helping to garner that which reestablishes the nations. If only for a little while, we have bent our backs over the splendid furrows, to save a shining gift that would otherwise rot, or vanish away.

THURSDAY AFTERNOON, JULY FOURTH, 1912. In the shadow of a lonely windmill between Raymond and Ellinwood, Kansas.

I arrived hot and ravenous at Raymond about eleven A.M. on this glorious Independence Day, having walked twelve miles facing a strange wind. At first it seemed fairly cool, because it travelled at the rate of an express train. But it was really hot and alkaline, and almost burnt me up. I had had for breakfast a cooky, some raisins and a piece of cheese, purchased with my booklet of rhymes at a grocery. By the time I reached Raymond I was fried and frantic.

The streets were deserted. I gathered from the station-master that almost everyone had gone to the Dutch picnic in the grove near Ellinwood. The returns for the Johnson-Flynn fight were to be received there beneath the trees, and a potent variety of dry-state beverage was to flow free. The unveracious station-master declared this beverage was made of equal parts iron-rust, patent medicine and rough-on-rats, added to a barrel of brown rain-water. He appeared to be prejudiced against it.

I walked down the street. Just as I had somehow anticipated, I spied out a certain type of man. He was alone in his restaurant and I crouched my soul to spring. The only man left in town is apt to be a soft-hearted party. ''Here, as sure as my name is tramp, I will wrestle with a defenceless fellow-being.''

Like many a restaurant in Kansas, it was a sort of farmhand's Saturday night paradise. If a man cannot loaf in a saloon he will loaf in a restaurant. Then certain problems of demand and supply arise according to circumstances and circumlocutions.

I obtained leave for the ice-water without wrestling. I almost emptied the tank. Then, with due art, I offered to recite twenty poems to the solitary man, a square meal to be furnished at the end, if the rhymes were sufficiently fascinating.

Assuming a judicial attitude on the lunch-counter stool he put me in the arm-chair by the ice-chest and told me to unwind myself. As usual, I began with *The Proud Farmer, The Illinois Village* and *The Building of Springfield,* which three in series contain my whole gospel, directly or by implication. Then I wandered on through all sorts of rhyme. He nodded his head like a mandarin, at the end of each recital. Then he began to get dinner. He said he liked my poetry, and he was glad I came in, for he would feel more like getting something to eat himself. I sat on and on by the ice-chest while he prepared a meal more heating than the morning wind or the smell of firecrackers in the street. First, for each man, a slice of fried ham large enough for a whole family. Then French fried potatoes by the platterful. Then three fried eggs apiece. There was milk with cream on top to be poured from a big granite bucket as we desired it. There was a can of beans with tomato sauce. There was sweet apple-butter. There were canned apples. There was a pot of coffee. I moved over from the ice-chest and we talked and ate till half-past one. I began to feel that I was solid as an iron man and big as a Colossus of Rhodes. I would like to report our talk, but this letter must end somewhere. I agreed with my host's opinions on everything but the temperance question. He did not believe in *total* abstinence. On that I remained noncommittal. Eating as I had, how could I take a stand against my benefactor even though the issue were the immortal one of man's sinful weakness for drink? The ham and ice water were going to my head as it was. And I could have eaten more. I could have eaten a fat Shetland pony.

My host explained that he also travelled at times, but did not carry poetry. He gave me much box-car learning. Then, curious to relate, he dug out maps and papers, and showed me how to take up a claim in Oregon, a thing I did not in the least desire to do. God bless him in basket and in store, afoot or at home.

This afternoon the ham kept on frying within me, not uncomfortably. I stopped and drank at every windmill. Now it is about four o'clock in the afternoon and I am in the shadow of one more. I have found a bottle which just fits my hip pocket which I have washed and will use as a canteen henceforth. When one knows he has his drink with him, he does not get so thirsty.

But I have put down little to show you the strange intoxication that has pervaded this whole day. The inebriating character of the air and the water and the intoxication that comes with the very sight of the windmills spinning alone, and the elation that comes with the companionship of the sun, and the gentleness of the occasional good Samaritans, are not easily conveyed in words. When one's spirit is just right for this sort of thing it all makes as good an Independence Day as folks are having anywhere in this United States, even at Ellinwood.

[FRIDAY], JULY 5, 1912. In the office of the Ellinwood livery stable in the morning.

Everyone came home drunk from the Dutch picnic last night. Ellinwood roared and Ellinwood snorted. I reached the place from the east just as the noisy revellers arrived from the south.

Ellinwood is an old German town full of bar-rooms, forced by the sentiment of the dry voters in surrounding territory to turn into restaurants, but only of late. The bar-fixtures are defiantly retained. Ever and anon Ellinwood takes to the woods with malicious intent.

Many of the citizens were in a mad-dog fury because Flynn had not licked Johnson. This town seems to be of the opinion that that battle was important. The proprietor of the most fashionable hotel monopolized the 'phone on his return from the woods. He called up everybody in town. His conversation was always the same. "What'd ya think of the fight?" And without waiting for answer: "I'll bet one hundred thousand dollars that Flynn can lick Johnson in a fair fight. It's a disgrace to this nation that black rascal kin lay hands on a white man. I'll bet a hundred thousand dollars. . . . A hundred thousand dollars . .," etc.

I sat a long time waiting for him to get through. At last I put in my petition at another hostelrie. This host was intoxicated, but gentle. In exchange for what I call the squarest kind of a meal I recited the most cooling verses I knew to a somewhat distracted, rather alcoholic company of harvest hands. First I recited a poem in praise of Lincoln and then one in praise of the uplifting influence of the village church. Then, amid qualified applause, I distributed my tracts, and retreated to this stable for the night.

V

In Kansas: the Second and Third Harvest

Two miles north of Great Bend. In the heart of the greatest wheat country in America, and in the midst of the harvest-time, Sunday, July 7, 1912.

I am meditating on the ways of Destiny. It seems to me I am here, not altogether by chance. But just why I am here, time must reveal.

Last Friday I had walked the ten miles from Ellinwood to Great Bend by 9 A.M. I went straight to the general delivery, where a package of tracts and two or three weeks' mail awaited me. I read about half through the letter-pile as I sat on a rickety bench in the public square. Some very loud-mouthed negroes were playing horse-shoe obstreperously. I began to wish Flynn had whipped Johnson. I was thinking of getting away from there, when two white men, evidently harvesters, sat down near me and diluted the color scheme.

One man said: "Harvest-wages this week are from two dollars and fifty cents up to four dollars. We are experienced men and worth three dollars and fifty cents." Then a German farmer came and negotiated with them in vain. He wanted to hold them down to three dollars apiece. He had his automobile to take his crew away that morning.

Then a fellow in citified clothes came to me and asked: "Can you follow a reaper and shock?" I said: *"Show me the wheat."* So far as I remember, it is the first time in my life anyone ever hunted me out and *asked* me to work for him. He put me into his buggy and drove me about two miles north to this place, just the region John Humphrey told me to find, though he did not specify this farm. I was offered $2.50 and keep, as the prophet foretold. The man who drove me out has put his place this year into the hands of a tenant who is my direct boss. I may not be able to last out, but all is well so far. I have made an acceptable hand, keeping up with the reaper by myself, and I feel something especial awaits me. But the reaper breaks down so often I do not know whether I can keep up with it without help when it begins going full-speed.

These people do not attend church like the Mennonites. The tenant wanted me to break the Sabbath and help him in the alfalfa today. He suggested that neither he nor I was so narrow-minded or superstitious as to be a "Sunday man." Besides he couldn't work the alfalfa at all without one more hand. I did not tell him so, but I felt I needed all Sunday to catch up on my tiredness. I suspect that my refusal to violate the Sabbath vexed him.

There has been a terrible row of some kind going on behind the barn all afternoon. Maybe he is working off his vexation. At last the tenant's wife has gone out to ''see about that racket.'' Now she comes in. She tells me they have been trying to break a horse.

The same farm, two miles north of Great Bend, July 8, 1912.

How many times in the counties further back I have asked with fear and misgiving for permission to work in the alfalfa, and have been repulsed when I confessed to the lack of experience! And now this morning I have pitched alfalfa hay with the best of them. We had to go to work early while the dew softened the leaves. It is a kind of clover. Once perfectly dry, the leaves crumble off when the hay is shaken. Then we must quit. The leaves are the nourishing part.

The owner of the place, the citified party who drove me out here the other day and who is generally back in town, was on top of that stack this morning, his collar off, his town shirt and pants somewhat the worse for the exertion. He puffed like a porpoise, for he was putting in place all the hay we men handed up to him. We lifted the alfalfa in a long bundle, using our three forks at one time. We worked like drilled soldiers, then went in to early dinner.

This is a short note written while the binder takes the necessary three turns round the new wheatfield that the tenant's brother and I are starting to conquer this afternoon. Three swaths of four bundles each must be cut, then I will start on my rounds, piling them into shocks of twelve bundles each.

I am right by the R.F.D. box that goes with this farm. I will put up the little tin flag that signals the postman. One of the four beasts hitched to the reaper is a broncho colt who came dancing to the field this afternoon, refusing to keep his head in line with the rest of the steeds, and, as a consequence, pulling the whole reaper. It transpires that the row in the horselot Sunday was caused by this colt. He jumped up and left his hoof-print on the chest of the man now driving him. So the two men tied him up and beat him all afternoon with a double-tree, cursing him between whacks, lashing themselves with Kansas whisky to keep up steam. Yet he comes dancing to the field.

On the farm two miles north of Great Bend, Wednesday evening, July 10, 1912.

I must write you a short note to-night while the rest are getting ready for supper. I will try to mail it to-morrow morning on the way to the wheat. Let me assure you that your letter will be heeded. I know pretty well, by this time, what I can stand, but if I feel the least bit unfit I will not go into the sun. That is my understanding with the tenant who runs the farm. I can eat and sweat like a Mennonite. I sleep like a top and wake up fresh as a little daisy. So far I have gone dancing to the field as the broncho did. But the broncho is a poor illustration. He is dead.

The broncho was the property of a little boy, the son of the man who owns the farm. The little boy had started with a lamb and raised it, then sold it for chickens, increasing his capital by trading and feeding till it was all concentrated to buy this colt. Then he and his people moved to town and left the colt, just at the breaking age, to be trained for a boy's pet by these men. Since he became obstreperous, they thought hitching him to the reaper would cure him, leaving a draught-horse in the barn to make place for the unruly one.

The tenant's brother, who drove the reaper, sent word to the little boy he had not the least idea what ailed Dick. He hinted to me later that whatever killed him must have come from some disease in his head.

Yes, it came from his head. That double-tree and that pitchfork handle probably missed his ribs once or twice and hit him somewhere around his eyes, in the course of the Sabbath afternoon services. Two whisky-lashed colt-breakers can do wonders without trying. I have been assured that this is the only way to subdue the beasts, that law and order must assert themselves or the whole barnyard will lead an industrial rebellion. It is past supper now. I have been writing till the lamp is dim. I must go to my quilts in the hay.

To-day was the only time the reaper did not break down every half hour for repairs. So it was one continuous dance for me and my friend the broncho till about three o'clock in the afternoon, when the sun really did its best. Then the broncho went crazy. He shoved his head over the backs of two mules twice his size, and almost pushed them into the teeth of the sickle.

He was bleeding at the mouth and his eyes almost popped out of his head. He had hardly an inch of hide that was whole, and his raw places were completely covered with Kansas flies. And the hot winds have made the flies so ravenous they draw blood from the back of the harvester's hand the moment they alight.

The broncho began to kick in all four directions at once. He did one good thing. He pulled the callouses off the hands of the tenant's brother, the driver, who still gripped the lines but surrendered his pride and yelled for me to help. I am as afraid of bronchos and mules as I am of buzz saws. Yet we separated the beasts somehow, the mules safely hitched to the fence, the broncho between us, held by two halter-ropes.

There was no reasoning with Dick. He was dying, and dying game. One of the small boys appeared just then and carried the alarm. Soon a more savage and indomitable man with a more eloquent tongue, the tenant himself, had my end of the rope. But not the most formidable cursing could stop Dick from bleeding at the mouth. Later the draught horse whose place he had taken was brought over from his pleasant rest in the barn and the two were tied head to head. The lordly tenant started to lead them toward home. But Dick fell down and died as soon as he reached a patch of unploughed prairie grass, which, I think, was the proper end for him. The peaceful draught horse was put in his place.

The reaper went back to work. The reaper cut splendidly the rest of the afternoon. As for me I never shocked wheat with such machine-like precision. I went at a dog-trot part of the time, and almost caught up with the machine.

The broncho should not have been called Dick. He should have been called Daniel Boone, or Davy Crockett or Custer or Richard, yes, Richard the Lion-Hearted. He came dancing to the field this morning, between the enormous overshadowing mules, and dancing feebly this noon. He pulled the whole reaper till three o'clock. I remember I asked the driver at noon what made the broncho dance. He answered: "The flies on his ribs, I suppose."

I fancy Dick danced because he was made to die dancing, just as the Spartans rejoiced and combed their long hair preparing to face certain death at Thermopylae.

I think I want on my coat of arms a broncho, rampant.

THURSDAY, JULY 11, 1912. Great Bend, Kansas.

Yesterday I could lift three moderate-sized sheaves on the run. This morning I could hardly lift one, walking. This noon the foreman of the ranch, the man who, with his brother, disciplined the broncho, was furiously angry with me, because, as I plainly explained, I was getting too much sun and wanted a bit of rest. He inquired, "Why didn't you tell me two days ago you were going to be overcome by the heat, so I could have had a man ready to take your place?" Also, "It's no wonder dirty homeless men are walking around the country looking for jobs." Also, a little later: "I have my opinion of any man on earth who is a quitter."

But I kept my serenity and told him that under certain circumstances I was apt to be a quitter, though, of course, I did not like to overdo the quitting business. I remained unruffled, as I say, and handed him and his brother copies of *The Gospel of Beauty* and *Rhymes to Be Traded for Bread* and bade them good-bye. Then I went to town and told the local editor on them for their horse-killing, which, I suppose, was two-faced of me.

The tenant's attitude was perfectly absurd. Hands are terribly scarce. A half day's delay in shocking that wheat would not have hurt it, or stopped the reaper, or altered any of the rest of the farm routine. He fired me without real hope of a substitute. I was working for rock-bottom wages and willing to have them docked all he pleased if he would only give me six hours to catch up in my tiredness.

Anyway, here I am in the Saddlerock Hotel, to which I have paid in advance a bit of my wages, in exchange for one night's rest. I enclose the rest to you. I will start out on the road to-morrow, bathed, clean, dead broke and fancy free. I have made an effort to graduate from beggary into the respectable laboring class, which you have so often exhorted me to do.

I shall try for employment again, as soon as I rest up a bit. I enjoyed the wheat and the second-hand reaper, and the quaintness of my employers and all till the death of Richard the Lion-Hearted.

I am wondering whether I ought to be as bitter as I am against the horse-killers. We cannot have green fields just for bronchos to gambol in, or roads where they can trot unharnessed and nibble by the way. We must have Law and Order and Discipline.

But, thanks to the Good St. Francis who marks out my path for me, I start to-morrow morning to trot unharnessed once again.

SUNDAY, JULY 14, 1912. In front of the general store at Wright Kansas, which same is as small as a town can get.

I have been wondering why Destiny sent me to that farm where the horse-killers flourished. I suppose it was that Dick might have at least one mourner. All the world's heroes are heroes because they had the qualities of constancy and dancing gameness that brought him to his death.

Some day I shall hunt up the right kind of a Hindu and pay him filthy gold and have him send the ghost of Dick to those wretched men. They will be unable to move, lying with eyes a-staring all night long. Dreadful things will happen in that room, dreadful things the Hindu shall devise after I have told him what the broncho endured.

They shall wake in the morning, thinking it all a dream till they behold the horse-shoe prints all over the counterpane. Then they will try to sit up and find that their ribs are broken—well, I will leave it to the Hindu.

I have been waiting many hours at this town of Wright. To-day and yesterday I made seventy-six miles. Thirty-five of these miles I made yesterday in the automobile of the genial and scholarly Father A.P. Heimann of Kinsley, who took me as far as that point. I have been loafing here at Wright since about four in the afternoon. It is nearly dark now. Dozens of harvesters, already engaged for the week, have been hanging about and the two stores have kept open to accommodate them. There is a man to meet me here at eight o'clock. I may harvest for him four days. I told him I would not promise for longer. He has taken the train to a station further east to try to get some men for all week. If he does not return with a full quota he will take me on. While I am perfectly willing to work for two dollars and a half, many hold out for three.

The man I am waiting for overtook me two miles east of this place. He was hurrying to catch his train. He took me into his rig and made the bargain. He turned his horse over to me and raced for the last car as we neared the station. So here I am a few yards from the depot, in front of the general store, watching the horse of an utter stranger. Of course the horse isn't worth stealing, and his harness is half twine and wire. But the whole episode is so careless and free and Kansas-like.

Most of the crowd have gone, and I am awfully hungry. I might steal off the harness in the dark, and eat it. Somehow I have not quite the nerve to beg where I expect to harvest. I am afraid to try again in this fight with the sun, yet when a man overtakes me in the road and trusts me with his best steed and urges me to work for him, I hardly know how to refuse.

SUNDAY AFTERNOON, JULY 21, 1912. Loafing and dozing on my bed in the granary on the farm near Wright, Kansas, where I have been harvesting a full week.

The man I waited for last Sunday afternoon returned with his full quota of hands on the "Plug" train about nine o'clock. Where was I to sleep? I began to think about a lumber pile I had seen, when I discovered that five other farmers had climbed off that train. They were poking around in all the dark corners for men just like me. I engaged with a German named Louis Lix for the whole week, all the time shaking with misgivings from the memory of my last break-down. Here it is, Sunday, before I know it. Lix wants me back again next year, and is sorry I will not work longer. I have totalled about sixteen days of harvesting in Kansas, and though I sagged in the middle I think I have ended in fair style. Enclosed find all my wages except enough for one day's stay at Dodge City and three real hotel meals there — sherbet and cheese and crackers, and finger bowls at the end, and all such folly. Harvest eating is grand in its way but somehow lacks frills. Ah, if eating were as much in my letters as in my thoughts, this would be nothing but a series of menus!

I have helped Lix harvest barley, oats and wheat, mainly wheat. This is the world of wheat. In this genial region one can stand on a soap-box and see nothing else to the horizon. Walking the Santa Fé Trail beside the railroad means walking till the enormous wheat-elevator behind one disappears because of the curvature of the earth, like the ships in the geography picture, and walking on and on till finally in the west the top of another elevator appears, being gradually revealed because this earth is not flat like a table, but, as the geography says, curved like an apple or an orange.

In these fields, instead of working a reaper with a sickle eight feet long, they work a header with a twelve-foot sickle. Instead of four horses to this machine, there are six. Instead of one man or two following behind to the left of the driver to pile sheaves into shocks, a barge, a most copious slatted receptacle, drives right beside the header, catching the unbound wheat which is thrown up loosely by the machine. One pitchfork man in the barge spreads this cataract of headed wheat so a full load can be taken in. His partner guides the team, keeping precisely with the header.

But these two bargemen do not complete the outfit. Two others with their barge or "header-box" come up behind as soon as the first box starts over to the stack to be unloaded. Here the sixth man, the stacker, receives it, and piles it into a small mountain nicely calculated to resist cyclones. The green men are broken in as bargemen. The stacker is generally an old hand.

Unloading the wheat is the hardest part of the bargeman's work. His fork must be full and he must be fast. Otherwise his partner, who takes turns driving and filling, and who helps to pitch the wheat out, will have more than half the pitching to do. And all the time will be used up. Neither man will have a rest-period while waiting for the other barge to come up. This rest-period is the thing toward which we all wrestle. If we save it out we drink from the water-jugs in the corner of the wagon. We examine where the grasshoppers have actually bitten little nicks out of our pitchfork handles, nicks that are apt to make blisters. We tell our adventures and, when the header breaks down, and must be tinkered endlessly, and we have a grand rest, the stacker sings a list of the most amazing cowboy songs. He is a young man, yet rode the range here for seven years before it became wheat-country. One day when the songs had become hopelessly, prosaically pornographic I yearned for a change. I quoted the first stanza of Atalanta's chorus:

> "When the hounds of Spring are on Winter's traces,
> The mother of months, in meadow or plain,
> Fills the shadows and windy places
> With lisp of leaves and ripple of rain—"

The stacker asked for more. I finished the chorus. Then I repeated it several times, while the header was being mended. We had to get to work. The next morning when my friend climbed into our barge to ride to the field he began:

> "'When the hounds of Spring are on Winter's traces,
> The mother of months, in meadow or plain,
> Fills the shadows—'

"Dammit, what's the rest of it? I've been trying to recite that piece all night."

Now he has the first four stanzas. And last evening he left for Dodge City to stay overnight and Sunday. He was resolved to purchase *Atalanta in Calydon* and find in the Public Library *The Lady of Shallot* and *The Blessed Damozel,* besides paying the usual visit to his wife and children.

Working in a header-barge is fun, more fun than shocking wheat, even when one is working for a Mennonite boss. The crew is larger. There is occasional leisure to be social. There is more cool wind, for one is higher in the air. There is variety in the work. One drives about a third of the time, guides the wheat into the header a third of the time and empties the barge a third of the time. The emptying was the back-breaking work.

And I was all the while fearful, lest, from plain awkwardness, or shaking from weariness, I should stick some man in the eye with my pitchfork. But I did not. I came nearer to being a real harvester every day. The last two days my hands were so hard I could work without gloves, this despite the way the grasshoppers had chewed the fork-handle.

Believe everything you have ever heard of the Kansas grasshoppers.

The heights of the header-barge are dramatically commanding. Kansas appears much larger than when we are merely standing in the field. We are just as high as upon a mountain-peak, for here, as there, we can see to the very edges of the eternities.

Now let me tell you of a new kind of weather.

Clouds thicken overhead. The wind turns suddenly cold. We shiver while we work. We are liable in five minutes to a hailstorm, a terrific cloudburst or a cyclone. The horses are unhitched. The barges are tied end to end. And *still* the barges may be blown away. They must be anchored even more safely. The long poles to lock the wheels are thrust under the bed through the spokes. It has actually been my duty to put this pole in the wheels every evening to keep the barges from being blown out of the barn-lot at night. Such is the accustomed weather excitement in Kansas. Just now we have excitement that is unusual. But as the storm is upon us it splits and passes to the north and south. There is not a drop of rain.

We are at work again in ten minutes. In two hours the sky is clear and the air is hot and alkaline. And ten thousand grasshoppers are glad to see that good old hot wind again, you may believe. They are preening themselves, each man in his place on the slats of the barge. They are enjoying their chewing tobacco the same as ever.

Wheat, wheat, wheat, wheat! States and continents and oceans and solar-systems of wheat! We poor ne'er-do-weels take our little part up there in the header half way between the sky and the earth, and in the evening going home, carrying Mister Stacker-Man in our barge, we sing *Sweet Rosy O'Grady* and the *Battle Hymn of the Republic*. And the most emphatic and unadulterated tramp among us harvesters, a giant Swiss fifty years old, gives the yodel he learned when a boy.

This is a German Catholic family for which I have been working. We have had grace before and after every meal, and we crossed ourselves before and after every meal, except the Swiss, who left the table early to escape being blest too much.

My employers are good folk, good as the Mennonites. My boss was absolutely on the square all the week, as kind as a hard-working man has time to be. It gave me great satisfaction to go to Mass with him this morning. Though some folks talk against religion, though it sometimes appears to be a nuisance, after weighing all the evidence of late presented, I prefer a religious farmer.

VI

The End of the Road; Moonshine; and Some Proclamations

AUGUST 1, 1912. Standing up at the Postoffice desk, Pueblo, Colorado.

Several times since going over the Colorado border I have had such a cordial reception for the Gospel of Beauty that my faith in this method of propaganda is reawakened. I confess to feeling a new zeal. But there are other things I want to tell in this letter.

I have begged my way from Dodge City on, dead broke, and keeping all the rules of the road. I have been asked dozens of times by frantic farmers to help them at various tasks in western Kansas and eastern Colorado. I have regretfully refused all but half-day jobs, having firmly resolved not to harvest again till I have well started upon a certain spiritual enterprise, namely, the writing of certain new poems that have taken possession of me in this high altitude, despite the physical stupidity that comes with strenuous walking. Thereby hangs a tale that I have not room for here.

Resolutely setting aside all recent wonders, I have still a few impressions of the wheatfield to record. Harvesting time in Kansas is such a distinctive institution! Whole villages that are dead any other season blossom with new rooming signs, fifty cents a room, or when two beds are in a room, twenty five cents a bed. The eating counters are generally separate from these. The meals are almost uniformly twenty-five cents each. The fact that Kansas has no bar-rooms makes these shabby food-sodden places into near-taverns, the main assembly halls for men wanting to be hired, or those spending their coin. Famous villages where an enormous amount of money changes hands in wages and the sale of wheat-crops are thus nothing but marvellous lines of dirty restaurants. In front of the dingy hotels are endless ancient chairs. Summer after summer fidgety, sun-fevered, sticky harvesters have gossiped from chair to chair or walked toward the dirty band-stand in the public square, sure, as of old, to be encountered by the anxious farmer, making up his crew.

A few harvesters are seen, carrying their own bedding; grasshopper bitten quilts with all their colors flaunting and their cotton gushing out, held together by a shawl-strap or a rope. Almost every harvester has a shabby suit-case of the paste-board variety banging round his ankles. When wages are rising the harvester, as I have said before, holds out for the top price. The poor farmer walks round and round the village half a day before he consents to the three dollars. Stacker's wages may be three to five simoleons and the obdurate farmer may have to consent to the five lest his wheat go to seed on the ground. It is a hard situation for a class that is constitutionally tightwad, often wisely so.

The roundhouses, water tanks, and all other places where men stealing freight rides are apt to pass, have enticing cards tacked on or near them by the agents of the mayors of the various towns, giving average wages, number of men wanted, and urging all harvesters good and true to come to some particular town between certain dates. The multitude of these little cards keeps the harvester on the alert, and, as the saying is: ''Independent as a hog on ice.''

To add to the farmer's distractions, still fresher news comes by word of mouth that three hundred men are wanted in a region two counties to the west, at fifty cents more a day. It sweeps through the harvesters' hotels, and there is a great banging of suit-cases, and the whole town is rushing for the train. Then there is indeed a nabbing of men at the station, and sudden surrender on the part of the farmers, before it is too late.

Harvesting season is inevitably placarded and dated too soon in one part of the State, and not soon enough in another. Kansas weather does not produce its results on schedule. This makes not one, but many hurry-calls. It makes the real epic of the muscle-market.

Stand with me at the station. Behold the trains rushing by, hour after hour, freight-cars and palace cars of dishevelled men! The more elegant the equipage the more do they put their feet on the seats. Behold a saturnalia of chewing tobacco and sunburn and hairy chests, disturbing the primness and crispness of the Santa Fé, jostling the tourist and his lovely daughter.

They are a happy-go-lucky set. They have the reverse of the tightwad's vices. The harvester, alas, is harvested. Gamblers lie in wait for him. The scarlet woman has her pit digged and ready. It is fun for the police to lock him up and fine him. No doubt he often deserves it. I sat half an afternoon in one of these towns and heard the local undertaker tell horrible stories of friendless field hands with no kinsfolk anywhere discoverable, sunstruck and buried in a day or so by the county. One man's story he told in great detail. The fellow had complained of a headache, and left the field. He fell dead by the roadside on the way to the house. He was face downward in an ant hill. He was eaten into an unrecognizable mass before they found him at sunset. The undertaker expatiated on how hard it was to embalm such folks. It was a discourse marshalled with all the wealth of detail one reads in *The Facts in the Case of M. Valdemar.*

The harvester is indeed harvested. He gambles with sunstroke, disease and damnation. In one way or another the money trickles from his loose fingers, and he drifts from the wheat in Oklahoma north to the wheat in Nebraska. He goes to Canada to shock wheat there as the season recedes, and then, perhaps, turns on his tracks and makes for Duluth, Minnesota, we will say. He takes up lumbering. Or he may make a circuit of the late fruit crops of Colorado and California. He is, pretty largely, so much crude, loose, ungoverned human strength, more useful than wise. Looked at closely, he may be the boy from the machine-shop, impatient for ready money, the farmer failure turned farm-hand, the bank-clerk or machine-shop mechanic tired of slow pay, or the college student on a lark, in more or less incognito. He may be the intermittent criminal, the gay-cat or the travelling religious crank, or the futile tract-distributer.

And I was three times fraternally accosted by harvesters who thought my oil-cloth package of poems was a kit of burglar's tools. It *is* a system of breaking in, I will admit.

A STORY LEFT OUT OF THE LETTERS

This ends the section of my letters home that in themselves make a consecutive story. But to finish with a bit of a nosegay, and show one of the unexpected rewards of troubadouring, let me tell the tale of the Five Little Children Eating Mush.

One should not be so vain as to recount a personal triumph. Still this is a personal triumph. And I shall tell it with all pride and vanity. Let those who dislike a conceited man drop the book right here.

I had walked all day straight west from Rocky Ford. It was pitch dark, threatening rain—the rain that never comes. It was nearly ten o'clock. At six I had entered a village, but had later resolved to press on to visit a man to whom I had a letter of introduction from my loyal friend Dr. Barbour of Rocky Ford.

There had been a wash-out. I had to walk around it, and was misdirected by the good villagers and was walking merrily on toward nowhere. Around nine o'clock I had been refused lodging at three different shanties. But from long experience I knew that something would turn up in a minute. And it did.

I walked right into the fat sides of a big country hotel on that interminable plain. It was not surrounded by a village. It was simply a clean hostelrie for the transient hands who worked at irrigating in that region.

I asked the looming figure I met in the dark: "Where is the boss of this place?"

"I am the boss." He had a Scandinavian twist to his tongue.

"I want a night's lodging. I will give in exchange an entertainment this evening, or half a day's work to-morrow."

"Come in."

I followed him up the outside stairway to the dining-room in the second story. There was his wife, a woman who greeted me cheerfully in the Scandinavian accent. She was laughing at her five little children who were laughing at her and eating their mush and milk.

Presumably the boarders had been delayed by their work, and had dined late. The children were at it still later.

They were real Americans, those little birds. And they had memories like parrots, as will appear.

"Wife," said the landlord, "here is a man that will entertain us to-night for his keep, or work for us to-morrow. I think we will take the entertainment to-night. Go ahead, mister. Here are the kids. Now listen, kids."

To come out of the fathomless, friendless dark and, almost in an instant, to look into such expectant fairy faces! They were laughing, laughing, laughing, not in mockery, but companionship. I recited every child-piece I had ever written—(not many).

They kept quite still till the end of each one. Then they pounded the table for more, with their tin spoons and their little red fists.

So, with misgivings, I began to recite some of my fairy-tales for grown-ups. I spoke slowly, to make the externals of each story plain. The audience squealed for more. . . . I decided to recite six jingles about the moon, that I had written long ago: How the Hyaena said the Moon was a Golden Skull, and how the Shepherd Dog contradicted him and said it was a Candle in the Sky—and all that and all that.

The success of the move was remarkable because I had never pleased either grown folks or children to any extent with those verses. But these children, through the accumulated excitements of a day that I knew nothing about, were in an ecstatic imaginative condition of soul that transmuted everything.

The last of the series recounted what Grandpa Mouse said to the Little Mice on the Moon question. I arranged the ketchup bottle on the edge of the table for Grandpa Mouse. I used the salts and peppers for the little mice in circle round. I used a black hat or so for the swooping, mouse-eating owls that came down from the moon. Having acted out the story first, I recited it, slowly, mind you.

At the end I asked for my room and retired. I slept maybe an hour. I was awakened by those tireless little rascals racing along the dark hall and saying in horrible solemn tones, pretending to scare one another:

> "The moon's a holy owl-queen:
> She keeps them in a jar
> Under her arm till night,
> Then 'allies out to war!
> She sicks the owls upon us,
> They 'OOT with 'orrid noise
> And eat . . . the naughty boys,
> And the MOON'S A HOLY OWL-QUEEN!
> SHE KEEPS THEM IN A JAR!"

And so it went on, over and over.

Thereupon I made a mighty and a rash resolve. I renewed that same resolve in the morning when I woke. I said within myself *"I shall write one hundred Poems on the Moon!"*

Of course I did not keep my resolve to write one hundred pieces about the moon.

PROCLAMATIONS

Immediately upon my return from my journey the following Proclamations were printed in Farm and Fireside, through the great kindness of the editors, as another phase of the same crusade.

A PROCLAMATION OF BALM IN GILEAD

Go to the fields, O city laborers, till your wounds are healed. Forget the streetcars, the skyscrapers, the slums, the Marseillaise song.

We proclaim to the broken-hearted, still able to labor, the glories of the ploughed land. The harvests are wonderful. And there is a spiritual harvest appearing. A great agricultural flowering of art and song is destined soon to appear. Where corn and wheat are growing, men are singing the psalms of David, not the Marseillaise.

You to whom the universe has become a blast-furnace, a coke-oven, a cinder-strewn freight-yard, to whom the history of all ages is a tragedy with the climax now, to whom our democracy and our flag are but playthings of the hypocrite, — turn to the soil, turn to the earth, your mother, and she will comfort you. Rest, be it ever so little, from your black broodings. Think with the farmer once more, as your fathers did. Revere with the farmer our centuries-old civilization, however little it meets the city's trouble. Revere the rural customs that have their roots in the immemorial benefits of nature.

With the farmer look again upon the Constitution as something brought by Providence, prepared for by the ages. Go to church, the cross-roads church, and say the Lord's Prayer again. Help them with their temperance crusade. It is a deeper matter than you think. Listen to the laughter of the farmer's children. Know that not all the earth is a-weeping. Know that so long as there is black soil deep on the prairie, so long as grass will grow on it, we have a vast green haven.

The roots of some of our trees are still in the earth. Our mountains need not to be moved from their places. Wherever there is tillable land, there is a budding and blooming of old-fashioned Americanism, which the farmer is making splendid for us against the better day.

There is perpetual balm in Gilead, and many city workmen shall turn to it and be healed. This by faith, and a study of the signs, we proclaim!

PROCLAMATION

Of the New Time for Farmers and the New New England

Let it be proclaimed and shouted over all the ploughlands of the United States that the same ripening that brought our first culture in New England one hundred years ago is taking place in America to-day. Every State is to have its Emerson, its Whittier, its Longfellow, its Hawthorne and the rest.

Our Puritan farmer fathers in our worthiest handful of States waited long for their first group of burnished, burning lamps. From the landing of the Pilgrims in 1620 to the delivery of Emerson's address on the American Scholar was a weary period of gestation well rewarded.

Therefore, let us be thankful that we have come so soon to the edge of this occasion, that the western farms, though scarcely settled, have the Chautauqua, which is New England's old rural lecture course; the temperance crusade, which is New England's abolitionism come again; the magazine militant, which is the old Atlantic Monthly combined with the Free-Soil Newspaper under a new dress, and educational reform, which is the Yankee school-house made glorious.

All these, and more, electrify the farmlands. Things are in that ferment where many-sided Life and Thought are born.

Because our West and South are richer and broader and deeper than New England, so much more worth while will our work be. We will come nearer to repeating the spirit of the best splendors of the old Italian villages than to multiplying the prunes and prisms of Boston.

The mystery-seeking, beauty-serving followers of Poe in their very revolt from democracy will serve it well. The Pan-worshipping disciples of Whitman will in the end be, perhaps, more useful brothers of the White Christ than all our coming saints. And men will not be infatuated by the written and spoken word only, as in New England. Every art shall have the finest devotion.

Already in this more tropical California, this airier Colorado, this black-soiled Illinois, in Georgia, with her fire-hearted tradition of chivalry and her new and most romantic prosperity, men have learned to pray to the God of the blossoming world, men have learned to pray to the God of Beauty. They meditate upon His ways. They have begun to sing.

As of old, their thoughts and songs begin with the land, and go directly back to the land. Their tap-roots are deep as those of the alfalfa. A new New England is coming, a New England of ninety million souls! An artistic Renaissance is coming. An America is coming such as was long ago prophesied in Emerson's address on the American Scholar. This by faith, and a study of the signs, we proclaim!

PROCLAMATION

Of the New Village, and the New Country Community,
as Distinct from the Village

This is a year of bumper crops, of harvesting festivals. Through the mists of the happy waning year, a new village rises, and the new country community, in visions revealed to the rejoicing heart of faith.

And yet it needs no vision to see them. Walking across this land I have found them, little ganglions of life, promise of thousands more. The next generation will be that of the eminent village. The son of the farmer will be no longer dazzled and destroyed by the fires of the metropolis. He will travel, but only for what he can bring back. Just as his father sends half-way across the continent for good corn, or melon-seed, so he will make his village famous by transplanting and growing this idea or that. He will make it known for its pottery or its processions, its philosophy or its peacocks, its music or its swans, its golden roofs or its great union cathedral of all faiths. There are a thousand miscellaneous achievements within the scope of the great-hearted village. Our agricultural land to-day holds the ploughboys who will bring these benefits. I have talked to these boys. I know them. I have seen their gleaming eyes.

And the lonely country neighborhood, as distinct from the village, shall make itself famous. There are river valleys that will be known all over the land for their tall men and their milk-white maidens, as now for their well-bred horses. There are mountain lands that shall cultivate the tree of knowledge, as well as the apple-tree. There are sandy tracts that shall constantly ripen red and golden citrus fruit, but as well, philosophers comforting as the moon, and strength-giving as the sun.

These communities shall have their proud circles. They shall have families joined hand in hand, to the end that new blood and new thoughts be constantly brought in, and no good force or leaven be lost. The country community shall awaken illustrious. This by faith, and a study of the signs, we proclaim!

PROCLAMATION

Welcoming the Talented Children of the Soil

Because of their closeness to the earth, the men on the farms increase in stature and strength.

And for this very reason a certain proportion of their children are being born with a finer strength. They are being born with all this power concentrated in their nerves. They have the magnificent thoughts that might stir the stars in their courses, were they given voice.

Yea, in almost every ranch-house is born one flower-like girl or boy, a stranger among the brothers and sisters. Welcome, and a thousand welcomes, to these fairy changelings! They will make our land lovely. Let all of us who love God give our hearts to these His servants. They are born with eyes that weep themselves blind, unless there is beauty to look upon. They are endowed with souls that are self-devouring, unless they be permitted to make rare music; with a desire for truth that will make them mad as the old prophets, unless they be permitted to preach and pray and praise God in their own fashion, each establishing his own dream visibly in the world.

The land is being jewelled with talented children, from Maine to California: souls dewy as the grass, eyes wondering and passionate, lips that tremble. Though they be born in hovels, they have slender hands, seemingly lost amid the heavy hands. They have hands that give way too soon amid the bitter days of labor, but are everlastingly patient with the violin, or chisel, or brush, or pen.

All these children as a sacred charge are appearing, coming down upon the earth like manna. Yet many will be neglected as the too-abundant mulberry, that is left upon the trees. Many will perish like the wild strawberries of Kansas, cut down by the roadside with the weeds. Many will be looked upon like an over-abundant crop of apples, too cheap to be hauled to market, often used as food for the beasts. There will be a great slaughter of the innocents, more bloody than that of Herod of old. But there will be a desperate hardy remnant, adepts in all the conquering necromancy of agricultural Song and democratic Craftsmanship. They will bring us our new time in its completeness.

This by faith, and a study of the signs, we proclaim!

PROCLAMATION

Of the Coming of Religion, Equality and Beauty

In our new day, so soon upon us, for the first time in the history of Democracy, art and the church shall be hand in hand and equally at our service. Neither craftsmanship nor prayer shall be purely aristocratic any more, nor at war with each other, nor at war with the State. The priest, the statesman and the singer shall discern one another's work more perfectly and give thanks to God.

Even now our best churches are blossoming in beauty. Our best political life, whatever the howlers may say, is tending toward equality, beauty and holiness.

Political speech will cease to turn only upon the price of grain, but begin considering the price of cross-roads fountains and people's palaces. Our religious life will no longer trouble itself with the squabbles of orthodoxy. It will give us the outdoor choral procession, the ceremony of dedicating the wheat-field or the new-built private house to God. That politician who would benefit the people will not consider all the world wrapped up in the defence or destruction of a tariff schedule. He will serve the public as did Pericles, with the world's greatest dramas. He will rebuild the local Acropolis. He will make his particular Athens rule by wisdom and philosophy, not trade alone. Our crowds shall be audiences, not hurrying mobs; dancers, not brawlers; observers, not restless curiosity-seekers. Our mobs shall become assemblies and our assemblies religious; devout in a subtle sense, equal in privilege and courtesy, delicate of spirit, a perfectly rounded democracy.

All this shall come through the services of three kinds of men in wise cooperation: the priests, the statesmen and the artists. Our priests shall be religious men like St. Francis, or John Wesley, or General Booth, or Cardinal Newman. They shall be many types, but supreme of their type.

Our statesmen shall find their exemplars and their inspiration in Washington, Jefferson and Lincoln, as all good Americans devoutly desire.

But even these cannot ripen the land without the work of men as versatile as William Morris or Leonardo. Our artists shall fuse the work of these other workers, and give expression to the whole cry and the whole weeping and rejoicing of the land. We shall have Shelleys with a heart for religion, Ruskins with a comprehension of equality.

Religion, equality and *beauty!* By these America shall come into a glory that shall justify the yearning of the sages for her perfection, and the prophecies of the poets, when she was born in the throes of Valley Forge.

This, by faith, and a study of the signs, we proclaim!

THE ART OF THE MOVING PICTURE

(December 1915)

We are no other than a moving row
Of magic shadow-shapes that come and go
Round with this sun-illumined lantern held
In midnight by the Master of the Show.
　　　　　　　　　　— Fitzgerald

DEDICATED to George Mather Richards
in memory of the art student days we spent together when
the Metropolitan Museum was our picture drama

[The revised edition of *The Art of the Moving Picture* was published in 1922 and includes a new opening chapter, a complete rewrite of chapter one, and three new pages for the beginning of chapter three. I have included these in their proper chronological order. The final sentence of chapter two was added in 1922. The copy-text is the 1922 edition, except for chapter one and the first two paragraphs of chapter three, where the 1915 edition is the copy-text.]

THE ART OF THE MOVING PICTURE

CHAPTER I

The Point of View

This book is primarily for photoplay audiences. It might be entitled: "How to Classify and Judge the Current Films." But I desire as well that the work shall have its influence upon producers, scenario-writers, actors, and those who are about to prepare and endow pictures for special crusades.

While many leading players and producers are mentioned, I do not presume to attempt a rigid roll of honor, but rather to supply a way of approach to the moving picture field.

Many of the productions discussed are but recently on the market, or lately reissued. In such neighborhoods as the book has the honor to be read enterprising local managers might combine to send for them, in the order named.

According to this work, there are three types of photoplays: pictures of (1) Action, (2) Intimacy, and (3) Splendor. The Action Pictures are those where the outpouring of physical force at high speed is the main source of drama. The Spoilers, from the novel of Rex Beach, is an example. It is the chronicle of a fight for a Klondike mine, played by William Farnum, Kathlyn Williams, and others. The Intimate Pictures are based on the ability to photograph and magnify small groups, "close up." They give us idyls, genre pictures, village comedies, and the like. An example is Enoch Arden, played by Alfred Paget and Lillian Gish. The Splendor Pictures may be subdivided into four sorts: (1) The Fairy Tale Splendor is such a production as Cinderella, played by Mabel Taliaferro. (2) The Patriotic Splendor is such a one as Cabiria, a story of ancient Italy. Gabriel D'Annunzio is the writer and producer thereof. (3) The Crowd Splendor is the panorama where the principal dramatic asset is in showing the changing moods of informal public gatherings, and putting the different types of mobs and assemblies in contrast with one another while they wave their characteristic flags, rags, or torches. Such gatherings of men are found in The Italian, the leading part of which is acted by George Beban. (4) The photoplay of Religious Splendor is such a one as the Story of Thomas à Becket. He dies in Canterbury Cathedral in his priestly vestments, surrounded by long-robed monks, a martyr-priest, defending his order.

Action, intimacy, and splendor blend in every kind of reel, but some one of these qualities is dominant in each production. To keep his action from becoming hysterical, the fastidious scenario-writer or producer should study those standard sculptures that are depicted in motion, such as the work of Myron of the ancient time, or MacMonnies of the present day. On the other hand the maker of the Intimate Photoplay should let his mind dwell upon the work of such artists as the Dutch little Masters of Painting. Here he finds interiors that are close-up, well composed, delineated with a realism that is quaint and kindly. But the maker of Splendor Pictures could key them with profit to standard mural painting and architecture. And I go on to suggest in another chapter that the makers of trick pictures of jumping furniture and the like evolve them into real fairy-tales, with fewer things moving, and give those things a ritualistic and architectural dignity. And completing the analogy, my position is that religious and patriotic pageants should be in the mood of nature-cathedrals like Stonehenge, or metropolitan Cathedrals, like Notre Dame, whatever the actual materials and subject-matter.

In short, by my hypothesis, Action Pictures are sculpture-in-motion, Intimate Pictures are paintings-in-motion, Splendor Pictures are architecture-in-motion.

This work tries to show that whatever the seeming emphasis on dramatic excitement, the tendency of the best motion pictures is to evolve quite a different thing; the mood of the standard art gallery, the spirit of Tintoretto rather than that of Molière. The ripe photoplay is the art exhibition, plus action. The speed limit is soon reached. But the limit of pictorial beauty cannot be reached. This is the substantial effect of the book to this point. Then follows chapter twelve giving a summary that is in part a review: thirty points of difference between the spoken drama and the photoplay.

Then I endeavor to show a certain surprising parallelism between Egyptian hieroglyphics and this new silent drama, a suggestion I owe in its inception to my friend, James Oppenheim. The development of the argument is confidently based on the diagram under the word Alphabet in the Standard Dictionary. Here ends the first and more dogmatic part of the book. The principal headings thus far are proposed as a basis for photoplay criticism in America.

The rest of the work is a series of afterthoughts and speculations not brought forward so dogmatically. In this more informal section I begin by airing my opinion that the best censorship is a public feeling for beauty. To this end the chapter advocates the acknowledgment of the photoplay house as an art gallery, the suppressing of the music, and making the moving picture audience even more conversational by taking a nightly ballot on the favorite film or episode.

Then since the restitution of picture-writing revives the cave-man point of view on a higher plane, I advocate the endowment of certain special films likely to be neglected by commerce, films that this cave-man needs.

The various types of plays suggest particular social thoughts. The Action Play, it seems to me, is especially adapted to the moral crusader. The Intimate Play is adapted to endowment and development by the pure aesthete, and is tentatively recommended to the imagist poets. Meditation in another field, that of the Crowd Picture, brings me to the contemporary fact that the cheap photoplay house is the best known rival and eliminator of the slum saloon, the erstwhile poor man's club. On this turns some political speculation.

Then I show how California, as the natural moving picture playground, has the possibility of developing a unique cultural leverage upon America. Then I bring forward the proposition that the photoplay is such a good natural medium for architectural propaganda that architects could use it to stimulate the rebuilding of America into a sort of perpetual World's Fair, if they had the courage of such persons as Alexander, Julius Caesar, or Napoleon. In the course of the effort to bring about a greater range of Fairy-Tale and Religious Splendors I advocate specifically a deeply considered rendition of The Egyptian Book of the Dead, or as it is better entitled: The Chapters on Coming Forth by Day.

The last discourse is on the forecasters of a newer civilization, and shows how Jules Verne, Edward Bellamy, and H.G. Wells need more mystical and less mechanical successors when we formulate our America of Tomorrow. And maintaining that the photoplay cuts deeper into some stratifications of society than the newspaper or the book have ever gone, I try to show that the destiny of America from many aspects may be bound up in what the prophet-wizards among her photoplaywrights and producers mark out for her, for those things which a whole nation dares to hope for, it may in the end attain.

CHAPTER II

The Photoplay of Action

Let us assume, friendly reader, that it is eight o'clock in the evening when you make yourself comfortable in your den, to peruse this chapter. I want to tell you about the Action Film, the simplest, the type most often seen. In the mind of the habitué of the cheaper theatre it is the only sort in existence. It dominates the slums, is announced there by red and green posters of the melodrama sort, and retains its original elements, more deftly handled, in places more expensive. The story goes at the highest possible speed to be still credible. When it is a poor thing, which is the case too often, the St. Vitus dance destroys the pleasure-value. The rhythmic quality of the picture-motions is twitched to death. In the bad photoplay even the picture of an express train more than exaggerates itself. Yet when the photoplay chooses to behave it can reproduce a race far more joyously than the stage. On that fact is based the opportunity of this form. Many Action Pictures are indoors, but the abstract theory of the Action Film is based on the out-of-door chase. You remember the first one you saw where the policeman pursues the comical tramp over hill and dale and across the town lots. You remember that other where the cowboy follows the horse thief across the desert, spies him at last and chases him faster, faster, faster, and faster, and finally catches him. If the film was made in the days before the National Board of Censorship, it ends with the cowboy cheerfully hanging the villain; all details given to the last kick of the deceased.

One of the best Action Pictures is an old Griffith Biograph, recently reissued, the story entitled ''Man's Genesis.'' In the time when cave-men-gorillas had no weapons, Weak-Hands (impersonated by Robert Harron) invents the stone club. He vanquishes his gorilla-like rival, Brute-Force (impersonated by Wilfred Lucas). Strange but credible manners and customs of the cave-men are detailed. They live in picturesque caves. Their half-monkey gestures are wonderful to see. But these things are beheld on the fly. It is the chronicle of a race between the brain of Weak-Hands and the body of the other, symbolized by the chasing of poor Weak-Hands in and out among the rocks until the climax. Brain desperately triumphs. Weak-Hands slays Brute-Force with the startling invention. He wins back his stolen bride, Lily-White (impersonated by Mae Marsh). It is a Griffith masterpiece, and every actor does sound work. The audience, mechanical Americans, fond of crawling on their stomachs to tinker their automobiles, are eager over the evolution of the first weapon from a stick to a hammer. They are as full of curiosity as they could well be over the history of Langley or the Wright brothers.

The dire perils of the motion pictures provoke the ingenuity of the audience, not their passionate sympathy. When, in the minds of the deluded producers, the beholders should be weeping or sighing with desire, they are prophesying the next step to one another in worldly George Ade slang. This is illustrated in another good Action Photoplay: the dramatization of The Spoilers. The original novel was written by Rex Beach. The gallant William Farnum as Glenister dominates the play. He has excellent support. Their team-work makes them worthy of chronicle: Thomas Santschi as McNamara, Kathlyn Williams as Cherry Malotte, Bessie Eyton as Helen Chester, Frank Clark as Dextry, Wheeler Oakman as Broncho Kid, and Jack McDonald as Slapjack.

There are, in The Spoilers, inspiriting ocean scenes and mountain views. There are interesting sketches of mining-camp manners and customs. There is a well-acted love-interest in it, and the element of the comradeship of loyal pals. But the chase rushes past these things to the climax, as in a policeman picture it whirls past blossoming gardens and front lawns till the tramp is arrested. The difficulties are commented on by the people in the audience as rah-rah boys on the side lines comment on hurdles cleared or knocked over by the men running in college field-day. The sudden cut-backs into side branches of the story are but hurdles also, not plot complications in the stage sense. This is as it should be. The pursuit progresses without St. Vitus dance or hysteria to the end of the film. There the spoilers are discomfited, the gold mine is recaptured, the incidental girls are won, in a flash, by the rightful owners.

These shows work like the express elevators in the Metropolitan Tower. The ideal is the maximum of speed in descending or ascending, not to be jolted into insensibility. There are two girl parts as beautifully thought out as the parts of ladies in love can be expected to be in Action Films. But in the end the love is not much more romantic in the eye of the spectator than it would be to behold a man on a motorcycle with the girl of his choice riding on the same machine behind him. And the highest type of Action Picture romance is not attained by having Juliet triumph over the motorcycle handicap. It is not achieved by weaving in a Sherlock Holmes plot. Action Picture romance comes when each hurdle is a tableau, when there is indeed an art-gallery-beauty in each one of these swift glimpses: when it is a race, but with a proper and golden-linked grace from action to action, and the goal is the most beautiful glimpse in the whole reel.

In the Action Picture there is no adequate means for the development of any full grown personal passion. The distinguished character-study that makes genuine the personal emotions in the legitimate drama, has no chance. People are but types, swiftly moved chessmen. More elaborate discourse on this subject may be found in chapter twelve on the differences between the films and the stage. But here, briefly: the Action Pictures are falsely advertised as having heart-interest, or abounding in tragedy. But though the actors glower and wrestle and even if they are the most skilful lambasters in the profession, the audience gossips and chews gum.

Why does the audience keep coming to this type of photoplay if neither lust, love, hate, nor hunger is adequately conveyed? Simply because such spectacles gratify the incipient or rampant speed-mania in every American.

To make the elevator go faster than the one in the Metropolitan Tower is to destroy even this emotion. To elaborate unduly any of the agonies or seductions in the hope of arousing lust, love, hate, or hunger, is to produce on the screen a series of misplaced figures of the order Frankenstein.

How often we have been horrified by these galvanized and ogling corpses. These are the things that cause the outcry for more censors. It is not that our moral codes are insulted, but what is far worse, our nervous systems are temporarily racked to pieces. These wriggling half-dead men, these over-bloody burglars, are public nuisances, no worse and no better than dead cats being hurled about by street urchins.

The cry for more censors is but the cry for the man with the broom. Sometimes it is a matter as simple as when a child is scratching with a pin on a slate. While one would not have the child locked up by the chief of police, after five minutes of it almost every one wants to smack him till his little jaws ache. It is the very cold-bloodedness of the proceeding that ruins our kindness of heart. And the best Action Film is impersonal and unsympathetic even if it has no scratching pins. Because it is cold-blooded it must take extra pains to be tactful. Cold-blooded means that the hero as we see him on the screen is a variety of amiable or violent ghost. Nothing makes his lack of human charm plainer than when we as audience enter the theatre at the middle of what purports to be the most passionate of scenes when the goal of the chase is unknown to us and the alleged "situation" appeals on its magnetic merits. Here is neither the psychic telepathy of Forbes Robertson's Caesar, nor the fire-breath of E.H. Sothern's Don Quixote. The audience is not worked up into the deadly still mob-unity of the speaking theatre. We late comers wait for the whole reel to start over and the goal to be indicated in the preliminary, before we can get the least bit wrought up. The prize may be a lady's heart, the restoration of a lost reputation, or the ownership of the patent for a churn. In the more effective Action Plays it is often what would be secondary on the stage, the recovery of a certain glove, spade, bull-calf, or rock-quarry. And to begin, we are shown a clean-cut picture of said glove, spade, bull-calf, or rock-quarry. Then when these disappear from ownership or sight, the suspense continues till they are again visible on the screen in the hands of the rightful owner.

In brief, the actors hurry through what would be tremendous passions on the stage to recover something that can be really photographed. For instance, there came to our town long ago a film of a fight between Federals and Confederates, with the loss of many lives, all for the recapture of a steam-engine that took on more personality in the end than private or general on either side, alive or dead. It was based on the history of the very engine photographed, or else that engine was given in replica. The old locomotive was full of character and humor amidst the tragedy, leaking steam at every orifice. The original is in one of the Southern Civil War museums. This engine in its capacity as a principal actor is going to be referred to more than several times in this work.

The highest type of Action Picture gives us neither the quality of Macbeth or Henry Fifth, the Comedy of Errors, or the Taming of the Shrew. It gives us rather that fine and special quality that was in the ink-bottle of Robert Louis Stevenson, that brought about the limitations and the nobility of the stories of Kidnapped, Treasure Island, and the New Arabian Nights.

This discussion will be resumed on another plane in the eighth chapter: Sculpture-in-Motion.

Having read thus far, why not close the book and go round the corner to a photoplay theatre? Give the preference to the cheapest one. *The Action Picture will be inevitable. Since this chapter was written, Charlie Chaplin and Douglas Fairbanks have given complete department store examples of the method, especially Chaplin in the brilliantly constructed Shoulder Arms, and Fairbanks in his one great piece of acting, in The Three Musketeers.*

CHAPTER III

The Intimate Photoplay

If you are one of the ten thousand people writing scenarios that have not been taken as yet, if you desire advice that will enable you to place your work, read along with this volume The Technique of the Photoplay by Epes Winthrop Sargent, to be had from The Moving Picture World. That book shows the devices whereby films akin to The Spoilers are evolved. It tells how to develop comedies and near-tragedies that are their cousins. Further acquaintance with this interesting practical field may be had by subscribing to The Moving Picture World. It is a trade-weekly primarily for operators of theatres the country over, but with items for all the people interested in the field. These chapters that we are developing together, friend reader, bring the artistic and not the commercial ruler to the measuring of the business. I hope that the fifty people who are manufacturing successful scenarios will think it worth their while to read further into these discourses for advice that I dare to hope, when combined with their practical sense, will have some influence in shaping their art. And I hope that some of the ten thousand who emulate them may be led by certain passages in this book nearer to the artistic side of the thing without destroying their commercial chances. The goal of the scenario-writer, be he commercially successful, or not, should be to manage his own scenarios, — be an author-producer. Not until he is in that commanding position will he be as well placed to work out his ideas as is the routine short-story writer or novelist. Further discussion of the producer's position is found in chapter twelve. In brief, he is the beginning and the end of the real photoplay, and the scenario-writer should be willing to be his slave only long enough to learn to invade his studio and replace him.

A bit of personal history may throw light on the method of approach in this book. I used to be one of a combined group of advanced students from the Art Students' League, the New York School of Art and the National Academy School, who assembled weekly for several winters in the Metropolitan Museum, for the discussion of the masterpieces in historic order, from Egypt to America. From that standpoint, the work least often found, hardest to make, least popular in the street, may be in the end the one most treasured in a world-museum as a counsellor and stimulus of mankind. Throughout this book I try to bring to bear the same simple standards of form, composition, mood, and motive that we used in finding the fundamental exhibits; the standards which are taken for granted in art histories and schools, radical or conservative, anywhere.

Again we assume it is eight o'clock in the evening, friend reader, when the chapter begins.

Just as the Action Picture has its photographic basis or fundamental metaphor in the long chase down the highway, so the Intimate Film has its photographic basis in the fact that any photoplay interior has a very small ground plan, and the cosiest of enclosing walls. Many a worth-while scene is acted out in a space no bigger than that which is occupied by an office boy's stool and hat. If there is a table in this room, it is often so near it is half out of the picture or perhaps it is against the front line of the triangular ground-plan. Only the top of the table is seen, and nothing close up to us is pictured below that. We in the audience are privileged characters. Generally attending the show in bunches of two or three, we are members of the household on the screen. Sometimes we are sitting on the near side of the family board. Or we are gossiping whispering neighbors, of the shoemaker, we will say, with our noses pressed against the pane of a metaphoric window.

Take for contrast the old-fashioned stage production showing the room and work table of a shoemaker. As it were the whole side of the house has been removed. The shop is as big as a banquet hall. There is something essentially false in what we see, no matter how the stage manager fills in with old boxes, broken chairs, and the like. But the photoplay interior is the size such a work-room should be. And there the awl and pegs and bits of leather, speaking the silent language of picture writing, can be clearly shown. They are sometimes like the engine in chapter two, the principal actors.

Though the Intimate-and-friendly Photoplay may be carried out of doors to the row of loafers in front of the country store, or the gossiping streets of the village, it takes its origin and theory from the snugness of the interior.

The restless reader replies that he has seen photoplays that showed ball-rooms that were grandiose, not the least cosy. These are to be classed as out-of-door scenery so far as theory goes, and are to be discussed under the head of Splendor Pictures. Masses of human beings pour by like waves, the personalities of none made plain. The only definite people are the hero and heroine in the foreground, and maybe one other. Though these three be in ball-costume, the little triangle they occupy next to the camera is in sort an interior, while the impersonal guests behind them conform to the pageant principles of out-of-doors, and the dancers are to the main actor as is the wind-shaken forest to the charcoal-burner, or the bending grain to the reaper.

The Intimate Motion Picture is the world's new medium for studying, not the great passions, such as black hate, transcendent love, devouring ambition, but rather the half relaxed or gently restrained moods of human creatures. It gives also our idiosyncrasies. It is gossip *in extremis*. It is apt to chronicle our petty little skirmishes, rather than our feuds. In it Colin Clout and his comrades return.

The Intimate Photoplay should not crowd its characters. It should not choke itself trying to dramatize the whole big bloody plot of Lorna Doone, or any other novel with a dozen leading people. Yet some gentle episode from the John Ridd farm, some half-chapter when Lorna and the Doones are almost forgotten, would be fitting. Let the duck-yard be parading its best, and Annie among the milk-pails, her work for the evening well nigh done. The Vicar of Wakefield has his place in this form. The Intimate-and-friendly Motion Picture might very well give humorous moments in the lives of the great, King Alfred burning the cakes, and other legendary incidents of him. Plato's writings give us glimpses of Socrates, in between the long dialogues. And there are intimate scraps in Plutarch.

Prospective author-producer, do you remember Landor's Imaginary Conversations, and Lang's Letters to Dead Authors? Can you not attain to that informal understanding in pictorial delineations of such people?

The photoplay has been unjust to itself in comedies. The late John Bunny's important place in my memory comes from the first picture in which I saw him. It is a story of high life below stairs. The hero is the butler at a governor's reception. John Bunny's work as this man is a delightful piece of acting. The servants are growing tipsier downstairs, but the more afraid of the chief functionary every time he appears, frozen into sobriety by his glance. At the last moment this god of the basement catches them at their worst and gives them a condescending but forgiving smile. The lid comes off completely. He himself has been imbibing. His surviving dignity in waiting on the governor's guests is worthy of the stage of Goldsmith and Sheridan. This film should be reissued in time as a Bunny memorial.

So far as my experience has gone, the best of the comedians is Sidney Drew. He could shine in the atmosphere of Pride and Prejudice or Cranford. But the best things I have seen of his are far from such. I beg the pardon of Miss Jane Austen and Mrs. Gaskell while I mention Who's Who in Hogg's Hollow, and A Regiment of Two. Over these I rejoiced like a yokel with a pocketful of butterscotch and peanuts. The opportunities to laugh on a higher plane than this, to laugh like Olympians, are seldom given us in this world.

The most successful motion picture drama of the intimate type ever placed before mine eyes was Enoch Arden, produced by Cabanne.

Lillian Gish takes the part of Annie, Alfred Paget impersonates Enoch Arden, and Wallace Reid takes the part of Philip Ray. The play is in four reels of twenty minutes each. It should have been made into three reels by shortening every scene just a bit. Otherwise it is satisfying, and I and my friends have watched it through many times as it has returned to Springfield.

The mood of the original poem is approximated. The story is told with fireside friendliness. The pale Lillian Gish surrounded by happy children gives us many a genre painting on the theme of domesticity. It is a photographic rendering in many ways as fastidious as Tennyson's versification. The scenes on the desert island are some of them commonplace. The shipwreck and the like remind one of other photoplays, but the rest of the production has a mood of its own. Seen several months ago it fills my eye-imagination and eye-memory more than that particular piece of Tennyson's fills word-imagination and word-memory. Perhaps this is because it is pleasing to me as a theorist. It is a sound example of the type of film to which this chapter is devoted. If you cannot get your local manager to bring Enoch Arden, reread that poem of Tennyson's and translate it in your own mind's eye into a gallery of six hundred delicately toned photographs hung in logical order, most of them cosy interior scenes, some of the faces five feet from chin to forehead in the more personal episodes, yet exquisitely fair. Fill in the out-of-door scenes and general gatherings with the appointments of an idyllic English fisher-village, and you will get an approximate conception of what we mean by the Intimate-and-friendly Motion Picture, or the Intimate Picture, as I generally call it, for convenience.

It is a quality, not a defect, of all photoplays that human beings tend to become dolls and mechanisms, and dolls and mechanisms tend to become human. But the haughty, who scorn the moving pictures, cannot rid themselves of the feeling that they are being seduced into going into some sort of a Punch-and-Judy show. And they think that of course one should not take seriously anything so cheap in price and so appealing to the cross-roads taste. But it is very well to begin in the Punch-and-Judy-show state of mind, and reconcile ourselves to it, and then like good democrats await discoveries. Punch and Judy is the simplest form of marionette performance, and the marionette has a place in every street in history just as the doll's house has its corner in every palace and cottage. The French in particular have had their great periods of puppet shows; and the Italian tradition survived in America's Little Italy, in New York for many a day; and I will mention in passing that one of Pavlova's unforgettable dance dramas is The Fairy Doll. Prospective author-producer, why not spend a deal of energy on the photoplay successors of the puppet-plays?

We have the queen of the marionettes already, without the play.

One description of the Intimate-and-friendly Comedy would be the Mary Pickford kind of a story. None has yet appeared. But we know the Mary Pickford mood. When it is gentlest, most roguish, most exalted, it is a prophecy of what this type should be, not only in the actress, but in the scenario and setting.

Mary Pickford can be a doll, a village belle, or a church angel. Her powers as a doll are hinted at in the title of the production: Such a Little Queen. I remember her when she was a village belle in that film that came out before producers or actors were known by name. It was sugar-sweet. It was called: What the Daisy Said. If these productions had conformed to their titles sincerely, with the highest photoplay art we would have had two more examples for this chapter.

Why do people love Mary? Not on account of the Daniel Frohman style of handling her appearances. He presents her to us in what are almost the old-fashioned stage terms: the productions energetic and full of painstaking detail but dominated by a dream that is a theatrical hybrid. It is neither good moving picture nor good stage play. Yet Mary could be cast as a cloudy Olympian or a church angel if her managers wanted her to be such. She herself was transfigured in the Dawn of Tomorrow, but the film-version of that play was merely a well mounted melodrama.

Why do people love Mary? Because of a certain aspect of her face in her highest mood. Botticelli painted her portrait many centuries ago when by some necromancy she appeared to him in this phase of herself. There is in the Chicago Art Institute at the top of the stairs on the north wall a noble copy of a fresco by that painter, the copy by

Mrs. MacMonnies. It is very near the Winged Victory of Samothrace. In the picture the muses sit enthroned. The loveliest of them all is a startling replica of Mary.

The people are hungry for this fine and spiritual thing that Botticelli painted in the faces of his muses and heavenly creatures. Because the mob catch the very glimpse of it in Mary's face, they follow her night after night in the films. They are never quite satisfied with the plays, because the managers are not artists enough to know they should sometimes put her into sacred pictures and not have her always the village hoyden, in plays not even hoydenish. But perhaps in this argument I have but betrayed myself as Mary's infatuated partisan.

So let there be recorded here the name of another actress who is always in the intimate-and-friendly mood and adapted to close-up interiors, Marguerite Clark. She is endowed by nature to act, in the same film, the eight-year-old village pet, the irrepressible sixteen-year-old, and finally the shining bride of twenty. But no production in which she acts that has happened to come under my eye has done justice to these possibilities. The transitions from one of these stages to the other are not marked by the producer with sufficient delicate graduation, emphasis, and contrast. Her plots have been but sugared nonsense, or swash-buckling ups and downs. She shines in a bevy of girls. She has sometimes been given the bevy.

But it is easier to find performers who fit this chapter, than to find films. Having read so far, it is probably not quite nine o'clock in the evening. Go around the corner to the nearest theatre. You will not be apt to find a pure example of the Intimate-and-friendly Moving Picture, but some one or two scenes will make plain the intent of the phrase. Imagine the most winsome tableau that passes before you, extended logically through one or three reels, with no melodramatic interruptions or awful smashes. For a further discussion of these smashes, and other items in this chapter, read the ninth chapter, entitled "Painting-in-Motion."

CHAPTER IV

The Motion Picture of Fairy Splendor

Again, kind reader, let us assume it is eight o'clock in the evening, for purposes of future climax which you no doubt anticipate.

Just as the Action Motion Picture has its photographic basis in the
race down the high-road, just as the Intimate Motion Picture has its
photographic basis in the close-up interior scene, so the Photoplay of
Splendor, in its four forms, is based on the fact that the kinetoscope
can take in the most varied of out-of-door landscapes. It can
reproduce fairy dells. It can give every ripple of the lily-pond. It can
show us cathedrals within and without. It can take in the panorama of
cyclopaean cloud, bending forest, storm-hung mountain. In like
manner it can put on the screen great impersonal mobs of men. It can
give us tremendous armies, moving as oceans move. The pictures of
Fairy Splendor, Crowd Splendor, Patriotic Splendor, and Religious
Splendor are but the embodiments of these backgrounds.

And a photographic corollary quite useful in these four forms is
that the camera has a kind of Hallowe'en witch-power. This power is
the subject of this chapter.

The world-old legends and revelations of men in connection with
the lovely out of doors, or lonely shrines, or derived from inspired
crusading humanity moving in masses, can now be fitly retold. Also
the fairy wand can do its work, the little dryad can come from the
tree. And the spirits that guard the Republic can be seen walking on
the clouds above the harvest-fields.

But we are concerned with the humblest voodooism at present.

Perhaps the world's oldest motion picture plot is a tale in Mother
Goose. It ends somewhat in this fashion: —

> The old lady said to the cat: —
> "Cat, cat, kill rat.
> Rat will not gnaw rope,
> Rope will not hang butcher,
> Butcher will not kill ox,
> Ox will not drink water,
> Water will not quench fire,
> Fire will not burn stick,
> Stick will not beat dog,
> Dog will not bite pig,
> Pig will not jump over the stile,
> And I cannot get home to-night.''

By some means the present writer does not remember, the cat was
persuaded to approach the rat. The rest was like a tale of European
diplomacy: —

The rat began to gnaw the rope,
The rope began to hang the butcher,
The butcher began to kill the ox,
The ox began to drink the water,
The water began to quench the fire,
The fire began to burn the stick,
The stick began to beat the dog,
The dog began to bite the pig,
The frightened little pig jumped over the stile,
And the old lady was able to get home that night.

Put yourself back to the state of mind in which you enjoyed this bit of verse.

Though the photoplay fairy-tale may rise to exquisite heights, it begins with pictures akin to this rhyme. Mankind in his childhood has always wanted his furniture to do such things. Arthur names his blade Excalibur. It becomes a person. The man in the Arabian tale speaks to the magic carpet. It carries him whithersoever he desires. This yearning for personality in furniture begins to be crudely worked upon in the so-called trick-scenes. The typical commercialized comedy of this sort is Moving Day. Lyman H. Howe, among many excellent reels of a different kind, has films allied to Moving Day.

But let us examine at this point, as even more typical, an old Pathe Film from France. The representatives of the moving-firm are sent for. They appear in the middle of the room with an astonishing jump. They are told that this household desires to have its goods and hearthstone gods transplanted two streets east. The agents salute. They disappear. Yet their wireless orders are obeyed with a military crispness. The books and newspapers climb out of the window. They go soberly down the street. In their wake are the dishes from the table. Then the more delicate porcelains climb down the shelves and follow. Then follow the hobble-de-hoy kitchen dishes, then the chairs, then the clothing, and the carpets from over the house. The most joyous and curious spectacle is to behold the shoes walking down the boulevard, from father's large boots to those of the youngest child. They form a complete satire of the family, yet have a masterful air of their own, as though they were the most important part of a human being.

The new apartment is shown. Everything enters in procession. In contrast to the general certainty of the rest, one or two pieces of furniture grow confused trying to find their places. A plate, in leaping upon a high shelf, misses and falls broken. The broom and dustpan sweep up the pieces, and consign them to the dustbin. Then the human family comes in, delighted to find everything in order. The moving agents appear and salute. They are paid their fee. They salute again and disappear with another gigantic leap.

The ability to do this kind of a thing is fundamental in the destinies of the art. Yet this resource is neglected because its special province is not understood. "People do not like to be tricked," the manager says. Certainly they become tired of mere contraptions. But they never grow weary of imagination. There is possible many a highly imaginative fairy-tale on this basis if we revert to the sound principles of the story of the old lady and the pig.

Moving Day is at present too crassly material. It has not the touch of the creative imagination. We are overwhelmed with a whole van of furniture. Now the mechanical or non-human object, beginning with the engine in the second chapter, is apt to be the hero in most any sort of photoplay while the producer remains utterly unconscious of the fact. Why not face this idiosyncrasy of the camera and make the non-human object the hero indeed? Not by filling the story with ropes, buckets, firebrands, and sticks, but by having these four unique. Make the fire the loveliest of torches, the water the most graceful of springs. Let the rope be the humorist. Let the stick be the outstanding hero, the D'Artagnan of the group, full of queer gestures and hoppings about. Let him be both polite and obdurate. Finally let him beat the dog most heroically.

Then, after the purely trick-picture is disciplined till it has fewer tricks, and those more human and yet more fanciful, the producer can move on up into the higher realms of the fairy-tale, carrying with him this riper workmanship.

Mabel Taliaferro's Cinderella, seen long ago, is the best film fairy-tale the present writer remembers. It has more of the fireside wonder-spirit and Hallowe'en-witch-spirit than the Cinderella of Mary Pickford.

There is a Japanese actor, Sessue Hayakawa, who takes the leading part with Blanche Sweet in The Clew, and is the hero in the film version of The Typhoon. He looks like all the actors in the old Japanese prints. He has a general dramatic equipment which enables him to force through the stubborn screen such stagy plays as these, that are more worth while in the speaking theatre. But he has that atmosphere of pictorial romance which would make him a valuable man for the retelling of the old Japanese legends of Kwannon and other tales that are rich, unused moving picture material, tales such as have been hinted at in the gleaming English of Lafcadio Hearn. The Japanese genius is eminently pictorial. Rightly viewed, every Japanese screen or bit of lacquer is from the Ancient Asia Columbus set sail to find.

It would be a noble thing if American experts in the Japanese principles of decoration, of the school of Arthur W. Dow, should tell stories of old Japan with the assistance of such men as Sessue Hayakawa. Such things go further than peace treaties. Dooming a talent like that of Mr. Hayakawa to the task of interpreting the Japanese spy does not conduce to accord with Japan, however the technique may move us to admiration. Let such of us as are at peace get together, and tell the tales of our happy childhood to one another.

This chapter is ended. You will of course expect to be exhorted to visit some photoplay emporium. But you need not look for fairy-tales. They are much harder to find than they should be. But you can observe even in the advertisements and cartoons the technical elements of the story of the old lady and the pig. And you can note several other things that show how much more quickly than on the stage the borderline of All Saints' Day and Hallowe'en can be crossed. Note how easily memories are called up, and appear in the midst of the room. In any plays whatever, you will find these apparitions and recollections. The dullest hero is given glorious visualizing power. Note the ''fadeaway'' at the beginning and the end of the reel, whereby all things emerge from the twilight and sink back into the twilight at last. These are some of the indestructible least common denominators of folk stories old and new. When skilfully used, they can all exercise a power over the audience, such as the crystal has over the crystal-gazer.

But this discussion will be resumed, on another plane, in the tenth chapter: ''Furniture, Trappings, and Inventions in Motion.''

CHAPTER V

The Picture of Crowd Splendor

Henceforth the reader will use his discretion as to when he will read the chapter and when he will go to the picture show to verify it.

The shoddiest silent drama may contain noble views of the sea. This part is almost sure to be good. It is a fundamental resource.

A special development of this aptitude in the hands of an expert gives the sea of humanity, not metaphorically but literally: the whirling of dancers in ballrooms, handkerchief-waving masses of people in balconies, hat-waving political ratification meetings, ragged glowering strikers, and gossiping, dickering people in the market-place. Only Griffith and his close disciples can do these as well as almost any manager can reproduce the ocean. Yet the sea of humanity is dramatically blood-brother to the Pacific, Atlantic, or Mediterranean. It takes this new invention, the kinetoscope, to bring us these panoramic drama-elements. By the law of compensation, while the motion picture is shallow in showing private passion, it is powerful in conveying the passions of masses of men. Bernard Shaw, in a recent number of the Metropolitan, answered several questions in regard to the photoplay. Here are two bits from his discourse: —

"Strike the dialogue from Molière's Tartuffe, and what audience would bear its mere stage-business? Imagine the scene in which Iago poisons Othello's mind against Desdemona, conveyed in dumb show. What becomes of the difference between Shakespeare and Sheridan Knowles in the film? Or between Shakespeare's Lear and any one else's Lear? No, it seems to me that all the interest lies in the new opening for the mass of dramatic talent formerly disabled by incidental deficiencies of one sort or another that do not matter in the picture-theatre. . . ."

"Failures of the spoken drama may become the stars of the picture palace. And there are the authors with imagination, visualization and first-rate verbal gifts who can write novels and epics, but cannot for the life of them write plays. Well, the film lends itself admirably to the succession of events proper to narrative and epic, but physically impracticable on the stage. Paradise Lost would make a far better film than Ibsen's John Gabriel Borkman, though Borkman is a dramatic masterpiece, and Milton could not write an effective play."

Note in especial what Shaw says about narrative, epic, and Paradise Lost. He has in mind, no doubt, the pouring hosts of demons and angels. This is one kind of a Crowd Picture.

There is another sort to be seen where George Beban impersonates The Italian in a film of that title, by Thomas H. Ince and G. Gardener Sullivan. The first part, taken ostensibly in Venice, delineates the festival spirit of the people on the bridges and in gondolas. It gives out the atmosphere of town-crowd happiness. Then comes the vineyard, the crowd sentiment of a merry grape-harvest, then the massed emotion of many people embarking on an Atlantic liner telling good-by to their kindred on the piers, then the drama of arrival in New York. The wonder of the steerage people pouring down their proper gangway is contrasted with the conventional at-home-ness of the first-class passengers above. Then we behold the seething human cauldron of the East Side, then the jolly little wedding-dance, then the life of the East Side, from the policeman to the peanut-man, and including the bar tender, for the crowd is treated on two separate occasions.

It is hot weather. The mobs of children follow the ice-wagon for chips of ice. They besiege the fountain-end of the street-sprinkling wagon quite closely, rejoicing to have their clothes soaked. They gather round the fire-plug that is turned on for their benefit, and again become wet as drowned rats.

Passing through these crowds are George Beban and Clara Williams as The Italian and his sweetheart. They owe the force of their acting to the fact that they express each mass of humanity in turn. Their child is born. It does not flourish. It represents in an acuter way another phase of the same child-struggle with the heat that the gamins indicate in their pursuit of the water-cart.

Then a deeper matter. The hero represents in a fashion the adventures of the whole Italian race coming to America: its natural southern gayety set in contrast to the drab East Side. The gondolier becomes boot-black. The grape-gathering peasant girl becomes the suffering slum mother. They are not specialized characters like Pendennis or Becky Sharp in the Novels of Thackeray.

Omitting the last episode, the entrance into the house of Corrigan, The Italian is a strong piece of work.

Another kind of Crowd Picture is The Battle, an old Griffith Biograph, first issued in 1911, before Griffith's name or that of any actor in films was advertised. Blanche Sweet is the leading lady, and Charles H. West the leading man. The psychology of a bevy of village lovers is conveyed in a lively sweethearting dance. Then the boy and his comrades go forth to war. The lines pass between hand-waving crowds of friends from the entire neighborhood. These friends give the sense of patriotism in mass. Then as the consequence of this feeling, as the special agents to express it, the soldiers are in battle. By the fortunes of war the onset is unexpectedly near to the house where once was the dance.

The boy is at first a coward. He enters the old familiar door. He appeals to the girl to hide him, and for the time breaks her heart. He goes forth a fugitive not only from battle, but from her terrible girlish anger. But later he rallies. He brings a train of powder wagons through fires built in his path by the enemy's scouts. He loses every one of his men, and all but the last wagon, which he drives himself. His return with that ammunition saves the hard-fought day.

And through all this, glimpses of the battle are given with a splendor that only Griffith has attained.

Blance Sweet stands as the representative of the bevy of girls in the house of the dance, and the whole body social of the village. How the costumes flash and the handkerchiefs wave around her! In the battle the hero represents the cowardice that all the men are resisting within themselves. When he returns, he is the incarnation of the hardihood they have all hoped to display. Only the girl knows he was first a failure. The wounded general honors him as the hero above all. Now she is radiant, she cannot help but be triumphant, though the side of the house is blown out by a shell and the dying are everywhere.

This one-reel work of art has been reissued of late by the Biograph Company. It should be kept in the libraries of the Universities as a standard. One-reel films are unfortunate in this sense that in order to see a favorite the student must wait through five other reels of a mixed programme that usually is bad. That is the reason one-reel masterpieces seldom appear now. The producer in a mood to make a special effort wants to feel that he has the entire evening, and that nothing before or after is going to be a bore or destroy the impression. So at present the painstaking films are apt to be five or six reels of twenty minutes each. These have the advantage that if they please at all, one can see them again at once without sitting through irrelevant slap-stick work put there to fill out the time. But now, having the whole evening to work in, the producer takes too much time for his good ideas. I shall reiterate throughout this work the necessity for restraint. A one hour programme is long enough for any one. If the observer is pleased, he will sit it through again and take another hour. There is not a good film in the world but is the better for being seen in immediate succession to itself. Six-reel programmes are a weariness to the flesh. The best of the old one-reel Biographs of Griffith contained more in twenty minutes than these ambitious incontinent six-reel displays give us in two hours. It would pay a manager to hang out a sign: ''This show is only twenty minutes long, but it is Griffith's great film 'The Battle.'''

But I am digressing. To continue the contrast between private passion in the theatre and crowd-passion in the photoplay, let us turn to Shaw again. Consider his illustration of Iago, Othello, and Lear. These parts, as he implies, would fall flat in motion pictures. The minor situations of dramatic intensity might in many cases be built up. The crisis would inevitably fail. Iago and Othello and Lear, whatever their offices in their governments, are essentially private persons, individuals *in extremis*. If you go to a motion picture and feel yourself suddenly gripped by the highest dramatic tension, as on the old stage, and reflect afterward that it was a fight between only two or three men in a room otherwise empty, stop to analyze what they stood for. They were probably representatives of groups or races that had been pursuing each other earlier in the film. Otherwise the conflict, however violent, appealed mainly to the sense of speed.

So, in The Birth of a Nation, which could better be called The Overthrow of Negro Rule, the Ku Klux Klan dashes down the road as powerfully as Niagara pours over the cliff. Finally the white girl Elsie Stoneman (impersonated by Lillian Gish) is rescued by the Ku Klux Klan from the mulatto politician, Silas Lynch (impersonated by George Seigmann). The lady is brought forward as a typical helpless white maiden. The white leader, Col. Ben Cameron (impersonated by Henry B. Walthall), enters not as an individual, but as representing the whole Anglo-Saxon Niagara. He has the mask of the Ku Klux Klan on his face till the crisis has passed. The wrath of the Southerner against the blacks and their Northern organizers has been piled up through many previous scenes. As a result this rescue is a real climax, something the photoplays that trace strictly personal hatreds cannot achieve.

The Birth of a Nation is a Crowd Picture in a triple sense. On the films, as in the audience, it turns the crowd into a mob that is either for or against the Reverend Thomas Dixon's poisonous hatred of the negro.

Griffith is a chameleon in interpreting his authors. Wherever the scenario shows traces of The Clansman, the original book, by Thomas Dixon, it is bad. Wherever it is unadulterated Griffith, which is half the time, it is good. The Reverend Thomas Dixon is a rather stagy Simon Legree: in his avowed views a deal like the gentleman with the spiritual hydrophobia in the latter end of Uncle Tom's Cabin. Unconsciously Mr. Dixon has done his best to prove that Legree was not a fictitious character.

Joel Chandler Harris, Harry Stillwell Edwards, George W. Cable, Thomas Nelson Page, James Lane Allen, and Mark Twain are Southern men in Mr. Griffith's class. I recommend their works to him as a better basis for future Southern scenarios.

The Birth of a Nation has been very properly denounced for its Simon Legree qualities by Francis Hackett, Jane Addams, and others. But it is still true that it is a wonder in its Griffith sections. In its handling of masses of men it further illustrates the principles that made notable the old one-reel Battle film described in the beginning of this chapter. The Battle in the end is greater, because of its self-possession and concentration: all packed into twenty minutes.

When, in The Birth of a Nation, Lincoln (impersonated by Joseph Henabery) goes down before the assassin, it is a master-scene. He falls as the representative of the government and a thousand high and noble crowd aspirations. The mimic audience in the restored Ford's Theatre rises in panic. This crowd is interpreted in especial for us by the two young people in the seats nearest, and the freezing horror of the treason sweeps from the Ford's Theatre audience to the real audience beyond them. The real crowd touched with terror beholds its natural face in the glass.

Later come the pictures of the rioting negroes in the streets of the Southern town, mobs splendidly handled, tossing wildly and rhythmically like the sea. Then is delineated the rise of the Ku Klux Klan, of which we have already spoken. For comment on the musical accompaniment to The Birth of a Nation, read the fourteenth chapter entitled "The Orchestra, Conversation and the Censorship."

In the future development of motion pictures mob-movements of anger and joy will go through fanatical and provincial whirlwinds into great national movements of anger and joy.

A book by Gerald Stanley Lee that has a score of future scenarios in it, a book that might well be dipped into by the reader before he goes to such a play as The Italian or The Battle, is the work which bears the title of this chapter: "Crowds."

Mr. Lee is far from infallible in his remedies for factory and industrial relations. But in sensitiveness to the flowing street of humanity he is indeed a man. Listen to the names of some of the divisions of his book: "Crowds and Machines; Letting the Crowds be Good; Letting the Crowds be Beautiful; Crowds and Heroes; Where are we Going? The Crowd Scare; The Strike, an Invention for making Crowds Think; The Crowd's Imagination about People; Speaking as One of the Crowd; Touching the Imagination of Crowds." Films in the spirit of these titles would help to make world-voters of us all.

The World State is indeed far away. But as we peer into the Mirror Screen some of us dare to look forward to the time when the pouring streets of men will become sacred in each other's eyes, in pictures and in fact.

A further discussion of this theme on other planes will be found in the eleventh chapter, entitled "Architecture-in-Motion," and the fifteenth chapter, entitled "The Substitute for the Saloon."

CHAPTER VI

Patriotic Splendor

The Patriotic Picture need not necessarily be in terms of splendor. It generally is. Beginning the chronicle is one that waves no banners.

The Typhoon, a film produced by Thomas H. Ince, is a story of the Japanese love of Nippon in which a very little of the landscape of the nation is shown, and that in the beginning. The hero (acted by Sessue Hayakawa), living in the heart of Paris, represents the far-off Empire. He is making a secret military report. He is a responsible member of a colony of Japanese gentlemen. The bevy of them appear before or after his every important action. He still represents this crowd when alone.

The unfortunate Parisian heroine, unable to fathom the mystery of the fanatical hearts of the colony, ventures to think that her love for the Japanese hero and his equally great devotion to her is the important human relation on the horizon. She flouts his obscure work, pits her charms against it. In the end there is a quarrel. The irresistible meets the immovable, and in madness or half by accident, he kills the girl.

The youth is protected by the colony, for he alone can make the report. He is the machine-like representative of the Japanese patriotic formula, till the document is complete. A new arrival in the colony, who obviously cannot write the book, confesses the murder and is executed. The other high fanatic dies soon after, of a broken heart, with the completed manuscript volume in his hand. The one impression of the play is that Japanese patriotism is a peculiar and fearful thing. The particular quality of the private romance is but vaguely given, for such things in their rise and culmination can only be traced by the novelist, or by the gentle alternations of silence and speech on the speaking stage, aided by the hot blood of players actually before us.

Here, as in most photoplays, the attempted lover-conversations in pantomime are but indifferent things. The details of the hero's last quarrel with the heroine and the precise thoughts that went with it are muffled by the inability to speak. The power of the play is in the adequate style the man represents the colony. Sessue Hayakawa should give us Japanese tales more adapted to the films. We should have stories of Iyeyasu and Hideyoshi, written from the ground up for the photoplay theatre. We should have the story of the Forty-seven Ronin, not a Japanese stage version, but a work from the source-material. We should have legends of the various clans, picturizations of the code of the Samurai.

The Typhoon is largely indoors. But the Patriotic Motion Picture is generally a landscape. This is for deeper reasons than that it requires large fields in which to manoeuvre armies. Flags are shown for other causes than that they are the nominal signs of a love of the native land.

In a comedy of the history of a newspaper, the very columns of the publication are actors, and may be photographed oftener than the human hero. And in the higher realms this same tendency gives particular power to the panorama and trappings. It makes the natural and artificial magnificence more than a narrative, more than a color-scheme, something other than a drama. In a photoplay by a master, when the American flag is shown, the thirteen stripes are columns of history and the stars are headlines. The woods and the templed hills are their printing press, almost in a literal sense.

Going back to the illustration of the engine, in chapter two, the non-human thing is a personality, even if it is not beautiful. When it takes on the ritual of decorative design, this new vitality is made seductive, and when it is an object of nature, this seductive ritual becomes a new pantheism. The armies upon the mountains they are defending are rooted in the soil like trees. They resist invasion with the same elementary stubbornness with which the oak resists the storm or the cliff resists the wave.

Let the reader consider Antony and Cleopatra, the Cines film. It was brought to America from Italy by George Klein. This and several ambitious spectacles like it are direct violations of the foregoing principles. True, it glorifies Rome. It is equivalent to waving the Italian above the Egyptian flag, quite slowly for two hours. From the stage standpoint, the magnificence is thoroughgoing. Viewed as a circus, the acting is elephantine in its grandeur. All that is needed is pink lemonade sold in the audience.

The famous Cabiria, a tale of war between Rome and Carthage, by D'Annunzio, is a prime example of a success, where Antony and Cleopatra and many European films founded upon the classics have been failures. With obvious defects as a producer, D'Annunzio appreciates spectacular symbolism. He has an instinct for the strange and the beautifully infernal, as they are related to decorative design. Therefore he is able to show us Carthage indeed. He has an Italian patriotism that amounts to frenzy. So Rome emerges body and soul from the past, in this spectacle. He gives us the cruelty of Baal, the intrepidity of the Roman legions. Everything Punic or Italian in the middle distance or massed background speaks of the very genius of the people concerned and actively generates their kind of lightning.

The principals do not carry out the momentum of this immense resource. The half a score of leading characters, with the costumes, gestures, and aspects of gods, are after all works of the taxidermist. They are stuffed gods. They conduct a silly nickelodeon romance while Carthage rolls on toward her doom. They are like sparrows fighting for grain on the edge of the battle.

The doings of his principals are sufficiently evident to be grasped with a word or two of printed insert on the films. But he sentimentalizes about them. He adds side-elaborations of the plot that would require much time to make clear, and a hard working novelist to make interesting. We are sentenced to stop and gaze long upon this array of printing in the darkness, just at the moment the tenth wave of glory seems ready to sweep in. But one hundred words cannot be a photoplay climax. The climax must be in a tableau that is to the eye as the rising sun itself, that follows the thousand flags of the dawn.

In the New York performance, and presumably in other large cities, there was also an orchestra. Behold then, one layer of great photoplay, one layer of bad melodrama, one layer of explanation, and a final cement of music. It is as though in an art museum there should be a man at the door selling would-be masterly short stories about the paintings, and a man with a violin playing the catalogue. But for further discourse on the orchestra read the fourteenth chapter.

I left Cabiria with mixed emotions. And I had to forget the distressful eye-strain. Few eyes submit without destruction to three hours of film. But the mistakes of Cabiria are those of the pioneer work of genius. It has in it twenty great productions. It abounds in suggestions. Once the classic rules of this art-unit are established, men with equal genius with D'Annunzio and no more devotion, will give us the world's masterpieces. As it is, the background and mass-movements must stand as monumental achievements in vital patriotic splendor.

D'Annunzio is Griffith's most inspired rival in these things. He lacks Griffith's knowledge of what is photoplay and what is not. He lacks Griffith's simplicity of hurdle-race plot. He lacks his avalanche-like action. The Italian needs the American's health and clean winds. He needs his foregrounds, leading actors, and types of plot. But the American has never gone as deep as the Italian into landscapes that are their own tragedians, and into Satanic and celestial ceremonials.

Judith of Bethulia and The Battle Hymn of the Republic have impressed me as the two most significant photoplays I have ever encountered. They may be classed with equal justice as religious or patriotic productions. But for reasons which will appear, The Battle Hymn of the Republic will be classed as a film of devotion and Judith as a patriotic one. The latter was produced by D.W. Griffith, and released by the Biograph Company in 1914. The original stage drama was once played by the famous Boston actress, Nance O'Neil. It is the work of Thomas Bailey Aldrich. The motion picture scenario, when Griffith had done with it, had no especial Aldrich flavor, though it contained several of the characters and events as Aldrich conceived them. It was principally the old apocryphal story plus the genius of Griffith and that inner circle of players whom he has endowed with much of his point of view.

This is his cast of characters: —

Judith .... Blanche Sweet
Holofernes .... Henry Walthall
His servant .... J.J. Lance
Captain of the Guards .... H. Hyde
Judith's maid .... Miss Bruce
General of the Jews .... C.H. Mailes
Priests .... Messrs. Oppleman and Lestina
Nathan .... Robert Harron
Naomi .... Mae Marsh
Keeper of the slaves for Holofernes .... Alfred Paget
The Jewish mother .... Lillian Gish

The Biograph Company advertises the production with the following Barnum and Bailey enumeration: ''In four parts. Produced in California. Most expensive Biograph ever produced. More than one thousand people and about three hundred horsemen. The following were built expressly for the production: a replica of the ancient city of Bethulia; the mammoth wall that protected Bethulia; a faithful reproduction of the ancient army camps, embodying all their barbaric splendor and dances; chariots, battering rams, scaling ladders, archer towers, and other special war paraphernalia of the period.

''The following spectacular effects: the storming of the walls of the city of Bethulia; the hand-to-hand conflicts; the death-defying chariot charges at break-neck speed; the rearing and plunging horses infuriated by the din of battle; the wonderful camp of the terrible

Holofernes, equipped with rugs brought from the far East; the dancing girls in their exhibition of the exquisite and peculiar dances of the period; the routing of the command of the terrible Holofernes, and the destruction of the camp by fire. And overshadowing all, the heroism of the beautiful Judith.''

This advertisement should be compared with the notice of Your Girl and Mine transcribed in the seventeenth chapter.

But there is another point of view by which this Judith of Bethulia production may be approached, however striking the advertising notice.

There are four sorts of scenes alternated: (1) the particular history of Judith; (2) the gentle courtship of Nathan and Naomi, types of the inhabitants of Bethulia; (3) pictures of the streets, with the population flowing like a sluggish river; (4) scenes of raid, camp, and battle, interpolated between these, tying the whole together. The real plot is the balanced alternation of all the elements. So many minutes of one, then so many minutes of another. As was proper, very little of the tale was thrown on the screen in reading matter, and no climax was ever a printed word, but always an enthralling tableau.

The particular history of Judith begins with the picture of her as the devout widow. She is austerely garbed, at prayer for her city, in her own quiet house. Then later she is shown decked for the eyes of man in the camp of Holofernes, where all is Assyrian glory. Judith struggles between her unexpected love for the dynamic general and the resolve to destroy him that brought her there. In either type of scene, the first gray and silver, the other painted with Paul Veronese splendor, Judith moves with a delicate deliberation. Over her face the emotions play like winds on a meadow lake. Holofernes is the composite picture of all the Biblical heathen chieftains. His every action breathes power. He is an Assyrian bull, a winged lion, and a god at the same time, and divine honors are paid to him every moment.

Nathan and Naomi are two Arcadian lovers. In their shy meetings they express the life of the normal Bethulia. They are seen among the reapers outside the city or at the well near the wall, or on the streets of the ancient town. They are generally doing the things the crowd behind them is doing, meanwhile evolving their own little heart affair. Finally when the Assyrian comes down like a wolf on the fold, the gentle Naomi becomes a prisoner in Holofernes' camp. She is in the foreground, a representative of the crowd of prisoners. Nathan is photographed on the wall as the particular defender of the town in whom we are most interested.

The pictures of the crowd's normal activities avoid jerkiness and haste. They do not abound in the boresome self-conscious quietude that some producers have substituted for the usual twitching. Each actor in the assemblies has a refreshing equipment in gentle gesticulation; for the manners and customs of Bethulia must needs be different from those of America. Though the population moves together as a river, each citizen is quite preoccupied. To the furthest corner of the picture, they are egotistical as human beings. The elder goes by, in theological conversation with his friend. He thinks his theology is important. The mother goes by, all absorbed in her child. To her it is the only child in the world.

Alternated with these scenes is the terrible rush of the Assyrian army, on to exploration, battle, and glory. The speed of their setting out becomes actual, because it is contrasted with the deliberation of the Jewish town. At length the Assyrians are along those hills and valleys and below the wall of defence. The population is on top of the battlements, beating them back the more desperately because they are separated from the water-supply, the wells in the fields where once the lovers met. In a lull in the siege, by a connivance of the elders, Judith is let out of a little door in the wall. And while the fortune of her people is most desperate she is shown in the quiet shelter of the tent of Holofernes. Sinuous in grace, tranced, passionately in love, she has forgotten her peculiar task. She is in a sense Bethulia itself, the race of Israel made over into a woman, while Holofernes is the embodiment of the besieging army. Though in a quiet tent, and on the terms of love, it is the essential warfare of the hot Assyrian blood and the pure and peculiar Jewish thoroughbredness.

Blanche Sweet as Judith is indeed dignified and ensnaring, the more so because in her abandoned quarter of an hour the Jewish sanctity does not leave her. And her aged woman attendant, coming in and out, sentinel and conscience, with austere face and lifted finger, symbolizes the fire of Israel that shall yet awaken within her. When her love for her city and God finally becomes paramount, she shakes off the spell of the divine honors which she has followed all the camp in according to that living heathen deity Holofernes, and by the very transfiguration of her figure and countenance we know that the deliverance of Israel is at hand. She beheads the dark Assyrian. Soon she is back in the city, by way of the little gate by which she emerged. The elders receive her and her bloody trophy.

The people who have been dying of thirst arise in a final whirlwind of courage. Bereft of their military genius, the Assyrians flee from the burning camp. Naomi is delivered by her lover Nathan. This act is taken by the audience as a type of the setting free of all the captives. Then we have the final return of the citizens to their town. As for Judith, hers is no crass triumph. She is shown in her gray and silvery room in her former widow's dress, but not the same woman. There is thwarted love in her face. The sword of sorrow is there. But there is also the prayer of thanksgiving. She goes forth. She is hailed as her city's deliverer. She stands among the nobles like a holy candle.

Providing the picture may be preserved in its original delicacy, it has every chance to retain a place in the affections of the wise, if a humble pioneer of criticism may speak his honest mind.

Though in this story the archaic flavor is well-preserved, the way the producer has pictured the population at peace, in battle, in despair, in victory gives me hope that he or men like unto him will illustrate the American patriotic crowd-prophecies. We must have Whitmanesque scenarios, based on moods akin to that of the poem By Blue Ontario's Shore. The possibility of showing the entire American population its own face in the Mirror Screen has at last come. Whitman brought the idea of democracy to our sophisticated literati, but did not persuade the democracy itself to read his democratic poems. Sooner or later the kinetoscope will do what he could not, bring the nobler side of the equality idea to the people who are so crassly equal.

The photoplay penetrates in our land to the haunts of the wildest or the dullest. The isolated prospector rides twenty miles to see the same film that is displayed on Broadway. There is not a civilized or half-civilized land but may read the Whitmanesque message in time, if once it is put on the films with power. Photoplay theatres are set up in ports where sailors revel, in heathen towns where gentlemen adventurers are willing to make one last throw with fate.

On the other hand, as a recorder Whitman approaches the wildest, rawest American material and conquers it, at the same time keeping his nerves in the state in which Swinburne wrote Only the Song of Secret Bird, or Lanier composed The Ballad of Trees and The Master. J.W. Alexander's portrait of Whitman in the Metropolitan Museum, New York, is not too sophisticated. The out-of-door profoundness of this poet is far richer than one will realize unless he has just returned from some cross-country adventure afoot. Then if one reads breathlessly by the page and the score of pages, there is a glory transcendent. For films of American patriotism to parallel the splendors of Cabiria and Judith of Bethulia, and to excel them, let us have Whitmanesque scenarios based on moods like that of By Blue

Ontario's Shore, The Salute au Monde, and The Passage to India. Then the people's message will reach the people at last.

The average Crowd Picture will cling close to the streets that are, and the usual Patriotic Picture will but remind us of nationality as it is at present conceived and aflame, and the Religious Picture will for the most part be close to the standard orthodoxies. The final forms of these merge into each other, though they approach the heights by different avenues. We Americans should look for the great photoplay of tomorrow, that will mark a decade or a century, that prophesies of the flags made one, the crowds in brotherhood.

CHAPTER VII

Religious Splendor

As far as the photoplay is concerned, religious emotion is a form of crowd-emotion. In the most conventional and rigid church sense this phase can be conveyed more adequately by the motion picture than by the stage. There is little, of course, for the anti-ritualist in the art-world anywhere. The thing that makes cathedrals real shrines in the eye of the reverent traveller makes them, with their religious processions and the like, impressive in splendor-films.

For instance, I have long remembered the essentials of the film, The Death of Thomas Becket. It may not compare in technique with some of our present moving picture achievements, but the idea must have been particularly adapted to the film medium. The story has stayed in my mind with great persistence, not only as a narrative, but as the first hint to me that orthodox religious feeling has here an undeveloped field.

Green tells the story in this way, in his History of the English People: —

"Four knights of the King's court, stirred to outrage by a passionate outburst of their master's wrath, crossed the sea and on the twenty-ninth of December forced their way into the Archbishop's palace. After a stormy parley with him in his chamber they withdrew to arm. Thomas was hurried by his clerks into the cathedral, but as he reached the steps leading from the transept into the choir his pursuers burst in from the cloisters. 'Where,' cried Reginald Fitzurse, 'is the traitor, Thomas Becket?' 'Here am I, no traitor, but a priest of God,' he replied. And again descending the steps he placed himself with his back against a pillar and fronted his foes. . . . The brutal murder was received with a thrill of horror throughout

Christendom. Miracles were wrought at the martyr's tomb, etc. . . .''

It is one of the few deaths in moving pictures that have given me the sense that I was watching a tragedy. Most of them affect one, if they have any effect, like exhibits in an art gallery, as does Josef Israels' oil painting, Alone in the World. We admire the technique, and as for emotion, we feel the picturesqueness only. But here the church procession, the robes, the candles, the vaulting overhead, the whole visualized cathedral mood has the power over the reverent eye it has in life, and a touch more.

It is not a private citizen who is struck down. Such a taking off would have been but nominally impressive, no matter how well acted. Private deaths in the films, to put it another way, are but narrative statements. It is not easy to convey their spiritual significance. Take, for instance, the death of John Goderic, in the film version of Gilbert Parker's The Seats of the Mighty. The major leaves this world in the first third of the story. The photoplay use of his death is, that he may whisper in the ear of Robert Moray to keep certain letters of La Pompadour well hidden. The fact that it is the desire of a dying man gives sharpness to his request. Later in the story Moray is hard-pressed by the villain for those same papers. Then the scene of the death is flashed for an instant on the screen, representing the hero's memory of the event. It is as though he should recollect and renew a solemn oath. The documents are more important than John Goderic. His departure is but one of their attributes. So it is in any film. There is no emotional stimulation in the final departure of a non-public character to bring tears, such tears as have been provoked by the novel or the stage over the death of Sidney Carton or Faust's Marguerite or the like.

All this, to make sharper the fact that the murder of Becket the archbishop is a climax. The great Church and hierarchy are profaned. The audience feels the same thrill of horror that went through Christendom. We understand why miracles were wrought at the martyr's tomb.

In the motion pictures the entrance of a child into the world is a mere family episode, not a climax, when it is the history of private people. For instance, several little strangers come into the story of Enoch Arden. They add beauty, and are links in the chain of events. Still they are only one of many elements of idyllic charm in the village of Annie. Something that in real life is less valuable than a child is the goal of each tiny tableau, some coming or departure or the like that affects the total plot. But let us imagine a production that would chronicle the promise to Abraham, and the vision that came with it.

Let the film show the final gift of Isaac to the aged Sarah, even the boy who is the beginning of a race that shall be as the stars of heaven and the sands of the sea for multitude. This could be made a pageant of power and glory. The crowd-emotions, patriotic fires, and religious exaltations on which it turns could be given in noble procession and the tiny fellow on the pillow made the mystic centre of the whole. The story of the coming of Samuel, the dedicated little prophet, might be told on similar terms.

The real death in the photoplay is the ritualistic death, the real birth is the ritualistic birth, and the cathedral mood of the motion picture which goes with these and is close to these in many of its phases, is an inexhaustible resource.

The film corporations fear religious questions, lest offence be given to this sect or that. So let such denominations as are in the habit of cooperating, themselves take over this medium, not gingerly, but whole-heartedly, as in mediaeval time the hierarchy strengthened its hold on the people with the marvels of Romanesque and Gothic architecture. This matter is further discussed in the seventeenth chapter, entitled ''Progress and Endowment.''

But there is a field wherein the commercial man will not be accused of heresy or sacrilege, which builds on ritualistic birth and death and elements akin thereto. This the established producer may enter without fear. Which brings us to The Battle Hymn of the Republic, issued by the American Vitagraph Company in 1911. This film should be studied in the High Schools and Universities till the canons of art for which it stands are established in America. The director was Larry Trimble. All honor to him.

The patriotism of The Battle Hymn of the Republic, if taken literally, deals with certain aspects of the Civil War. But the picture is transfigured by so marked a devotion, that it is the main illustration in this work of the religious photoplay.

The beginning shows President Lincoln in the White House brooding over the lack of response to his last call for troops. (He is impersonated by Ralph Ince.) He and Julia Ward Howe are looking out of the window on a recruiting headquarters that is not busy. (Mrs. Howe is impersonated by Julia S. Gordon.) Another scene shows an old mother in the West refusing to let her son enlist. (This woman is impersonated by Mrs. Maurice.) The father has died in the war. The sword hangs on the wall. Later Julia Ward Howe is shown in her room asleep at midnight, then rising in a trance and writing the Battle Hymn at a table by the bed.

The pictures that might possibly have passed before her mind during the trance are thrown upon the screen. The phrases they illustrate are not in the final order of the poem, but in the possible sequence in which they went on the paper in the first sketch. The dream panorama is not a literal discussion of abolitionism or states' rights. It illustrates rather the Hebraic exultation applied to all lands and times. "Mine eyes have seen the glory of the coming of the Lord''; a gracious picture of the nativity. (Edith Storey impersonates Mary the Virgin.) "I have seen him in the watchfires of a hundred circling camps" and "They have builded him an altar in the evening dews and damps'' — for these are given symbolic pageants of the Holy Sepulchre crusaders.

Then there is a visible parable, showing a marketplace in some wicked capital, neither Babylon, Tyre, nor Nineveh, but all of them in essential character. First come spectacles of rejoicing, cruelty, and waste. Then from Heaven descend flood and fire, brimstone and lightning. It is like the judgment of the Cities of the Plain. Just before the overthrow, the line is projected upon the screen: "He hath loosed the fateful lightning of his terrible swift sword." Then the heavenly host becomes gradually visible upon the air, marching toward the audience, almost crossing the footlights, and blowing their solemn trumpets. With this picture the line is given us to read: "Our God is marching on." This host appears in the photoplay as often as the refrain sweeps into the poem. The celestial company, its imperceptible emergence, its spiritual power when in the ascendant, is a thing never to be forgotten, a tableau that proves the motion picture a great religious instrument.

Then comes a procession indeed. It is as though the audience were standing at the side of the throne at Doomsday looking down the hill of Zion toward the little earth. There is a line of those who are to be judged, leaders from the beginning of history, barbarians with their crude weapons, classic characters, Caesar and his rivals for fame; mediaeval figures including Dante meditating; later figures, Richelieu, Napoleon. Many people march toward the strange glorifying eye of the camera, growing larger than men, filling the entire field of vision, disappearing when they are almost upon us. The audience weighs the worth of their work to the world as the men themselves with downcast eyes seem to be doing also. The most thrilling figure is Tolstoi in his peasant smock, coming after the bitter egotists and conquerors. (The impersonation is by Edward Thomas.) I shall never forget that presence marching up to the throne invisible with bowed head. This procession is to illustrate the line: "He is sifting out the hearts of men before his Judgment Seat.'' Later Lincoln is pictured on the steps of the White House. It is a quaint tableau, in the spirit of the old-fashioned Rogers group. Yet it is masterful for all that. Lincoln is taking the chains from a cowering slave. This tableau is to illustrate the line: ''Let the hero born of woman crush the serpent with his heel.'' Now it is the end of the series of visions. It is morning in Mrs. Howe's room. She rises. She is filled with wonder to find the poem on her table.

Written to the rousing glory-tune of John Brown's Body the song goes over the North like wildfire. The far-off home of the widow is shown. She and the boy read the famous chant in the morning news column. She takes the old sword from the wall. She gives it to her son and sends him to enlist with her blessing. In the next picture Lincoln and Mrs. Howe are looking out the window where was once the idle recruiting tent. A new army is pouring by, singing the words that have rallied the nation. Ritualistic birth and death have been discussed. This film might be said to illustrate ritualistic birth, death, and resurrection.

The writer has seen hundreds of productions since this one. He has described it from memory. It came out in a time when the American people paid no attention to the producer or the cast. It may have many technical crudities by present-day standards. But the root of the matter is there. And Springfield knew it. It was brought back to our town many times. It was popular in both the fashionable picture show houses and the cheapest, dirtiest hole in the town. It will soon be reissued by the Vitagraph Company. Every student of American Art should see this film.

The same exultation that went into it, the faculty for commanding the great spirits of history and making visible the unseen powers of the air, should be applied to Crowd Pictures which interpret the non-sectarian prayers of the broad human race.

The pageant of Religious Splendor is the final photoplay form in the classification which this work seeks to establish. Much of what follows will be to reenforce the heads of these first discourses. Further comment on the Religious Photoplay may be found in the eleventh chapter, entitled ''Architecture-in-Motion.''

CHAPTER VIII

Sculpture-In-Motion

The outline is complete. Now to reenforce it. Pictures of Action Intimacy and Splendor are the foundation colors in the photoplay, as red, blue, and yellow are the basis of the rainbow. Action Films might be called the red section; Intimate Motion Pictures, being colder and quieter, might be called blue; and Splendor Photoplays called yellow, since that is the hue of pageants and sunshine.

Another way of showing the distinction is to review the types of gesture. The Action Photoplay deals with generalized pantomime: the gesture of the conventional policeman in contrast with the mannerism of the stereotyped preacher. The Intimate Film gives us more elusive personal gestures: the difference between the table manners of two preachers in the same restaurant, or two policemen. A mark of the Fairy Play is the gesture of incantation, the sweep of the arm whereby Mab would transform a prince into a hawk. The other Splendor Films deal with the total gestures of crowds: the pantomime of a torch-waving mass of men, the drill of an army on the march, or the bending of the heads of a congregation receiving the benediction.

Another way to demonstrate the thesis is to use the old classification of poetry: dramatic, lyric, epic. The Action Play is a narrow form of the dramatic. The Intimate Motion Picture is an equivalent of the lyric. In the seventeenth chapter it is shown that one type of the Intimate might be classed as imagist. And obviously the Splendor Pictures are the equivalent of the epic.

But perhaps the most adequate way of showing the meaning of this outline is to say that the Action Film is sculpture in motion, the Intimate Photoplay is painting-in-motion, and the Fairy Pageant, along with the rest of the Splendor Pictures, may be described as architecture-in-motion. This chapter will discuss the bearing of the phrase sculpture-in-motion. It will relate directly to chapter two.

First, gentle and kindly reader, let us discuss sculpture in its most literal sense; after that, less realistically, but perhaps more adequately. Let us begin with Annette Kellerman in Neptune's Daughter. This film has a crude plot constructed to show off Annette's various athletic resources. It is good photography, and a big idea so far as the swimming episodes are concerned. An artist haunted by picture-conceptions equivalent to the musical thoughts back of Wagner's Rhine-maidens could have made of Annette, in her mermaid's dress, a notable figure. Or a story akin to the mermaid tale of Hans Christian Andersen, or Matthew Arnold's poem of the forsaken merman, could have made this picturesque witch of the salt water truly significant, and still retained the most beautiful parts of the photoplay as it was exhibited. It is an exceedingly irrelevant imagination that shows her in other scenes as a duellist, for instance, because forsooth she can fence. As a child of the ocean, half fish, half woman, she is indeed convincing. Such mermaids as this have haunted sailors, and lured them on the rocks to their doom, from the day the siren sang till the hour the Lorelei sang no more. The scene with the baby mermaid, when she swims with the pretty creature on her back, is irresistible. Why are our managers so mechanical? Why do they flatten out at the moment the fancy of the tiniest reader of fairy-tales begins to be alive? Most of Annette's support were stage dummies. Neptune was a lame Santa Claus with cotton whiskers.

But as for the bearing of the film on this chapter: the human figure is within its rights whenever it is as free from self-consciousness as was the life-radiating Annette in the heavenly clear waters of Bermuda. On the other hand, Neptune and his pasteboard diadem and wooden-pointed pitchfork, should have put on his dressing-gown and retired. As a toe dancer in an alleged court scene, on land, Annette was a mere simperer. Possibly Pavlova as a swimmer in Bermuda waters would have been as much of a mistake. Each queen to her kingdom.

For living, moving sculpture, the human eye requires a costume and a part in unity with the meaning of that particular figure. There is the Greek dress of Mordkin in the arrow dance. There is Annette's breast covering of shells, and wonderful flowing mermaid hair, clothing her as the midnight does the moon. The new costume freedom of the photoplay allows such limitation of clothing as would be probable when one is honestly in touch with wild nature and preoccupied with vigorous exercise. Thus the cave-man and desert island narratives, though seldom well done, when produced with verisimilitude, give an opportunity for the native human frame in the logical wrappings of reeds and skins. But those who in a silly hurry seek excuses, are generally merely ridiculous, like the barefoot man who is terribly tender about walking on the pebbles, or the wild man who is white as celery or grass under a board. There is no short cut to vitality.

A successful literal use of sculpture is in the film Oil and Water. Blanche Sweet is the leader of the play within a play which occupies the first reel. Here the Olympians and the Muses, with a grace that we fancy was Greek, lead a dance that traces the story of the spring, summer, and autumn of life. Finally the supple dancers turn gray and old and die, but not before they have given us a vision from the Ionian islands. The play might have been inspired from reading Keats' Lamia, but is probably derived from the work of Isadora Duncan. This chapter has hereafter only a passing word or two on literal sculptural effects. It has more in mind the carver's attitude toward all that passes before the eye.

The sculptor George Gray Barnard is responsible for none of the views in this discourse, but he has talked to me at length about his sense of discovery in watching the most ordinary motion pictures, and his delight in following them with their endless combinations of masses and flowing surfaces.

The little far-away people on the old-fashioned speaking stage do not appeal to the plastic sense in this way. They are, by comparison, mere bits of pasteboard with sweet voices, while, on the other hand, the photoplay foreground is full of dumb giants. The bodies of these giants are in high sculptural relief. Where the lights are quite glaring and the photography is bad, many of the figures are as hard in their impact on the eye as lime-white plaster-casts, no matter what the clothing. There are several passages of this sort in the otherwise beautiful Enoch Arden, where the shipwrecked sailor is depicted on his desert island in the glaring sun.

What materials should the photoplay figures suggest? There are as many possible materials as there are subjects for pictures and tone schemes to be considered. But we will take for illustration wood, bronze, and marble, since they have been used in the old sculptural art.

There is found in most art shows a type of carved wood gargoyle where the work and the subject are at one, not only in the color of the wood, but in the way the material masses itself, in bulk betrays its qualities. We will suppose a moving picture humorist who is in the same mood as the carver. He chooses a story of quaint old ladies, street gamins, and fat aldermen. Imagine the figures with the same massing and interplay suddenly invested with life, yet giving to the eye a pleasure kindred to that which is found in carved wood, and bringing to the fancy a similar humor.

Or there is a type of Action Story where the mood of the figures is that of bronze, with the aesthetic resources of that metal: its elasticity; its emphasis on the tendon, ligament, and bone, rather than on the muscle; and an attribute that we will call the panther-like quality. Hermon A. MacNeil has a memorable piece of work in the yard of the architect Shaw, at Lake Forest, Illinois. It is called "The Sun Vow." A little Indian is shooting toward the sun, while the old warrior, crouching immediately behind him, follows with his eye the direction of the arrow. Few pieces of sculpture come readily to mind that show more happily the qualities of bronze as distinguished from other materials. To imagine such a group done in marble, carved wood, or Della Robbia ware is to destroy the very image in the fancy.

The photoplay of the American Indian should in most instances be planned as bronze in action. The tribes should not move so rapidly that the panther-like elasticity is lost in the riding, running, and scalping. On the other hand, the aborigines should be far from the temperateness of marble.

Mr. Edward S. Curtis, the super-photographer, has made an Ethnological collection of photographs of our American Indians. This work of a life-time, a supreme art achievement, shows the native as a figure in bronze. Mr. Curtis' photoplay, The Land of the Head Hunters (World Film Corporation), a romance of the Indians of the North-West, abounds in noble bronzes.

I have gone through my old territories as an art student, in the Chicago Art Institute and the Metropolitan Museum, of late, in special excursions, looking for sculpture, painting, and architecture that might be the basis for the photoplays of the future.

The Bacchante of Frederick MacMonnies is in bronze in the Metropolitan Museum and in bronze replica in the Boston Museum of Fine Arts. There is probably no work that more rejoices the hearts of the young art students in either city. The youthful creature illustrates a most joyous leap into the air. She is high on one foot with the other knee lifted. She holds a bunch of grapes full-arm's length. Her baby, clutched in the other hand, is reaching up with greedy mouth toward the fruit. The bacchante body is glistening in the light. This is joy-in-bronze as the Sun Vow is power-in-bronze. This special story could not be told in another medium. I have seen in Paris a marble copy of this Bacchante. It is as though it were done in soap. On the other hand, many of the renaissance Italian sculptors have given us children in marble in low relief, dancing like lilies in the wind. They could not be put into bronze.

The plot of the Action Photoplay is literally or metaphorically a chase down the road or a hurdle-race. It might be well to consider how typical figures for such have been put into carved material. There are two bronze statues that have their replicas in all museums. They are generally one on either side of the main hall, towering above the second-story balustrade. First, the statue of Gattamelata, a Venetian general, by Donatello. The original is in Padua. Then there is the figure of Bartolommeo Colleoni. The original is in Venice. It is by Verrocchio and Leopardi. These equestrians radiate authority. There is more action in them than in any cowboy hordes I have ever beheld zipping across the screen. Look upon them and ponder long, prospective author-producer. Even in a simple chase-picture, the speed must not destroy the chance to enjoy the modelling. If you would give us mounted legions, destined to conquer, let any one section of the film, if it is stopped and studied, be grounded in the same bronze conception. The Assyrian commanders in Griffith's Judith would, without great embarrassment, stand this test.

But it may not be the pursuit of an enemy we have in mind. It may be a spring celebration, horsemen in Arcadia, going to some happy tournament. Where will we find our precedents for such a cavalcade? Go to any museum. Find the Parthenon room. High on the wall is the copy of the famous marble frieze of the young citizens who are in the procession in praise of Athena. Such a rhythm of bodies and heads and the feet of proud steeds, and above all the profiles of thoroughbred youths, no city has seen since that day. The delicate composition relations, ever varying, ever refreshing, amid the seeming sameness of formula of rider behind rider, have been the delight of art students the world over, and shall so remain. No serious observer escapes the exhilaration of this company. Let it be studied by the author-producer though it be but an idyl in disguise that his scenario calls for: merry young farmers hurrying to the State Fair parade, boys making all speed to the political rally.

Buy any three moving picture magazines you please. Mark the illustrations that are massive, in high relief, with long lines in their edges. Cut out and sort some of these. I have done it on the table where I write. After throwing away all but the best specimens, I have four different kinds of sculpture. First, behold the inevitable cowboy. He is on a ramping horse, filling the entire outlook. The steed rears, while facing us. The cowboy waves his hat. There is quite such an animal by Frederick MacMonnies, wrought in bronze, set up on a gate to a park in Brooklyn. It is not the identical color of the photoplay animal, but the bronze elasticity is the joy in both.

Here is a scene of a masked monk, carrying off a fainting girl. The hero intercepts him. The figures of the lady and the monk are in sufficient sculptural harmony to make a formal sculptural group for an art exhibition. The picture of the hero, strong, with well-massed surfaces, is related to both. The fact that he is in evening dress does not alter his monumental quality. All three are on a stone balcony that relates itself to the general largeness of spirit in the group, and the semi-classic dress of the maiden. No doubt the title is: The Morning Following the Masquerade Ball. This group could be made in unglazed clay, in four colors.

Here is an American lieutenant with two ladies. The three are suddenly alert over the approach of the villain, who is not yet in the picture. In costume it is an everyday group, but those three figures are related to one another, and the trees behind them, in simple sculptural terms. The lieutenant, as is to be expected, looks forth in fierce readiness. One girl stands with clasped hands. The other points to the danger. The relations of these people to one another may seem merely dramatic to the superficial observer, but the power of the group is in the fact that it is monumental. I could imagine it done in four different kinds of rare tropical wood, carved unpolished.

Here is a scene of storm and stress in an office where the hero is caught with seemingly incriminating papers. The table is in confusion. The room is filling with people, led by one accusing woman. Is this also sculpture? Yes. The figures are in high relief. Even the surfaces of the chairs and the littered table are massive, and the eye travels without weariness, as it should do in sculpture, from the hero to the furious woman, then to the attorney behind her, then to the two other revilers, then to the crowd in three loose rhythmic ranks. The eye makes this journey, not from space to space, or fabric to fabric, but first of all from mass to mass. It is sculpture, but it is the sort that can be done in no medium but the moving picture itself, and therefore it is one goal of this argument.

But there are several other goals. One of the sculpturesque resources of the photoplay is that the human countenance can be magnified many times, till it fills the entire screen. Some examples are in rather low relief, portraits approximating certain painters. But if they are on sculptural terms, and are studies of the faces of thinking men, let the producer make a pilgrimage to Washington for his precedent. There, in the rotunda of the capitol, is the face of Lincoln by Gutzon Borglum. It is one of the eminently successful attempts to get at the secret of the countenance by enlarging it much, and concentrating the whole consideration there.

The photoplay producer, seemingly without taking thought, is apt to show a sculptural sense in giving us Newfoundland fishermen, clad in oilskins. The background may have an unconscious Winslow Homer reminiscence. In the foreground our hardy heroes fill the screen, and dripping with sea-water become wave-beaten granite, yet living creatures none the less. Imagine some one chapter from the story of Little Em'ly in David Copperfield, retold in the films. Show us Ham Peggotty and old Mr. Peggotty in colloquy over their nets. There are many powerful bronze groups to be had from these two, on to the heroic and unselfish death of Ham, rescuing his enemy in storm and lightning.

I have seen one rich picture of alleged cannibal tribes. It was comedy about a missionary. But the aborigines were like living ebony and silver. That was long ago. Such things come too much by accident. The producer is not sufficiently aware that any artistic element in his list of productions that is allowed to go wild, that has not had full analysis, reanalysis, and final conservation, wastes his chance to attain supreme mastery.

Open your history of sculpture, and dwell upon those illustrations which are not the normal, reposeful statues, but the exceptional, such as have been listed for this chapter. Imagine that each dancing, galloping, or fighting figure comes down into the room life-size. Watch it against a dark curtain. Let it go through a series of gestures in harmony with the spirit of the original conception, and as rapidly as possible, not to lose nobility. If you have the necessary elasticity, imagine the figures wearing the costumes of another period, yet retaining in their motions the same essential spirit. Combine them in your mind with one or two kindred figures, enlarged till they fill the end of the room. You have now created the beginning of an Action Photoplay in your own fancy.

Do this with each most energetic classic till your imagination flags. I do not want to be too dogmatic, but it seems to me this is one way to evolve real Action Plays. It would, perhaps, be well to substitute this for the usual method of evolving them from old stage material or newspaper clippings.

There is in the Metropolitan Museum a noble modern group, the Mares of Diomedes, by the aforementioned Gutzon Borglum. It is full of material for the meditations of a man who wants to make a film of a stampede. The idea is that Hercules, riding his steed bareback, guides it in a circle. He is fascinating the horses he has been told to capture. They are held by the mesmerism of the circular path and follow him round and round till they finally fall from exhaustion. Thus the Indians of the West capture wild ponies, and Borglum, a far western man, imputes the method to Hercules. The bronze group shows a segment of this circle. The whirlwind is at its height. The mares are wild to taste the flesh of Hercules. Whoever is to photograph horses, let him study the play of light and color and muscle-texture in this bronze. And let no group of horses ever run faster than these of Borglum.

An occasional hint of a Michelangelo figure or gesture appears for a flash in the films. Young artist in the audience, does it pass you by? Open your history of sculpture again and look at the usual list of

Michelangelo groups. Suppose the seated majesty of Moses should rise, what would be the quality of the action? Suppose the sleeping figures of the Medician tombs should wake, or those famous slaves should break their bands, or David again hurl the stone. Would not their action be as heroic as their quietness? Is it not possible to have a Michelangelo of photoplay sculpture? Should we not look for him in the fulness of time? His figures might come to us in the skins of the desert island solitary, or as cave men and women, or as mermaids and mermen, and yet have a force and grandeur akin to that of the old Italian.

Rodin's famous group of the citizens of Calais is an example of the expression of one particular idea by a special technical treatment. The producer who tells a kindred story to that of the siege of Calais, and the final going of these humble men to their doom, will have a hero-tale indeed. It will be not only sculpture-in-action, but a great Crowd Picture. It begins to be seen that the possibilities of monumental achievement in the films transcend the narrow boundaries of the Action Photoplay. Why not conceptions as heroic as Rodin's Hand of God, where the first pair are clasped in the gigantic fingers of their maker in the clay from which they came?

Finally, I desire in moving pictures, not the stillness, but the majesty of sculpture. I do not advocate for the photoplay the mood of the Venus of Milo. But let us turn to that sister of hers, the great Victory of Samothrace, that spreads her wings at the head of the steps of the Louvre, and in many an art gallery beside. When you are appraising a new film, ask yourself: "Is this motion as rapid, as godlike, as the sweep of the wings of the Samothracian?" Let her be the touchstone of the Action Drama, for nothing can be more swift than the winged Gods, nothing can be more powerful than the oncoming of the immortals.

CHAPTER IX

Painting-In-Motion

This chapter is founded on the delicate effects that may be worked out from cosy interior scenes, close to the camera. It relates directly to chapter three.

While the Intimate-and-friendly Motion Picture may be in high sculptural relief, its characteristic manifestations are in low relief. The situations show to better advantage when they seem to be paintings rather than monumental groups.

Turn to your handful of motion picture magazines and mark the illustrations that look the most like paintings. Cut them out. Winnow them several times. I have before me, as a final threshing from such an experiment, five pictures. Each one approximates a different school.

Here is a colonial Virginia maiden by the hearth of the inn. Bending over her in a cherishing way is the negro maid. On the other side, the innkeeper shows a kindred solicitude. A dishevelled traveller sleeps huddled up in the corner. The costume of the man fades into the velvety shadows of the wall. His face is concealed. His hair blends with the soft background. The clothing of the other three makes a patch of light gray. Added to this is the gayety of special textures: the turban of the negress, a trimming on the skirt of the heroine, the silkiness of the innkeeper's locks, the fabric of the broom in the hearth-light, the pattern of the mortar lines round the bricks of the hearth. The tableau is a satisfying scheme in two planes and many textures.

Here is another sort of painting. The young mother in her pretty bed is smiling on her infant. The cot and covers and flesh tints have gentle scales of difference, all within one tone of the softest gray. Her hair is quite dark. It relates to the less luminous black of the coat of the physician behind the bed and the dress of the girl-friend bending over her. The nurse standing by the doctor is a figure of the same gray-white as the bed. Within the pattern of the velvety blacks there are as many subtle gradations as in the pattern of the gray-whites. The tableau is a satisfying scheme in black and gray, with practically one non-obtrusive texture throughout.

Here is a picture of an Englishman and his wife, in India. It might be called sculptural, but for the magnificence of the turban of the rajah who converses with them, the glitter of the light round his shoulders, and the scheme of shadow out of which the three figures rise. The arrangement remotely reminds one of several of Rembrandt's semi-oriental musings.

Here is a picture of Mary Pickford as Fanchon the Cricket. She is in the cottage with the strange old mother. I have seen a painting in this mood by the Greek Nickolas Gysis.

The Intimate-and-friendly Moving Picture, the photoplay of painting-in-motion, need not be indoors as long as it has the native-heath mood. It is generally keyed to the hearth-stone, and keeps quite close to it. But how well I remember when the first French photoplays began to come. Though unintelligent in some respects, the photography and subject-matter of many of them made one think of that painter of gentle out-of-door scenes, Jean Charles Cazin. Here is our last clipping, which is also in a spirit allied to Cazin. The heroine, accompanied by an aged shepherd and his dog, are in the foreground. The sheep are in the middle distance on the edge of the river. There is a noble hill beyond the gently flowing water. Here is intimacy and friendliness in the midst of the big out of doors.

If these five photo-paintings were on good paper enlarged to twenty by twenty-four inches, they would do to frame and hang on the wall of any study, for a month or so. And after the relentless test of time, I would venture that some one of the five would prove a permanent addition to the household gods.

Hastily made photographs selected from the films are often put in front of the better theatres to advertise the show. Of late they are making them two by three feet and sometimes several times larger. Here is a commercial beginning of an art gallery, but not enough pains are taken to give the selections a complete art gallery dignity. Why not have the most beautiful scenes in front of the theatres, instead of those alleged to be the most thrilling? Why not rest the fevered and wandering eye, rather than make one more attempt to take it by force?

Let the reader supply another side of the argument by looking at the illustrations in any history of painting. Let him select the pictures that charm him most, and think of them enlarged and transferred bodily to one corner of the room, as he has thought of the sculpture. Let them take on motion without losing their charm of low relief, or their serene composition within the four walls of the frame. As for the motion, let it be a further extension of the drawing. Let every gesture be a bolder but not less graceful brush-stroke.

The Metropolitan Museum has a Van Dyck that appeals equally to one's sense of beauty and one's feeling for humor. It is a portrait of James Stuart, Duke of Lennox, and I cannot see how the author-producer-photographer can look upon it without having it set his imagination in a glow. Every small town dancing set has a James like this. The man and the greyhound are the same witless breed, the kind that achieve a result by their clean-limbed elegance alone. Van Dyck has painted the two with what might be called a greyhound brush-stroke, a style of handling that is nothing but courtly convention and strut to the point of genius. He is as far from the meditative spirituality of Rembrandt as could well be imagined.

Conjure up a scene in the hereditary hall after a hunt (or golf tournament), in which a man like this Duke of Lennox has a noble parley with his lady (or dancing partner), she being a sweet and stupid swan (or a white rabbit) by the same sign that he is a noble and stupid greyhound. Be it an ancient or modern episode, the story could be told in the tone and with well-nigh the brushwork of Van Dyck.

Then there is a picture my teachers, Chase and Henri, were never weary of praising, the Girl with the Parrot, by Manet. Here continence in nervous force, expressed by low relief and restraint in tone, is carried to its ultimate point. I should call this an imagist painting, made before there were such people as imagist poets. It is a perpetual sermon to those that would thresh around to no avail, be they orators, melodramatists, or makers of photoplays with an alleged heart-interest.

Let us consider Gilbert Stuart's portrait of Washington. This painter's notion of personal dignity has far more of the intellectual quality than Van Dyck. He loves to give us stately, able, fairly conscientious gentry, rather than overdone royalty. His work represents a certain mood in design that in architecture is called colonial. Such portraits go with houses like Mount Vernon. Let the photographer study the flat blacks in the garments. Let him note the transparent impression of the laces and flesh-tints that seem to be painted on glass, observing especially the crystalline whiteness of the wigs. Let him inspect also the silhouette-like outlines, noting the courtly self-possession they convey. Then let the photographer, the producer, and the author, be they one man or six men, stick to this type of picturization through one entire production, till any artist in the audience will say, "This photoplay was painted by a pupil of Gilbert Stuart"; and the layman will say, "It looks like those stately days." And let us not have battle, but a Mount Vernon fireside tale.

Both the Chicago and New York museums contain many phases of one same family group, painted by George de Forest Brush. There is a touch of the hearthstone priestess about the woman. The force of sex has turned to the austere comforting passion of motherhood. From the children, under the wings of this spirit, come special delicate powers of life. There is nothing tense or restless about them, yet they embody action, the beating of the inner fire, without which all outer action is mockery. Hearthstone tales keyed to the mood and using the brush stroke that delineates this especial circle would be unmistakable in their distinction.

Charles W. Hawthorne has pictures in Chicago and New York that imply the Intimate-and-friendly Photoplay. The Trousseau in the Metropolitan Museum shows a gentle girl, an unfashionable home-body with a sweetly sheltered air. Behind her glimmers the patient mother's face. The older woman is busy about fitting the dress. The picture is a tribute to the qualities of many unknown gentlewomen. Such an illumination as this, on faces so innocently eloquent, is the light that should shine on the countenance of the photoplay actress who really desires greatness in the field of the Intimate Motion Picture. There is in Chicago, Hawthorne's painting of Sylvia: a little girl standing with her back to a mirror, a few blossoms in one hand and a vase of flowers on the mirror shelf. It is as sound a composition as Hawthorne ever produced. The painting of the child is another tribute to the physical-spiritual textures from which humanity is made. Ah, you producer who have grown squeaky whipping your people into what you called action, consider the dynamics of these figures that would be almost motionless in real life. Remember there must be a spirit-action under the other, or all is dead.

Yet that soul may be the muse of Comedy. If Hawthorne and his kind are not your fashion, turn to models that have their feet on the earth always, yet successfully aspire. Key some of your intimate humorous scenes to the Dutch Little Masters of Painting, such pictures as Gerard Terburg's Music Lesson in the Chicago Art Institute. The thing is as well designed as a Dutch house, wind-mill, or clock. And it is more elegant than any of these. There is humor enough in the picture to last one reel through. The society dame of the period, in her pretty raiment, fingers the strings of her musical instrument, while the master stands by her with the baton. The painter has enjoyed the satire, from her elegant little hands to the teacher's well-combed locks. It is very plain that she does not want to study music with any sincerity, and he does not desire to develop the ability of this particular person. There may be a flirtation in the background. Yet these people are not hollow as gourds, and they are not caricatured. The Dutch Little Masters have indulged in numberless characterizations of mundane humanity. But they are never so preoccupied with the story that it is an anecdote rather than a picture. It is, first of all, a piece of elegant painting-fabric. Next it is a scrap of Dutch philosophy or aspiration.

Let Whistler turn over in his grave while we enlist him for the cause of democracy. One view of the technique of this man might summarize it thus: fastidiousness in choice of subject, the picture well within the frame, low relief, a Velasquez study of tones and a Japanese study of spaces. Let us, dear and patient reader, particularly dwell upon the spacing. A Whistler, or a good Japanese print, might be described as a kaleidoscope suddenly arrested and transfixed at the moment of most exquisite relations in the pieces of glass. An Intimate Play of a kindred sort would start to turning the kaleidoscope again, losing fine relations only to gain those which are more exquisite and novel. All motion pictures might be characterized as *space measured without sound, plus time measured without sound*. This description fits in a special way the delicate form of the Intimate Motion Picture, and there can be studied out, free from irrelevant issues.

As to *space measured without sound*. Suppose it is a humorous characterization of comfortable family life, founded on some Dutch Little Master. The picture measures off its spaces in harmony. The triangle occupied by the little child's dress is in definite relation to the triangle occupied by the mother's costume. To these two patterns the space measured off by the boy's figure is adjusted, and all of them are as carefully related to the shapes cut out of the background by the figures. No matter how the characters move about in the photoplay, these pattern shapes should relate to one another in a definite design. The exact tone value of each one and their precise nearness or distance to one another have a deal to do with the final effect.

We go to the photoplay to enjoy right and splendid picture-motions, to feel a certain thrill when the pieces of kaleidoscope glass slide into new places. Instead of moving on straight lines, as they do in the mechanical toy, they progress in strange curves that are part of the very shapes into which they fall.

Consider: first came the photograph. Then motion was added to the photograph. We must use this order in our judgment. If it is ever to evolve into a national art, it must first be good picture, then good motion.

Belasco's attitude toward the stage has been denounced by the purists because he makes settings too large a portion of his story-telling, and transforms his theatre into the paradise of the property-man. But this very quality of the well spaced setting, if you please, has made his chance for the world's moving picture anthology. As reproduced by Jesse K. Lasky the Belasco production is the only type of the old-line drama that seems really made to be the basis of a moving picture play. Not always, but as a general rule, Belasco suffers less detriment in the films than other men. Take, for instance, the Belasco-Lasky production of The Rose of the Rancho with Bessie Barriscale as the heroine. It has many highly modelled action-tableaus, and others that come under the classification of this chapter. When I was attending it not long ago, here in my home town, the fair companion at my side said that one scene looked like a painting by Sorolla y Bastida, the Spaniard. It is the episode where the Rose sends back her servant to inquire the hero's name. As a matter of fact there were Sorollas and Zuloagas all through the piece. The betrothal reception with flying confetti was a satisfying piece of Spanish splendor. It was space music indeed, space measured without sound. Incidentally the cast is to be congratulated on its picturesque acting, especially Miss Barriscale in her impersonation of the Rose.

It is harder to grasp the other side of the paradox, picture-motions considered as *time measured without sound.* But think of a lively and humoresque clock that does not tick and takes only an hour to record a day. Think of a noiseless electric vehicle, where you are looking out of the windows, going down the smooth boulevard of Wonderland. Consider a film with three simple time-elements: (1) that of the pursuer, (2) the pursued, (3) the observation vehicle of the camera following the road and watching both of them, now faster, now slower than they, as the photographer overtakes the actors or allows them to hurry ahead. The plain chase is a bore because there are only these three time-elements. But the chase principle survives in every motion picture and we simply need more of this sort of time measurement, better considered. The more the non-human objects, the human actors, and the observer move at a varying pace, the greater chances there are for what might be called time-and-space music.

No two people in the same room should gesture at one mechanical rate, or lift their forks or spoons, keeping obviously together. Yet it stands to reason that each successive tableau should be not only a charming picture, but the totals of motion should be an orchestration of various speeds, of abrupt, graceful, and seemingly awkward progress, worked into a silent symphony.

Supposing it is a fisher-maiden's romance. In the background the waves toss in one tempo. Owing to the sail, the boat rocks in another. In the foreground the tree alternately bends and recovers itself in the breeze, making more opposition than the sail. In still another time-unit the smoke rolls from the chimney, making no resistance to the wind. In another unit, the lovers pace the sand. Yet there is one least common multiple in which all move. This the producing genius should sense and make part of the dramatic structure, and it would have its bearing on the periodic appearance of the minor and major crises.

Films like this, you say, would be hard to make. Yes. Here is the place to affirm that the one-reel Intimate Photoplay will no doubt be the form in which this type of time-and-space music is developed. The music of silent motion is the most abstract of moving picture attributes and will probably remain the least comprehended. Like the quality of Walter Pater's Marius the Epicurean, or that of Shelley's Hymn to Intellectual Beauty, it will not satisfy the sudden and the brash.

The reader will find in his round of the picture theatres many single scenes and parts of plays that elucidate the title of this chapter. Often the first two-thirds of the story will fit it well. Then the producers, finding that, for reasons they do not understand, with the best and most earnest actors they cannot work the three reels into an emotional climax, introduce some stupid disaster and rescue utterly irrelevant to the character-parts and the paintings that have preceded. Whether the alleged thesis be love, hate, or ambition, cottage charm, daisy dell sweetness, or the ivy beauty of an ancient estate, the resource for the final punch seems to be something like a train-wreck. But the transfiguration of the actors, not their destruction or rescue, is the goal. The last moment of the play is great, not when it is a grandiose salvation from a burning house, that knocks every delicate preceding idea in the head, but a tableau that is as logical as the awakening of the Sleeping Beauty after the hero has explored all the charmed castle.

CHAPTER X

Furniture, Trappings, and Inventions in Motion

The Action Pictures are sculpture-in-motion, the Intimate Pictures, paintings-in-motion, the Splendor Pictures, many and diverse. It seems far-fetched, perhaps, to complete the analogy and say they are architecture-in-motion; yet, patient reader, unless I am mistaken, that assumption can be given a value in time without straining your imagination.

Landscape gardening, mural painting, church building, and furniture making as well, are some of the things that come under the head of architecture. They are discussed between the covers of any architectural magazine. There is a particular relation in the photoplay between Crowd Pictures and landscape conceptions, between Patriotic Films and mural paintings, between Religious Films and architecture. And there is just as much of a relation between Fairy Tales and furniture, which same is discussed in this chapter.

Let us return to Moving Day, chapter four. This idea has been represented many times with a certain sameness because the producers have not thought out the philosophy behind it. A picture that is all action is a plague, one that is all elephantine and pachydermatous pageant is a bore, and, most emphatically, a film that is all mechanical legerdemain is a nuisance. The possible charm in a so-called trick picture is in eliminating the tricks, giving them dignity till they are no longer such, but thoughts in motion and made visible. In Moving Day the shoes are the most potent. They go through a drama that is natural to them. To march without human feet inside is but to exaggerate themselves. It would not be amusing to have them walk upside down, for instance. As long as the worn soles touch the pavement, we unconsciously conjure up the character of the absent owners, about whom the shoes are indeed gossiping. So let the remainder of the furniture keep still while the shoes do their best. Let us call to mind a classic fairy-tale involving shoes that are magical: The Seven Leagued Boots, for example, or The Enchanted Moccasins, or the footwear of Puss in Boots. How gorgeous and embroidered any of these should be, and at a crisis what sly antics they should be brought to play, without fidgeting all over the shop! Cinderella's Slipper is not sufficiently the heroine in moving pictures of that story. It should be the tiny leading lady of the piece, in the same sense the mighty steam-engine is the hero of the story in chapter two. The peasants when they used to tell the tale by the hearth fire said the shoe was made of glass. This was in mediaeval Europe, at a time when glass was much more of a rarity. The material was chosen to imply a sort of jewelled strangeness from the start. When Cinderella loses it in her haste, it should flee at once like a white mouse, to hide under the sofa. It should be pictured there with special artifice, so that the sensuous little foot of every girl-child in the audience will tingle to wear it. It should move a bit when the prince comes frantically hunting his lady, and peep out just in time for that royal personage to spy it. Even at the coronation it should be the centre of the ritual, more gazed at than the crown, and on as dazzling a cushion. The final taking on of the slipper by the lady should be as stately a ceremony as the putting of the circlet of gold on her aureole hair. So much for Cinderella. But there are novel stories that should be evolved by preference, about new sorts of magic shoes.

We have not exhausted Moving Day. The chairs kept still through the Cinderella discourse. Now let them take their innings. Instead of having all of them dance about, invest but one with an inner life. Let its special attributes show themselves but gradually, reaching their climax at the highest point of excitement in the reel, and being an integral part of that enthusiasm. Perhaps, though we be inventing a new fairy-tale, it will resemble the Siege Perilous in the Arthurian story, the chair where none but the perfect knight could sit. A dim row of flaming swords might surround it. When the soul entitled to use this throne appears, the swords might fade away and the gray cover hanging in slack folds roll back because of an inner energy and the chair might turn from gray to white, and with a subtle change of line become a throne.

The photoplay imagination which is able to impart vital individuality to furniture will not stop there. Let the buildings emanate conscious life. The author-producer-photographer, or one or all three, will make into a personality some place akin to the House of the Seven Gables till the ancient building dominates the fancy as it does in Hawthorne's tale. There are various ways to bring about this result: by having its outlines waver in the twilight, by touches of phosphorescence, or by the passing of inexplicable shadows or the like. It depends upon what might be called the genius of the building. There is the Poe story of The Fall of the House of Usher, where with the death of the last heir the castle falls crumbling into the tarn. There are other possible tales on such terms, never yet imagined, to be born tomorrow. Great structures may become in sort villains, as in the old Bible narrative of the origin of the various languages. The producer can show the impious Babel Tower, going higher and higher into the sky, fascinating and tempting the architects till a confusion of tongues turns those masons into quarrelling mobs that become departing caravans, leaving her blasted and forsaken, a symbol of every Babylon that rose after her.

There are fables where the rocks and the mountains speak. Emerson has given us one where the Mountain and the Squirrel had a quarrel. The Mountain called the Squirrel "Little Prig." And then continues a clash of personalities more possible to illustrate than at first appears. Here we come to the second stage of the fairy-tale where the creature seems so unmanageable in his physical aspect that some actor must be substituted who will embody the essence of him. To properly illustrate the quarrel of the Mountain and the Squirrel, the steep height should quiver and heave and then give forth its personality in the figure of a vague smoky giant, capable of human argument, but with oak-roots in his hair, and Bun, perhaps, become a jester in squirrel's dress.

Or it may be our subject matter is a tall Dutch clock. Father Time himself might emerge therefrom. Or supposing it is a chapel, in a knight's adventure. An angel should step from the carving by the door: a design that is half angel, half flower. But let the clock first tremble a bit. Let the carving stir a little, and then let the spirit come forth, that there may be a fine relation between the impersonator and the thing represented. A statue too often takes on life by having the actor abruptly substituted. The actor cannot logically take on more personality than the statue has. He can only give that personality expression in a new channel. In the realm of letters, a real transformation scene, rendered credible to the higher fancy by its slow cumulative movement, is the tale of the change of the dying Rowena to the living triumphant Ligeia in Poe's story of that name. Substitution is not the fairy-story. It is transformation, transfiguration, that is the fairy-story, be it a divine or a diabolical change. There is never more than one witch in a forest, one Siege Perilous at any Round Table. But she is indeed a witch and the other is surely a Siege Perilous.

We might define Fairy Splendor as furniture transfigured, for without transfiguration there is no spiritual motion of any kind. But the phrase ''furniture-in-motion'' serves a purpose. It gets us back to the earth for a reason. Furniture is architecture, and the fairy-tale picture should certainly be drawn with architectural lines. The normal fairy-tale is a sort of tiny informal child's religion, the baby's secular temple, and it should have for the most part that touch of delicate sublimity that we see in the mountain chapel or grotto, or fancy in the dwellings of Aucassin and Nicolette. When such lines are drawn by the truly sophisticated producer, there lies in them the secret of a more than ritualistic power. Good fairy architecture amounts to an incantation in itself.

If it is a grown-up legend, it must be more than monumental in its lines, like the great stone face of Hawthorne's tale. Even a chair can reach this estate. For instance, let it be the throne of Wodin, illustrating some passage in Norse mythology. If this throne has a language, it speaks with the lightning; if it shakes with its threat, it moves the entire mountain range beneath it. Let the wizard-author-producer climb up from the tricks of Moving Day to the foot-hills where he can see this throne against the sky, as a superarchitect would draw it. But even if he can give this vision in the films, his task will not be worth while if he is simply a teller of old stories. Let us have magic shoes about which are more golden dreams than those concerning Cinderella. Let us have stranger castles than that of Usher, more dazzling chairs than the Siege Perilous. Let us have the throne of Liberty, not the throne of Wodin.

There is one outstanding photoplay that I always have in mind when I think of film magic. It illustrates some principles of this chapter and chapter four, as well as many others through the book. It is Griffith's production of The Avenging Conscience. It is also an example of that rare thing, a use of old material that is so inspired that it has the dignity of a new creation. The raw stuff of the plot is pieced together from the story of The Tell-Tale Heart and the poem Annabel Lee. It has behind it, in the further distance, Poe's conscience stories of The Black Cat, and William Wilson. I will describe the film here at length, and apply it to whatever chapters it illustrates.

An austere and cranky bachelor (well impersonated by Spottis-woode Aitken) brings up his orphan nephew with an awkward affection. The nephew is impersonated by Henry B. Walthall. The uncle has an ambition that the boy will become a man of letters. In his attempts at literature the youth is influenced by Poe. This brings about the Poe quality of his dreams at the crisis. The uncle is silently exasperated when he sees his boy's writing-time broken into, and wasted, as he thinks, by an affair with a lovely Annabel (Blanche Sweet). The intimacy and confidence of the lovers has progressed so far that it is a natural thing for the artless girl to cross the gardens and after hesitation knock at the door. She wants to know what has delayed her boy. She is all in a flutter on account of the overdue appointment to go to a party together. The scene of the pretty hesitancy on the step, her knocking, and the final impatient tapping with her foot is one of the best illustrations of the intimate mood in photoplay episodes. On the girl's entrance the uncle overwhelms her and the boy by saying she is pursuing his nephew like a common woman of the town. The words actually burst through the film, not as a melodramatic, but as an actual insult. This is a thing almost impossible to do in the photoplay. This outrage in the midst of an atmosphere of chivalry is one of Griffith's master-moments. It accounts for the volcanic fury of the nephew that takes such trouble to burn itself out afterwards. It is not easy for the young to learn that they must let those people flay them for an hour who have made every sacrifice for them through a lifetime.

This scene of insult and the confession scene, later in this film, moved me as similar passages in high drama would do; and their very rareness, even in the hands of photoplay masters, indicates that such purely dramatic climaxes cannot be the main asset of the moving picture. Over and over, with the best talent and producers, they fail.

The boy and girl go to the party in spite of the uncle. It is while on the way that the boy looks on the face of a stranger who afterwards mixes up in his dream as the detective. There is a mistake in the printing here. There are several minutes of a worldly-wise oriental dance to amuse the guests, while the lovers are alone at another end of the garden. It is, possibly, the aptest contrast with the seriousness of our hero and heroine. But the social affair could have had a better title than the one that is printed on the film "An Old-fashioned Sweetheart Party." Possibly the dance was put in after the title.

The lovers part forever. The girl's pride has had a mortal wound. About this time is thrown on the screen the kind of a climax quite surely possible to the photoplay. It reminds one, not of the mood of Poe's verse, but of the spirit of the paintings of George Frederick Watts. It is allied in some way, in my mind, with his "Love and Life," though but a single draped figure within doors, and "Love and Life" are undraped figures, climbing a mountain.

The boy, having said good-by, remembers the lady Annabel. It is a crisis after the event. In his vision she is shown in a darkened passageway, all in white, looking out of the window upon the moonlit sky. Simple enough in its elements, this vision is shown twice in glory. The third replica has not the same glamour. The first two are transfigurations into divinity. The phrase thrown on the screen is "The moon never beams without bringing me dreams of the beautiful Annabel Lee." And the sense of loss goes through and through one like a flight of arrows. Another noble picture, more realistic, more sculpturesque, is of Annabel mourning on her knees in her room. Her bended head makes her akin to "Niobe, all tears."

The boy meditating on a park-path is meanwhile watching the spider in his web devour the fly. Then he sees the ants in turn destroy the spider. These pictures are shown on so large a scale that the spiderweb fills the end of the theatre. Then the ant-tragedy does the same. They can be classed as particularly apt hieroglyphics in the sense of chapter thirteen. Their horror and decorative iridescence are of the Poe sort. It is the first hint of the Poe hieroglyphic we have had except the black patch over the eye of the uncle, along with his jaundiced, cadaverous face. The boy meditates on how all nature turns on cruelty and the survival of the fittest.

He passes just now an Italian laborer (impersonated by George Seigmann). This laborer enters later into his dream. He finally goes to sleep in his chair, the resolve to kill his uncle rankling in his heart.

The audience is not told that a dream begins. To understand that, one must see the film through twice. But it is perfectly legitimate to deceive us. Through our ignorance we share the young man's hallucinations, entering into them as imperceptibly as he does. We think it is the next morning. Poe would start the story just here, and here the veritable Poe-esque quality begins.

After debate within himself as to means, the nephew murders his uncle and buries him in the thick wall of the chimney. The Italian laborer witnesses the death-struggle through the window. While our consciences are aching and the world crashes round us, he levies blackmail. Then for due compensation the Italian becomes an armed sentinel. The boy fears detection.

Yet the foolish youth thinks he will be happy. But every time he runs to meet his sweetheart he is appalled by hallucinations over her shoulder. The cadaverous ghost of the uncle is shown on the screen several times. It is an appearance visible to the young man and the audience only. Later the ghost is implied by the actions of the guilty one. We merely imagine it. This is a piece of sound technique. We no more need a dray full of ghosts than a dray full of jumping furniture.

The village in general has never suspected the nephew. Only two people suspect him: the broken-hearted girl and an old friend of his father. This gentleman puts a detective on the trail. (The detective is impersonated by Ralph Lewis.) The gradual breakdown of the victim is traced by dramatic degrees. This is the second case of the thing I have argued as being generally impossible in a photoplay chronicle of a private person, and which the considerations of chapter twelve indicate as exceptional. We trace the innermost psychology of one special citizen step by step to the crisis, and that path is actually the primary interest of the story. The climax is the confession to the detective. With this self-exposure the direct Poe-quality of the technique comes to an end. Moreover, Poe would end the story here. But the Poe-dream is set like a dark jewel in a gold ring, of which more anon.

Let us dwell upon the confession. The first stage of this conscience-climax is reached by the dramatization of The Tell-Tale Heart reminiscence in the memory of the dreaming man. The episode makes a singular application of the theories with which this chapter begins. For furniture-in-motion we have the detective's pencil. For trappings and inventions in motion we have his tapping shoe and the busy clock pendulum. Because this scene is so powerful the photoplay is described in this chapter rather than any other, though the application is more spiritual than literal. The half-mad boy begins to divulge that he thinks that the habitual ticking of the clock is satanically timed to the beating of the dead man's heart. Here more unearthliness hovers round a pendulum than any merely mechanical trick-movements could impart. Then the merest commonplace of the detective tapping his pencil in the same time — the boy trying in vain to ignore it—increases the strain, till the audience has well-nigh the hallucinations of the victim. Then the bold tapping of the detective's foot, who would do all his accusing without saying a word, and the startling coincidence of the owl hoot-hooting outside the window to the same measure, bring us close to the final breakdown. These realistic material actors are as potent as the actual apparitions of the dead man that preceded them. Those visions prepared the mind to invest trifles with significance. The pencil and the pendulum conducting themselves in an apparently everyday fashion, satisfy in a far nobler way the thing in the cave-man attending the show that made him take note in other centuries of the rope that began to hang the butcher, the fire that began to burn the stick, and the stick that began to beat the dog.

Now the play takes a higher demoniacal plane reminiscent of Poe's Bells. The boy opens the door. He peers into the darkness. There he sees them. They are the nearest to the sinister Poe quality of any illustrations I recall that attempt it. "They are neither man nor woman, they are neither brute nor human; they are ghouls." The scenes are designed with the architectural dignity that the first part of this chapter has insisted wizard trappings should take on. Now it is that the boy confesses and the Poe story ends.

Then comes what the photoplay people call the punch. It is discussed at the end of chapter nine. It is a kind of solar plexus blow to the sensibilities, certainly by this time an unnecessary part of the film. Usually every soul movement carefully built up to where the punch begins is forgotten in the material smash or rescue. It is not so bad in this case, but it is a too conventional proceeding for Griffith.

The boy flees interminably to a barn too far away. There is a siege by a posse, led by the detective. It is veritable border warfare. The Italian leads an unsuccessful rescue party. The unfortunate youth finally hangs himself. The beautiful Annabel bursts through the siege a moment too late; then, heart broken, kills herself. These things are carried out by good technicians. But it would have been better to have had the suicide with but a tiny part of the battle, and the story five reels long instead of six. This physical turmoil is carried into the spiritual world only by the psychic momentum acquired through the previous confession scene. The one thing with intrinsic pictorial heart-power is the death of Annabel by jumping off the sea cliff.

Then comes the awakening. To every one who sees the film for the first time it is like the forgiveness of sins. The boy finds his uncle still alive. In revulsion from himself, he takes the old man into his arms. The uncle has already begun to be ashamed of his terrible words, and has prayed for a contrite heart. The radiant Annabel is shown in the early dawn rising and hurrying to her lover in spite of her pride. She will bravely take back her last night's final word. She cannot live without him. The uncle makes amends to the girl. The three are in the inconsistent but very human mood of sweet forgiveness for love's sake, that sometimes overtakes the bitterest of us after some crisis in our days.

The happy pair are shown, walking through the hills. Thrown upon the clouds for them are the moods of the poet-lover's heart. They look into the woods and see his fancies of Spring, the things that he will some day write. These pageants might be longer. They furnish the great climax. They make a consistent parallel and contrast with the ghoul-visions that end with the confession to the detective. They wipe that terror from the mind. They do not represent Poe. The rabbits, the leopard, the fairies, Cupid and Psyche in the clouds, and the little loves from the hollow trees are contributions to the original poetry of the eye.

Finally, the central part of this production of the Avenging Conscience is no dilution of Poe, but an adequate interpretation, a story he might have written. Those who have the European respect for Poe's work will be most apt to be satisfied with this section, including the photographic texture which may be said to be an authentic equivalent of his prose. How often Poe has been primly patronized for his majestic quality, the wizard power which looms above all his method and subject-matter and furnishes the only reason for its existence!

For Griffith to embroider this Poe Interpretation in the centre of a fairly consistent fabric, and move on into a radiant climax of his own that is in organic relation to the whole, is an achievement indeed. The final criticism is that the play is derivative. It is not built from new material in all its parts, as was the original story. One must be a student of Poe to get its ultimate flavor. But in reading Poe's own stories, one need not be a reader of any one special preceding writer to get the strange and solemn exultation of that literary enchanter. He is the quintessence of his own lonely soul.

Though the wizard element is paramount in the Poe episode of this film, the appeal to the conscience is only secondary to this. It is keener than in Poe, owing to the human elements before and after. The Chameleon producer approximates in The Avenging Conscience the type of mystic teacher, discussed in the twentieth chapter: "The Prophet-Wizard."

CHAPTER XI

Architecture-In-Motion

This chapter is a superstructure upon the foundations of chapters five, six, and seven.

I have said that it is a quality, not a defect, of the photoplays that while the actors tend to become types and hieroglyphics and dolls, on the other hand, dolls and hieroglyphics and mechanisms tend to become human. By an extension of this principle, non-human tones, textures, lines, and spaces take on a vitality almost like that of flesh and blood. It is partly for this reason that some energy is hereby given to the matter of reenforcing the idea that the people with the proper training to take the higher photoplays in hand are not veteran managers of vaudeville circuits, but rather painters, sculptors, and architects, preferably those who are in the flush of their first reputation in these crafts. Let us imagine the centres of the experimental drama, such as the Drama League, the Universities, and the stage societies, calling in people of these professions and starting photoplay competitions and enterprises. Let the thesis be here emphasized that the architects, above all, are the men to advance the work in the ultra-creative photoplay. "But few architects," you say, "are creative, even in their own profession."

Let us begin with the point of view of the highly trained pedantic young builder, the type that, in the past few years, has honored our landscape with those paradoxical memorials of Abraham Lincoln the railsplitter, memorials whose Ionic columns are straight from Paris. Pericles is the real hero of such a man, not Lincoln. So let him for the time surrender completely to that great Greek. He is worthy of a monument nobler than any America has set up to any one. The final pictures may be taken in front of buildings with which the architect or his favorite master has already edified this republic, or if the war is over, before some surviving old-world models. But whatever the method, let him study to express at last the thing that moves within him as a creeping fire, which Americans do not yet understand and the loss of which makes the classic in our architecture a mere piling of elegant stones upon one another. In the arrangement of crowds and flow of costuming and study of tableau climaxes, let the architect bring an illusion of that delicate flowering, that brilliant instant of time before the Peloponnesian war. It does not seem impossible when one remembers the achievements of the author of Cabiria in approximating Rome and Carthage.

Let the principal figure of the pageant be the virgin Athena, walking as a presence visible only to us, yet among her own people, and robed and armed and panoplied, the guardian of Pericles, appearing in those streets that were herself. Let the architect show her as she came only in a vision to Phidias, while the dramatic writers and mathematicians and poets and philosophers go by. The crowds should be like pillars of Athens, and she like a great pillar. The crowds should be like the tossing waves of the Ionic Sea and Athena like the white ship upon the waves. The audiences in the tragedies should be shown like wheat-fields on the hill-sides, always stately yet blown by the wind, and Athena the one sower and reaper. Crowds should descend the steps of the Acropolis, nymphs and fauns and Olympians, carved as it were from the marble, yet flowing like a white cataract down into the town, bearing with them Athena, their soul. All this in the Photoplay of Pericles.

No civic or national incarnation since that time appeals to the poets like the French worship of the Maid of Orleans. In Percy MacKaye's book, The Present Hour, he says on the French attitude toward the war: —

"Half artist and half anchorite,
Part siren and part Socrates,
Her face—alluring fair, yet recondite—
Smiled through her salons and academics.

Lightly she wore her double mask,
Till sudden, at war's kindling spark,
Her inmost self, in shining mail and casque,
Blazed to the world her single soul—Jeanne d'Arc!"

To make a more elaborate showing of what is meant by architecture-in-motion, let us progress through the centuries and suppose that the builder has this enthusiasm for France, that he is slowly setting about to build a photoplay around the idea of the Maid.

First let him take the mural painting point of view. Bear in mind these characteristics of that art: it is wall-painting that is an organic part of the surface on which it appears: it is on the same lines as the building and adapted to the colors and forms of the structure of which it is a part.

The wall-splendors of America that are the most scattered about in inexpensive copies are the decorations of the Boston Public Library. Note the pillar-like quality of Sargent's prophets, the solemn dignity of Abbey's Holy Grail series, the grand horizontals and perpendiculars of the work of Puvis de Chavannes. The last is the orthodox mural painter of the world, but the other two will serve the present purpose also. These architectural paintings if they were dramatized, still retaining their powerful lines, would be three exceedingly varied examples of what is meant by architecture-in-motion. The visions that appear to Jeanne d'Arc might be delineated in the mood of some one of these three painters. The styles will not mix in the same episode.

A painter from old time we mention here, not because he was orthodox, but because of his genius for the drawing of action, and because he covered tremendous wall-spaces with Venetian tone and color, is Tintoretto. If there is a mistrust that the mural painting standard will tend to destroy the sense of action, Tintoretto will restore confidence in that regard. As the Winged Victory represents flying in sculpture, so his work is the extreme example of action with the brush. The Venetians called him the furious painter. One must understand a man through his admirers. So explore Ruskin's sayings on Tintoretto.

I have a dozen moving picture magazine clippings, which are in their humble way first or second cousins of mural paintings. I will describe but two, since the method of selection has already been amply indicated, and the reader can find his own examples. For a Crowd Picture, for instance, here is a scene at a masquerade ball. The glitter of the costumes is an extension of the glitter of the candelabra overhead. The people are as it were chandeliers, hung lower down. The lines of the candelabra relate to the very ribbon streamers of the heroine, and the massive wood-work is the big brother of the square-shouldered heroes in the foreground, though one is a clown, one is a Russian Duke, and one is Don Caesar De Bazan. The building is the father of the people. These relations can be kept in the court scenes of the production of Jeanne d'Arc.

Here is a night picture from a war story in which the light is furnished by two fires whose coals and brands are hidden by earth heaped in front. The sentiment of tenting on the old camp-ground pervades the scene. The far end of the line of those keeping bivouac disappears into the distance, and the depths of the ranks behind them fade into the thick shadows. The flag, a little above the line, catches the light. One great tree overhead spreads its leafless half-lit arms through the gloom. Behind all this is unmitigated black. The composition reminds one of a Hiroshige study of midnight. These men are certainly a part of the architecture of out of doors, and mysterious as the vault of Heaven. This type of a camp-fire is possible in our Jeanne d'Arc.

These pictures, new and old, great and unknown, indicate some of the standards of judgment and types of vision whereby our conception of the play is to be evolved.

By what means shall we block it in? Our friend Tintoretto made use of methods which are here described from one of his biographers, W. Roscoe Osler: "They have been much enlarged upon in the different biographies as the means whereby Tintoretto obtained his power. They constituted, however, his habitual method of determining the effect and general grouping of his compositions. He moulded with extreme care small models of his figures in wax and clay. Titian and other painters as well as Tintoretto employed this method as the means of determining the light and shade of their design. Afterwards the later stages of their work were painted from the life. But in Tintoretto's compositions the position and arrangement of his figures as he began to dwell upon his great conceptions were such as to render the study from the living model a matter of great difficulty and at times an impossibility. . . . He . . . modelled his sculptures . . . imparting to his models a far more complete character than had been customary. These firmly moulded figures, sometimes draped, sometimes free, he suspended in a box made of wood, or of cardboard for his smaller work, in whose walls he made an aperture to admit a lighted candle. . . . He sits moving the light about amidst his assemblage of figures. Every aspect of sublimity of light suitable to a Madonna surrounded with angels, or a heavenly choir, finds its miniature response among the figures as the light moves.

"This was the method by which, in conjunction with a profound study of outward nature, sympathy with the beauty of different types of face and varieties of form, with the many changing hues of the Venetian scene, with the great laws of color and a knowledge of literature and history, he was able to shadow forth his great imagery of the intuitional world."

This method of Tintoretto suggests several possible derivatives in the preparation of motion pictures. Let the painters and sculptors be now called upon for painting models and sculptural models, while the architect, already present, supplies the architectural models, all three giving us visible scenarios to furnish the cardinal motives for the acting, from which the amateur photoplay company of the university can begin their interpretation.

For episodes that follow the precedent of the simple Action Film tiny wax models of the figures, toned and costumed to the heart's delight, would tell the high points of the story. Let them represent, perhaps, seven crucial situations from the proposed photoplay. Let them be designed as uniquely in their dresses as are the Russian dancers' dresses, by Léon Bakst. Then to alternate with these, seven little paintings of episodes, designed in blacks, white, and grays, each representing some elusive point in the intimate aspects of the story. Let there be a definite system of space and texture relations retained throughout the set.

The models for the splendor scenes would, of course, be designed by the architect, and these other scenes alternated with and subordinated to his work. The effects which he would conceive would be on a grander scale. The models for these might be mere extensions of the methods of those others, but in the typical and highest let us imagine ourselves going beyond Tintoretto in preparation.

Let the principal splendor moods and effects be indicated by actual structures, such miniatures as architects offer along with their plans of public buildings, but transfigured beyond that standard by the light of inspiration combined with experimental candle-light, spotlight, sunlight, or torchlight. They must not be conceived as stage arrangements of wax figures with harmonious and fitting backgrounds, but as backgrounds that clamor for utterance through the figures in front of them, as Athens finds her soul in the Athena with which we began. These three sorts of models, properly harmonized, should have with them a written scenario constructed to indicate all the scenes between. The scenario will lead up to these models for climaxes and hold them together in the celestial hurdle-race.

We have in our museums some definite architectural suggestions as to the style of these models. There are in Blackstone Hall in the Chicago Art Institute several great Romanesque and Gothic portals, pillars, and statues that might tell directly upon certain settings of our Jeanne d'Arc pageant. They are from Notre Dame du Port at Clermont-Ferrand, the Abbey church of St. Gilles, the Abbey of Charlieu, the Cathedral of Amiens, Notre Dame at Paris, the Cathedral of Bordeaux, and the Cathedral of Rheims. Perhaps the object I care for most in the Metropolitan Museum, New York, is the complete model of Notre Dame, Paris, by M. Joly. Why was this model of Notre Dame made with such exquisite pains? Certainly not as a matter of mere information or cultivation. I venture the first right these things have to be taken care of in museums is to stimulate to new creative effort.

I went to look over the Chicago collection with a friend and poet Arthur Davison Ficke. He said something to this effect: ''The first thing I see when I look at these fragments is the whole cathedral in all its original proportions. Then I behold the mediaeval marketplace hunched against the building, burying the foundations, the life of man growing rank and weedlike around it. Then I see the bishop coming from the door with his impressive train. But a crusade may go by on the way to the Holy Land. A crusade may come home battered and in rags. I get the sense of life, as of a rapid in a river flowing round a great rock.''

The cathedral stands for the age-long meditation of the ascetics in the midst of battling tribes. This brooding architecture has a blood-brotherhood with the meditating, saint-seeing Jeanne d'Arc.

There is in the Metropolitan Museum a large and famous canvas painted by the dying Bastien-Lepage; — Jeanne Listening to the Voices. It is a picture of which the technicians and the poets are equally enamored. The tale of Jeanne d'Arc could be told, carrying this particular peasant girl through the story. And for a piece of architectural pageantry akin to the photoplay ballroom scene already described, yet far above it, there is nothing more apt for our purpose than the painting by Boutet de Monvel filling the space at the top of the stair at the Chicago Art Institute. Though the Bastien-Lepage is a large painting, this is many times the size. It shows Joan's visit at the court of Chinon. It is big without being empty. It conveys a glitter which expresses one of the things that is meant by the phrase: Splendor Photoplay. But for moving picture purposes it is the Bastien-Lepage Joan that should appear here, set in dramatic contrast to the Boutet de Monvel Court. Two valuable neighbors to whom I have read this chapter suggest that the whole Boutet de Monvel illustrated child's book about our heroine could be used on this grand scale, for a background.

The Inness room at the Chicago Art Institute is another school for the meditative producer, if he would evolve his tribute to France on American soil. Though no photoplay tableau has yet approximated the brush of Inness, why not attempt to lead Jeanne through an Inness landscape? The Bastien-Lepage trees are in France. But here is an American world in which one could see visions and hear voices. Where is the inspired camera that will record something of what Inness beheld?

Thus much for the atmosphere and trappings of our Jeanne d'Arc scenario. Where will we get our story? It should, of course, be written from the ground up for this production, but as good Americans we would probably find a mass of suggestions in Mark Twain's Joan of Arc.

Quite recently a moving picture company sent its photographers to Springfield, Illinois, and produced a story with our city for a background, using our social set for actors. Backed by the local commercial association for whose benefit the thing was made, the resources of the place were at the command of routine producers. Springfield dressed its best, and acted with fair skill. The heroine was a charming debutante, the hero the son of Governor Dunne. The Mine Owner's Daughter was at best a mediocre photoplay. But this type of social-artistic event, that happened once, may be attempted a hundred times, each time slowly improving. Which brings us to something that is in the end very far from The Mine Owner's Daughter. By what scenario method the following film or series of films is to be produced I will not venture to say. No doubt the way will come if once the dream has a sufficient hold.

I have long maintained that my hometown should have a goddess like Athena. The legend should be forthcoming. The producer, while not employing armies, should use many actors and the tale be told with the same power with which the productions of Judith of Bethulia and The Battle Hymn of the Republic were evolved. While the following story may not be the form which Springfield civic religion will ultimately take, it is here recorded as a second cousin of the dream that I hope will some day be set forth.

Late in an afternoon in October, a light is seen in the zenith like a dancing star. The clouds form round it in the approximation of a circle. Now there becomes visible a group of heads and shoulders of presences that are looking down through the ring of clouds, watching the star, like giant children that peep down a well. The jewel descends by four sparkling chains, so far away they look to be dewy threads of silk. As the bright mystery grows larger it appears to be approaching the treeless hill of Washington Park, a hill that is surrounded by many wooded ridges. The people come running from everywhere to watch. Here indeed will be a Crowd Picture with as many phases as a stormy ocean. Flying machines appear from the Fair Ground north of the city, and circle round and round as they go up, trying to reach the slowly descending plummet.

At last, while the throng cheers, one birdman has attained it. He brings back his message that the gift is an image, covered loosely with a wrapping that seems to be of spun gold. Now the many aviators whirl round the descending wonder, like seagulls playing about a ship's mast. Soon, amid an awestruck throng, the image is on the hillock. The golden chains, and the giant children holding them there above, have melted into threads of mist and nothingness. The shining wrapping falls away. The people look upon a seated statue of marble and gold. There is a branch of wrought-gold maple leaves in her hands. Then beside the image is a fluttering transfigured presence of which the image seems to be a representation. This spirit, carrying a living maple branch in her hand, says to the people: ''Men and Women of Springfield, this carving is the Lady Springfield sent by your Lord from Heaven. Build no canopy over her. Let her ever be under the prairie-sky. Do her perpetual honor.'' The messenger, who is the soul and voice of Springfield, fades into the crowd, to emerge on great and terrible occasions.

This is only one story. Round this public event let the photoplay romancer weave what tales of private fortune he will, narratives bound up with the events of that October day, as the story of Nathan and Naomi is woven into Judith of Bethulia.

Henceforth the city officers are secular priests of Our Lady Springfield. Their failure in duty is a profanation of her name. A yearly pledge of the first voters is taken in her presence like the old Athenian oath of citizenship. The seasonal pageants march to the statue's feet, scattering flowers. The important outdoor festivals are given on the edge of her hill. All the roads lead to her footstool. Pilgrims come from the Seven Seas to look upon her face that is carved by Invisible Powers. Moreover, the living messenger that is her actual soul appears in dreams, or visions of the open day, when the days are dark for the city, when her patriots are irresolute, and her children are put to shame. This spirit with the maple branch rallies them, leads them to victories like those that were won of old in the name of Jeanne d'Arc or Pallas Athena herself.

CHAPTER XII

Thirty Differences between the Photoplays and the Stage

The stage is dependent upon three lines of tradition: first, that of Greece and Rome that came down through the French. Second, the English style, ripened from the miracle play and the Shakespearian stage. And third, the Ibsen precedent from Norway, now so firmly established it is classic. These methods are obscured by the commercialized dramas, but they are behind them all. Let us discuss for illustration the Ibsen tradition.

Ibsen is generally the vitriolic foe of pageant. He must be read aloud. He stands for the spoken word, for the iron power of life that may be concentrated in a phrase like the "All or nothing" of Brand. Though Peer Gynt has its spectacular side, Ibsen generally comes in through the ear alone. He can be acted in essentials from end to end with one table and four chairs in any parlor. The alleged punch with which the "movie" culminates has occurred three or ten years before the Ibsen curtain goes up. At the close of every act of the dramas of this Norwegian one might inscribe on the curtain "This the magnificent moving picture cannot achieve." Likewise after every successful film described in this book could be inscribed "This the trenchant Ibsen cannot do."

But a photoplay of Ghosts came to our town. The humor of the prospect was the sort too deep for tears. My pastor and I reread the William Archer translation that we might be alert for every antithesis. Together we went to the services. Since then the film has been furiously denounced by the literati. Floyd Dell's discriminating assault upon it is quoted in Current Opinion, October, 1915, and Margaret Anderson prints a denunciation of it in a recent number of The Little Review. But it is not such a bad film in itself. It is not Ibsen. It should be advertised "The Iniquities of the Fathers, an American drama of Eugenics, in a Palatial Setting."

Henry Walthall as Alving, afterward as his son, shows the men much as Ibsen outlines their characters. Of course the only way to be Ibsen is to be so precisely. In the new plot all is open as the day. The world is welcome, and generally present when the man or his son go forth to see the elephant and hear the owl. Provincial hypocrisy is not implied. But Ibsen can scarcely exist without an atmosphere of secrecy for his human volcanoes to burst through in the end.

Mary Alden as Mrs. Alving shows in her intelligent and sensitive countenance that she has a conception of that character. She does not always have the chance to act the woman written in her face, the tart, thinking, handsome creature that Ibsen prefers. Nigel Debrullier looks the buttoned-up Pastor Manders, even to caricature. But the crawling, bootlicking carpenter, Jacob Engstrand, is changed into a respectable, guileless man with an income. And his wife and daughter are helpless, conventional, upper-class rabbits. They do not remind one of the saucy originals.

The original Ibsen drama is the result of mixing up five particular characters through three acts. There is not a situation but would go to pieces if one personality were altered. Here are two, sadly tampered with: Engstrand and his daughter. Here is the mother, who is only referred to in Ibsen. Here is the elder Alving, who disappears before the original play starts. So the twenty great Ibsen situations in the stage production are gone. One new crisis has an Ibsen irony and psychic tension. The boy is taken with the dreaded intermittent pains in the back of his head. He is painting the order that is to make him famous: the King's portrait. While the room empties of people he writhes on the floor. If this were all, it would have been one more moving picture failure to put through a tragic scene. But the thing is reiterated in tableau-symbol. He is looking sideways in terror. A hairy arm with clutching demon claws comes thrusting in toward the back of his neck. He writhes in deadly fear. The audience is appalled for him.

This visible clutch of heredity is the nearest equivalent that is offered for the whispered refrain: ''Ghosts,'' in the original masterpiece. This hand should also be reiterated as a refrain, three times at least, before this tableau, each time more dreadful and threatening. It appears but the once, and has no chance to become a part of the accepted hieroglyphics of the piece, as it should be, to realize its full power.

The father's previous sins have been acted out. The boy's consequent struggle with the malady has been traced step by step, so the play should end here. It would then be a rough equivalent of the Ibsen irony in a contrary medium. Instead of that, it wanders on through paraphrases of scraps of the play, sometimes literal, then quite alien, on to the alleged motion picture punch, when the Doctor is the god from the machine. There is no doctor on the stage in the original Ghosts. But there is a physician in the Doll's House, a scientific, quietly moving oracle, crisp, Spartan, sophisticated.

Is this photoplay physician such a one? The boy and his half-sister are in their wedding-clothes in the big church. Pastor Manders is saying the ceremony. The audience and building are indeed showy. The doctor charges up the aisle at the moment people are told to speak or forever hold their peace. He has tact. He simply breaks up the marriage right there. He does not tell the guests why. But he takes the wedding party into the pastor's study and there blazes at the bride and groom the long-suppressed truth that they are brother and sister. Always an orotund man, he has the Chautauqua manner indeed in this exigency.

He brings to one's mind the tearful book, much loved in childhood, Parted at the Altar, or Why Was it Thus? And four able actors have the task of telling the audience by facial expression only, that they have been struck by moral lightning. They stand in a row, facing the people, endeavoring to make the crisis of an alleged Ibsen play out of a crashing melodrama.

The final death of young Alving is depicted with an approximation of Ibsen's mood. But the only ways to suggest such feelings in silence, do not convey them in full to the audience, but merely narrate them. Wherever in Ghosts we have quiet voices that are like the slow drip of hydrochloric acid, in the photoplay we have no quiet gestures that will do trenchant work. Instead there are endless writhings and rushings about, done with a deal of skill, but destructive of the last remnants of Ibsen.

Up past the point of the clutching hand this film is the prime example for study for the person who would know once for all the differences between the photoplays and the stage dramas. Along with it might be classed Mrs. Fiske's decorative moving picture Tess, in which there is every determination to convey the original Mrs. Fiske illusion without her voice and breathing presence. To people who know her well it is a surprisingly good tintype of our beloved friend, for the family album. The relentless Thomas Hardy is nowhere to be found. There are two moments of dramatic life set among many of delicious pictorial quality: when Tess baptizes her child, and when she smooths its little grave with a wavering hand. But in the stage-version the dramatic poignancy begins with the going up of the curtain, and lasts till it descends.

The prime example of complete failure is Sarah Bernhardt's Camille. It is indeed a tintype of the consumptive heroine, with every group entire, and taken at full length. Much space is occupied by the floor and the overhead portions of the stage setting. It lasts as long as would the spoken performance, and wherever there is a dialogue we must imagine said conversation if we can. It might be compared to watching Camille from the top gallery through smoked glass, with one's ears stopped with cotton.

It would be well for the beginning student to find some way to see the first two of these three, or some other attempts to revamp the classic, for instance Mrs. Fiske's painstaking reproduction of Vanity Fair, bearing in mind the list of differences which this chapter now furnishes.

There is no denying that many stage managers who have taken up photoplays are struggling with the Shakespearian French and Norwegian traditions in the new medium. Many of the moving pictures discussed in this book are rewritten stage dramas, and one, Judith of Bethulia, is a pronounced success. But in order to be real photoplays the stage dramas must be overhauled indeed, turned inside out and upside down. The successful motion picture expresses itself through mechanical devices that are being evolved every hour.

Upon those many new bits of machinery are founded novel methods of combination in another field of logic, not dramatic logic, but tableau logic. But the old-line managers, taking up photoplays, begin by making curious miniatures of stage presentations. They try to have most things as before. Later they take on the moving picture technique in a superficial way, but they, and the host of talented actors in the prime of life and Broadway success, retain the dramatic state of mind.

It is a principle of criticism, the world over, that the distinctions between the arts must be clearly marked, even by those who afterwards mix those arts. Take, for instance, the perpetual quarrel between the artists and the half-educated about literary painting. Whistler fought that battle in England. He tried to beat it into the head of John Bull that a painting is one thing, a mere illustration for a story another thing. But the novice is always stubborn. To him Hindu and Arabic are both foreign languages, therefore just alike. The book illustration may be said to come in through the ear, by reading the title aloud in imagination. And the other is effective with no title at all. The scenario writer who will study to the bottom of the matter in Whistler's Gentle Art of Making Enemies will be equipped to welcome the distinction between the old-fashioned stage, where the word rules, and the photoplay, where splendor and ritual are all. It is not the same distinction, but a kindred one.

But let us consider the details of the matter. The stage has its exits and entrances at the side and back. The standard photoplays have their exits and entrances across the imaginary footlight line, even in the most stirring mob and battle scenes. In Judith of Bethulia, though the people seem to be coming from everywhere and going everywhere, when we watch close, we see that the individuals enter at the near right-hand corner and exit at the near left-hand corner, or enter at the near left-hand corner and exit at the near right-hand corner.

Consider the devices whereby the stage actor holds the audience as he goes out at the side and back. He sighs, gestures, howls, and strides. With what studious preparation he ripens his quietness, if he goes out that way. In the new contraption, the moving picture, the hero or villain in exit strides past the nose of the camera, growing much bigger than a human being, marching toward us as though he would step on our heads, disappearing when largest. There is an explosive power about the mildest motion picture exit, be the actor skilful or the reverse. The people left in the scene are pygmies compared with each disappearing cyclops. Likewise, when the actor enters again, his mechanical importance is overwhelming. Therefore, for his first entrance the motion picture star does not require the preparations that are made on the stage. The support does not need to warm the spectators to the problem, then talk them into surrender.

When the veteran stage-producer as a beginning photoplay producer tries to give us a dialogue in the motion pictures, he makes it so dull no one follows. He does not realize that his camera-born opportunity to magnify persons and things instantly, to interweave them as actors on one level, to alternate scenes at the slightest whim, are the big substitutes for dialogue. By alternating scenes rapidly, flash after flash: cottage, field, mountain-top, field, mountain-top, cottage, we have a conversation between three places rather than three persons. By alternating the picture of a man and the check he is forging, we have his soliloquy. When two people talk to each other, it is by lifting and lowering objects rather than their voices. The collector presents a bill: the adventurer shows him the door. The boy plucks a rose: the girl accepts it. Moving objects, not moving lips, make the words of the photoplay.

The old-fashioned stage producer, feeling he is getting nowhere, but still helpless, puts the climax of some puzzling lip-debate, often the climax of the whole film, as a sentence on the screen. Sentences should be used to show changes of time and place and a few such elementary matters before the episode is fully started. The climax of a motion picture scene cannot be one word or fifty words. As has been discussed in connection with Cabiria, the crisis must be an action sharper than any that has gone before in organic union with a tableau more beautiful than any that has preceded: the breaking of the tenth wave upon the sand. Such remnants of pantomimic dialogue as remain in the main chase of the photoplay film are but guide-posts in the race toward the goal. They should not be elaborate toll-gates of plot, to be laboriously lifted and lowered while the horses stop, mid-career.

The Venus of Milo, that comes directly to the soul through the silence, requires no quotation from Keats to explain her, though Keats is the equivalent in verse. Her setting in the great French Museum is enough. We do not know that her name is Venus. She is thought by many to be another statue of Victory. We may some day evolve scenarios that will require nothing more than a title thrown upon the screen at the beginning, they come to the eye so perfectly. This is not the only possible sort, but the self-imposed limitation in certain films might give them a charm akin to that of the Songs without Words.

The stage audience is a unit of three hundred or a thousand. In the beginning of the first act there is much moving about and extra talk on the part of the actors, to hold the crowd while it is settling down, and enable the latecomer to be in his seat before the vital part of the story starts. If he appears later, he is glared at. In the motion picture art gallery, on the other hand, the audience is around two hundred, and these are not a unit, and the only crime is to obstruct the line of vision. The high-school girls can do a moderate amount of giggling without breaking the spell. There is no spell, in the stage sense, to break. People can climb over each other's knees to get in or out. If the picture is political, they murmur war-cries to one another. If the film suggests what some of the neighbors have been doing, they can regale each other with the richest sewing society report.

The people in the motion picture audience total about two hundred, any time, but they come in groups of two or three at no specified hour. The newcomers do not, as in Vaudeville, make themselves part of a jocular army. Strictly as individuals they judge the panorama. If they disapprove, there is grumbling under their breath, but no hissing. I have never heard an audience in a photoplay theatre clap its hands even when the house was bursting with people. Yet they often see the film through twice. When they have had enough, they stroll home. They manifest their favorable verdict by sending some other member of the family to "see the picture." If the people so delegated are likewise satisfied, they may ask the man at the door if he is going to bring it back. That is the moving picture kind of cheering.

It was a theatrical sin when the old-fashioned stage actor was rendered unimportant by his scenery. But the motion picture actor is but the mood of the mob or the landscape or the department store behind him, reduced to a single hieroglyphic.

The stage-interior is large. The motion-picture interior is small. The stage out-of-door scene is at best artificial and little and is generally at rest, or its movement is tainted with artificiality. The waves dash, but not dashingly, the water flows, but not flowingly. The motion picture out-of-door scene is as big as the universe. And only pictures of the Sahara are without magnificent motion.

The photoplay is as far from the stage on the one hand as it is from the novel on the other. Its nearest analogy in literature is, perhaps, the short story, or the lyric poem. The key-words of the stage are *passion* and *character;* of the photoplay, *splendor* and *speed.* The stage in its greatest power deals with pity for some one especially unfortunate, with whom we grow well acquainted; with some private revenge against some particular despoiler; traces the beginning and culmination of joy based on the gratification of some preference, or love for some person, whose charm is all his own. The drama is concerned with the slow, inevitable approaches to these intensities. On the other hand, the motion picture, though often appearing to deal with these things, as a matter of fact uses substitutes, many of which have been listed. But to review: its first substitute is the excitement of speed-mania stretched on the framework of an obvious plot. Or it deals with delicate informal anecdote as the short story does, or fairy legerdemain, or patriotic banners, or great surging mobs of the proletariat, or big scenic outlooks, or miraculous beings made visible. And the further it gets from Euripides, Ibsen, Shakespeare, or Molière—the more it becomes like a mural painting from which flashes of lightning come—the more it realizes its genius. Men like Gordon Craig and Granville Barker are almost wasting their genius on the theatre. The Splendor Photoplays are the great outlet for their type of imagination.

The typical stage performance is from two hours and a half upward. The movie show generally lasts five reels, that is, an hour and forty minutes. And it should last but three reels, that is, an hour. Edgar Poe said there was no such thing as a long poem. There is certainly no such thing as a long moving picture masterpiece.

The stage-production depends most largely upon the power of the actors, the movie show upon the genius of the producer. The performers and the dumb objects are on equal terms in his paint-buckets. The star-system is bad for the stage because the minor parts are smothered and the situations distorted to give the favorite an orbit. It is bad for the motion pictures because it obscures the producer. While the leading actor is entitled to his glory, as are all the actors, their mannerisms should not overshadow the latest inspirations of the creator of the films.

The display of the name of the corporation is no substitute for giving the glory to the producer. An artistic photoplay is not the result of a military efficiency system. It is not a factory-made staple article, but the product of the creative force of one soul, the flowering of a spirit that has the habit of perpetually renewing itself.

Once I saw Mary Fuller in a classic. It was the life and death of Mary Queen of Scots. Not only was the tense, fidgety, over-American Mary Fuller transformed into a being who was a poppy and a tiger-lily and a snow-queen and a rose, but she and her company, including Marc Macdermott, radiated the old Scotch patriotism. They made the picture a memorial. It reminded one of Maurice Hewlett's novel The Queen's Quair. Evidently all the actors were fused by some noble managerial mood.

There can be no doubt that so able a group have evolved many good films that have escaped me. But though I did go again and again, never did I see them act with the same deliberation and distinction, and I laid the difference to a change in the state of mind of the producer. Even baseball players must have managers. A team cannot pick itself, or it surely would. And this rule may apply to the stage. But by comparison to motion picture performers, stage-actors are their own managers, for they have an approximate notion of how they look in the eye of the audience, which is but the human eye. They can hear and gauge their own voices. They have the same ears as their listeners. But the picture producer holds to his eyes the seven-leagued demon spy-glass called the kinetoscope, as the audience will do later. The actors have not the least notion of their appearance. Also the words in the motion picture are not things whose force the actor can gauge. The book under the table is one word, the dog behind the chair is another, the window curtain flying in the breeze is another.

This chapter has implied that the performers were but paint on the canvas. They are both paint and models. They are models in the sense that the young Ellen Terry was the inspiration for Watts' Sir Galahad. They resemble the persons in private life who furnish the basis for novels. Dickens' mother was the original of Mrs. Nickleby. His father entered into Wilkins Micawber. But these people are not perpetually thrust upon us as Mr. and Mrs. Dickens. We are glad to find them in the Dickens biographies. When the stories begin, it is Micawber and Mrs. Nickleby we want, and the Charles Dickens atmosphere.

The photoplays of the future will be written from the foundations for the films. The soundest actors, photographers, and producers will be those who emphasize the points wherein the photoplay is unique. What is adapted to complete expression in one art generally secures but half expression in another. The supreme photoplay will give us things that have been but half expressed in all other mediums allied to it.

Once this principle is grasped there is every reason why the same people who have interested themselves in the advanced experimental drama should take hold of the super-photoplay. The good citizens who can most easily grasp the distinction should be there to perpetuate the higher welfare of these institutions side by side. This parallel development should come, if for no other reason, because the two arts are still roughly classed together by the public. The elect cannot teach the public what the drama is till they show them precisely what the photoplay is and is not. Just as the university has departments of both History and English teaching in amity, each one illuminating the work of the other, so these two forms should live in each other's sight in fine and friendly contrast. At present they are in blind and jealous warfare.

CHAPTER XIII

Hieroglyphics

I have read this chapter to a pretty neighbor who has approved of the preceding portions of the book, whose mind, therefore, I cannot but respect. My neighbor classes this discussion of hieroglyphics as a fanciful flight rather than a sober argument. I submit the verdict, then struggle against it while you read.

The invention of the photoplay is as great a step as was the beginning of picture-writing in the stone age. And the cave-men and women of our slums seem to be the people most affected by this novelty, which is but an expression of the old in that spiral of life which is going higher while seeming to repeat the ancient phrase.

There happens to be here on the table a book on Egypt by Rawlinson that I used to thumb long ago. A footnote says: "The font of hieroglyphic type used in this work contains eight hundred forms. But there are many other forms beside." There is more light on Egypt in later works than in Rawlinson, but the statement quoted will serve for our text.

Several complex methods of making visible scenarios are listed in this work. Here is one that is mechanically simple. Let the man searching for tableau combinations, even if he is of the practical commercial type, prepare himself with eight hundred signs from Egypt. He can construct the outlines of his scenarios by placing these little pictures in rows. It may not be impractical to cut his hundreds of them from black cardboard and shuffle them on his table every morning. The list will contain all elementary and familiar things. Let him first give the most literal meaning to the patterns. Then if he desires to rise above the commercial field, let him turn over each cardboard, making the white undersurface uppermost, and there write a more abstract meaning of the hieroglyphic, one that has a fairly close relation to his way of thinking about the primary form. From a proper balance of primary and secondary meanings photoplays with souls could come. Not that he must needs become an expert Egyptologist. Yet it would profit any photoplay man to study to think like the Egyptians, the great picture-writing people. There is as much reason for this course as for the Bible student's apprenticeship in Hebrew.

Hieroglyphics can prove their worth, even without the help of an Egyptian history. Humorous and startling analogies can be pointed out by opening the Standard Dictionary, page fifty-nine. Look under the word *alphabet*. There is the diagram of the evolution of inscriptions from the Egyptian and Phoenician idea of what letters should be, on through the Greek and Roman systems.

In the Egyptian row is the picture of a throne, that has its equivalent in the Roman letter C. And a throne has as much place in what might be called the moving-picture alphabet as the letter C has in ours. There are sometimes three thrones in this small town of Springfield in an evening. When you see one flashed on the screen, you know instantly you are dealing with royalty or its implications. The last one I saw that made any particular impression was when Mary Pickford acted in Such a Little Queen. I only wished then that she had a more convincing throne. Let us cut one out of black cardboard. Turning the cardboard over to write on it the spirit-meaning, we inscribe some such phrase as The Throne of Wisdom or The Throne of Liberty.

Here is the hieroglyphic of a hand: Roman equivalent, the letter D. The human hand, magnified till it is as big as the whole screen, is as useful in the moving picture alphabet as the letter D in the printed alphabet. This hand may open a lock. It may pour poison in a bottle. It may work a telegraph key. Then turning the white side of the cardboard uppermost we inscribe something to the effect that this hand may write on the wall, as at the feast of Belshazzar. Or it may represent some such conception as Rodin's Hand of God, discussed in the Sculpture-in-motion chapter.

Here is a duck: Roman equivalent, the letter Z. In the motion pictures this bird, a somewhat z-shaped animal, suggests the finality of Arcadian peace. It is the last and fittest ornament of the mill-pond. Nothing very terrible can happen with a duck in the foreground. There is no use turning it over. It would take Maeterlinck or Swedenborg to find the mystic meaning of a duck. A duck looks to me like a caricature of an alderman.

Here is a sieve: Roman equivalent, H. A sieve placed on the kitchen-table, close-up, suggests domesticity, hired girl humors, broad farce. We will expect the bride to make her first cake, or the flour to begin to fly into the face of the intrusive ice-man. But, as to the other side of the cardboard, the sieve has its place in higher symbolism. It has been recorded by many a sage and singer that the Almighty Powers sift men like wheat.

Here is the picture of a bowl: ▬▬ ○ Roman equivalent, the letter K. A bowl seen through the photoplay window on the cottage table suggests Johnny's early supper of bread and milk. But as to the white side of the cardboard, out of a bowl of kindred form Omar may take his moonlit wine, or the higher gods may lift up the very wine of time to the lips of men, as Swinburne sings in Atalanta in Calydon.

Here is a lioness: ◣◣◣ Roman equivalent, the letter L. The lion or lioness creeps through the photoplay jungle to give the primary picture-word of terror in this new universal alphabet. The present writer has seen several valuable lions unmistakably shot and killed in the motion pictures, and charged up to profit and loss, just as steam-engines or houses are sometimes blown up or burned down. But of late there is a disposition to use the trained lion (or lioness) for all sorts of effects. No doubt the king and queen of beasts will become as versatile and humbly useful as the letter L itself: that is, in the commonplace routine photoplay. We turn the cardboard over and the lion becomes a resource of glory and terror, a symbol of cruel persecutions or deathless courage, sign of the zodiac that Poe in Ulalume calls the Lair of the Lion.

Here is an owl: ▮ Roman equivalent, the letter M. The only use of the owl I can record is to be inscribed on the white surface. In The Avenging Conscience, as described in chapter ten, the murderer marks the ticking of the heart of his victim while watching the swinging of the pendulum of the old clock, then in watching the tapping of the detective's pencil on the table, then in the tapping of his foot on the floor. Finally a handsome owl is shown in the branches outside hoot-hooting in time with the action of the pencil, and the pendulum, and the dead man's heart.

But here is a wonderful thing, an actual picture that has lived on, retaining its ancient imitative sound and form: ∧∧∧∧∧∧ the letter N, the drawing of a wave, with the sound of a wave still within it. One could well imagine the Nile in the winds of the dawn making such a sound: "NN,N,N," lapping at the reeds upon its banks. Certainly the glittering water scenes are a dominant part of moving picture Esperanto. On the white reverse of the symbol, the spiritual meaning of water will range from the metaphor of the purity of the dew to the sea as a sign of infinity.

Here is a window with closed shutters: Latin equivalent, the letter P. It is a reminder of the technical outline of this book. The Intimate Photoplay, as I have said, is but a window where we open the shutters and peep into some one's cottage. As to the soul meaning in the opening or closing of the shutters, it ranges from Noah's opening the hatches to send forth the dove, to the promises of blessing when the Windows of Heaven should be opened.

Here is the picture of an angle: Latin equivalent, Q. This is another reminder of the technical outline. The photoplay interior, as has been reiterated, is small and three-cornered. Here the heroine does her plotting, flirting, and primping, etc. I will leave the spiritual interpretation of the angle to Emerson, Swedenborg, or Maeterlinck.

Here is the picture of a mouth: Latin equivalent, the letter R. If we turn from the dictionary to the monuments, we will see that the Egyptians used all the human features in their pictures. We do not separate the features as frequently as did that ancient people, but we conventionalize them as often. Nine-tenths of the actors have faces as fixed as the masks of the Greek chorus: they have the hero-mask with the protruding chin, the villain-frown, the comedian-grin, the fixed innocent-girl simper. These formulas have their place in the broad effects of Crowd Pictures and in comedies. Then there are sudden abandonments of the mask. Griffith's pupils, Henry Walthall and Blanche Sweet, seem to me to be the greatest people in the photoplays: for one reason their faces are as sensitive to changing emotion as the surfaces of fair lakes in the wind. There is a passage in Enoch Arden where Annie, impersonated by Lillian Gish, another pupil of Griffith, is waiting in suspense for the return of her husband. She changes from lips of waiting, with a touch of apprehension, to a delighted laugh of welcome, her head making a half-turn toward the door. The audience is so moved by the beauty of the slow change they do not know whether her face is the size of the screen or the size of a postage-stamp. As a matter of fact it fills the whole end of the theatre.

Thus much as to faces that are not hieroglyphics. Yet fixed facial hieroglyphics have many legitimate uses. For instance in The Avenging Conscience, as the play works toward the climax and the guilty man is breaking down, the eye of the detective is thrown on the screen with all else hid in shadow, a watching, relentless eye. And this suggests a special talisman of the old Egyptians, a sign called the Eyes of Horus, meaning the all-beholding sun.

Here is the picture of an inundated garden: ▨▨▨ Latin equivalent, the letter S. In our photoplays the garden is an ever-present resource, and at an instant's necessity suggests the glory of nature, or sweet privacy, and kindred things. The Egyptian lotus garden had to be inundated to be a success. Ours needs but the hired man with the hose, who sometimes supplies broad comedy. But we turn over the cardboard, for the deeper meaning of this hieroglyphic. Our gardens can, as of old, run the solemn range from those of Babylon to those of the Resurrection.

If there is one sceptic left as to the hieroglyphic significance of the photoplay, let him now be discomfited by page fifty-nine, Standard Dictionary. The last letter in this list is a lasso: ◗ The equivalent of the lasso in the Roman alphabet is the letter T. The crude and facetious would be apt to suggest that the equivalent of the lasso in the photoplay is the word trouble, possibly for the hero, but probably for the villain. We turn to the other side of the symbol. The noose may stand for solemn judgment and the hangman, it may also symbolize the snare of the fowler, temptation. Then there is the spider web, close kin, representing the cruelty of evolution, in The Avenging Conscience.

This list is based on the rows of hieroglyphics most readily at hand. Any volume on Egypt, such as one of those by Maspero, has a multitude of suggestions for the man inclined to the idea.

If this system of pasteboard scenarios is taken literally, I would like to suggest as a beginning rule that in a play based on twenty hieroglyphics, nineteen should be the black realistic signs with obvious meanings, and only one of them white and inexplicably strange. It has been proclaimed further back in this treatise that there is only one witch in every wood. And to illustrate further, there is but one scarlet letter in Hawthorne's story of that name, but one wine-cup in all of Omar, one Bluebird in Maeterlinck's play.

I do not insist that the prospective author-producer adopt the hieroglyphic method as a routine, if he but consents in his meditative hours to the point of view that it implies.

The more fastidious photoplay audience that uses the hieroglyphic hypothesis in analyzing the film before it, will acquire a new tolerance and understanding of the avalanche of photoplay conceptions, and find a promise of beauty in what have been properly classed as mediocre and stereotyped productions.

The nineteenth chapter has a discourse on the Book of the Dead. As a connecting link with that chapter the reader will note that one of the marked things about the Egyptian wall-paintings, pictures on the mummy-case wrappings, papyrus inscriptions, and architectural conceptions, is that they are but enlarged hieroglyphics, while the hieroglyphics are but reduced fac-similes of these. So when a few characters are once understood, the highly colored Egyptian wall-paintings of the same things are understood. The hieroglyphic of Osiris is enlarged when they desire to represent him in state. The hieroglyphic of the soul as a human-headed hawk may be in a line of writing no taller than the capitals of this book. Immediately above may be a big painting of the soul, the same hawk placed with the proper care with reference to its composition on the wall, a pure decoration.

The transition from reduction to enlargement and back again is as rapid in Egypt as in the photoplay. It follows, among other things, that in Egypt, as in China and Japan, literary style and mere penmanship and brushwork are to be conceived as inseparable. No doubt the Egyptian scholar was the man who could not only compose a poem, but write it down with a brush. Talent for poetry, deftness in inscribing, and skill in mural painting were probably gifts of the same person. The photoplay goes back to this primitive union in styles.

The stages from hieroglyphics through Phoenician and Greek letters to ours, are of no particular interest here. But the fact that hieroglyphics can evolve is important. Let us hope that our new picture alphabets can take on richness and significance, as time goes on, without losing their literal values. They may develop into something more all-pervading, yet more highly wrought, than any written speech. Languages when they evolve produce stylists, and we will some day distinguish the different photoplay masters as we now delight in the separate tang of O. Henry and Mark Twain and Howells. When these are ancient times, we will have scholars and critics learned in the flavors of early moving picture traditions with their histories of movements and schools, their grammars, and anthologies.

Now some words as to the Anglo-Saxon language and its relation to pictures. In England and America our plastic arts are but beginning. Yesterday we were preeminently a word-civilization. England built her mediaeval cathedrals, but they left no legacy among craftsmen. Art had to lean on imported favorites like Van Dyck till the days of Sir Joshua Reynolds and the founding of the Royal Society. Consider that the friends of Reynolds were of the circle of Doctor Johnson. Literary tradition had grown old. Then England had her beginning of landscape gardening. Later she saw the rise of Constable, Ruskin, and Turner, and their iridescent successors. Still to-day in England the average leading citizen matches word against word, — using them as algebraic formulas, — rather than picture against picture, when he arranges his thoughts under the eaves of his mind. To step into the Art world is to step out of the beaten path of British dreams. Shakespeare is still king, not Rossetti, nor yet Christopher Wren. Moreover, it is the book-reading colonial who led our rebellion against the very royalty that founded the Academy. The public-speaking American wrote the Declaration of Independence. It was not the work of the painting or cathedral-building Englishman. We were led by Patrick Henry, the orator, Benjamin Franklin, the printer.

The more characteristic America became, the less she had to do with the plastic arts. The emigrant-train carried many a Bible and Dictionary packed in beside the guns and axes. It carried the Elizabethan writers, Æsop's Fables, Blackstone's Commentaries, the revised statutes of Indiana, Bunyan's Pilgrim's Progress, Parson Weems' Life of Washington. But, obviously, there was no place for the Elgin marbles. Giotto's tower could not be loaded in with the dried apples and the seedcorn.

Yesterday morning, though our arts were growing every day, we were still more of a word-civilization than the English. Our architectural, painting, and sculptural history is concerned with men now living, or their immediate predecessors. And even such work as we have is pretty largely a cult by the wealthy. This is the more a cause for misgiving because, in a democracy, the arts, like the political parties, are not founded till they have touched the county chairman, the ward leader, the individual voter. The museums in a democracy should go as far as the public libraries. Every town has its library. There are not twenty Art museums in the land.

Here then comes the romance of the photoplay. A tribe that has thought in words since the days that it worshipped Thor and told legends of the cunning of the tongue of Loki, suddenly begins to think in pictures. The leaders of the people, and of culture, scarcely know the photoplay exists. But in the remote villages the players mentioned in this work are as well known and as fairly understood in their general psychology as any candidates for president bearing political messages. There is many a babe in the proletariat not over four years old who has received more pictures into its eye than it has had words enter its ear. The young couple go with their firstborn and it sits gaping on its mother's knee. Often the images are violent and unseemly, a chaos of rawness and squirm, but scattered through the experience is a delineation of the world. Pekin and China, Harvard and Massachusetts, Portland and Oregon, Benares and India, become imaginary playgrounds. By the time the hopeful has reached its geography lesson in the public school it has travelled indeed. Almost any word that means a picture in the text of the geography or history or third reader is apt to be translated unconsciously into moving picture terms. In the next decade, simply from the development of the average eye, cities akin to the beginnings of Florence will be born among us as surely as Chaucer came, upon the first ripening of the English tongue, after Caedmon and Beowulf. Sculptors, painters, architects, and park gardeners who now have their followers by the hundreds will have admirers by the hundred thousand. The voters will respond to the aspirations of these artists as the backwoodsmen followed Poor Richard's Almanac, or the trappers in their coon-skin caps were fired to patriotism by Patrick Henry.

This ends the second section of the book. Were it not for the passage on The Battle Hymn of the Republic, the chapters thus far might be entitled: ''an open letter to Griffith and the producers and actors he has trained.'' Contrary to my prudent inclinations, he is the star of the piece, except on one page where he is the villain. This stardom came about slowly. In making the final revision, looking up the producers of the important reels, especially those from the beginning of the photoplay business, numbers of times the photoplays have turned out to be the work of this former leading man of Nance O'Neil.

No one can pretend to a full knowledge of the films. They come faster than rain in April. It would take a man every day of the year, working day and night, to see all that come to Springfield. But in the photoplay world, as I understand it, D.W. Griffith is the king-figure.

So far, in this work I have endeavored to keep to the established dogmas of Art. I hope that the main lines of the argument will appeal to the people who have classified and related the beautiful works of man that have preceded the moving pictures. Let the reader make his own essay on the subject for the local papers and send the clipping to me. The next photoplay book that may appear from this hand may be construed to meet his point of view. It will try to agree or disagree in clear language. Many a controversy must come before a method of criticism is fully established.

     *   *   *   *   *   *

At this point I climb from the oracular platform and go down through my own chosen underbrush for haphazard adventure. I renounce the platform. Whatever it may be that I find, pawpaw or may-apple or spray of willow, if you do not want it, throw it over the edge of the hill, without ado, to the birds or squirrels or kine, and do not include it in your controversial discourse. It is not a part of the dogmatic system of photoplay criticism.

CHAPTER XIV

The Orchestra, Conversation, and the Censorship

Whenever the photoplay is mixed in the same programme with vaudeville, the moving picture part of the show suffers. The film is rushed through, it is battered, it flickers more than commonly, it is a little out of focus. The house is not built for it. The owner of the place cannot manage an art gallery with a circus on his hands. It takes more brains than one man possesses to pick good vaudeville talent and bring good films to the town at the same time. The best motion picture theatres are built for photoplays alone. But they make one mistake.

Almost every motion picture theatre has its orchestra, pianist, or mechanical piano. The perfect photoplay gathering-place would have no sound but the hum of the conversing audience. If this is too ruthless a theory, let the music be played at the intervals between programmes, while the advertisements are being flung upon the screen, the lights are on, and the people coming in.

If there is something more to be done on the part of the producer to make the film a telling one, let it be a deeper study of the pictorial arrangement, with the tones more carefully balanced, the sculpture vitalized. This is certainly better than to have a raw thing bullied through with a music-programme, furnished to bridge the weak places in the construction. A picture should not be released till it is completely thought out. A producer with this goal before him will not have the time or brains to spare to write music that is as closely and delicately related to the action as the action is to the background. And unless the tunes are at one with the scheme they are an intrusion. Perhaps the moving picture maker has a twin brother almost as able in music, who possesses the faculty of subordinating his creations to the work of his more brilliant coadjutor. How are they going to make a practical national distribution of the accompaniment? In the metropolitan theatres Cabiria carried its own musicians and programme with a rich if feverish result. In the Birth of a Nation, music was used that approached imitative sound devices. Also the orchestra produced a substitute for old-fashioned stage suspense by long drawn-out syncopations. The finer photoplay values were thrown askew. Perhaps these two performances could be successfully vindicated in musical policy. But such a defence proves nothing in regard to the typical film. Imagine either of these put on in Rochester, Illinois, population one hundred souls. The reels run through as well as on Broadway or Michigan Avenue, but the local orchestra cannot play the music furnished in annotated sheets as skilfully as the local operator can turn the reel (or watch the motor turn it!).

The big social fact about the moving picture is that it is scattered like the newspaper. Any normal accompaniment thereof must likewise be adapted to being distributed everywhere. The present writer has seen, here in his home place, population sixty thousand, all the films discussed in this book but Cabiria and The Birth of a Nation. It is a photoplay paradise, the spoken theatre is practically banished. Unfortunately the local moving picture managers think it necessary to have orchestras. The musicians they can secure make tunes that are most squalid and horrible. With fathomless imbecility, hoochey koochey strains are on the air while heroes are dying. The Miserere is in our ears when the lovers are reconciled. Ragtime is imposed upon us while the old mother prays for her lost boy. Sometimes the musician with this variety of sympathy abandons himself to thrilling improvisation.

My thoughts on this subject began to take form several years ago, when the film this book has much praised, The Battle Hymn of the Republic, came to town. The proprietor of one theatre put in front of his shop a twenty-foot sign "The Battle Hymn of the Republic, by Harriet Beecher Stowe, brought back by special request." He had probably read Julia Ward Howe's name on the film forty times before the sign went up. His assistant, I presume his daughter, played "In the Shade of the Old Apple Tree" hour after hour, while the great film was rolling by. Many old soldiers were coming to see it. I asked the assistant why she did not play and sing the Battle Hymn. She said they "just couldn't find it." Are the distributors willing to send out a musician with each film?

Many of the Springfield producers are quite able and enterprising, but to ask for music with photoplays is like asking the man at the news stand to write an editorial while he sells you the paper. The picture with a great orchestra in a far-off metropolitan Opera House, may be classed by fanatic partisanship with Grand Opera. But few can get at it. It has nothing to do with Democracy.

Of course people with a mechanical imagination, and no other kind, begin to suggest the talking moving picture at this point, or the phonograph or the mechanical piano. Let us discuss the talking moving picture only. That disposes of the others.

If the talking moving picture becomes a reliable mirror of the human voice and frame, it will be the basis of such a separate art that none of the photoplay precedents will apply. It will be the *phonoplay,* not the photoplay. It will be unpleasant for a long time. This book is a struggle against the non-humanness of the undisciplined photograph. Any film is correct, realistic, forceful, many times before it is charming. The actual physical storage-battery of the actor is many hundred miles away. As a substitute, the human quality must come in the marks of the presence of the producer. The entire painting must have his brush-work. If we compare it to a love-letter it must be in his handwriting rather than worked on a typewriter. If he puts his autograph into the film, it is after a fierce struggle with the uncanny scientific quality of the camera's work. His genius and that of the whole company of actors is exhausted in the task.

The raw phonograph is likewise unmagnetic. Would you set upon the shoulders of the troupe of actors the additional responsibility of putting an adequate substitute for human magnetism in the phonographic disk? The voice that does not actually bleed, that contains no heart-beats, fails to meet the emergency. Few people have wept over a phonographic selection from Tristan and Isolde. They are moved at the actual performance. Why? Look at the opera singer after the last act. His eyes are burning. His face is flushed. His pulse is high. Reaching his hotel room, he is far more weary than if he had sung the opera alone there. He has given out of his brain-fire and blood-beat the same magnetism that leads men in battle. To speak of it in the crassest terms, this resource brings him a hundred times more salary than another man with just as good a voice can command. The output that leaves him drained at the end of the show cannot be stored in the phonograph machine. That device is as good in the morning as at noon. It ticks like a clock.

To perfect the talking moving picture, human magnetism must be put into the mirror-screen and into the clock. Not only is this imperative, but clock and mirror must be harmonized, one gently subordinated to the other. Both cannot rule. In the present talking moving picture the more highly developed photoplay is dragged by the hair in a dead faint, in the wake of the screaming savage phonograph. No talking machine on the market reproduces conversation clearly unless it be elaborately articulated in unnatural tones with a stiff interval between each question and answer. Real dialogue goes to ruin.

The talking moving picture came to our town. We were given for one show a line of minstrels facing the audience, with the interlocutor repeating his immemorial question, and the end-man giving the immemorial answer. Then came a scene in a blacksmith shop where certain well-differentiated rackets were carried over the footlights. No one heard the blacksmith, unless he stopped to shout straight at us.

The *phonoplay* can quite possibly reach some divine goal, but it will be after the speaking powers of the phonograph excel the photographing powers of the reel, and then the pictures will be brought in as comment and ornament to the speech. The pictures will be held back by the phonograph as long as it is more limited in its range. The pictures are at present freer and more versatile without it. If the *phonoplay* is ever established, since it will double the machinery, it must needs double its prices. It will be the illustrated phonograph, in a more expensive theatre.

The orchestra is in part a blundering effort by the local manager to supply the human-magnetic element which he feels lacking in the pictures on which the producer has not left his autograph. But there is a much more economic and magnetic accompaniment, the before-mentioned buzzing commentary of the audience. There will be some people who disturb the neighbors in front, but the average crowd has developed its manners in this particular, and when the orchestra is silent, murmurs like a pleasant brook.

Local manager, why not an advertising campaign in your town that says: "Beginning Monday and henceforth, ours shall be known as the Conversational Theatre"? At the door let each person be handed the following card: —

"You are encouraged to discuss the picture with the friend who accompanies you to this place. Conversation, of course, must be sufficiently subdued not to disturb the stranger who did not come with you to the theatre. If you are so disposed, consider your answers to these questions: What play or part of a play given in this theatre did you like most to-day? What the least? What is the best picture you have ever seen anywhere? What pictures, seen here this month, shall we bring back?" Here give a list of the recent productions, with squares to mark by the Australian ballot system: approved or disapproved. The cards with their answers could be slipped into the ballot-box at the door as the crowd goes out.

It may be these questions are for the exceptional audiences in residence districts. Perhaps with most crowds the last interrogation is the only one worth while. But by gathering habitually the answers to that alone the place would get the drift of its public, realize its genius, and become an art-gallery, the people bestowing the blue ribbons. The photoplay theatres have coupon contests and balloting already: the most popular young lady, money prizes to the best vote-getter in the audience, etc. Why not ballot on the matter in hand?

If the cards are sent out by the big producers, a referendum could be secured that would be invaluable in arguing down to rigid censorship, and enable them to make their own private censorship more intelligent. Various styles of experimental cards could be tried till the vital one is found.

There is growing up in this country a clan of half-formed moving picture critics. The present stage of their work is indicated by the eloquent notice describing Your Girl and Mine, in the chapter on "Progress and Endowment." The metropolitan papers give their photoplay reporters as much space as the theatrical critics. Here in my home town the twelve moving picture places take one half a page of chaotic notices daily. The country is being badly led by professional photoplay newswriters who do not know where they are going, but are on the way.

But they aptly describe the habitual attendants as moving picture fans. The fan at the photoplay, as at the base-ball grounds, is neither a low-brow nor a high-brow. He is an enthusiast who is as stirred by the charge of the photographic cavalry as by the home runs that he watches from the bleachers. In both places he has the privilege of comment while the game goes on. In the photoplay theatre it is not so vociferous, but as keenly felt. Each person roots by himself. He has his own judgment, and roasts the umpire: who is the keeper of the local theatre: or the producer, as the case may be. If these opinions of the fan can be collected and classified, an informal censorship is at once established. The photoplay reporters can then take the enthusiasts in hand and lead them to a realization of the finer points in awarding praise and blame. Even the sporting pages have their expert opinions with due influence on the betting odds. Out of the work of the photoplay reporters let a super-structure of art criticism be reared in periodicals like The Century, Harper's, Scribner's, The Atlantic, The Craftsman, and the architectural magazines. These are our natural custodians of art. They should reproduce the most exquisite tableaus, and be as fastidious in their selection of them as they are in the current examples of the other arts. Let them spread the news when photoplays keyed to the Rembrandt mood arrive. The reporters for the newspapers should get their ideas and refreshment in such places as the Ryerson Art Library of the Chicago Art Institute. They should begin with such books as Richard Muther's History of Modern Painting, John C. Van Dyke's Art for Art's Sake, Marquand and Frothingham's History of Sculpture, A.D.F. Hamlin's History of Architecture. They should take the business of guidance in this new world as a sacred trust, knowing they have the power to influence an enormous democracy.

The moving picture journals and the literati are in straits over the censorship question. The literati side with the managers, on the principles of free speech and a free press. But few of the aesthetically super-wise are persistent fans. They rave for freedom, but are not, as a general thing, living back in the home town. They do not face the exigency of having their summer and winter amusement spoiled day after day.

Extremists among the pious are railing against the moving pictures as once they railed against novels. They have no notion that this institution is penetrating to the last backwoods of our civilization, where its presence is as hard to prevent as the rain. But some of us are destined to a reaction, almost as strong as the obsession. The religionists will think they lead it. They will be self-deceived. Moving picture nausea is already taking hold of numberless people, even when they are in the purely pagan mood. Forced by their limited purses, their inability to buy a Ford car, and the like, they go in their loneliness to film after film till the whole world seems to turn on a reel. When they are again at home, they see in the dark an imaginary screen with tremendous pictures, whirling by at a horribly accelerated pace, a photoplay delirium tremens. Faster and faster the reel turns in the back of their heads. When the moving picture sea-sickness is upon one, nothing satisfies but the quietest out of doors, the companionship of the gentlest of real people. The non-movie-life has charms such as one never before conceived. The worn citizen feels that the cranks and legislators can do what they please to the producers. He is through with them.

The moving picture business men do not realize that they have to face these nervous conditions in their erstwhile friends. They flatter themselves they are being pursued by some reincarnations of Anthony Comstock. There are several reasons why photoplay corporations are callous, along with the sufficient one that they are corporations.

First, they are engaged in a financial orgy. Fortunes are being found by actors and managers faster than they were dug up in 1849 and 1850 in California. Forty-niner lawlessness of soul prevails. They talk each other into a lordly state of mind. All is dash and experiment. Look at the advertisements in the leading moving picture magazines. They are like the praise of oil stock or Peruna. They bawl about films founded upon little classics. They howl about plots that are ostensibly from the soberest of novels, whose authors they blasphemously invoke. They boo and blow about twisted, callous scenarios that are bad imitations of the world's most beloved lyrics.

The producers do not realize the mass effect of the output of the business. It appears to many as a sea of unharnessed photography: sloppy conceptions set forth with sharp edges and irrelevant realism. The jumping, twitching, cold-blooded devices, day after day, create the aforesaid sea-sickness, that has nothing to do with the questionable subject. When on top of this we come to the picture that is actually insulting, we are up in arms indeed. It is supplied by a corporation magnate removed from his audience in location, fortune, interest, and mood: an absentee landlord. I was trying to convert a talented and noble friend to the films. The first time we went there was a prize-fight between a black and a white man, not advertised, used for a filler. I said it was queer, and would not happen again. The next time my noble friend was persuaded to go, there was a cock-fight, incidental to a Cuban romance. The third visit we beheld a lady who was dying for five minutes, rolling her eyes about in a way that was fearful to see. The convert was not made.

It is too easy to produce an unprovoked murder, an inexplicable arson, neither led up to nor followed by the ordinary human history of such acts, and therefore as arbitrary as the deeds of idiots or the insane. A villainous hate, an alleged love, a violent death, are flashed at us, without being in any sort of tableau logic. The public is ceaselessly played upon by tactless devices. Therefore it howls, just as children in the nursery do when the awkward governess tries the very thing the diplomatic governess, in reasonable time, may bring about.

The producer has the man in the audience who cares for the art peculiarly at his mercy. Compare him with the person who wants to read a magazine for an evening. He can look over all the periodicals in the local bookstore in fifteen minutes. He can select the one he wants, take this bit of printed matter home, go through the contents, find the three articles he prefers, get an evening of reading out of them, and be happy. Every day as many photoplays come to our town as magazines come to the book-store in a week or a month. There are good ones and bad ones buried in the list. There is no way to sample the films. One has to wait through the first third of a reel before he has an idea of the merits of a production, his ten cents is spent, and much of his time is gone. It would take five hours at least to find the best film in our town for one day. Meanwhile, nibbling and sampling, the seeker would run such a gantlet of plot and dash and chase that his eyes and patience would be exhausted. Recently there returned to the city for a day one of Griffith's best Biographs, The Last Drop of Water. It was good to see again. In order to watch this one reel twice I had to wait through five others of unutterable miscellany.

Since the producers and theatre-managers have us at their mercy, they are under every obligation to consider our delicate susceptibilities — granting the proposition that in an ideal world we will have no legal censorship. As to what to do in this actual nation, let the reader follow what John Collier has recently written in The Survey. Collier was the leading force in founding the National Board of Censorship. As a member of that volunteer extra-legal board which is independent and high minded, yet accepted by the leading picture companies, he is able to discuss legislation in a manner which the present writer cannot hope to match. Read John Collier. But I wish to suggest that the ideal censorship is that to which the daily press is subject, the elastic hand of public opinion, if the photoplay can be brought as near to newspaper conditions in this matter as it is in some others.

How does public opinion grip the journalist? The editor has a constant report from his constituency. A popular scoop sells an extra at once. An attack on the wrong idol cancels fifty subscriptions. People come to the office to do it, and say why. If there is a piece of real news on the second page, and fifty letters come in about it that night, next month when that character of news reappears it gets the front page. Some human peculiarities are not mentioned, some phrases not used. The total attribute of the blue-pencil man is diplomacy. But while the motion pictures come out every day, they get their discipline months afterwards in the legislation that insists on everything but tact. A tentative substitute for the letters that come to the editor, the personal call and cancelled subscription, and the rest, is the system of balloting on the picture, especially the answer to the question, "What picture seen here this month, or this week, shall we bring back?" Experience will teach how to put the queries. By the same system the public might dictate its own cut-outs. Let us have a democracy and a photoplay business working in daily rhythm.

CHAPTER XV

The Substitute for the Saloon

This is a special commentary on chapter five, The Picture of Crowd Splendor. It refers as well to every other type of moving picture that gets into the slum. But the masses have an extraordinary affinity for the Crowd Photoplay. As has been said before, the mob comes nightly to behold its natural face in the glass. Politicians on the platform have swayed the mass below them. But now, to speak in an Irish way, the crowd takes the platform, and looking down, sees itself swaying. The slums are an astonishing assembly of cave-men crawling out of their shelters to exhibit for the first time in history a common interest on a tremendous scale in an art form. Below the cliff caves were bar rooms in endless lines. There are almost as many bar rooms to-day, yet this new thing breaks the lines as nothing else ever did. Often when a moving picture house is set up, the saloon on the right hand or the left declares bankruptcy.

Why do men prefer the photoplay to the drinking place? For no pious reason, surely. Now they have fire pouring into their eyes instead of into their bellies. Blood is drawn from the guts to the brain. Though the picture be the veriest mess, the light and movement cause the beholder to do a little reptilian thinking. After a day's work a street-sweeper enters the place, heavy as King Log. A ditch-digger goes in, sick and surly. It is the state of the body when many men drink themselves into insensibility. But here the light is as strong in the eye as whiskey in the throat. Along with the flare, shadow, and mystery, they face the existence of people, places, costumes, utterly novel. Immigrants are prodded by these swords of darkness and light to guess at the meaning of the catch-phrases and headlines that punctuate the play. They strain to hear their neighbors whisper or spell them out.

The photoplays have done something to reunite the lower-class families. No longer is the fire-escape the only summer resort for big and little folks. Here is more fancy and whim than ever before blessed a hot night. Here, under the wind of an electric fan, they witness everything, from a burial in Westminster to the birthday parade of the ruler of the land of Swat.

The usual saloon equipment to delight the eye is one so-called ''leg'' picture of a woman, a photograph of a prize-fighter, and some colored portraits of goats to advertise various brands of beer. Many times, no doubt, these boys and young men have found visions of a sordid kind while gazing on the actress, the fighter, or the goats. But what poor material they had in the wardrobes of memory for the trimmings and habiliments of vision, to make this lady into Freya, this prize-fighter into Thor, these goats into the harnessed steeds that drew his chariot! Man's dreams are rearranged and glorified memories. How could these people reconstruct the torn carpets and tin cans and waste-paper of their lives into mythology? How could memories of Ladies' Entrance squalor be made into Castles in Granada or Carcassonne? The things they drank to see, and saw but grotesquely, and paid for terribly, now roll before them with no after pain or punishment. The mumbled conversation, the sociability for which they leaned over the tables, they have here in the same manner with far more to talk about. They come, they go home, men and women together, as casually and impulsively as the men alone ever entered a drinking-place, but discoursing now of far-off mountains and star-crossed lovers. As Padraic Colum says in his poem on the herdsman: —

> "With thoughts on white ships
> And the King of Spain's Daughter."

This is why the saloon on the right hand and on the left in the slum is apt to move out when the photoplay moves in.

But let us go to the other end of the temperance argument. I beg to be allowed to relate a personal matter. For some time I was a field-worker for the Anti-Saloon League of Illinois, being sent every Sunday to a new region to make the yearly visit on behalf of the league. Such a visitor is apt to speak to one church in a village, and two in the country, on each excursion, being met at the station by some leading farmer-citizen of the section, and driven to these points by him. The talk with this man was worth it all to me.

The agricultural territory of the United States is naturally dry. This is because the cross-roads church is the only communal institution, and the voice of the cross-roads pastor is for teetotalism. The routine of the farm-hand, while by no means ideal in other respects, keeps him from craving drink as intensely as other toilers do. A day's work in the open air fills his veins at nightfall with an opiate of weariness instead of a high-strung nervousness. The strong men of the community are church elders, not through fanaticism, but by right of leadership. Through their office they are committed to prohibition. So opposition to the temperance movement is scattering. The

Anti-Saloon League has organized these leaders into a nation-wide machine. It sees that they get their weekly paper, instructing them in the tactics whereby local fights have been won. A subscription financing the State League is taken once a year. It counts on the regular list of church benevolences. The state officers come in to help on the critical local fights. Any country politician fears their non-partisan denunciation as he does political death. The local machines thus backed are incurable mugwumps, hold the balance of power, work in both parties, and have voted dry the agricultural territory of the United States everywhere, by the township, county, or state unit.

The only institutions that touch the same territory in a similar way are the Chautauquas in the prosperous agricultural centres. These, too, by the same sign are emphatically anti-saloon in their propaganda, serving to intellectualize and secularize the dry sentiment without taking it out of the agricultural caste.

There is a definite line between our farm-civilization and the rest. When a county goes dry, it is generally in spite of the county-seat. Such temperance people as are in the court-house town represent the church-vote, which is even then in goodly proportion a retired-farmer vote. The larger the county-seat, the larger the non-church-going population and the more stubborn the fight. The majority of miners and factory workers are on the wet side everywhere. The irritation caused by the gases in the mines, by the dirty work in the blackness, by the squalor in which the company houses are built, turns men to drink for reaction and lamplight and comradeship. The similar fevers and exasperations of factory life lead the workers to unstring their tense nerves with liquor. The habit of snuggling up close in factories, conversing often, bench by bench, machine by machine, inclines them to get together for their pleasures at the bar. In industrial America there is an anti-saloon minority in moral sympathy with the temperance wave brought in by the farmers. But they are outstanding groups. Their leadership seldom dries up a factory town or a mining region, with all the help the Anti-Saloon League can give.

In the big cities the temperance movement is scarcely understood. The choice residential districts are voted dry for real estate reasons. The men who do this, drink freely at their own clubs or parties. The temperance question would be fruitlessly argued to the end of time were it not for the massive agricultural vote rolling and roaring round each metropolis, reawakening the town churches whose vote is a pitiful minority but whose spokesmen are occasionally strident.

There is a prophecy abroad that prohibition will be the issue of a national election. If the question is squarely put, there are enough farmers and church-people to drive the saloon out of legal existence. The women's vote, a little more puritanical than the men's vote, will make the result sure. As one anxious for this victory, I have often speculated on the situation when all America is nominally dry, at the behest of the American farmer, the American preacher, and the American woman. When the use of alcohol is treason, what will become of those all but unbroken lines of slum saloons? No lesser force than regular troops could dislodge them, with yesterday's intrenchment.

The entrance of the motion picture house into the arena is indeed striking, the first enemy of King Alcohol with real power where that king has deepest hold. If every one of those saloon doors is nailed up by the Chautauqua orators, the photoplay archway will remain open. The people will have a shelter where they can readjust themselves, that offers a substitute for many of the lines of pleasure in the groggery. And a whole evening costs but a dime apiece. Several rounds of drinks are expensive, but the people can sit through as many repetitions of this programme as they desire, for one entrance fee. The dominant genius of the moving picture place is not a gentleman with a red nose and an eye like a dead fish, but some producer who, with all his faults, has given every person in the audience a seven-leagued angel-and-demon telescope.

Since I have announced myself a farmer and a puritan, let me here list the saloon evils not yet recorded in this chapter. They are separate from the catalogue of the individualistic woes of the drunkard that are given in the Scripture. The shame of the American drinking place is the bar-tender who dominates its thinking. His cynical and hardened soul wipes out a portion of the influence of the public school, the library, the self-respecting newspaper. A stream rises no higher than its source, and through his dead-fish eye and dead-fish brain the group of tired men look upon all the statesmen and wise ones of the land. Though he says worse than nothing, his furry tongue, by endless reiteration, is the American slum oracle. At the present the bar-tender handles the neighborhood group, the ultimate unit in city politics.

So, good citizen, welcome the coming of the moving picture man as a local social force. Whatever his private character, the mere formula of his activities makes him a better type. He may not at first sway his group in a directly political way, but he will make himself the centre of more social ideals than the bar-tender ever entertained. And he is beginning to have as intimate a relation to his public as the bar-tender. In many cases he stands under his arch in the sheltered lobby and is on conversing terms with his habitual customers, the length of the afternoon and evening.

Voting the saloon out of the slums by voting America dry, does not, as of old, promise to be a successful operation that kills the patient. In the past some of the photoplay magazines have contained denunciations of the temperance people for refusing to say anything in behalf of the greatest practical enemy of the saloon. But it is not too late for the dry forces to repent. The Anti-Saloon League officers and the photoplay men should ask each other to dinner. More moving picture theatres in doubtful territory will help make dry voters. And wet territory voted dry will bring about a greatly accelerated patronage of the photoplay houses. There is every strategic reason why these two forces should patch up a truce.

Meanwhile, the cave-man, reader of picture-writing, is given a chance to admit light into his mind, whatever he puts to his lips. Let us look for the day, be it a puritan triumph or not, when the sons and the daughters of the slums shall prophesy, the young men shall see visions, the old men dream dreams.

CHAPTER XVI

California and America

The moving picture captains of industry, like the California gold finders of 1849, making colossal fortunes in two or three years, have the same glorious irresponsibility and occasional need of the sheriff. They are Californians more literally than this. Around Los Angeles the greatest and most characteristic moving picture colonies are being built. Each photoplay magazine has its California letter, telling of the putting-up of new studios, and the transfer of actors, with much slap-you-on-the-back personal gossip. This is the outgrowth of the fact that every type of the photoplay but the intimate is founded on some phase of the out-of-doors. Being thus dependent, the plant can best be set up where there is no winter. Besides this, the Los Angeles region has the sea, the mountains, the desert, and many kinds of grove and field. Landscape and architecture are sub-tropical. But for a description of California, ask any traveller or study the background of almost any photoplay.

If the photoplay is the consistent utterance of its scenes, if the actors are incarnations of the land they walk upon, as they should be, California indeed stands a chance to achieve through the films an utterance of her own. Will this land furthest west be the first to capture the inner spirit of this newest and most curious of the arts? It certainly has the opportunity that comes with the actors, producers, and equipment. Let us hope that every region will develop the silent photographic pageant in a local form as outlined in the chapter on Progress and Endowment. Already the California sort, in the commercial channels, has become the broadly accepted if mediocre national form. People who revere the Pilgrim Fathers of 1620 have often wished those gentlemen had moored their bark in the region of Los Angeles rather than Plymouth Rock, that Boston had been founded there. At last that landing is achieved.

Patriotic art students have discussed with mingled irony and admiration the Boston domination of the only American culture of the nineteenth century, namely, literature. Indianapolis has had her day since then, Chicago is lifting her head. Nevertheless Boston still controls the text-book in English and dominates our high schools. Ironic feelings in this matter on the part of western men are based somewhat on envy and illegitimate cussedness, but are also grounded in the honest hope of a healthful rivalry. They want new romanticists and artists as indigenous to their soil as was Hawthorne to witch-haunted Salem or Longfellow to the chestnuts of his native heath. Whatever may be said of the patriarchs, from Oliver Wendell Holmes to Amos Bronson Alcott, they were true sons of the New England stone fences and meeting houses. They could not have been born or nurtured anywhere else on the face of the earth.

Some of us view with a peculiar thrill the prospect that Los Angeles may become the Boston of the photoplay. Perhaps it would be better to say the Florence, because California reminds one of colorful Italy more than of any part of the United States. Yet there is a difference.

The present-day man-in-the-street, man-about-town Californian has an obvious magnificence about him that is allied to the eucalyptus tree, the pomegranate. California is a gilded state. It has not the sordidness of gold, as has Wall Street, but it is the embodiment of the natural ore that the ragged prospector finds. The gold of California is the color of the orange, the glitter of dawn in the Yosemite, the hue of the golden gate that opens the sunset way to mystic and terrible Cathay and Hindustan.

The enemy of California says the state is magnificent but thin. He declares it is as though it were painted on a Brobdingnagian piece of gilt paper, and he who dampens his finger and thrusts it through finds an alkali valley on the other side, the lonely prickly pear, and a heap of ashes from a deserted campfire. He says the citizens of this state lack the richness of an aesthetic and religious tradition. He says there is no substitute for time. But even these things make for coincidence. This apparent thinness California has in common with the routine photoplay, which is at times as shallow in its thought as the shadow it throws upon the screen. This newness California has in common with all photoplays. It is thrillingly possible for the state and the art to acquire spiritual tradition and depth together.

Part of the thinness of California is not only its youth, but the result of the physical fact that the human race is there spread over so many acres of land. They try not only to count their mines and enumerate their palm trees, but they count the miles of their sea-coast, and the acres under cultivation and the height of the peaks, and revel in large statistics and the bigness generally, and forget how a few men rattle around in a great deal of scenery. They shout their statistics across the Rockies and the deserts to New York. The Mississippi Valley is non-existent to the Californian. His fellow-feeling is for the opposite coast-line. Through the geographical accident of separation by mountain and desert from the rest of the country, he becomes a mere shouter, hurrahing so assiduously that all variety in the voice is lost. Then he tries gestures, and becomes flamboyant, rococo.

These are the defects of the motion picture qualities also. Its panoramic tendency runs wild. As an institution it advertises itself with the sweeping gesture. It has the same passion for coast-line. These are not the sins of New England. When, in the hands of masters, they become sources of strength, they will be a different set of virtues from those of New England.

There is no more natural place for the scattering of confetti than this state, except the moving picture scene itself. Both have a genius for gardens and dancing and carnival.

When the Californian relegates the dramatic to secondary scenes, both in his life and his photoplay, and turns to the genuinely epic and lyric, he and this instrument may find their immortality together as New England found its soul in the essays of Emerson. Tide upon tide of Spring comes to California through all four seasons. Fairy beauty overwhelms the lumbering grand-stand players. The tiniest garden is a jewelled pathway of wonder. But the Californian cannot shout ''orange blossoms, orange blossoms; heliotrope, heliotrope!'' He cannot boom forth ''roseleaves, roseleaves'' so that he does their beauties justice. Here is where the photoplay can begin to give him a more delicate utterance. And he can go on into stranger things and evolve all the Splendor Films into higher types, for the very name of California is splendor. The California photoplaywright can base his Crowd Picture upon the city-worshipping mobs of San Francisco. He can derive his Patriotic and Religious Splendors from something older and more magnificent than the aisles of the Romanesque, namely: the groves of the giant redwoods.

The campaign for a beautiful nation could very well emanate from the west coast, where with the slightest care grow up models for all the world of plant arrangement and tree-luxury. Our mechanical East is reproved, our tension is relaxed, our ugliness is challenged every time we look upon those garden paths and forests.

It is possible for Los Angeles to lay hold of the motion picture as our national text-book in Art as Boston appropriated to herself the guardianship of the national text-books of Literature. If California has a shining soul, and not merely a golden body, let her forget her seventeen-year-old melodramatics, and turn to her poets who understand the heart underneath the glory. Edwin Markham, the dean of American singers, Clark Ashton Smith, the young star treader, George Sterling, that son of Ancient Merlin, have in their songs the seeds of better scenarios than California has sent us. There are two poems by George Sterling that I have had in mind for many a day as conceptions that should inspire mystic films akin to them. These poems are The Night Sentries and Tidal King of Nations.

But California can tell us stories that are grim children of the tales of the wild Ambrose Bierce. Then there is the lovely unforgotten Nora May French and the austere Edward Rowland Sill.

Edison is the new Gutenberg. He has invented the new printing. The state that realizes this may lead the soul of America, day after to-morrow.

CHAPTER XVII

Progress and Endowment

The moving picture goes almost as far as journalism into the social fabric in some ways, further in others. Soon, no doubt, many a little town will have its photographic newspress. We have already the weekly world-news films from the big centres.

With local journalism will come devices for advertising home enterprises. Some staple products will be made attractive by having film-actors show their uses. The motion pictures will be in the public schools to stay. Text-books in geography, history, zoölogy, botany, physiology, and other sciences will be illustrated by standardized films. Along with these changes, there will be available at certain centres collections of films equivalent to the Standard Dictionary and the Encyclopaedia Britannica.

And sooner or later we will have a straight-out capture of a complete film expression by the serious forces of civilization. The merely impudent motion picture will be relegated to the leisure hours with yellow journalism. Photoplay libraries are inevitable, as active if not as multitudinous as the book-circulating libraries. The oncoming machinery and expense of the motion picture is immense. Where will the money come from? No one knows. What the people want they will get. The race of man cannot afford automobiles, but has them nevertheless. We cannot run away into non-automobile existence or non-steam-engine or non-movie life long at a time. We must conquer this thing. While the more stately scientific and educational aspects just enumerated are slowly on their way, the artists must be up and about their ameliorative work.

Every considerable effort to develop a noble idiom will count in the final result, as the writers of early English made possible the language of the Bible, Shakespeare, and Milton. We are perfecting a medium to be used as long as Chinese ideographs have been. It will no doubt, like the Chinese language, record in the end massive and classical treatises, imperial chronicles, law-codes, traditions, and religious admonitions. All this by the *motion picture* as a recording instrument, not necessarily the *photoplay,* a much more limited thing, a form of art.

What shall be done in especial by this generation of idealists, whose flags rise and go down, whose battle line wavers and breaks a thousand times? What is the high quixotic splendid call? We know of a group of public-spirited people who advocate, in endowed films, "safety first," another that champions total abstinence. Often their work seems lost in the mass of commercial production, but it is a good beginning. Such citizens take an established studio for a specified time and at the end put on the market a production that backs up their particular idea. There are certain terms between the owners of the film and the proprietors of the studio for the division of the income, the profits of the cult being spent on further propaganda. The product need not necessarily be the type outlined in chapter two, The Photoplay of Action. Often some other sort might establish the cause more deeply. But most of the propaganda films are of the action variety, because of the dynamic character of the people who produce them. Fired by fanatic zeal, the auto speeds faster, the rescuing hero runs harder, the stern policeman and sheriff become more jumpy, all that the audience may be converted. Here if anywhere meditation on the actual resources of charm and force in the art is a fitting thing. The crusader should realize that it is not a good Action Play nor even a good argument unless it is indeed the Winged Victory sort. The gods are not always on the side of those who throw fits.

There is here appended a newspaper description of a crusading film, that, despite the implications of the notice, has many passages of charm. It is two-thirds Action Photoplay, one-third Intimate-and-friendly. The notice does not imply that at times the story takes pains to be gentle. This bit of writing is all too typical of film journalism.

"Not only as an argument for suffrage but as a play with a story, a punch, and a mission, 'Your Girl and Mine' is produced under the direction of the National Woman's Suffrage Association at the Capitol to-day.

"Olive Wyndham forsook the legitimate stage for the time to pose as the heroine of the play. Katherine Kaelred, leading lady of 'Joseph and his Brethren,' took the part of a woman lawyer battling for the right. Sydney Booth, of the 'Yellow Ticket' company posed as the hero of the experiment. John Charles and Katharine Henry played the villain and the honest working girl. About three hundred secondaries were engaged along with the principals.

"It is melodrama of the most thrilling sort, in spite of the fact that there is a moral concealed in the very title of the play. But who is worried by a moral in a play which has an exciting hand-to-hand fight between a man and a woman in one of the earliest acts, when the quick march of events ranges from a wedding to a murder and an automobile abduction scene that breaks all former speed-records. 'The Cause' comes in most symbolically and poetically, a symbolic figure that 'fades out' at critical periods in the plot. Dr. Anna Howard Shaw, the famous suffrage leader, appears personally in the film.

" 'Your Girl and Mine' is a big play with a big mission built on a big scale. It is a whole evening's entertainment, and a very interesting evening at that." Here endeth the newspaper notice. Compare it with the Biograph advertisement of Judith in chapter six.

There is nothing in the film that rasps like this account of it. The clipping serves to give the street-atmosphere through which our Woman's Suffrage Joan of Arcs move to conquest and glory with unstained banners.

The obvious amendments to the production as an instrument of persuasion are two. Firstly there should be five reels instead of six, every scene shortened a bit to bring this result. Secondly, the lieutenant governor of the state, who is the Rudolf Rassendyll of the production, does not enter the story soon enough, and is too James K. Hacketty all at once. We are jerked into admiration of him, rather than ensnared. But after that the gentleman behaves more handsomely than any of the distinguished lieutenant governors in real life the present writer happens to remember. The figure of Aunt Jane, the queenly serious woman of affairs, is one to admire and love. Her effectiveness without excess or strain is in itself an argument for giving woman the vote. The newspaper notice does not state the facts in saying the symbolical figure ''fades out'' at critical periods in the plot. On the contrary, she appears at critical periods, clothed in white, solemn and royal. She comes into the groups with an adequate allurement, pointing the moral of each situation while she shines brightest. The two children for whom the contest is fought are winsome little girls. By the side of their mother in the garden or in the nursery they are a potent argument for the natural rights of femininity. The film is by no means ultra-aesthetic. The implications of the clipping are correct to that degree. But the resources of beauty within the ready command of the advising professional producer are used by the women for all they are worth. It could not be asked of them that they evolve technical novelties.

Yet the figures of Aunt Jane and the Goddess of Suffrage are something new in their fashion. Aunt Jane is a spiritual sister to that unprecedented woman, Jane Addams, who went to the Hague conference for Peace in the midst of war, which heroic action the future will not forget. Aunt Jane does justice to that breed of women amid the sweetness and flowers and mere scenario perils of the photoplay story. The presence of the ''Votes for Women'' figure is the beginning of a line of photoplay goddesses that serious propaganda in the new medium will make part of the American Spiritual Hierarchy. In the imaginary film of Our Lady Springfield, described in the chapter on Architecture-in-Motion, a kindred divinity is presumed to stand by the side of the statue when it first reaches the earth.

High-minded graduates of university courses in sociology and schools of philanthropy, devout readers of The Survey, The Chicago Public, The Masses, The New Republic, La Follette's, are going to advocate increasingly, their varied and sometimes contradictory causes, in films. These will generally be produced by heroic exertions in the studio, and much passing of the subscription paper outside.

Then there are endowments already in existence that will no doubt be diverted to the photoplay channel. In every state house, and in Washington, D.C., increasing quantities of dead printed matter have been turned out year after year. They have served to kindle various furnaces and feed the paper-mills a second time. Many of these routine reports will remain in innocuous desuetude. But one-fourth of them, perhaps, are capable of being embodied in films. If they are scientific demonstrations, they can be made into realistic motion picture records. If they are exhortations, they can be transformed into plays with a moral, brothers of the film Your Girl and Mine. The appropriations for public printing should include such work hereafter.

The scientific museums distribute routine pamphlets that would set the whole world right on certain points if they were but read by said world. Let them be filmed and started. Whatever the congressman is permitted to frank to his constituency, let him send in the motion picture form when it is the expedient and expressive way.

When men work for the high degrees in the universities, they labor on a piece of literary conspiracy called a thesis which no one outside the university hears of again. The gist of this research work that is dead to the democracy, through the university merits of thoroughness, moderation of statement, and final touch of discovery, would have a chance to live and grip the people in a motion picture transcript, if not a photoplay. It would be University Extension. The relentless fire of criticism which the heads of the departments would pour on the production before they allowed it to pass would result in a standardization of the sense of scientific fact over the land. Suppose the film has the coat of arms of the University of Chicago along with the name of the young graduate whose thesis it is. He would have a chance to reflect credit on the university even as much as a foot-ball player.

Large undertakings might be under way, like those described in the chapter on Architecture-in-Motion. But these would require much more than the ordinary outlay for thesis work, less, perhaps, than is taken for Athletics. Lyman Howe and several other world-explorers have already set the pace in the more human side of the educative film. The list of Mr. Howe's offerings from the first would reveal many a one that would have run the gantlet of a university department. He points out a new direction for old energies, whereby professors may become citizens.

Let the cave-man, reader of picture-writing, be allowed to ponder over scientific truth. He is at present the victim of the alleged truth of the specious and sentimental variety of photograph. It gives the precise edges of the coat or collar of the smirking masher and the exact fibre in the dress of the jumping-jack. The eye grows weary of sharp points and hard edges that mean nothing. All this idiotic precision is going to waste. It should be enlisted in the cause of science and abated everywhere else. The edges in art are as mysterious as in science they are exact.

Some of the higher forms of the Intimate Moving Picture play should be endowed by local coteries representing their particular region. Every community of fifty thousand has its group of the cultured who have heretofore studied and imitated things done in the big cities. Some of these coteries will in exceptional cases become creative and begin to express their habitation and name. The Intimate Photoplay is capable of that delicacy and that informality which should characterize neighborhood enterprises.

The plays could be acted by the group who, season after season, have secured the opera house for the annual amateur show. Other dramatic ability could be found in the high-schools. There is enough talent in any place to make an artistic revolution, if once that region is aflame with a common vision. The spirit that made the Irish Players, all so racy of the soil, can also move the company of local photoplayers in Topeka, or Indianapolis, or Denver. Then let them speak for their town, not only in great occasional enterprises, but steadily, in little fancies, genre pictures, developing a technique that will finally make magnificence possible.

There was given not long ago, at the Illinois Country Club here, a performance of The Yellow Jacket by the Coburn Players. It at once seemed an integral part of this chapter.

The two flags used for a chariot, the bamboo poles for oars, the red sack for a decapitated head, etc., were all convincing, through a direct resemblance as well as the passionate acting. They suggest a possible type of hieroglyphics to be developed by the leader of the local group.

Let the enthusiast study this westernized Chinese play for primitive representative methods. It can be found in book form, a most readable work. It is by G.C. Hazelton, Jr., and J.H. Benrimo. The resemblance between the stage property and the thing represented is fairly close. The moving flags on each side of the actor suggest the actual color and progress of the chariot, and abstractly suggest its magnificence. The red sack used for a bloody head has at least the color and size of one. The dressed-up block of wood used for a child is the length of an infant of the age described and wears the general costume thereof. The farmer's hoe, though exaggerated, is still an agricultural implement.

The evening's list of properties is economical, filling one wagon, rather than three. Photographic realism is splendidly put to rout by powerful representation. When the villager desires to embody some episode that if realistically given would require a setting beyond the means of the available endowment, and does not like the near-Egyptian method, let him evolve his near-Chinese set of symbols.

The Yellow Jacket was written after long familiarity with the Chinese Theatre in San Francisco. The play is a glory to that city as well as to Hazelton and Benrimo. But every town in the United States has something as striking as the Chinese Theatre, to the man who keeps the eye of his soul open. It has its Ministerial Association, its boys' secret society, its red-eyed political gang, its grubby Justice of the Peace court, its free school for the teaching of Hebrew, its snobbish chapel, its fire-engine house, its milliner's shop. All these could be made visible in photoplays as flies are preserved in amber.

Edgar Lee Masters looked about him and discovered the village graveyard, and made it as wonderful as Noah's Ark, or Adam naming the animals, by supplying honest inscriptions to the headstones. Such stories can be told by the Chinese theatrical system as well. As many different films could be included under the general title: "Seven Old Families, and Why they Went to Smash." Or a less ominous series would be "Seven Victorious Souls." For there are triumphs every day under the drab monotony of an apparently defeated town: conquests worthy of the waving of sun-banners.

Above all, The Yellow Jacket points a moral for this chapter because there was conscience behind it. First: the rectitude of the Chinese actors of San Francisco who kept the dramatic tradition alive, a tradition that was bequeathed from the ancient generations. Then the artistic integrity of the men who readapted the tradition for western consumption, and their religious attitude that kept the high teaching and devout feeling for human life intact in the play. Then the zeal of the Drama League that indorsed it for the country. Then the earnest work of the Coburn Players who embodied it devoutly, so that the whole company became dear friends forever.

By some such ladder of conscience as this can the local scenario be endowed, written, acted, filmed, and made a real part of the community life. The Yellow Jacket was a drama, not a photoplay. This chapter does not urge that it be readapted for a photoplay in San Francisco or anywhere else. But a kindred painting-in-motion, something as beautiful and worthy and intimate, in strictly photoplay terms, might well be the flower of the work of the local groups of film actors.

Harriet Monroe's magazine, ''Poetry'' (Chicago), has given us a new sect, the Imagists: — Ezra Pound, Richard Aldington, John Gould Fletcher, Amy Lowell, F.S. Flint, D.H. Lawrence, and others. They are gathering followers and imitators. To these followers I would say: the Imagist impulse need not be confined to verse. Why would you be imitators of these leaders when you might be creators in a new medium? There is a clear parallelism between their point of view in verse and the Intimate-and-friendly Photoplay, especially when it is developed from the standpoint of the last part of chapter nine, *space measured without sound plus time measured without sound.*

There is no clan to-day more purely devoted to art for art's sake than the Imagist clan. An Imagist film would offer a noble challenge to the overstrained emotion, the overloaded splendor, the mere repetition of what are at present the finest photoplays. Now even the masterpieces are incontinent. Except for some of the old one-reel Biographs of Griffith's beginning, there is nothing of Doric restraint from the best to the worst. Read some of the poems of the people listed above, then imagine the same moods in the films. Imagist photoplays would be Japanese prints taking on life, animated Japanese paintings, Pompeian mosaics in kaleidoscopic but logical succession, Beardsley drawings made into actors and scenery, Greek vase-paintings in motion.

Scarcely a photoplay but hints at the Imagists in one scene. Then the illusion is lost in the next turn of the reel. Perhaps it would be a sound observance to confine this form of motion picture to a half reel or quarter reel, just as the Imagist poem is generally a half or quarter page. A series of them could fill a special evening.

The Imagists are colorists. Some people do not consider that photographic black, white, and gray are color. But here for instance are seven colors which the Imagists might use: (1) The whiteness of swans in the light. (2) The whiteness of swans in a gentle shadow. (3) The color of a sunburned man in the light. (4) His color in a gentle shadow. (5) His color in a deeper shadow. (6) The blackness of black velvet in the light. (7) The blackness of black velvet in a deep shadow. And to use these colors with definite steps from one to the other does not militate against an artistic mystery of edge and softness in the flow of line. There is a list of possible Imagist textures which is only limited by the number of things to be seen in the world. Probably only seven or ten would be used in one scheme and the same list kept through one production.

The Imagist photoplay will put discipline into the inner ranks of the enlightened and remind the sculptors, painters, and architects of the movies that there is a continence even beyond sculpture and that seas of realism may not have the power of a little well-considered elimination.

The use of the scientific film by established institutions like schools and state governments has been discussed. Let the Church also, in her own way, avail herself of the motion picture, whole-heartedly, as in mediaeval time she took over the marvel of Italian painting. There was a stage in her history when religious representation was by Byzantine mosaics, noble in color, having an architectural use, but curious indeed to behold from the standpoint of those who crave a sensitive emotional record. The first paintings of Cimabue and Giotto, giving these formulas a touch of life, were hailed with joy by all Italy. Now the Church Universal has an opportunity to establish **her new painters if she will. She has taken over in the course of** history, for her glory, miracle plays, Romanesque and Gothic architecture, stained glass windows, and the music of St. Cecilia's organ. Why not this new splendor? The Cathedral of St. John the Divine, on Morningside Heights, should establish in its crypt motion pictures as thoroughly considered as the lines of that building, if possible designed by the architects thereof, with the same sense of permanency.

This chapter does not advocate that the Church lay hold of the photoplays as one more medium for reillustrating the stories of the Bible as they are given in the Sunday-school papers. It is not pietistic simpering that will feed the spirit of Christendom, but a steady church-patronage of the most skilful and original motion picture artists. Let the Church follow the precedent which finally gave us Fra Angelico, Botticelli, Andrea del Sarto, Leonardo da Vinci, Raphael, Michelangelo, Correggio, Titian, Paul Veronese, Tintoretto, and the rest.

Who will endow the successors of the present woman's suffrage film, and other great crusading films? Who will see that the public documents and university researches take on the form of motion picture? Who will endow the local photoplay and the Imagist photoplay? Who will take the first great measures to insure motion picture splendors in the church?

Things such as these come on the winds of to-morrow. But let the crusader look about him, and where it is possible, put in the diplomatic word, and coöperate with the Gray Norns.

CHAPTER XVIII

Architects as Crusaders

Many a worker sees his future America as a Utopia, in which his own profession, achieving dictatorship, alleviates the ills of men. The militarist grows dithyrambic in showing how war makes for the blessings of peace. The economic teacher argues that if we follow his political economy, none of us will have to economize. The church-fanatic says if all churches will merge with his organization, none of them will have to try to behave again. They will just naturally be good. The physician hopes to abolish the devil by sanitation. We have our Utopias. Despite levity, the present writer thinks that such hopes are among the most useful things the earth possesses.

A normal man in the full tide of his activities finds that a world-machinery could logically be built up by his profession. At least in the heyday of his working hours his vocation satisfies his heart. So he wants the entire human race to taste that satisfaction. Approximate Utopias have been built from the beginning. Many civilizations have had some dominant craft to carry them the major part of the way. The priests have made India. The classical student has preserved Old China to its present hour of new life. The samurai knights have made Japan. Sailors have evolved the British Empire. One of the enticing future Americas is that of the architect. Let the architect appropriate the photoplay as his means of propaganda and begin. From its intrinsic genius it can give his profession a start beyond all others in dominating this land. Or such is one of many speculations of the present writer.

The photoplay can speak the language of the man who has a mind World's Fair size. That we are going to have successive generations of such builders may be reasonably implied from past expositions. Beginning with Philadelphia in 1876, and going on to San Francisco and San Diego in 1915, nothing seems to stop us from the habit. Let us enlarge this proclivity into a national mission in as definite a movement, as thoroughly thought out as the evolution of the public school system, the formation of the Steel Trust, and the like. After duly weighing all the world's fairs, let our architects set about making the whole of the United States into a permanent one. Supposing the date to begin the erection be 1930. Till that time there should be tireless if indirect propaganda that will further the architectural state of mind, and later bring about the elucidation of the plans while they are being perfected. For many years this America, founded on the psychology of the Splendor Photoplay, will be evolving. It might be conceived as a going concern at a certain date within the lives of men now living, but it should never cease to develop.

To make films of a more beautiful United States is as practical and worth while a custom as to make military spy maps of every inch of a neighbor's territory, putting in each fence and cross-roads. Those who would satisfy the national pride with something besides battle flags must give our people an objective as shining and splendid as war when it is most glittering, something Napoleonic, and with no outward pretence of excessive virtue. We want a substitute as dramatic internationally, yet world-winning, friend making. If America is to become the financial centre through no fault of her own, that fact must have a symbol other than guns on the sea-coast.

If it is inexpedient for the architectural patriarchs and their young hopefuls to take over the films bodily, let a board of strategy be formed who make it their business to eat dinner with the scenario writers, producers, and owners, conspiring with them in some practical way.

Why should we not consider ourselves a deathless Panama-Pacific Exposition on a coast-to-coast scale? Let Chicago be the transportation building, Denver the mining building. Let Kansas City be the agricultural building and Jacksonville, Florida, the horticultural building, and so around the states.

Even as in mediaeval times men rode for hundreds of miles through perils to the permanent fairs of the free cities, the world-travellers will attend this exhibit, and many of them will in the end become citizens. Our immigration will be something more than tide upon tide of raw labor. The Architects would send forth publicity films which are not only delineations of a future Cincinnati, Cleveland, or St. Louis, but whole counties and states and groups of states could be planned at one time, with the development of their natural fauna, flora, and forestry. Wherever nature has been rendered desolate by industry or mere haste, there let the architect and park-architect proclaim the plan. Wherever she is still splendid and untamed, let her not be violated.

America is in the state of mind where she must visualize herself again. If it is not possible to bring in the New Jerusalem to-day, by public act, with every citizen eating bread and honey under his vine and fig-tree, owning forty acres and a mule, singing hymns and saying prayers all his leisure hours, it is still reasonable to think out tremendous things the American people can do, in the light of what they have done, without sacrificing any of their native cussedness or kick. It was sprawling Chicago that in 1893 achieved the White City. The automobile routes bind the states together closer than muddy counties were held in 1893. A "Permanent World's Fair" may be a phrase distressing to the literal mind. Perhaps it would be better to say "An Architect's America."

Let each city take expert counsel from the architectural demigods how to tear out the dirty core of its principal business square and erect a combination of civic centre and permanent and glorious bazaar. Let the public debate the types of state flower, tree, and shrub that are expedient, the varieties of villages and middle-sized towns, farm-homes, and connecting parkways.

Sometimes it seems to me the American expositions are as characteristic things as our land has achieved. They went through without hesitation. The difficulties of one did not deter the erection of the next. The United States may be in many things slack. Often the democracy looks hopelessly shoddy. But it cannot be denied that our people have always risen to the dignity of these great architectural projects.

Once the population understand they are dealing with the same type of idea on a grander scale, they will follow to the end. We are not proposing an economic revolution, or that human nature be suddenly altered. If California can remain in the World's Fair state of mind for four or five years, and finally achieve such a splendid result, all the states can undertake a similar project conjointly, and because of the momentum of a nation moving together, remain in that mind for the length of the life of a man.

Here we have this great instrument, the motion picture, the fourth largest industry in the United States, attended daily by ten million people, and in ten days by a hundred million, capable of interpreting the largest conceivable ideas that come within the range of the plastic arts, and those ideas have not been supplied. It is still the plaything of newly rich vaudeville managers. The nation goes daily, through intrinsic interest in the device, and is dosed with such continued stories as the Adventures of Kathlyn, What Happened to Mary, and the Million Dollar Mystery, stretched on through reel after reel, week after week. Kathlyn had no especial adventures. Nothing in particular happened to Mary. The million dollar mystery was: why did the millionaires who owned such a magnificent instrument descend to such silliness and impose it on the people? Why cannot our weekly story be henceforth some great plan that is being worked out, whose history will delight us? For instance, every stage of the building of the

Panama Canal was followed with the greatest interest in the films. But there was not enough of it to keep the films busy.

The great material projects are often easier to realize than the little moral reforms. Beautiful architectural undertakings, while appearing to be material, and succeeding by the laws of American enterprise, bring with them the healing hand of beauty. Beauty is not directly pious, but does more civilizing in its proper hour than many sermons or laws.

The world seems to be in the hands of adventurers. Why not this for the adventure of the American architects? If something akin to this plan does not come to pass through photoplay propaganda, it means there is no American builder with the blood of Julius Caesar in his veins. If there is the old brute lust for empire left in any builder, let him awake. The world is before him.

As for the other Utopians, the economist, the physician, the puritan, as soon as the architects have won over the photoplay people, let these others take sage counsel and ensnare the architects. Is there a reform worth while that cannot be embodied and enforced by a builder's invention? A mere city plan, carried out, or the name or intent of a quasi-public building and the list of offices within it may bring about more salutary economic change than all the debating and voting imaginable. So without too much theorizing, why not erect our new America and move into it?

CHAPTER XIX

On Coming Forth by Day

If he will be so indulgent with his author, let the reader approach the photoplay theatre as though for the first time, having again a new point of view. Here the poorest can pay and enter from the glaring afternoon into the twilight of an Ali Baba's cave. The dime is the single open-sesame required. The half-light wherein the audience is seated, by which they can read in an emergency, is as bright and dark as that of some candle-lit churches. It reveals much in the faces and figures of the audience that cannot be seen by common day. Hard edges are the main things that we lose. The gain is in all the delicacies of modelling, tone-relations, form, and color. A hundred evanescent impressions come and go. There is often a tenderness of appeal about the most rugged face in the assembly. Humanity takes on its sacred aspect. It is a crude mind that would insist that these appearances are not real, that the eye does not see them when all eyes behold them. To say dogmatically that any new thing seen by half-light is an illusion, is like arguing that a discovery by the telescope or microscope is unreal. If the appearances are beautiful besides, they are not only facts, but assets in our lives.

Book-reading is not done in the direct noon-sunlight. We retire to the shaded porch. It takes two more steps toward quietness of light to read the human face and figure. Many great paintings and poems are records of things discovered in this quietness of light.

It is indeed ironical in our Ali Baba's cave to see sheer everydayness and hardness upon the screen, the audience dragged back to the street they have escaped. One of the inventions to bring the twilight of the gathering into brotherhood with the shadows on the screen is a simple thing known to the trade as the fade-away, that had its rise in a commonplace fashion as a method of keeping the story from ending with the white glare of the empty screen. As a result of the device the figures in the first episode emerge from the dimness and in the last one go back into the shadow whence they came, as foam returns to the darkness of an evening sea. In the imaginative pictures the principle begins to be applied more largely, till throughout the fairy story the figures float in and out from the unknown, as fancies should. This method in its simplicity counts more to keep the place an Ali Baba's cave than many a more complicated procedure. In luxurious scenes it brings the soft edges of Correggio, and in solemn ones a light and shadow akin to the effects of Rembrandt.

Now we have a darkness on which we can paint, an unspoiled twilight. We need not call it the Arabian's cave. There is a tomb we might have definitely in mind, an Egyptian burying-place where with a torch we might enter, read the inscriptions, and see the illustrations from the Book of the Dead on the wall, or finding that ancient papyrus in the mummy-case, unroll it and show it to the eager assembly, and have the feeling of return. Man is an Egyptian first, before he is any other type of civilized being. The Nile flows through his heart. So let this cave be Egypt, let us incline ourselves to revere the unconscious memories that echo within us when we see the hieroglyphics of Osiris, and Isis. Egypt was our long brooding youth. We built the mysteriousness of the Universe into the pyramids, carved it into every line of the Sphinx. We thought always of the immemorial.

The reel now before us is the mighty judgment roll dealing with the question of our departure in such a way that any man who beholds it will bear the impress of the admonition upon his heart forever. Those

Egyptian priests did no little thing, when amid their superstitions they still proclaimed the Judgment. Let no one consider himself ready for death, till like the men by the Nile he can call up every scene, face with courage every exigency of the ordeal.

There is one copy of the Book of the Dead of especial interest, made for the Scribe Ani, with exquisite marginal drawings. Copies may be found in our large libraries. The particular fac-simile I had the honor to see was in the Lenox Library, New York, several years ago. Ani, according to the formula of the priesthood, goes through the adventures required of a shade before he reaches the court of Osiris. All the Egyptian pictures on tomb-wall and temple are but enlarged picture-writing made into tableaus. Through such tableaus Ani moves. The Ani manuscript has so fascinated some of the Egyptologists that it is copied in figures fifteen feet high on the walls of two of the rooms of the British Museum. And you can read the story eloquently told in Maspero.

Ani knocks at many doors in the underworld. Monstrous gatekeepers are squatting on their haunches with huge knives to slice him if he cannot remember their names or give the right password, or by spells the priests have taught him, convince the sentinels that he is Osiris himself. To further the illusion the name of Osiris is inscribed on his breast. While he is passing these perils his little wife is looking on by a sort of clairvoyant sympathy, though she is still alive. She is depicted mourning him and embracing his mummy on earth at the same time she accompanies him through the shadows.

Ani ploughs and sows and reaps in the fields of the underworld. He is carried past a dreadful place on the back of the cow Hathor. After as many adventures as Browning's Childe Roland he steps into the judgment-hall of the gods. They sit in majestic rows. He makes the proper sacrifices, and advances to the scales of justice. There he sees his own heart weighed against the ostrich-feather of Truth, by the jackal-god Anubis, who has already presided at his embalming. His own soul, in the form of a human-headed hawk, watches the ceremony. His ghost, which is another entity, looks through the door with his little wife. Both of them watch with tense anxiety. The fate of every phase of his personality depends upon the purity of his heart.

Lying in wait behind Anubis is a monster, part crocodile, part lion, part hippopotamus. This terror will eat the heart of Ani if it is found corrupt. At last he is declared justified. Thoth, the ibis-headed God of Writing, records the verdict on his tablet. The justified Ani moves on past the baffled devourer, with the mystic presence of his little wife rejoicing at his side. They go to the awful court of Osiris. She makes sacrifice with him there. The God of the Dead is indeed a strange deity, a seated semi-animated mummy, with all the appurtenances of royalty, and with the four sons of Horus on a lotus before him, and his two wives, Isis and Nephthys, standing behind his throne with their hands on his shoulders.

The justified soul now boards the boat in which the sun rides as it journeys through the night. He rises a glorious boatman in the morning, working an oar to speed the craft through the high ocean of the noon sky. Henceforth he makes the eternal round with the sun. Therefore in Ancient Egypt the roll was called, not the Book of the Dead, but *The Chapters on Coming Forth by Day*.

This book on motion pictures does not profess to be an expert treatise on Egyptology as well. The learned folk are welcome to amend the modernisms that have crept into it. But the fact remains that something like this story in one form or another held Egypt spell-bound for many hundred years. It was the force behind every mummification. It was the reason for the whole Egyptian system of life, death, and entombment, for the man not embalmed could not make the journey. So the explorer finds the Egyptian with a roll of this papyrus as a guide-book on his mummy breast. The soul needed to return for refreshment periodically to the stone chamber, and the mummy mutilated or destroyed could not entertain the guest. Egypt cried out through thousands of years for the ultimate resurrection of the whole man, his *coming forth by day*.

We need not fear that a story that so dominated a race will be lost on modern souls when vividly set forth. Is it too much to expect that some American prophet-wizard of the future will give us this film in the spirit of an Egyptian priest?

The Greeks, the wisest people in our limited system of classics, bowed down before the Egyptian hierarchy. That cult must have had a fine personal authority and glamour to master such men. The unseen mysteries were always on the Egyptian heart as a burden and a consolation, and though there may have been jugglers in the outer courts of these temples, as there have been in the courts of all temples, no mere actor could make an Egyptian priest of himself. Their very alphabet has a regal enchantment in its lines, and the same aesthetic-mystical power remains in their pylons and images under the blaze of the all-revealing noonday sun.

Here is a nation, America, going for dreams into caves as shadowy as the tomb of Queen Thi. There they find too often, not that ancient priestess and ruler, nor any of her kin, nor yet Ani the scribe, nor yet any of the kings, but shabby rags of fancy, or circuses that were better in the street.

Because ten million people daily enter into the cave, something akin to Egyptian wizardry, certain national rituals, will be born. By studying the matter of being an Egyptian priest for a little while, the author-producer may learn in the end how best to express and satisfy the spirit-hungers that are peculiarly American. It is sometimes out of the oldest dream that the youngest vision is born.

CHAPTER XX

The Prophet-Wizard

The whirlwind of cowboys and Indians with which the photoplay began, came about because this instrument, in asserting its genius, was feeling its way toward the most primitive forms of life it could find.

Now there is a tendency for even wilder things. We behold the half-draped figures living in tropical islands or our hairy forefathers acting out narratives of the stone age. The moving picture conventionality permits an abbreviation of drapery. If the primitive setting is convincing, the figure in the grass-robe or buffalo hide at once has its rights over the healthful imagination.

There is in this nation of moving-picture-goers a hunger for tales of fundamental life that are not yet told. The cave-man longs with an incurable homesickness for his ancient day. One of the fine photoplays of primeval life is the story called Man's Genesis, described in chapter two.

We face the exigency the world over of vast instruments like national armies being played against each other as idly and aimlessly as the checker-men on the cracker-barrels of corner groceries. And this invention, the kinetoscope, which affects or will affect as many people as the guns of Europe, is not yet understood in its powers, particularly those of bringing back the primitive in a big rich way. The primitive is always a new and higher beginning to the man who understands it. Not yet has the producer learned that the feeling of the crowd is patriarchal, splendid. He imagines the people want nothing but a silly lark.

All this apparatus and opportunity, and no immortal soul! Yet by faith and a study of the signs we proclaim that this lantern of wizard-drama is going to give us in time the visible things in the fulness of their primeval force, and some that have been for a long time invisible. To speak in a metaphor, we are going to have the primitive life of Genesis, then all that evolution after: Exodus,

Leviticus, Numbers, Deuteronomy, Joshua, Judges, and on to a new revelation of St. John. In this adolescence of Democracy the history of man is to be retraced, the same round on a higher spiral of life.

Our democratic dream has been a middle-class aspiration built on a bog of toil-soddened minds. The piles beneath the castle of our near-democratic arts were rotting for lack of folk-imagination. The Man with the Hoe had no spark in his brain. But now a light is blazing. We can build the American soul broad-based from the foundations. We can begin with dreams the veriest stone-club warrior can understand, and as far as an appeal to the eye can do it, lead him in fancy through every phase of life to the apocalyptic splendors.

This progress, according to the metaphor of this chapter, will be led by prophet-wizards. These were the people that dominated the cave-men of old. But what, more specifically, are prophet-wizards?

Let us consider two kinds of present-day people: scientific inventors, on the one hand, and makers of art and poetry and the like, on the other. The especial producers of art and poetry that we are concerned with in this chapter we will call prophet-wizards: men like Albert Dürer, Rembrandt, Blake, Elihu Vedder, Watts, Rossetti, Tennyson, Coleridge, Poe, Maeterlinck, Yeats, Francis Thompson.

They have a certain unearthly fascination in some one or many of their works. A few other men might be added to the list. Most great names are better described under other categories, though as much beloved in their own way. But these are especially adapted to being set in opposition to a list of mechanical inventors that might be called realists by contrast: the Wright brothers, and H. Pierpont Langley, Thomas A. Edison, Charles Steinmetz, John Hays Hammond, Hudson Maxim, Graham Bell.

The prophet-wizards are of various schools. But they have a common tendency and character in bringing forth a type of art peculiarly at war with the realistic civilization science has evolved. It is one object of this chapter to show that, when it comes to a clash between the two forces, the wizards should rule, and the realists should serve them.

The two functions go back through history, sometimes at war, other days in alliance. The poet and the scientist were brethren in the centuries of alchemy. Tennyson, bearing in mind such a period, took the title of Merlin in his veiled autobiography, Merlin and the Gleam.

Wizards and astronomers were one when the angels sang in Bethlehem, "Peace on Earth, Good Will to Men." There came magicians, saying, "Where is he that is born king of the Jews, for we have seen his star in the east and have come to worship him?" The modern world in its gentler moments seems to take a peculiar thrill of delight from these travellers, perhaps realizing what has been lost from parting with such gentle seers and secular diviners. Every Christmas half the magazines set them forth in richest colors, riding across the desert, following the star to the same manger where the shepherds are depicted.

Those wizard kings, whatever useless charms and talismans they wore, stood for the unknown quantity in spiritual life. A magician is a man who lays hold on the unseen for the mere joy of it, who steals, if necessary, the holy bread and the sacred fire. He is often of the remnant of an ostracized and disestablished priesthood. He is a free-lance in the soul-world, owing final allegiance to no established sect. The fires of prophecy are as apt to descend upon him as upon members of the established faith. He loves the mysterious for the beauty of it, the wildness and the glory of it, and not always to compel stiff-necked people to do right.

It seems to me that the scientific and poetic functions of society should make common cause again, if they are not, as in Merlin's time, combined in one personality. They must recognize that they serve the same society, but with the understanding that the prophetic function is the most important, the wizard vocation the next, and the inventors' and realists' genius important indeed, but the third consideration. The war between the scientists and the prophet-wizards has come about because of the half-defined ambition of the scientists to rule or ruin. They give us the steam-engine, the skyscraper, the steam-heat, the flying machine, the elevated railroad, the apartment house, the newspaper, the breakfast food, the weapons of the army, the weapons of the navy, and think that they have beautified our existence.

Moreover some one rises at this point to make a plea for the scientific imagination. He says the inventor-scientists have brought us the mystery of electricity, which is no hocus-pocus, but a special manifestation of the Immanent God within us and about us. He says the student in the laboratory brought us the X-ray, the wireless telegraph, the mystery of radium, the mystery of all the formerly unharnessed power of God which man is beginning to gather into the hollow of his hand.

The one who pleads for the scientific imagination points out that Edison has been called the American Wizard. All honor to Edison and his kind. And I admit specifically that Edison took the first great mechanical step to give us the practical kinetoscope and make it possible that the photographs, even of inanimate objects thrown upon the mirror-screen, may become celestial actors. But the final phase of the transfiguration is not the work of this inventor or any other. As long as the photoplays are in the hands of men like Edison they are mere voodooism. We have nothing but Moving Day, as heretofore described. It is only in the hands of the prophetic photoplaywright and allied artists that the kinetoscope reels become as mysterious and dazzling to the thinking spirit as the wheels of Ezekiel in the first chapter of his prophecy. One can climb into the operator's box and watch the sword-like stream of light till he is as dazzled in flesh and spirit as the moth that burns its wings in the lamp. But this is while a glittering vision and not a mere invention is being thrown upon the screen.

The scientific man can explain away the vision as a matter of the technique of double exposure, double printing, trick-turning, or stopping down. And having reduced it to terms and shown the process, he expects us to become secular and casual again. But of course the sun itself is a mere trick of heat and light, a dynamo, an incandescent globe, to the man in the laboratory. To us it must be a fire upon the altar.

Transubstantiation must begin. Our young magicians must derive strange new pulse-beats from the veins of the earth, from the sap of the trees, from the lightning of the sky, as well as the alchemical acids, metals, and flames. Then they will kindle the beginning mysteries for our cause. They will build up a priesthood that is free, yet authorized to freedom. It will be established and disestablished according to the intrinsic authority of the light revealed.

Now for a closer view of this vocation.

The picture of Religious Splendor has its obvious form in the delineation of Biblical scenes, which, in the hands of the best commercial producers, can be made as worth while as the work of men like Tissot. Such films are by no means to be thought of lightly. This sort of work will remain in the minds of many of the severely orthodox as the only kind of a religious picture worthy of classification. But there are many further fields.

Just as the wireless receiving station or the telephone switchboard become heroes in the photoplay, so Aaron's rod that confounded the Egyptians, the brazen serpent that Moses uplifted in the wilderness, the ram's horn that caused the fall of Jericho, the mantle of Elijah descending upon the shoulders of Elisha from the chariot of fire, can take on a physical electrical power and a hundred times spiritual meaning that they could not have in the dead stage properties of the old miracle play or the realism of the Tissot school. The waterfall and the tossing sea are dramatis personae in the ordinary film romance. So the Red Sea overwhelming Pharaoh, the fires of Nebuchadnezzar's furnace sparing and sheltering the three holy children, can become celestial actors. And winged couriers can appear, in the pictures, with missions of import, just as an angel descended to Joshua, saying, "As captain of the host of the Lord am I now come."

The pure mechanic does not accept the doctrine. "Your alleged supernatural appearance," he says, "is based on such a simple fact as this: two pictures can be taken on one film."

But the analogy holds. Many primitive peoples are endowed with memories that are double photographs. The world faiths, based upon centuries of these appearances, are none the less to be revered because machine-ridden men have temporarily lost the power of seeing their thoughts as pictures in the air, and for the time abandoned the task of adding to tradition.

Man will not only see visions again, but machines themselves, in the hands of prophets, will see visions. In the hands of commercial men they are seeing alleged visions, and the term *"vision"* is a part of moving-picture studio slang, unutterably cheapening religion and tradition. When Confucius came, he said one of his tasks was the rectification of names. The leaders of this age should see that this word *"vision"* comes to mean something more than a piece of studio slang. If it is the conviction of serious minds that the mass of men shall never again see pictures out of Heaven except through such mediums as the kinetoscope lens, let all the higher forces of our land courageously lay hold upon this thing that saves us from perpetual spiritual blindness.

When the thought of primitive man, embodied in misty forms on the landscape, reached epic proportions in the Greek, he saw the Olympians more plainly than he beheld the Acropolis. Myron, Polykleitos, Phidias, Scopas, Lysippus, Praxiteles, discerned the gods and demigods so clearly they afterward cut them from the hard marble without wavering. Our guardian angels of to-day must be as clearly seen and nobly hewn.

A double mental vision is as fundamental in human nature as the double necessity for air and light. It is as obvious as that a thing can be both written and spoken. We have maintained that the kinetoscope in the hands of artists is a higher form of picture writing. In the hands of prophet-wizards it will be a higher form of vision-seeing.

I have said that the commercial men are seeing alleged visions. Take, for instance, the large Italian film that attempts to popularize Dante. Though it has a scattering of noble passages, and in some brief episodes it is an enhancement of Gustave Doré, taking it as a whole, it is a false thing. It is full of apparitions worked out with mechanical skill, yet Dante's soul is not back of the fires and swords of light. It gives to the uninitiated an outline of the stage paraphernalia of the Inferno. It has an encyclopaedic value. If Dante himself had been the high director in the plenitude of his resources, it might still have had that hollowness. A list of words making a poem and a set of apparently equivalent pictures forming a photoplay may have an entirely different outcome. It may be like trying to see a perfume or listen to a taste. Religion that comes in wholly through the eye has a new world in the films, whose relation to the old is only discovered by experiment and intuition, patience and devotion.

But let us imagine the grandson of an Italian immigrant to America, a young seer, trained in the photoplay technique by the high American masters, knowing all the moving picture resources as Dante knew Italian song and mediaeval learning. Assume that he has a genius akin to that of the Florentine. Let him be a Modernist Catholic if you will. Let him begin his message in the timber lands of Minnesota or the forests of Alaska. "In midway of this our mortal life I found me in a gloomy wood astray." Then let him paint new pictures of just punishment beyond the grave, and merciful rehabilitation and great reward. Let his Hell, Purgatory, and Paradise be built of those things which are deepest and highest in the modern mind, yet capable of emerging in picture-writing form.

Men are needed, therefore they will come. And lest they come weeping, accursed, and alone, let us ask, how shall we recognize them? There is no standard by which to discern the true from the false prophet, except the mood that is engendered by contemplating the messengers of the past. Every man has his own roll call of noble magicians selected from the larger group. But here are the names with which this chapter began, with some words on their work.

Albert Dürer is classed as a Renaissance painter. Yet his art has its dwelling-place in the early Romanesque savageness and strangeness. And the reader remembers Dürer's brooding muse called Melancholia that so obsessed Kipling in The Light that Failed. But the wonder-quality went into nearly all the Dürer wood-cuts and etchings. Rembrandt is a prophet-wizard, not only in his shadowy portraits, but in his etchings of holy scenes even his simplest cobweb lines become incantations. Other artists in the high tides of history have had kindred qualities, but coming close to our day, Elihu Vedder, the American, the illustrator of the Rubáiyát, found it a poem questioning all things, and his very illustrations answer in a certain fashion with winds of infinity, and bring the songs of Omar near to the Book of Job. Vedder's portraits of Lazarus and Samson are conceptions that touch the hem of the unknown. George Frederick Watts was a painter of portraits of the soul itself, as in his delineations of Burne-Jones and Morris and Tennyson.

It is a curious thing that two prophet-wizards have combined pictures and song. Blake and Rossetti, whatever the failure of their technique, never lacked in enchantment. Students of the motion picture side of poetry would naturally turn to such men for spiritual precedents. Blake, that strange Londoner, in his book of Job, is the paramount example of the enchanter doing his work with the engraving tool in his hand.

Rossetti's Dante's Dream is a painting on the edge of every poet's paradise. As for the poetry of these two men, there are Blake's Songs of Innocence, and Rossetti's Blessed Damozel and his Burden of Nineveh.

As for the other poets, we have Coleridge, the author of Christabel, that piece of winter witchcraft, Kubla Khan, that oriental dazzlement, and the Ancient Mariner, that most English of all this list of enchantments. Of Tennyson's work, besides Merlin and the Gleam, there are the poems when the mantle was surely on his shoulders: The Lady of Shalott, The Lotus Eaters, Sir Galahad, and St. Agnes' Eve.

Edgar Poe, always a magician, blends this power with the prophetical note in the poem, The Haunted Palace, and in the stories of William Wilson, The Black Cat and The Tell-tale Heart. This prophet-wizard side of a man otherwise a wizard only, has been well illustrated in The Avenging Conscience photoplay.

From Maeterlinck we have The Bluebird and many another dream. I devoutly hope I will never see in the films an attempt to paraphrase this master. But some disciple of his should conquer the photoplay medium, giving us great original works.

Yeats has bestowed upon us The Land of Heart's Desire, The Secret Rose, and many another piece of imaginative glory. Let us hope that we may be spared any attempts to hastily paraphrase his wonders for the motion pictures. But the man that reads Yeats will be better prepared to do his own work in the films, or to greet the young new masters when they come.

Finally, Francis Thompson, in The Hound of Heaven, has written a song that the young wizard may lean upon forevermore for private guidance. It is composed of equal parts of wonder and conscience. With this poem in his heart, the roar of the elevated railroad will be no more in his ears, and he will dream of palaces of righteousness, and lead other men to dream of them till the houses of mammon fade away.

CHAPTER XXI

The Acceptable Year of the Lord

Without airing my private theology I earnestly request the most sceptical reader of this book to assume that miracles in a Biblical sense have occurred. Let him take it for granted in the fashion of the strictly aesthetic commentator who writes in sympathy with a Fra Angelico painting, or as that great modernist, Paul Sabatier, does as he approaches the problems of faith in the life of St. Francis. Let him also assume, for the length of time that he is reading this chapter if no longer, that miracles, in a Biblical sense, as vivid and as real to the body of the Church, will again occur two thousand years in the future: events as wonderful as those others, twenty centuries back. Let us anticipate that many of these will be upon American soil. Particularly as sons and daughters of a new country it is a spiritual necessity for us to look forward to traditions, because we have so few from the past identified with the six feet of black earth beneath us.

The functions of the prophet whereby he definitely painted future sublimities have been too soon abolished in the minds of the wise. Mere forecasting is left to the weather bureau so far as a great section of the purely literary and cultured are concerned. The term prophet has survived in literature to be applied to men like Carlyle: fiery spiritual leaders who speak with little pretence of revealing to-morrow.

But in the street, definite forecasting of future events is still the vulgar use of the term. Dozens of sober historians predicted the present war with a clean-cut story that was carried out with much faithfulness of detail, considering the thousand interests involved. They have been called prophets in a congratulatory secular tone by the man in the street. These felicitations come because well-authorized merchants in futures have been put out of countenance from the days of Jonah and Balaam till now. It is indeed a risky vocation. Yet there is an undeniable line of successful forecasting by the hardy, to be found in the Scripture and in history. In direct proportion as these men of fiery speech were free from sheer silliness, their outlook has been considered and debated by the gravest people round them. The heart of man craves the seer. Take, for instance, the promise of the restoration of Jerusalem in glory that fills the latter part of the Old Testament. It moves the Jewish Zionist, the true race-Jew, to this hour. He is even now endeavoring to fulfil the prophecy.

Consider the words of John the Baptist, "One mightier than I cometh, the latchet of whose shoes I am not worthy to unloose: he shall baptize you with the Holy Ghost and with fire." A magnificent foreshadowing, being both a spiritual insight and the statement of a great definite event.

The heeded seers of the civilization of this our day have been secular in their outlook. Perhaps the most striking was Karl Marx, in the middle of the capitalistic system tracing its development from feudalism and pointing out as inevitable, long before they came, such modern institutions as the Steel Trust and the Standard Oil Company. It remains to be seen whether the Marxian prophecy of the international alliance of workingmen that is obscured by the present conflict in Europe, and other of his forecastings, will be ultimately verified.

There have been secular teachers like Darwin, who, by a scientific reconstruction of the past, have implied an evolutionary future based on the biological outlook. Deductions from the teachings of Darwin are said to control those who mould the international doings of Germany and Japan.

There have been inventor-seers like Jules Verne. In Twenty Thousand Leagues under the Sea he dimly discerned the submarine. There is a type of social prophet allied to Verne. Edward Bellamy, in Looking Backward, reduced the world to a matter of pressing the button, turning on the phonograph. It was a combination of glorified department-store and Coney Island, on a coöperative basis. A seventeen-year-old boy from the country, making his first visit to the Woolworth building in New York, and riding in the subway when it is not too crowded, might be persuaded by an eloquent city relative that this is Bellamy's New Jerusalem.

A soul with a greater insight is H.G. Wells. But he too, in spite of his humanitarian heart, has, in a great mass of his work, the laboratory imagination. Serious Americans pronounce themselves beneficiaries of Wells' works, and I confess myself edified and thoroughly grateful. Nevertheless, one smells chemicals in the next room when he reads most of Wells' prophecies. The X-ray has moved that Englishman's mind more dangerously than moonlight touches the brain of the chanting witch. One striking and typical story is The Food of the Gods. It is not only a fine speculation, but a great parable. The reader may prefer other tales. Many times Wells has gone into his laboratory to invent our future, in the same state of mind in which an automobile manufacturer works out an improvement in his car. His disposition has greatly mellowed of late, in this respect, but underneath he is the same Wells.

Citizens of America, wise or foolish, when they look into the coming days, have the submarine mood of Verne, the press-the-button complacency of Bellamy, the wireless telegraph enthusiasm of Wells. If they express hopes that can be put into pictures with definite edges, they order machinery piled to the skies. They see the redeemed United States running deftly in its jewelled sockets, ticking like a watch.

This, their own chosen outlook, wearies the imaginations of our people, they do not know why. It gives no full-orbed apocalyptic joy. Only to the young mechanical engineer does such a hope express real Utopia. He can always keep ahead of the devices that herald its approach. No matter what day we attain and how busy we are adjusting ourselves, he can be moving on, inventing more to-morrows; ruling the age, not being ruled by it.

Because this Utopia is in the air, a goodly portion of the precocious boys turn to mechanical engineering. Youths with this bent are the most healthful and inspiring young citizens we have. They and their like will fulfil a multitude of the hopes of men like Verne, Bellamy, and Wells.

But if every mechanical inventor on earth voiced his dearest wish and lived to see it worked out, the real drama of prophecy and fulfilment, as written in the imagination of the human race, would remain uncompleted.

As Mrs. Browning says in Lady Geraldine's Courtship: —

> If we trod the deeps of ocean, if we struck the stars in rising,
> If we wrapped the globe intensely with one hot electric breath,
> 'Twere but power within our tether, no new spirit-power comprising,
> And in life we were not greater men, nor bolder men in death.

St. John beheld the New Jerusalem coming down out of Heaven prepared as a bride adorned for her husband, not equipped as a touring car varnished for its owner.

It is my hope that the moving picture prophet-wizards will set before the world a new group of pictures of the future. The chapter on The Architect as a Crusader endeavors to show how, by proclaiming that America will become a permanent World's Fair, she can be made so within the lives of men now living, if courageous architects have the campaign in hand. There are other hopes that look a long way further. They peer as far into the coming day as the Chinese historian looks into the past. And then they are but halfway to the millennium.

Any standard illustrator could give us Verne or Bellamy or Wells if he did his best. *But we want pictures beyond the skill of any delineator in the old mediums, yet within the power of the wizard photoplay producer.* Oh you who are coming to-morrow, show us everyday America as it will be when we are only halfway to the millennium yet thousands of years in the future! Tell what type of honors men will covet, what property they will still be apt to steal, what murders they will commit, what the law court and the jail will be or what will be the substitutes, how the newspaper will appear, the office, the busy street.

Picture to America the lovers in her half-millennium, when usage shall have become iron-handed once again, when noble sweethearts must break beautiful customs for the sake of their dreams. Show us the gantlet of strange courtliness they must pass through before they reach one another, obstacles brought about by the immemorial distinctions of scholarship gowns or service badges.

Make a picture of a world where machinery is so highly developed it utterly disappeared long ago. Show us the antique United States, with ivy vines upon the popular socialist churches, and weather-beaten images of socialist saints in the niches of the doors. Show us the battered fountains, the brooding universities, the dusty libraries. Show us houses of administration with statues of heroes in front of them and gentle banners flowing from their pinnacles. Then paint pictures of the oldest trees of the time, and tree-revering ceremonies, with unique costumes and a special priesthood.

Show us the marriage procession, the christening, the consecration of the boy and girl to the state. Show us the political processions and election riots. Show us the people with their graceful games, their religious pantomimes. Show us impartially the memorial scenes to celebrate the great men and women, and the funerals of the poor. And then moving on toward the millennium itself, show America after her victories have been won, and she has grown old, as old as the Sphinx. Then give us the Dragon and Armageddon and the Lake of Fire.

Author-producer-photographer, who would prophesy, read the last book in the Bible, not to copy it in form and color, but that its power and grace and terror may enter into you. Delineate in your own way, as you are led on your own Patmos, the picture of our land redeemed. After fasting and prayer, let the Spirit conduct you till you see in definite line and form the throngs of the brotherhood of man, the colonnades where the arts are expounded, the gardens where the children dance.

That which man desires, that will man become. He largely fulfils his own prediction and vision. Let him therefore have a care how he prophesies and prays. We shall have a tin heaven and a tin earth, if the scientists are allowed exclusive command of our highest hours.

Let us turn to Luke iv. 17.

''And there was delivered unto him the book of the prophet Esaias. And when he had opened the book he found the place where it was written: —

''The Spirit of the Lord is upon me because he hath anointed me to preach the Gospel to the poor; he hath sent me to heal the broken-hearted, to preach deliverance to the captives, and recovering of sight to the blind, to set at liberty them that are bruised, to preach the acceptable year of the Lord.

''And he closed the book, and he gave it again to the minister, and sat down. And the eyes of all them that were in the synagogue were fastened on him. And he began to say unto them: 'This day is this Scripture fulfilled in your ears.'

''And all bare him witness, and wondered at the gracious words which proceeded out of his mouth. And they said: 'Is not this Joseph's son?'''

I am moved to think Christ fulfilled that prophecy because he had read it from childhood. It is my entirely personal speculation, not brought forth dogmatically, that Scripture is not so much inspired as it is curiously and miraculously inspiring.

If the New Isaiahs of this time will write their forecastings in photoplay hieroglyphics, the children in times to come, having seen those films from infancy, or their later paraphrases in more perfect form, can rise and say, ''This day is this Scripture fulfilled in your ears.'' But without prophecy there is no fulfilment, without Isaiah there is no Christ.

America is often shallow in her dreams because she has no past in the European and Asiatic sense. Our soil has no Roman coin or buried altar or Buddhist tope. For this reason multitudes of American artists have moved to Europe, and only the most universal of wars has driven them home. Year after year Europe drained us of our beauty-lovers, our highest painters and sculptors and the like. They have come pouring home, confused expatriates, trying to adjust themselves. It is time for the American craftsman and artist to grasp the fact that we must be men enough to construct a to-morrow that grows rich in forecastings in the same way that the past of Europe grows rich in sweet or terrible legends as men go back into it.

* * * * * *

Scenario writers, producers, photoplay actors, endowers of exquisite films, sects using special motion pictures for a predetermined end, all you who are taking the work as a sacred trust, I bid you God-speed. Let us resolve that whatever America's to-morrow may be, she shall have a day that is beautiful and not crass, spiritual, not material. Let us resolve that she shall dream dreams deeper than the sea and higher than the clouds of heaven, that she shall come forth crowned and transfigured with her statesmen and wizards and saints and sages about her, with magic behind her and miracle before her.

Pray that you be delivered from the temptation to cynicism and the timidities of orthodoxy. Pray that the workers in this your glorious new art be delivered from the mere lust of the flesh and pride of life. Let your spirits outflame your burning bodies.

Consider what it will do to your souls, if you are true to your trust. Every year, despite earthly sorrow and the punishment of your mortal sins, despite all weakness and all of Time's revenges upon you, despite Nature's reproofs and the whips of the angels, new visions will come, new prophecies will come. You will be seasoned spirits in the eyes of the wise. The record of your ripeness will be found in your craftsmanship. You will be God's thoroughbreds.

* * * * * *

It has come then, this new weapon of men, and the face of the whole earth changes. In after centuries its beginning will be indeed remembered.

It has come, this new weapon of men, and by faith and a study of the signs we proclaim that it will go on and on in immemorial wonder.

VACHEL LINDSAY.

Springfield, Illinois,
   Nov. 1, 1915.